CHOICES
A Text for Writing and Reading

CHOICES
A Text for Writing and Reading

Lila Fink
Phyllis Levy
Charlotte Miller
Gwen Brewer
with the assistance of
Andrea White

California State University, Northridge

Little, Brown and Company
Boston   Toronto

Library of Congress Cataloging in Publication Data
Main entry under title:

Choices, a text for writing and reading.

Includes index.
 1. College readers. 2. English language--
Rhetoric. I. Fink, Lila.
PE1417.C56 1983   808'.0427   82-14827
ISBN 0-316-28317-7

Copyright © 1983 by Lila Fink, Phyllis Levy, Charlotte Miller, Gwen Brewer, and Andrea White

All rights reserved. No part of this book may be reproduced in any form or by any electronic or mechanical means including information storage and retrieval systems without permission in writing from the publisher, except by a reviewer who may quote brief passages in a review.

Library of Congress Catalog Card No. 82-14827

ISBN 0-316-28317-7

9 8 7 6 5 4 3 2 1

BP

Published simultaneously in Canada by Little, Brown & Company (Canada) Limited

Printed in the United States of America

CREDITS

Isaac Asimov, "Our Destiny in Space." Reprinted by permission of the author. This material originally appeared in *Science Digest*, Special Edition (Summer 1980).

George Basalla, "The Fallacy of the Energy = Civilization Equation," *Saturday Review* (24 November 1979). Copyright © 1979 by *Saturday Review*. All rights reserved. Reprinted by permission.

Marc Bekoff and Michael C. Wells, excerpt from "The Social Ecology of Coyotes," *Scientific American* (April 1980). Used by permission.

Anthony Brandt, "Symbol of Success: The Real Horatio Alger," *Quest/80* (April 1980). Reprinted by permission of the author.

(Continued on page 463)

To the Teacher

For the past several years, college and university English departments have been confronted with an increasing number of entering students who lack the traditional college-level language skills. These students have often faced difficulties, not only in their English composition classes, but also in other classes in which writing and reading are essential. Indeed, many of these students, though bright and possessing good potential, flounder and ultimately drop out of school. Facing this problem, our English department began to reevaluate its composition curriculum, seeking to establish a language-skills program to meet student needs. Our findings showed that although a small number of students would need a year or more to achieve college-level competency, most students would be able to reach this level in a shorter time through intensive work. This last group, then, became our primary focus.

Those of us involved in this effort worked as a team to develop an introductory program for middle-level students. We searched the available literature for theories and suggestions, we experimented with techniques, and we exchanged ideas based on our individual training and past teaching experience. Our review of literature offered helpful theories on which to base some classroom lessons, such as work on sentence combining, yet we could not find a traditional text to meet all of our needs. So we based many lessons on our students' writings; typed out and dittoed supplementary lessons until our fingers became permanently stained purple; and conferred with each other, adapting and adjusting each others' experiments. From all of this we wrenched out a course outline for students with moderate language skills and weaknesses and for students for whom English is a second language. This outline has served as a basis for our text. Both our program and this text are founded on the following concepts and observations.

1. Reading and writing are interrelated skills and therefore should be taught within the same textbook as well as in the same course. Well-read students generally use more sophisticated sentence structure, have more fluent styles and larger vocabularies, and can develop their ideas logically; experienced writers usually analyze written communications with more depth, have greater comprehension, and find more pleasure in well-written essays.

2. Vocabulary acquisition should be considered as a reading component. Most inexperienced readers need help in expanding their vocabularies so that they can comprehend all their college reading assignments. They must learn to form and alter words by adding roots, prefixes, and suffixes. They must also dare to risk an educated guess based on contextual meaning.

3. Reading effectiveness and comprehension should be taught as part of a language-skills program. Weak readers plod along, reading word by word; good readers anticipate. In short, some readers need lessons on skimming, phrase perception, scanning, analyzing, making inferences, and recognizing a writer's tone and subtleties. Weaker readers also need to reach *beyond* their present level of competency; with the help of a teacher, they must *begin* to tackle college-level and professional readings such as those assigned in their other classes.

4. The paragraph is the major unit of written communication, using the sentence as the basic building block. In other words, when good writers express themselves, they explain their meaning, rephrase, cite examples, describe situations or things, compare, contrast, and analyze. Inexperienced writers, however, often rely on undeveloped statements. These writers, therefore, should practice writing paragraphs before attempting lengthy essays.

5. Students need some sort of system of invention or brainstorming to establish their thesis and points of discussion. Most inexperienced writers lack the ability to retrieve knowledge they already possess or to manipulate this knowledge to suit their purpose.

6. A writer's conscious choices involve consideration of the intended audience. Inexperienced writers must learn to adjust diction, tone, language level, sentence structure, and organization with their audience in mind.

7. To be effective, ideas must be organized. Most inexperienced writers have little understanding of the need to organize their ideas consciously; they simply write down thoughts as they come. These writers need direction, patterns to follow such as those developed by Young and Becker.* Once students have become adept with certain standard patterns or organizations, they are capable of creating their own sophisticated variations.

---

* Richard E. Young and Alton I. Becker, "Toward a Modern Theory of Rhetoric: a Tagmemic Contribution," *Harvard Educational Review* 35 (1965): 456.

8. Good writing requires precise diction. Most inexperienced writers and readers are so accustomed to communicating orally that they cannot communicate concisely, clearly, or concretely on paper. In fact, many do not even realize that their language is embedded with clichés, colloquialisms, and slang.

9. Good writing incorporates syntactic fluency. Most inexperienced writers fail to vary their sentence structure, have problems with punctuation, and lack awareness of their own ability to manipulate their readers' speed of reading, focus, comprehension, and phrase perception through sentence organization and adjustment of punctuation.

10. Writing involves certain necessary steps. Most inexperienced writers, however, have little awareness of these steps. Some write a first draft, then correct a few glaring spelling errors, copy over, and submit the work; some do minor reorganization and correction; few if any attempt thorough revision or understand the need for final editing.

11. Comprehensive proofreading is a vital last step in the process of writing.

This text, then, incorporates these concepts and observations by gradually developing student skills and awareness. Since we believe that all language skills are interrelated, each unit of the text coordinates reading and writing assignments, offers reading and vocabulary lessons, and introduces writing concepts and techniques. In addition, each unit leads the student through the writing process, beginning with brainstorming and shaping to the first draft; from first draft through revision of content and organization; and on to editing words, sentences, and punctuation.

Each unit also offers three reading selections, ranging from easy to difficult, provides exercises for skill development and reinforcement, and reviews past assignments before introducing more sophisticated concepts and techniques. Writing assignments grow progressively more difficult as the student works through the book and range from the first one-paragraph narrative essay to a five-section analytical essay.

Finally, the appendices include a supplementary writing assignment on persuasion; additional cloze exercises; a section on taking notes in class; and tables of prefixes, suffixes, and roots.

We wrote this book for our own courses, but also to meet the demands created by the growing number of courses which combine instruction in reading and writing. We thank the following teachers who are sympathetic to this trend for their useful comments and criticisms: Robert Cosgrove of Saddleback Community College, Kim Flachmann of California State University at Bakersfield, Darwin Hayes of Brigham Young University, Cecilia Macheski of LaGuardia Community College and Toby Rose of Northern Michigan University.

To the Student

All of us find writing difficult. Even professional writers complain that they must write, rewrite, and rewrite again before they are satisfied with their work. In addition, many of us have reading difficulties, finding ourselves plugging along at a slow rate or struggling to understand the materials under discussion. Such problems may have bothered you before, but your school workload might not have been so heavy that you couldn't complete assignments on time. Now, however, you are enrolled in a college or university program and faced with hours and hours of weekly reading assignments, term papers, and essay examinations. Now, knowing how to write and read effectively becomes necessary for you to deal with your tasks and to participate in all courses with enjoyment and understanding.

    This term you have an opportunity to increase your reading and writing skills so that you can succeed in school. Working with your instructor and this text, you can develop your writing and reading to a level required at your school. Perhaps a few comments about the relationship between reading and writing will give you some understanding of the work you are about to begin. Consider this: writers are like puppeteers. Their strings are the *conscious choices* they make to manipulate their puppets; that is, through the manipulation of wording, punctuation, organization, sentence structure, and tone, writers produce unified performances to which readers can react. If writers manipulate these strings skillfully, they accomplish their purpose — to entertain, inform, or persuade their audience. In other words, an interplay takes place between writers and their audience/readers that involves mutual obligations. Writers have an obligation to communicate clearly to their audience; readers have an obligation to be attentive, to analyze, and to evaluate.

    Because of this interplay between writer and reader, we have integrated reading and writing activities in this text in order to help you acquire not only a conscious control of your writing, but also an analytical reading ability. As you complete your assignments, then, you will notice how your improved reading skills help you to grow more aware of language manipulation as you write and how your increased writing ability helps you to understand written materials better. But don't become impatient with your progress. If you find you aren't improving your skills as rapidly as you would like, remember that everyone needs time and practice to develop language competence and effectiveness. Confer with your teacher about any problems you might have and trust your own intelligence and talent. We promise that improvement will come!

Contents

UNIT 1 Narrative   1

READING: Narrative   1

Reading Strategies: The Preparation — Surveying, Anticipating, and Skimming   1
    Reading Preparation by Surveying a Book   1
    Reading Preparation by Anticipating and Skimming   2
Words and the Language: Words in Context — Definitions   4
Reading Narratives   6

READINGS: SELECTION ONE   8
    Ideas to Think About   8
    Vocabulary   8
    from Autobiography by Agatha Christie   8
    Discussion   10

READINGS: SELECTION TWO   11
    Ideas to Think About   11
    Vocabulary   11
    from Maud Martha by Gwendolyn Brooks   11
    Discussion   13

READINGS: SELECTION THREE   15
    Ideas to Think About   15
    Vocabulary   15

In the Islands *from* The White Album by Joan
        Didion   15
    Discussion   17

WRITING: Narrative   19

Writing Assignment: A One-Paragraph Narrative Essay   19
    Assignment   19
Brainstorming, Shaping, and Writing the First Draft   21
Revising the One-Paragraph Narrative Essay   22
    Basic Revision Questions   22
    Additional Questions   23
Editing   24
    Word Choice: Strong and Weak Verbs
        (1)   24
    Sentence Structure: Kernel Sentences,
        Subjects and Verbs, and Fragments   26
    Punctuation: A Review of Terminal
        Punctuation   30
Preparing the Final Copy and Proofreading   31

UNIT 2 Description   33

READING: Description   33

Reading Strategies: Reading for Controlling Ideas   33
    Words   33
    Sentences   34
    Paragraphs   35
    Essays and Extended Passages   38
Words and the Language: Words in Context — Restatement
    and Example   39
Reading Descriptions   41

READINGS: SELECTION ONE   43
    Ideas to Think About   43
    Vocabulary   43
    from My Journal by Henry David Thoreau   43
    Discussion   44

READINGS: SELECTION TWO   45
    Ideas to Think About   45
    Vocabulary   45
    from Rain Song by Frank Waters   45
    Discussion   48

READINGS: SELECTION THREE   50
    Ideas to Think About   50

Vocabulary   50
from The Other Side of the Bull Mountains by John Heminway   50
Discussion   56

WRITING: Description   58

Writing Assignment: A One-Paragraph Descriptive Essay   58
    Assignment   59
Brainstorming and Shaping   60
Writing the First Draft   62
Revising the One-Paragraph Descriptive Essay   63
    Basic Revision Questions   63
    Additional Questions   63
Editing   64
    Word Choice: Abstract and Concrete Nouns; Relative and Specific Adjectives   64
    Sentence Structure: Coordination   68
    Punctuation: The Compound Sentence   73
Preparing the Final Copy and Proofreading   76

UNIT 3   Exposition: The Development of Ideas   77

READING: Exposition: The Development of Ideas   77

Reading Strategies: Comprehension through Supporting Ideas; Recognition of Levels of Generality   77
    Types of Supporting Ideas   77
Words and the Language: Words in Context — Contrast and Negation   80
Reading Exposition: Information   82

READINGS: SELECTION ONE   83
    Ideas to Think About   83
    Vocabulary   83
    from The Magic of Memory by Laurence Cherry   83
    Discussion   86

READINGS: SELECTION TWO   88
    Ideas to Think About   88
    Vocabulary   88
    Mankind's Better Moments by Barbara Tuchman   88
    Discussion   95

READINGS: SELECTION THREE   96
    Ideas to Think About   96
    Vocabulary   96
    Symbol of Success: The Real Horatio Alger by
        Anthony Brandt   96
    Discussion   101

WRITING: Exposition: Information   102

Writing Assignment: A One-Paragraph Topic, Restriction,
    Illustration Essay   102
    Assignment   105
Brainstorming and Shaping   109
    Identifying Your Audience   109
    Choosing the Illustration   109
Writing the First Draft   112
Revising the One-paragraph Topic, Restriction, Illustration
    Essay   112
    Basic Revision Questions   112
    Additional Questions   112
Editing   113
    Word Choice: Denotation and
        Connotation   113
    Sentence Structure: Subordination   116
    Punctuation: Commas with
        Subordinators   121
Preparing the Final Copy and Proofreading   124

UNIT 4   Exposition: Definition   125

READING: Exposition: Definition   125

Reading Strategies: Phrase Reading   125
Cloze Exercise   128
Words and the Language: Using Context to Infer
    Meaning   129

READINGS: SELECTION ONE   131
    Ideas to Think About   131
    Vocabulary   131
    Your Better Basic Supermother by Ellen
        Goodman   131
    Discussion   133

READINGS: SELECTION TWO   **134**
    Ideas to Think About   **134**
    Vocabulary   **134**
    Why Man Explores (1) by Philip Morrison   **134**
    Discussion   **135**

READINGS: SELECTION THREE   **137**
    Ideas to Think About   **137**
    Vocabulary   **137**
    from Confessions of a City Woodcutter by George H. Haas   **137**
    Discussion   **143**

WRITING: Exposition: Definition   145

Writing Assignment: A Three-Paragraph Definition Essay   **145**
    Assignment   **146**
Brainstorming and Shaping   **149**
    Group Work   **149**
    Individual Work   **149**
Writing the First Draft   **150**
Revising the Three-Paragraph Definition Essay   **150**
    Basic Revision Questions   **150**
    Special Questions for a Three-Paragraph Essay   **150**
Editing   **151**
    Word Choice: Strong and Weak Verbs (2)   **151**
    Sentence Structure: Combining for Style   **155**
    Punctuation: Commas with Items in a Series; Comma Review   **159**
Preparing the Final Copy and Proofreading   **161**

UNIT 5   Exposition: Problems and Solutions; Questions and Answers   **163**

READING: Exposition: Problems and Solutions; Questions and Answers   163

Reading Strategies: Scanning   **163**
Cloze Exercise: Focus on Nouns and Coordinators   **164**
Words and the Language: The Structure of Words — Roots   **167**

READINGS: SELECTION ONE **170**
    Ideas to Think About **170**
    Vocabulary **170**
    Reflections on My Brother's Murder by David Finn **170**
    Discussion **173**

READINGS: SELECTION TWO **174**
    Ideas to Think About **174**
    Vocabulary **174**
    We'd Better Not Make Book on U.S. Literacy by Robert C. Solomon **174**
    Discussion **176**

READINGS: SELECTION THREE **178**
    Ideas to Think About **178**
    Vocabulary **178**
    from Vegetarianism: Can You Get by Without Meat? from *Consumer Reports* **178**
    Discussion **184**

WRITING: Exposition: Problems and Solutions; Questions and Answers **185**

Writing Assignment: A Three-Paragraph Problem/Solution or Question/Answer Essay **185**
    The Thesis Statement **185**
    Assignment **189**
Brainstorming and Shaping **194**
    Choosing Materials for Your Solution or Answer Section **196**
Writing the First Draft **196**
Revising the Three-Paragraph Problem/Solution or Question/Answer Essay **196**
    Basic Revision Questions **197**
    Additional Questions **197**
Editing **198**
    Word Choice: Appropriate Language — Levels of Usage; Clichés **198**
    Sentence Structure: Combining through Relative Clauses **202**
    Punctuation: Midbranch Commas **207**
Preparing the Final Copy and Proofreading **210**

UNIT 6 Exposition: Comparison and Contrast 213

READING: Exposition: Comparison and Contrast 213

Reading Strategies: Reading and Recognizing
   Transitions 213
      Signal Words 214
      Illustration Words 215
      Order or Time Sequence Words 215
      Addition Words 215
      Comparison Words 215
      Contrast Words 216
      Cause-Effect Words 216
      Summary Words 216
      Heading and Subheading Words 217
Cloze Exercise — Focus on Adjectives 218
Words and the Language: The Structure of Words —
   Prefixes 219

READINGS: SELECTION ONE 222
      Ideas to Think About 222
      Vocabulary 222
      The Silent Generation: An Essay by Anatole
         Broyard 222
      Discussion 224

READINGS: SELECTION TWO 226
      Ideas to Think About 226
      Vocabulary 226
      Rails: From Old World to New by John H.
         White, Jr. 226
      Discussion 231

READINGS: SELECTION THREE 232
      Ideas to Think About 232
      Vocabulary 232
      from Modernized Ritual of Rodeo by Paul
         O'Neill 232
      Discussion 239

WRITING: Exposition: Comparison and Contrast 240

Writing Assignment: A Three-Paragraph Comparison and
   Contrast Essay 240
      Assignment 240
   Brainstorming and Shaping 244
   Writing the First Draft 248

Revising the Three-Paragraph Comparison and Contrast
   Essay   248
      Basic Revision Questions   249
      Additional Questions   249
   Editing   250
      Word Choice: Transitions   250
      Sentence Structure: Review of Style   252
      Punctuation: Review of Comma Usage   256
      Preparing the Final Copy and
         Proofreading   258

UNIT 7   Exposition: Cause and Effect; Effect and Cause   259

READING: Exposition: Cause and Effect; Effect and Cause   259

Reading Strategies: Reading for Different Purposes —
   Reports, Articles, and Essays in Various
   Disciplines   259
      The Précis   260
Cloze Exercise: Focus on Pronouns   260
Words and the Language: The Structure of Words —
   Suffixes   262

READINGS: SELECTION ONE   265
   Ideas to Think About   265
   Vocabulary   265
   Fear of Dearth by Carll Tucker   265
   Discussion   267

READINGS: SELECTION TWO   268
   Ideas to Think About   268
   Vocabulary   268
   Pomp and Civil Engineering by Samuel C.
      Florman   268
   Discussion   273

READINGS: SELECTION THREE   274
   Ideas to Think About   274
   Vocabulary   274
   Memories of a Bilingual Education by Richard
      Rodriguez   274
   Discussion   287

WRITING: Exposition: Cause and Effect; Effect and Cause   **288**

Writing Assignment: A Three-Paragraph Cause-and-Effect or Effect-and-Cause Essay   **288**
    Assignment   **289**
Brainstorming and Shaping   **293**
    Cause and Effect   **294**
    Effect and Cause   **296**
Writing the First Draft   **298**
Revising the Three-Paragraph Cause-and-Effect or Effect-and-Cause Essay   **298**
    Basic Revision Questions   **298**
    Additional Questions   **299**
Editing   **300**
    Word Choice: Transitions in the Longer Essay   **300**
    Sentence Structure: Participles   **301**
    Punctuation: Capitalization   **304**
Preparing the Final Copy and Proofreading   **308**

UNIT 8   Exposition: Opinion   309

READING: Exposition: Opinion   **309**

Reading Strategies: Reviewing for Tests   **309**
    Scheduling Time   **309**
    Rereading By Scanning   **310**
    Organizing the Material   **310**
    Anticipating Test Questions   **312**
    Objective Tests   **313**
Cloze Exercise: Focus on Adverbs   **313**
Words and the Language: The Dictionary   **315**
    Using the Dictionary   **316**

READINGS: SELECTION ONE   **319**
    Ideas to Think About   **319**
    Vocabulary   **319**
    Indian Food: A Rich Harvest by Evan Jones   **319**
    Discussion   **323**

READINGS: SELECTION TWO   **324**
    Ideas to Think About   **324**
    Vocabulary   **324**

from The Mysterious Rise and Decline of Monte
    Albán by John E. Pfeiffer   **324**
    Discussion   **330**
READINGS: SELECTION THREE   **331**
    Ideas to Think About   **331**
    Vocabulary   **331**
    Wrong Ism by J. B. Priestley   **331**
    Discussion   **334**

WRITING: Exposition: Opinion   **336**

The Three-Paragraph Essay Exam   **336**
    Thesis and Support   **336**
    Paragraph One: Support 1   **339**
    Paragraph Two: Support 2   **340**
    Paragraph Three: Support 3 and
        Conclusion   **340**
    Comparison and Contrast Essay   **341**
    Organization: Paragraph One   **342**
    Organization: The Divided or Separated
        Pattern   **342**
    Organization Choice 2: The Point-by-Point
        Pattern   **344**
    Choosing the Right Pattern   **345**
Brainstorming and Shaping   **346**
    Writing the Essay Exam   **346**
Revising the Three-Paragraph Essay Exam   **346**
    Basic Revision Questions   **346**
Editing   **347**
    Word Choice: Tone   **347**
    Sentence Structure: Noun Choices —
        Contracting and Expanding through
        Noun Clauses and Verbals   **349**
    Punctuation: Apostrophes and Quotation
        Marks   **352**
Preparing the Final Copy and Proofreading   **356**

UNIT 9   Exposition: Analysis and Evaluation   359

READING: Exposition: Analysis and Evaluation   **359**

Reading Strategies: Analysis and Evaluation   **359**
    Speaker/Writer   **359**
    Audience/Reader   **360**

Argument/Discussion 360
Style and Language 362
Cloze Exercise — Focus on Prepositional Phrases 362
Words and the Language: Technical Words 364

READINGS: SELECTION ONE 369
    Ideas to Think About 369
    Vocabulary 369
    Why Man Explores (2) by Norman Cousins 369
    Discussion 371

READINGS: SELECTION TWO 372
    Ideas to Think About 372
    Vocabulary 372
    Beware the Intellectual by Eric Hoffer 372
    Discussion 376

READINGS: SELECTION THREE 378
    Ideas to Think About 378
    Vocabulary 378
    The Fallacy of the Energy-Civilization Equation by George Basalla 378
    Discussion 385

WRITING: Exposition: Analysis and Evaluation 387

Writing Assignment: A Five-Paragraph Analytical Essay 387
    Assignment 387
Brainstorming and Shaping 390
Writing the First Draft 396
    Sample First Draft 396
Revising the Five-Paragraph Analysis Essay 397
    Basic Revision Questions 397
    Sample Revised Draft 397
Editing 399
    Word Choice: Point of View and Voice 399
    Sentence Structure: Parallel Structure for Style and Coherence 404
    Punctuation: Parentheses, Dashes, and Colons 406
    Final Draft of Sample Essay 410
Preparing the Final Copy and Proofreading 412

UNIT 10 Review 415

READING: Review 415

READINGS: SELECTION ONE 416
The Prodigal Son, Luke, XV: 11–32, *New Testament* 416

READINGS: SELECTION TWO 417
from America's Green Gold by Kathleen K. Wigner 417

READINGS: SELECTION THREE 426
Our Destiny in Space by Isaac Asimov 426

WRITING: Review 431

Writing Assignment: An Extended Essay 431
Assignment 431
Brainstorming and Shaping 432
Revising the Essay 434
Basic Revision Questions 435

APPENDIX A Supplementary Writing Lesson: Persuasion 437

APPENDIX B Additional Cloze Exercises 449

APPENDIX C Taking Lecture Notes 453

APPENDIX D Latin and Greek Prefixes, Suffixes, and Roots Commonly Used in Technical Vocabulary 459

Index 465

UNIT 1
Narrative

READING:
Narrative

Reading Strategies: The Preparation — Surveying, Anticipating, and Skimming

We read for many reasons. Sometimes we read simply for pleasure, sometimes to acquire information or knowledge, sometimes to analyze, and sometimes to review material. In other words, we don't always have the same purpose in mind when we open a book. And therefore we don't always read at the same speed or use the same reading techniques. Throughout this book you will be given a variety of reading strategies to help you adjust to many types of college reading assignments. In this unit, for example, you will learn to approach two different types of reading assignments: first, the college textbook and then, in the Readings section, the narrative.

Reading Preparation by Surveying a Book

Whenever you are assigned a textbook, you should *survey* or get an overview of the entire book; this process helps you become familiar with the general purpose and content of the material. Survey to find out how the book is organized and what kinds of aids are included to help your reading, studying, and understanding. To place the book into the proper perspective and link it clearly to your course, look at the following parts of the reading selection.

1. Read and remember the title, subtitle, and author's name. Notice where and when the book was published. Such information allows you to place the book in terms of time and place.

2. Look over the *Table of Contents*. Read through the main headings to discover the particular areas considered most important by the author. Check to see whether a *Glossary* is included to help you find specialized vocabulary definitions of words used in the text. If an *Appendix* is included, notice what it contains. Look for maps, graphs, or charts.
3. Read the *Introduction* or *Preface*. If it is very long, read only the first and last paragraphs, which will often state the main purpose of the book. If there is a *Conclusion* (or *Summary*), read it.

Reading Preparation by Anticipating and Skimming
A basic fact to accept is that every college assignment must be read more than once and sometimes more than twice, not counting review for tests! If you can accept this fact of college life, instead of feeling terrible about it, you should feel relieved — relieved to know that no one can be expected to understand difficult material after only one reading. What then should you expect to accomplish the first time you read an assignment? You should feel some kind of *anticipation* or expectation about what the material deals with. To some degree, you have already experienced anticipation when you surveyed the entire book. But when you focus on one or more chapters or even read a narrative, as you will later in this unit, you should anticipate by consciously using the reading technique of *skimming*.

When you skim, look for general ideas, rapidly trying to gain an overview. Don't seek out all details, and don't try for full understanding. Keep moving your eyes forward, never rereading, for skimming is not the same as careful reading. Skimming simply helps you preview difficult material that requires more than one reading for complete comprehension.

Skimming also has other advantages. It allows, and even encourages, you to read faster, knowing that you will be going back over the same material later for details. It also helps you to avoid becoming bogged down in a line-by-line struggle to understand everything the first time through. Skimming helps you to push on, to keep moving forward before you attempt a serious understanding of everything you have read. In other words, it is a basic step in learning to read more effectively.

Since your main purpose in skimming an assignment is to preview it for a general impression of its content, you should try to look for only the most important ideas. Use the following steps for the skimming procedure.

1. Note the chapter title. Most titles help you focus on the topic about to be discussed. If an essay or article is assigned, note the title, the date and place of original publication, and the author's name.
2. Read the introduction or first paragraph of the chapter to find the main focus. Read any "Preview" questions to help you anticipate.
3. Read any boldface headings or subheadings. They may form a clear outline of the main ideas.

4. Read the first sentence of each paragraph of the chapter or article. Seventy-five to 90 percent of expository (nonfiction) paragraphs in English express the main idea in the first sentence. (Unit 2 will show you how to find the main idea in the remaining 10–25 percent.)
5. Look at any illustrations, maps, or graphs that may emphasize important main ideas.
6. Look for any unusual **boldface** or *italicized* words or phrases but don't stop to check definitions.
7. Read the summary or the last paragraph, either of which may pull the material together for you.
8. Read through any discussion questions at the end of the reading. They will help you focus on key elements for your close reading procedure.
9. Read through the entire selection as rapidly as possible to get an overview of materials before you reread slowly.

EXERCISE 1

Skim the following paragraph, allowing yourself no more than three minutes. If you are going to skim this paragraph at home, set your alarm clock so you will not be tempted to check how much time you might have left. Remember: do not worry about learning "facts" or understanding the concepts discussed. Force your eyes to brush over all the words as fast as possible and don't reread anything.

COLOR PHOTOGRAPHY

Color photography is based upon a phenomenon of light first discovered by Sir Isaac Newton in the seventeenth century. Allowing a ray of sunlight to pass through a glass prism, Newton broke the light into a spectrum, a rainbow of colors arranged according to wave lengths. He then allowed the light reflecting from these colors to pass through a second glass prism to regain the original "white" light. The results of this experiment explain why objects appear to have color. For example, a tomato appears red because it reflects only the red wavelength of light and absorbs all others while grass appears green because it reflects the green wavelength and absorbs all others. Colors of the light spectrum visible to the human eye, that is, the colors of the rainbow, are hues of red, orange, yellow, green, blue, and violet. Those colors whose rays can combine to form other colors are called *primary* colors and those colors whose rays can combine to form white are called *secondary* colors. The three Primary colors used in photography are red, green, and blue (a bluish-violet); the three Secondary colors of photography are yellow, cyan (bluish-green), and magenta. Incorporating these principles of light and color, photographic film manufacturers produce camera film by layering chemical emulsions sensitive to blue, green, and red wavelengths on a film's surface.

After you have finished skimming, try to state the paragraph's main idea in one sentence. Then jot down any information you can recall. Now reread the paragraph more slowly, noting the primary points of discussion. This second reading should proceed rather smoothly since you already have some idea of the paragraph's contents.

EXERCISE 2

Take a few minutes to preread one of this unit's reading selections to acquaint yourself with its main idea. After you have finished surveying, anticipating, and skimming, jot down the selection's main idea in one sentence and note any other information or ideas you might remember. After you have completed your reading assignment, look over your notes to see how accurate you were.

Words and the Language: Words in Context — Definitions

We all have four vocabularies — one for listening, one for speaking, one for reading, and one for writing. These vocabularies overlap, of course, since we use certain common words such as *come, mother,* and *mountain* in our listening, speaking, reading, and writing vocabularies. Other words we might write but do not ordinarily use in speech, often because they are more formal: *pragmatic* for *useful, reiterate* for *repeat,* or *condescend* for *look down on.* Still others words we might recognize if we heard or read them, often because we have a context to help with meaning, but we might not be familiar enough with them to use them in speaking or writing. Examples of such words are: *ameliorate, felicity,* and *harbinger.*

When you were a child, new words entered your working vocabulary — your speaking and writing vocabulary — largely through listening. Now that you are an adult, most words enter your working vocabulary through your reading. In this section of each unit, you will learn strategies for increasing your reading vocabulary. The strategies can be divided into three major groups: *context, structure,* and *dictionary.* You will be studying the context of words in the next four units. (By *context,* we mean the environment of the word, the sentence, and the paragraph in which it occurs.) The structure of a word, discussed in Units 5, 6, and 7, concerns its parts and their relationship: the prefixes, roots, and suffixes. The dictionary, which you will study at the end of this text, is a reference tool that will tell you not only what words mean, but also how they should be pronounced and where they come from. To increase your reading vocabulary, then, you need to learn to use these strategies.

1. *Context* — guessing at the meaning of a word by picking up clues in the surrounding words.
2. *Structure* — looking for clues to meaning in the parts of the word.
3. *Dictionary* — looking up the meaning of the word if the other two strategies do not work, if you want to check yourself, or if you want to find out extra information about the word.

Good readers take chances. Rather than stopping to look up each unfamiliar word in a dictionary and thus interrupting the flow of thought, they take chances by guessing at the meaning of new words and in so doing become fast readers with good comprehension. You can learn to take chances too, and even though some of your chances will result in mistakes, the habit of taking chances will make you a faster, more efficient reader. However, in order to guess intelligently, you need to learn to pick up the clues to meaning in the context.

The most obvious kind of contextual clue is the author's definitions that are sometimes placed within the discussion. The author can offer a *full definition*, a *partial definition*, or a *synonym*. Study the following examples of definitions carefully, noting the care given by the authors to provide all necessary information to the reader.

Examples

FULL DEFINITION

Another philosophy that can lead to a vegetarian regimen is *Zen macrobiotics*, a system devised by a writer named George Ohsawa in the 1960's. Ohsawa prescribed a series of ten diets, a progression from meals that include some animal protein, such as fish, to a very restricted diet consisting mainly of brown rice (the perfect balanced food, according to Ohsawa). The "higher" macrobiotic diets have become notorious for sometimes causing severe malnutrition and even death. They are especially dangerous for children.

— *"Vegetarianism: Can You Get By Without Meat?"* from *Consumer Reports*

The total vegetarian, a rarity in the United States, eats no animal products at all. Some total vegetarians, called *vegans*, also refuse to use fur, leather, wool, and other inedible animal products, because they believe it wrong to exploit animals for any reason.

— *"Vegetarianism: Can You Get By Without Meat?"*

PARTIAL DEFINITION

Alzheimer's disease, a progressive ailment that leads to almost total memory loss.

— Cherry, *"The Magic of Memory"*

A photographic memory — the ability to look at something, such as a printed page, for just a few seconds, and then read it back as if they were looking at a photograph of the page in their minds.

— Cherry, *"The Magic of Memory"*

SYNONYM

My father was *adamant* (unyielding), refusing to raise my allowance.

Henry VII was the first Tudor *monarch* of England, serving as the nation's King after the defeat of Richard III.

EXERCISE 1

Look through the daily newspaper or a magazine to find examples of full definitions, partial definitions, and definitions through the use of synonyms. Remember, these definitions may take the form of a full paragraph, a sentence, a phrase, or a single word. Sometimes they might be enclosed within parentheses, and sometimes they might be preceded by the phrase "that is."

EXERCISE 2

Throughout this text, we have defined many terms for you. As you work through your assignments in this unit, place asterisks (*) in the margin next to each definition. Be prepared to discuss the types of definitions used.

Reading Narratives

In the Reading Strategies section of this unit, skimming was discussed in connection with textbook reading, a type of composition called *exposition*. But skimming is equally important when you read *narration*, the type of composition seen in the three reading selections in this unit. By understanding the purpose and definition of narration, you will see how skimming can also help you to approach this kind of reading material.

The first reading in this unit, by Agatha Christie, is part of an autobiography; the second, by Gwendolyn Brooks, is a section of a novel; and the third, by Joan Didion, is a personal essay. Yet even though these forms differ, they are all narratives, and *the purpose of any narration is to tell about an event or a series of events.*

There are two types of narration. A *simple narrative* tells about an event or events by arranging the details mainly in a natural (chronological) time sequence, such as in a newspaper or television report of an automobile accident. A *narrative with plot* also relates an event or events but is often not entirely chronological. The details may be arranged according to the *plot* (the interaction or interrelationship of opposing forces), which builds to a high point (climax), and then to a solution. In a sense, the plot is an artificial or artistic arrangement of events. It is usually thought of in connection with fiction, yet sometimes even writers of nonfiction manipulate the time sequence of their narrative, either to create suspense or to make a special point about an event.

Understanding a sequence of events is basic to understanding narrative. To grasp time sequence, keep the following ideas in mind as you skim.

1. If the main details of the event or events fall into a chronological order, the writing is *simple narrative*, and by skimming you have gained a quick, simple overview.
2. If the main details of the event or events shift back and forth in time, the writing is *narrative with plot* and therefore more complicated than the simple narrative. In such a case, you have gained a general idea as a *preliminary* step toward sorting out time sequence when you read closely.

As you read, also look closely at the author's treatment of setting and character. *Setting* is the word used to refer to the physical (and sometimes spiritual or emotional) background for the action of a narrative. When authors establish their settings, they often use description, a form of composition that will be discussed more fully in the next unit. Think of description here as details. As you skim, notice the following things about setting.

1. If many descriptive details are given, setting may be important. Make a note to look closely, when you reread, for a tie-in to the mood or emotions of a character.
2. Note where and when the events take place and remember to consider them when you reread.

Characters are usually involved in events; so, as you skim, focus on any people associated with the narrative. Consider the following as you reread carefully.

1. Notice whether the speaker is the only character (a narrative essay *may* focus only on the speaker and his or her experiences with something — a car, an earthquake, a fire).
2. Look for characters who appear throughout the narrative; observe their actions, alone or with others; and note their outstanding characteristics (e.g., age, appearance).

Immediately preceding each reading selection you'll find "Ideas to Think About." In a sense these ideas are related to the skimming strategy, because they offer you general ideas about the reading selection or materials to reinforce your reading. In some cases, these ideas even suggest particular things to look for in an essay. Always read "Ideas to Think About" before you skim. You might even want to glance at the Discussion Questions listed after each selection. Although you may not consciously remember these questions at this point, you will automatically become more aware of things to look for. Later, of course, you will use these questions when you read closely.

READINGS: SELECTION ONE
from Autobiography
by Agatha Christie

Ideas to Think About

1. The following excerpt from Agatha Christie's *Autobiography* relates moments of childhood fear. Why do you think this author would focus upon such incidents in a book directed primarily at her adult life? In what ways do childhood fears affect adult personalities?
2. We all have recurring dreams, some pleasurable, some frightening. Can you recall one of yours? Can you suggest its relevance to your life?
3. As you read this excerpt, look for the basic division of the piece into two parts. How do these parts interact?

Vocabulary

Look at each word as it is used in the article. (The number in parentheses indicates the paragraph in which it appears.) First, try to understand the meaning from the way it is used in the sentence. Then, use the dictionary to clarify the meaning.

autobiography (headnote)   soothingly (6)
visualized (5)   placid (8)
cauldron (5)

from Autobiography

Agatha Christie (1890–1976) wrote sixty-eight detective novels, one hundred detective short stories, and seventeen plays, earning her the title the "Queen of Crime." She wrote for almost sixty years, beginning after the end of World War I and ending shortly before her death. Her works have been translated into 103 languages, produced on both English and American stages, and made into many motion pictures. Among her best-loved works are *The Murder at the Vicarage, Ten Little Indians, Murder on the Orient Express,* and *Death on the Nile*. Her autobiography,° from which the following excerpt has been taken, was started in 1950 and completed in 1965.

It was just before I was five years old that I first met fear. Nursie and I were primrosing one spring day. We had crossed the railway line and gone up Shiphay Lane, picking primroses[1] from the hedges, where they grew thickly.

We turned in through an open gate and went on picking. Our basket was growing full when a voice shouted at us, angry and rough:

---

[1] A flower.

"Wot d'you think you're doing 'ere?"

He seemed to me a giant of a man, angry and red-faced.

Nursie said we were doing no harm, only primrosing.

"Trespassing, that's what you're at. Get out of it. If you're not out of that gate in one minute, I'll boil you alive, see?"

I tugged desperately at Nursie's hand as we went. Nursie could not go fast, and indeed did not try to do so. My fear mounted. When we were at last safely in the lane I almost collapsed with relief. I was white and sick as Nursie suddenly noticed.

"Dearie," she said gently, "you didn't think he *meant* it, did you? Not to boil you or whatever it was?"

I nodded dumbly. I had visualized° it. A great steaming cauldron° on a fire, myself being thrust into it. My agonized screams. It was all deadly real to me.

Nursie talked soothingly.° It was a way people had of speaking. A kind of joke, as it were. Not a nice man, a very rude, unpleasant man, but he hadn't meant what he said. It was a joke.

It had been no joke to me, and even now when I go into a field a slight tremor goes down my spine. From that day to this I have never known so real a terror.

Yet in nightmares I never relived this particular experience. All children have nightmares, and I doubt if they are a result of nursemaids or others "frightening" them, or of any happening in real life. My own particular nightmare centered on someone I called "The Gunman." I never read a story about anyone of the kind. I called him The Gunman because he carried a gun, not because I was frightened of his shooting me, or for any reason connected with the gun. The gun was part of his appearance, which seems to me now to have been that of a Frenchman in grey-blue uniform, powdered hair in a queue[2] and a kind of three-cornered hat, and the gun was some old-fashioned kind of musket. It was his mere presence that was frightening. The dream would be quite ordinary — a tea party, or a walk with various people, usually a mild festivity of some kind. Then suddenly a feeling of uneasiness would come. There was someone — *someone who ought not to be there* — a horrid feeling of fear: and then I would see him — sitting at the tea table, walking along the beach, joining in the game. His pale blue eyes would meet mine, and I would wake up shrieking:

"The Gunman, the Gunman!"

"Miss Agatha had one of her gunman dreams last night," Nursie would report in her placid° voice.

"Why is he so frightening, darling?" my mother would ask. "What do you think he will do to you?"

---

[2] A braid.

But I didn't know why he was frightening. Later the dream varied. The Gunman was not always in costume. Sometimes, as we sat round a tea table, I would look across at a friend, or a member of the family, and I would suddenly realize that it was *not* Dorothy or Phyllis or Monty, or my mother or whoever it might be. The pale blue eyes in the familiar face met mine — under the familiar appearance. *It was really the Gunman.*

Discussion
1. What clues in this selection forecast the author's career?
2. How does Christie organize this selection? Is it all chronological? Why do you think the author chose this pattern of organization?
3. The author tells of a frightening episode from her childhood and an often repeated nightmare. How does she link them to each other? What relationships are not mentioned but are obvious to you?
4. The first sentence of this excerpt introduces the main idea. Which sentence shows a shift from one kind of fear to another?

READINGS: SELECTION TWO

from Maud Martha
by Gwendolyn Brooks

Ideas to Think About

1. This excerpt from Gwendolyn Brooks's novel *Maud Martha* concerns the character's experience as the plain sister of a beautiful girl. Before reading, consider how our society reacts to females who are not physically attractive.
2. Psychologists often comment upon the rivalry among children in a family. Do you believe such rivalry must bring about hatred? Resentment? Jealousy? Pain? Alienation? Can "sibling° rivalry" have positive effects?
3. In the following selection, Maud Martha remembers three disappointments, each centering on a different male character. Look for these disappointments as you read.

Vocabulary

Look at each word as it is used in the article. (The number in parentheses indicates the paragraph in which it appears.) First, try to understand the meaning from the way it is used in the sentence. Then, use the dictionary to clarify the meaning.

sibling (Ideas to Think About) prestige (9)
autobiography (headnote) pathetic (9)
consolation (5) vicariously (Discussion)

from Maud Martha

Gwendolyn Brooks (1917–   ) grew up in the slums of Chicago in a family of music lovers. She began writing poetry while still in her teens and still writes and teaches writing in Chicago. She won the Pulitzer Prize in 1950 for her second book of poetry, *Annie Allen*. In addition to her poetry, collected in *The World of Gwendolyn Brooks* (1970), she has written an autobiography° (1972) and the short novel *Maud Martha* (1953) from which the excerpt is taken. Her writings communicate the experience of growing up as a black in America.

What she remembered was Emmanuel: laughing, glinting in the sun; kneeing his wagon toward them, as they walked tardily home from school. Six years ago.

"How about a ride?" Emmanuel had hailed.

She had, daringly — it was not her way, not her native way — made a quip.¹ A "sophisticated" quip. "Hi, handsome!" Instantly he had scowled, his dark face darkening.

---

¹ A remark.

"I don't mean you, you old black gal," little Emmanuel had exclaimed. "I mean Helen."

He had meant Helen, and Helen on the reissue of the invitation had climbed, without a word, into the wagon and was off and away.

Even now, at seventeen — high school graduate, mistress of her fate, and a ten-dollar-a-week file clerk in the very Forty-seventh Street lawyer's office where Helen was a fifteen-dollar-a-week typist — as she sat on Helen's bed and watched Helen primp for a party, the memory hurt. There was no consolation° in the thought that not now and not then would she have *had* Emmanuel "off a Christmas tree." For the basic situation had never changed. Helen was still the one they wanted in the wagon, still "the pretty one," "the dainty one." The lovely one.

She did not know what it was. She had tried to find the something that must be there to imitate, that she might imitate it. But she did not know what it was. I wash as much as Helen does, she thought. My hair is longer and thicker, she thought. I'm much smarter. I read books and newspapers and old folks like to talk with me, she thought.

But the kernel of the matter was that, in spite of these things, she was poor, and Helen was still the ranking queen, not only with the Emmanuels of the world, but even with their father — their mother — their brother. She did not blame the family. It was not their fault. She understood. They could not help it. They were enslaved, were fascinated, and they were not at all to blame.

Her noble understanding of their blamelessness did not make any easier to bear such a circumstance as Harry's springing to open a door so that Helen's soft little hands might not have to cope with the sullying[2] of a doorknob, or running her errands, to save the sweet and fine little feet, or shouldering Helen's part against Maud Martha. Especially could these items burn when Maud Martha recalled her comradely rompings with Harry, watched by the gentle Helen from the clean and gentle harbor of the porch: take the day, for example, when Harry had been chased by those five big boys from Forty-first and Wabash, cursing, smelling, beast-like boys with bats and rocks, and little stones that were more worrying than rocks; on that occasion, out Maud Martha had dashed, when she saw from the front-room window Harry, panting and torn, racing for home; out she had dashed and down into the street with one of the smaller porch chairs held high over her head, and while Harry gained first the porch and next the safety side of the front door she had swung left, swung right, clouting[3] a head here, a head there, and screaming at the top of her lungs, "Y' leave my brother alone!" And who had washed those bloody wounds, and afterward vaselined them down? Really — in spite of every-

---

[2] Making dirty.
[3] Hitting.

thing she could not understand why Harry had to hold open doors for Helen, and calmly let them slam in her, Maud Martha's, his friend's face.

It did not please her either, at the breakfast table, to watch her father drink his coffee and contentedly think (oh, she knew it!), as Helen started on her grapefruit, how daintily she ate, how gracefully she sat in her chair, how pure was her robe and unwrinkled, how neatly she had arranged her hair. Their father preferred Helen's hair to Maud Martha's (Maud Martha knew), which impressed him, not with its length and body, but simply with its apparent untamableness; for he would never get over that zeal of his for order in all things, in character, in housekeeping, in his own labor, in grooming, in human relationships. Always he had worried about Helen's homework, Helen's health. And now that the boys were taking her out, he believed not one of them worthy of her, not one of them good enough to receive a note of her sweet voice: he insisted that she be returned before midnight. Yet who was it who sympathized with him in his decision to remain, for the rest of his days, the simple janitor! when everyone else was urging him to get out, get prestige,° make more money? Who was it who sympathized with him in his almost desperate love for his old house? Who followed him about, emotionally speaking, loving this, doting on that? The kitchen, for instance, that was not beautiful in any way! The walls and ceilings, that were cracked. The chairs, which cried when people sat in them. The tables, that grieved audibly if anyone rested more than two fingers upon them. The huge cabinets, old and tired (when you shut their doors or drawers there was a sick, bickering little sound). The radiators, high and hideous. And underneath the low sink coiled unlovely pipes, that Helen said made her think of a careless woman's underwear, peeping out. In fact, often had Helen given her opinion, unasked, of the whole house, of the whole "hulk of rotten wood." Often had her cool and gentle eyes sneered, gently and coolly, at her father's determination to hold his poor estate. But take that kitchen, for instance! Maud Martha, taking it, saw herself there, up and down her seventeen years, eating apples after school; making sweet potato tarts; drawing, on the pathetic° table, the horse that won her the sixth grade prize; getting her hair curled for her first party, at that stove; washing dishes by summer twilight, with the back door wide open; making cheese and peanut butter sandwiches for a picnic. And even crying, crying in that pantry, when no one knew. The old sorrows brought there! — now dried, flattened out, breaking into interesting dust at the merest look . . .

"You'll never get a boy friend," said Helen, fluffing on her Golden Peacock powder, "if you don't stop reading those books."

Discussion

1. A major difficulty in writing narratives is to create excitement and tension, bringing a situation to life so that the reader can experience it vicariously.°

Some ways to achieve this are by using dialogue, offering vivid descriptions, building to a climax, and leaving some conclusions unstated. Which of these techniques are used by Brooks?
2. Evaluate the interlocking situations and time periods in this excerpt. Does the writer use a straightforward chronological organization? If not, how does she organize this section?
3. Compare the two sisters and assess their personalities.
4. Maud Martha either refuses to "play the game" to get a boyfriend, or else does not know how to. Should she try to change in order to be more popular with men? Should girls and women in real life "play the game"? Why? What games do men feel pressured to play?
5. How does Maud Martha feel toward her sister? Parents? Friends?
6. During adolescence, Maud Martha experiences much pain. What effect do the three male characters have on Maud Martha? Discuss whether or not the wounds or scars of adolescence can ever be healed.

READINGS: SELECTION THREE
"In the Islands" *from* The White Album
by Joan Didion

Ideas to Think About
1. Recall a sudden moment of self-awareness. What brought it about? For example, have you ever realized why you dislike a certain acquaintance or need constant approval of your actions from friends? What brought about these new understandings of your behavior?
2. Have you ever felt miserable, depressed, and alone on a beautiful day or at a place where the surroundings have been in complete and even terrible contrast to what you were feeling? What did you learn from these situations?
3. "In the Islands" deals with the writer's thoughts, emotions, and actions. As you read, notice when she describes her extreme situation and when she describes her feelings. Why does she include them both in one piece of writing?

Vocabulary

Look at each word as it is used in the article. (The number in parentheses indicates the paragraph in which it appears.) First, try to understand the meaning from the way it is used in the sentence. Then, use the dictionary to clarify the meaning.

translucent (1)
anticlimax (2)
alienation (4)
microcosm (4)

restorative (5)
rancor (5)
vicarious (Discussion)

"In the Islands" *from* The White Album

Joan Didion (1934–) is one of America's finest contemporary writers of essays and novels. A native Californian, she reveals a Western sensibility as she interprets the fears, concerns, and realities of our time. Among her best-known works are *Slouching Towards Bethlehem, Play It As It Lays,* and *The Book of Common Prayer*. In the following excerpt from her latest book, *The White Album*, she comments on the problem of alienation through a focus on her own inner and outer worlds.

1969: I had better tell you where I am, and why. I am sitting in a high-ceiling room in the Royal Hawaiian Hotel in Honolulu watching the long translucent° curtains billow in the trade winds and trying to put my life back together. My husband is here, and our daughter, age three. She is blonde and barefoot, a child of paradise in a frangipani lei, and she does not understand why she cannot go to the beach. She cannot go to the beach because there has been an earthquake in the Aleutians, 7.5 on the Richter scale, and a tidal wave is expected. In two or three minutes the wave, if there is one, will hit Midway Island, and we are awaiting word from Midway. My husband watches the television screen. I watch the curtains, and imagine the swell of the water.

The bulletin, when it comes, is a distinct anticlimax:° Midway reports no unusual wave action. My husband switches off the television set and stares out the window. I avoid his eyes, and brush the baby's hair. In the absence of a natural disaster we are left again to our own uneasy devices. We are here on this island in the middle of the Pacific in lieu of filing for divorce.

I tell you this not as aimless revelation but because I want you to know, as you read me, precisely who I am and where I am and what is on my mind. I want you to understand exactly what you are getting; you are getting a woman who for some time now has felt radically separated from most of the ideas that seem to interest other people. You are getting a woman who somewhere along the line misplaced whatever slight faith she ever had in the social contract, in the meliorative[1] principle, in the whole grand pattern of human endeavor. Quite often during the past several years I have felt myself a sleepwalker, moving through the world unconscious of the moment's high issues, oblivious to its data, alert only to the stuff of bad dreams, the children burning in the locked car in the supermarket parking lot, the bike boy stripping down stolen cars on the captive cripple's ranch, the freeway sniper who feels "real bad" about picking off the family of five, the hustlers, the insane, the cunning Okie faces that turn up in military investigations, the sullen lurkers in doorways, the lost children, all the ignorant armies, jostling in the night. Acquaintances read *The New York Times,* and try to tell me the news of the world. I listen to call-in shows.

You will perceive that such a view of the world presents difficulties. I have trouble making certain connections. I have trouble maintaining the basic notion that keeping promises matters in a world where everything I was taught seems beside the point. The point itself seems increasingly obscure. I came into adult life equipped with an essentially romantic ethic, holding always before me the examples of Axel Heyst in *Victory* and Milly Theale in *The Wings of the Dove* and Charlotte Rittenmayer in *The Wild Palms* and a few dozen others like them, believing as they did that salvation lay in extreme and doomed commitments, promises made and somehow kept outside the range of normal social experience. I still believe that, but I have trouble reconciling salvation with those ignorant

---

[1] Leading to improvement.

armies camped in my mind. I could indulge here in a little idle generalization, could lay off my own state of profound emotional shock on the larger cultural breakdown, could talk fast about convulsions in the society and alienation° and anomie² and maybe even assassination, but that would be just one more stylish shell game. I am not the society microcosm.° I am a thirty-four-year-old woman with long straight hair and an old bikini bathing suit and bad nerves sitting on an island in the middle of the Pacific waiting for a tidal wave that will not come.

We spend, my husband and I and the baby, a restorative° week in paradise. We are each other's model of consideration, tact, restraint at the very edge of the precipice. He refrains from noticing when I am staring at nothing, and in turn I refrain from dwelling at length upon a newspaper story about a couple who apparently threw their infant and then themselves into the boiling crater of a live volcano in Maui. We also refrain from mentioning any kicked-down doors, hospitalized psychotics, any chronic anxieties or packed suitcases. We lie in the sun, drive out through the cane to Waimea Bay. We breakfast on the terrace, and gray-haired women smile benevolently at us. I smile back. Happy families are all alike on the terrace of the Royal Hawaiian Hotel in Honolulu. My husband comes in from Kalakaua Avenue one morning and tells me that he has seen a six-foot-two drag queen we know in Los Angeles. Our acquaintance was shopping, my husband reports, for a fishnet bikini and did not speak. We both laugh. I am reminded that we laugh at the same things, and read him this complaint from a very old copy of *Honolulu* Magazine I picked up in someone's office: "When President Johnson recently came to Honolulu, the morning paper's banner read something like 'Pickets to Greet President.'" Would it not have been just as newsworthy to say "Warm Aloha to Greet President?" At the end of the week I tell my husband that I am going to try harder to make things matter. My husband says that he had heard that before, but the air is warm and the baby has another frangipani lei and there is no rancor° in his voice. Maybe it can be all right, I say. Maybe, he says.

Discussion

1. Notice that Didion uses present-tense verbs, such as *am sitting, are waiting*, in this selection. Can you justify her choice? For example, does the present tense add excitement? Interest? Intensity? What kinds of vicarious° feelings does the present tense allow?
2. Didion's descriptive choices are particularly effective because they are concise. Notice, for example, "I am a thirty-four-year-old woman with long straight hair and an old bikini bathing suit and bad nerves. . . ." There are only five details: age, sex, hair style, clothing, and a psychological clue.

---

² Absence of social norms.

Try changing any one of the details without changing the exact impression the author gives. With only these sparse details, can you describe the author more fully? What does each of the five details reveal about her?
3. Notice Didion's list of the "stuff of bad dreams." In what way might this "stuff" be considered "high issues"? How does her phrase "ignorant armies" relate to high issues? "In the Islands" deals with the writer's emotions, thoughts, and actions. Where does she describe her outer situation and where does she describe feelings?

WRITING:
Narrative

Writing Assignment: A One-Paragraph Narrative Essay

Narration not only forms the basis for novels, short stories, biographies, and autobiographies, but also enriches letters and informative essays. Varying in length from brief paragraphs to many pages, narrations capture the interest of readers through a story-like recounting of events or series of events. At times, these narrative passages dramatize an author's theme; at other times, they set the scenes for formal presentations of ideas; and at still other times, they animate points of interest within a discussion. Although in this unit you will be asked to write only a one-paragraph narrative essay to help you develop your story-telling abilities, you should remember that the techniques you learn can be used for writing longer pieces and for inclusion as sections in informative essays.

This writing assignment offers you many choices of *content* or topics for a one-paragraph narrative essay. The *form* or organization, however, is set up in a rather rigid pattern to help you arrange your material in a logical and interesting way. Using this pattern may seem frustrating at first, but it will help you avoid rambling and assist you in communicating your ideas clearly. Use your imagination freely to develop your subject matter but then learn how to organize it effectively. You might find this assignment somewhat difficult, but trying to write without practice in organization is like trying to compete in a swimming meet without learning the basic strokes or going through a rigorous training period — you might survive, but you will never succeed.

The pattern of organization presented here, while not the only one possible for a narrative, will help you first to think out a purpose for your one-paragraph essay and then to develop it into a coherent unit that makes a point. More important, the pattern will allow your reader to understand the effect that a particular incident or experience has had on your life.

Assignment

Select one of the following topics based on a reading selection in this unit and write a narrative paragraph of at least eight to ten sentences. To arrange your material, use the *S-N-E* pattern of organization:

- S — *Statement* introducing the focal point of an incident or experience in the present tense. (one to two sentences)
- N — *Narrative* developing the who, when, where, why, and what of that incident or experience in the past tense. (seven to eight sentences)

> E — *Evaluation* of the incident or experience in the present tense. (one to two sentences)

As indicated above, the *S* part of the pattern leads your reader quickly and briefly into your personal experience, with an introductory statement in the present tense:

> I sit here alone, in darkness, a little afraid, remembering the night we had a prowler.

The *N* section is the narration itself, told in past tense, filling in appropriate details of what happened, where, when, why it happened, or who was involved:

> I sit here alone, in darkness, a little afraid, but not as frightened as I was the night we had a prowler. That night had an eerie feeling and the weather outside contributed to it. The rain beating against the windows as I walked toward the stairs had already made me unpleasantly aware that I was alone in the house, but the sudden, sharp noise from the kitchen downstairs terrified me. I couldn't move. Rather than going back into the bedroom and calling the police or hiding somewhere, I stood in that hall terrified, afraid to make a sound. Then I heard footsteps; someone was definitely walking around in the kitchen, and still I stood, incapable of action. Just then the rain let up slightly, and I could hear the squeaking brakes of my brother's car as it came to a stop in the driveway. The prowler heard the car too, and, one minute after his noisy exit out the window, I heard my brother's key in the lock. Finally released from my fear, I ran downstairs to meet him.

Finally, the *E* segment evaluates what the incident or experience means to you now, what it taught you, what scars it left, or why it was important:

> That night I realized that I do not respond bravely in tense, danger-filled moments.

TOPICS

CHRISTIE

1. Write about one of your dreams or nightmares that has affected you in some meaningful way.
2. Write about a moment of terror in your childhood that has had either a positive or negative effect on your life.

BROOKS

1. Each day we are faced with various "game playing" situations. These may not be exactly like the ones Maud Martha faced, but they are often as

painful. For example, sometimes we feel pressured to "game play" with our friends in order to be accepted by them. At other times, we "game play" to influence or impress our teachers, employers, parents, or dates. Write about a time you *did* or *did not* play the game. Discuss the situation and evaluate the results.
2. Write about an incident in which competition with a brother or sister affected you — maybe permanently — in some positive or negative way.

DIDION

1. Write about a time you felt alienated from those around you or from your environment, perhaps a time you felt so isolated that even the sunshine seemed hostile. Discuss what that time meant to you or what you learned from it.
2. Write about a moment when you became suddenly aware of something you never realized before. For example, perhaps you had a nightmare or an experience that made you see yourself or your world in a new way.

Brainstorming, Shaping, and Writing the First Draft

Writing assignments in this text suggest essay topics that have been designed so you will not need to do library research. They ask you, instead, to recall information and past experiences that are stored in your memory, to develop ideas, and then to shape your materials so they can become meaningful to your readers. These tasks can be very difficult, but they can be made easier if you develop some basic "brainstorming" and shaping techniques to help you along. This unit's techniques, for example, stress sharing ideas with other people so you can receive immediate reactions to your ideas before you begin to write.

EXERCISE 1

Form a group with four or five classmates. Take turns describing the events you plan to use in your paragraphs. Listen carefully and ask questions about each episode that might need clarification. Discuss possible opening statements and final evaluations. After you talk about your own episode, take careful notes on any suggestions and comments offered by the group.

EXERCISE 2

Before you begin your first draft, decide upon the focal point of your narrative section. For example, if your memorable episode concerns an adoption, the climax of your episode could be a friend shouting, "They're not your real parents! You're adopted!" Next decide upon supporting details that will give excitement and interest to that focus.

EXERCISE 3

Review your notes taken during your group session and consider how you can incorporate the suggestions of your classmates into your paragraph.

EXERCISE 4

Write your first draft.

Revising the One-Paragraph Narrative Essay

Writers and readers have a precarious relationship: writers promise to inform, persuade, or entertain, to communicate clearly, and to treat readers with respect. On the other hand, readers promise to be attentive and to evaluate the writer's evidence fairly. For, as we have said in the Introduction, writers are like puppeteers manipulating strings. Two of these strings are the writer's choices about content and organization. If writers fail to honor their responsibilities by offering misinformation, by neglecting to explain fully or to provide concrete examples, by drowning readers in excessive unnecessary details, or by failing to organize their ideas so that readers can readily grasp the information, readers may put aside the communication, dispute the evidence, or deny the writers' conclusions. In other words, once writers lose control of their material, they no longer are effective puppeteers. Their strings become tangled, and their reading audience cannot respond appropriately.

Revision, then, involves shaping and controlling an essay's content and organization, two of the most important "strings" in the writer/reader relationship. Thus, certain basic revision questions need to be asked by all writers as they read over their first drafts.

Basic Revision Questions

1. Is all my information accurate? Appropriate?
2. Is this information organized so that my reader can comprehend what I have said? Could I reorganize my paper so that it would be more effective?
3. Do I have a clear, unified focus; that is, does my paragraph telescope in on one major theme?
4. Do I offer sufficient details, examples, or explanations so that my reader gains a complete understanding of what I am trying to say?

The writing pattern for your narrative paragraph assignment is S (statement of introduction to the incident, written in the present tense), N (narrative, written in the past tense), and E (evaluation, written in the present tense). Look back at the S, N, E model beginning on page 19 and note the verb tenses used in the paragraph. Your paragraph should be easy to outline in its final version if you have followed the pattern. Your rough draft, however, may not be so clear-cut. Don't be surprised or discouraged when you reread your paragraph and find some errors of organization. We all have to put words on paper before beginning the true tasks of revision: shaping and reshaping and organizing and reorganizing. But as we reorganize, we must keep in mind that we are writing for an audience, not for ourselves; we must communicate clearly.

The following questions to ask yourself are modifications of the basic revision questions adjusted to fit this particular assignment.

Additional Questions

1. Is my opening statement clear? Does it prepare my reader for my narration?
2. Do all details in my narrative relate to the focal point?
3. Do I give my readers sufficient details so that they can follow the narrative clearly? Have I omitted any important details?
4. Have I included details that because they are unnecessary might bore my readers?
5. Is my evaluation clear? Does it relate to my focal point and the narrative itself?
6. Is my organization logical, that is, does my narrative form a clear, easily followed pattern of development?

EXERCISE 1

1. The assignment asked that you offer an opening statement in the present tense (*S*), a narration of an event in the past tense (*N*), and an evaluation of the meaning of the situation in the present tense (*E*). If we were to outline the model paragraph, the outline would look like this:

   I. Statement — present tense:
   I *sit* here alone . . .

   II. Narration — past tense:
   That night *had* an eerie feeling . . .
   I walked toward the stairs . . .

   III. Evaluation — present tense:
   I do not respond bravely in tense, danger-filled moments.

   Read over your first draft and outline it as we have done, that is, divide it into three parts. Now check over your outline. Are parts I and III in the present tense? Now consider the narration. Is it all in some form of the past tense? Check each verb carefully and correct any mistakes in tense.

2. Again read through your paragraph, but this time role play. Pretend you are, for example, an adult living in London. As this person, do you understand what the writer has said? Do you need more information, explanations, or details in order to understand the statement, experience, or evaluation? Do you empathize with the speaker in the paragraph, that is, do you feel as if you shared the narrated experience? If you cannot answer these questions with a yes, you must further revise the paragraph.

3. Choose a classmate sitting near you and exchange and read each other's papers. You should ask yourselves the same questions you posed during role playing, this time in reference to each other's papers. You should also ask yourselves if any details are unnecessary. Now discuss any problems that either of you have uncovered and revise your papers accordingly.
4. After all adjustments to your paragraph have been completed, read it over once more, this time checking to be sure that no extra materials have crept in. Are the opening statement and evaluation clearly related to the narrative? Are all situations and details in the narrative interrelated and focused on the same situation? Does the narrative follow a chronological order? If not, make the necessary adjustments before you begin to edit the paragraph. Perhaps you should make a clean copy of your revised paragraph to make editing easier.

Editing

Word Choice: Strong and Weak Verbs (1)

The first element of writing is word choice. Writers struggling to express themselves exactly need to put much effort into finding the best word for each situation. This search for the most effective word can be very frustrating, but carelessness or indifference can block any attempt to communicate clearly, that is, to transmit ideas faithfully to the reader.

Each word in an essay must therefore be chosen with care, but one type of word that requires extra attention is the *verb*. Verbs are those words that bring *action* to a communication or express a *state of being* or *existence*. This concept might sound difficult at first, but a brief review of the *function* of verbs will help you recall what you already know.

Some common *action* verbs are: *go, eat, walk, look, talk, touch, speak, throw, drown, write, take, hate,* and *love*. Notice how *action verbs* operate in the following sentences.

I *see* the stars.

She *hates* spinach.

Joshua *eats* too much.

An easy way to help locate these action verbs is to ask the following questions. "What does _____ do?" For example, "What do *I* do?" — I see the stars"; "What does *she* do?" — "She hates spinach"; "What does *Joshua* do?" — "He eats too much."

Some common *verbs of being* are: *am, is, are, was,* and *were*. Notice how *verbs of being* function in the following sentences.

I *am* happy.

Anita *was* an artist.

Michael and Gabriel *are* cousins.

Note that these three sentences have no action — nothing happens. While such statements of being are sometimes necessary in a piece of writing, they tend to be boring when used imprecisely or too frequently because they lack excitement, movement, or interest.

Two other words that lack excitement are *have* and *do*. For example, notice the lack of action in the following sentences.

I *do* many favors for her. (perform? agree to? prepare?)

I *had* a new bicycle. (bought? own? borrowed? found?)

These *verbs of being* and *have* and *do* can be joined to *action* verbs to form *verb phrases*, that is, groups of verbs that act together. For example: I *have read*. She *did sing*. He *was eating*. When used in this way, as auxiliaries, verbs of being, *have*, and *do* complement or extend the action verb; but, when used alone, they often dull communication. With these ideas in mind, work through the following exercises.

EXERCISE 1

Rewrite the following sentences, substituting more direct and precise *action verbs* for *verbs of being* and *have* and *do*.

Example:
The man at the door is a book salesman.

Revision:
The man at the door *wants to sell* us some books.

Example:
The baseball team has a record of seven wins and no losses.

Revision:
The baseball team *has won* seven games and *lost* none.

1. The president of the United States is also the commander-in-chief of the armed forces.
2. He is on the train to Chicago.
3. The parents of that boy have little control over him.
4. Whenever I am at school, I do little work.
5. The doctor has a gentle approach to her patients.
6. A newspaper is a good source of information.

7. Both of the men are engineers at Hughes Aircraft Company.
8. The children have a new teacher this year.
9. This is the first day of the semester.
10. Both Mary and Sally are pretty, but Sally has the prettier smile.

EXERCISE 2

Examine the following paragraph to see how many effective action verbs the author has used. Read the paragraph aloud. Then in a few sentences describe the effect of these action words.

> Her noble understanding of their blamelessness did not *make* any easier *to bear* such a circumstance as Harry's *springing* to open a door so that Helen's soft little hands might not have *to cope* with the sullyings of a doorknob, or *running* her errands, to *save* the sweet and fine little feet, or *shouldering* Helen's part against Maud Martha. Especially could these items *burn* when Maud Martha *recalled* her comradely rompings with Harry, *watched* by those five big boys from Forty-first and Wabash, *cursing*, *smelling*, beast-like boys! with bats and rocks, and little stones that were more worrying than rocks; on that occasion out Maud Martha had *dashed*, when she *saw* from the front-room window Harry, *panting* and *torn*, *racing* for home; out she had *dashed* and down into the street with one of the smaller porch chairs *held* high over her head, and while Harry *gained* first the porch and next the safety side of the front door she had *swung* left, *swung* right, *clouting* a head here, a head there, and *screaming* at the top of her lungs. "Y' *leave* my brother alone! Y' *leave* my brother alone!" And who had *washed* those bloody wounds, and afterward *vaselined* them down? Really — in spite of everything she could not *understand* why Harry had *to hold* open doors for Helen, and calmly *let* them *slam* in her, Maud Martha's, his friend's, face.
>
> — Brooks, *Maud Martha*

EXERCISE 3

Read over the narrative paragraph you have written. Go through each sentence carefully, underlining all your verbs. Now reexamine those verbs and circle *verbs of being* and all forms of *have* and *do*. Do these verbs of being contribute to the narrative? Would your essay be more exciting, active, and interesting if you reworked your sentences, substituting *action verbs* for verbs of being? If so, make appropriate changes.

Sentence Structure: Kernel Sentences, Subjects and Verbs, and Fragments

A sentence, not a word or phrase, is the basic *unit* of communication, and even the sentence is but a building block in a larger structure of communication, the paragraph. Though single words or phrases communicate meaning, they occur usually only in conversation. And even then, the context (the placement among other words), tone of voice, and body language help supply the listener with the missing words that would make the word or phrase into a complete sentence.

    "New here?"   "No, not exactly.   Been here six months."
        pause   pause   pause

When you hear these sentences, you receive signals to indicate that they are complete. Oral signals are heard in the tone of voice, the intensity of sound, and the pauses. Note that in the question "New here?" the speaker begins at a middle tone but ends on a higher tone and then pauses. In the two statements above, note that the voice begins on a middle level, rises to a higher tone just before the end, and then drops to a low level, again followed by a pause.

In writing, visual signals parallel those oral signals. The beginning of a sentence is signaled by a capital letter and its end by a question mark (high-pitch pause or low-pitch pause), an exclamation point (emphatic low-pitch pause), or more commonly a period (low-pitch pause).

These same sentence signals appear in the essays you will be reading and writing this semester. But essays demand a more formal style than conversation. In essays you can't leave out words or phrases, expecting your reader to supply them. So when you edit your rough drafts, you can check for complete sentences by reading your essay aloud to see if you have put periods only where your voice drops. A second way to test for complete sentences in your writing is to make sure every sentence has a subject, a verb, and a completed thought. In other words, a sentence can be defined as a complete thought using a subject and a verb and which, when written, begins with a capital letter and ends with a period.

The shortest, simplest sentence with its subject and verb is called a *kernel*. The subject is the person or thing that works with the verb to describe an action or to make an assertion.

    S   V
    Cars *jam* the freeways. (action verb)

    S   V
    Cars *are* dangerous. (verb of being)

      S   V
    Motorists *speed*. (action verb)

        S   V V V
    Such motorists *should be cited*. (action verb)

A kernel sentence can stand alone, making a complete statement by itself, or, more often, it can grow by the addition of modifiers: those words and word groups that add detail and interest to a generalization. But whether the sentence is a bare kernel or a richly modified sentence, it can be divided into subject and verb, often with modifiers clustered around them. Read the following sentences aloud to hear the clusters of words:

Cars jam the freeways at nearly every hour of the day.

Cars that emit black exhaust are dangerous to all life — people, animals, and plants.

Motorists of such cars procrastinate instead of getting their engines overhauled.

Such irresponsible *motorists* should be cited and given substantial fines.

The *rain* fell heavily.

The long-awaited *rain* fell heavily for almost a week.

The *clouds* were black.

The thunder *clouds* moving in from the Pacific were black, threatening rain.

The *lightning* split the tree.

The sudden *lightning* split the old oak tree in the front yard.

The *class* bored me.

The late afternoon *class* bored me the whole semester.

In each of these examples, the subject identifies the "what" or "who" of the sentence, and the verb describes an action involving the subject (if the verb is an action verb) or makes an assertion about the subject (if the verb is a verb of being).

EXERCISE 1

In each kernel sentence below, underline the subject and its modifiers once, the verb and its modifiers twice, then add details or modification to each part.

Example

The ballplayers lost the game.

The ballplayers on my little sister's team lost the last game of the season because of poor hitting.

1. The government granted freedom to the prisoners.
2. John sleeps late.
3. Some vandals broke into the school.
4. The women ate some hamburgers.
5. A sailboat bobbed in the water.

EXERCISE 2

The following phrases are fragments of sentences; they are subjects without verbs. Supply verbs and modifiers to make the phrases into complete sentences.

Example
Feeding the cat each morning and evening.

Revision
Feeding the cat each morning and evening can be a bothersome chore.

1. Weary after the long plane ride, the Dodgers
2. Building sand castles
3. All the King's horses and all the King's men
4. The ride to camp
5. The football players who were living in the university dorm

The following phrases are also fragments of sentences; they are verbs without subjects. Supply subjects to make the phrases into complete sentences.

6. walked slowly towards the barracks.
7. stopped wanting his usual ham and egg breakfast.
8. expects us all to get married.
9. often fail to vote in municipal elections.
10. willingly allowed me to travel in Europe.

EXERCISE 3

Now, apply these two tests to check for complete sentences. First, does the word group *sound* complete? Does your voice drop and pause at the period? Second, does it have a subject, verb, and a complete thought? If the statement is incomplete, convert it into a sentence by adding the missing subject or verb. Now add capitals and end punctuation to indicate to your reader that the sentence is complete (most written sentences end with periods, not question marks or exclamation points). Notice also that in some of the following groups of words subjects and verbs may be present, but signal words, such as *after*, *who*, *because*, *if*, or *since*, indicate a lack of completeness. In other words, your voice would drop down to the middle level, not the low level.

Example
After moving to New York last July, we

Revision
After moving to New York last July, we settled in quickly.

1. The Chinese student who left Taiwan to attend Harvard University
2. If I can buy a new car, I

3. The 1984 Olympics, scheduled to take place in Los Angeles,
4. Foreign students from Israel
5. Going nowhere

EXERCISE 4

Read your *S-N-E* paragraph aloud. Does each sentence sound complete? Does each sentence have a subject and a verb with appropriate, precise modification?

EXERCISE 5

Put your paragraph aside for a day. When you come back to it the next day, approach it as a reader rather than as a writer. Now reread your paragraph, editing it for word choice and for sentence structure.

Punctuation: A Review of Terminal Punctuation

All sentences must end with an appropriate punctuation mark. Terminal punctuation, that is, those marks that denote the end of a sentence, includes a period (.), a question mark (?), and an exclamation point(!). *Periods* mark the end of a statement.

Frances knew her multiplication tables quite well.

A university offers many different kinds of degrees.

Mark Twain wrote *Huckleberry Finn* in 1890.

Question marks signify that a question has been asked.

Did you pass Chemistry 1A?

Who is that woman standing in the corner?

Where have you been today?

Exclamation points signify a forceful or emotional order, shout, or warning.

Watch out!

I hate him!

Don't touch that!

Help!

One point to remember about exclamation points is that they can jar the reader if overused. In general, academic and professional writers seldom use forceful shouts, orders, strong emotions, or warnings, so use this punctuation mark with caution.

EXERCISE 1

Punctuate the following sentences.

1. Why I hate professional football is not difficult to explain
2. Why don't you sit down somewhere
3. Take each lesson and file it for future use
4. Stop that
5. The price of gold has risen dramatically in the past year
6. Few vegetarians will eat eggs or butter
7. The accident occurred yesterday at 8:00 A.M.
8. What thrills me most is this gift from my boyfriend
9. Are you going to stay at a hotel or are you planning to camp out
10. Nothing ever happens to encourage me to try harder

EXERCISE 2

Check each sentence in your essay for terminal punctuation marks. Have you used the proper marks for each sentence? Make necessary corrections.

Preparing the Final Copy and Proofreading

You are now ready to type or write your final copy. As you do, observe the following conventions that are usually required in all college and professional work.

1. Provide one-inch margins on the top, bottom, and right side of your paper, provide a 1½-inch margin on the left side of the paper, and write or type on only one side of the paper.
2. Include a title that previews your topic for the reader. Do not underline the title or enclose it with quotation marks.
3. Indent the beginning of each paragraph (five spaces if you are typing).
4. Correct all errors using correction fluid, erasing neatly, or crossing out neatly in ink.

Now you are ready to proofread your final copy. Again, read it aloud. This time you should read slowly, word by word, looking for errors. You might even ask a friend or relative to read it aloud as well. Ask the following questions.

1. Have I spelled words correctly?
2. Have I omitted any words or made any accidental changes in my text?
3. Have I included all necessary punctuation? Does each sentence end with a period, question mark, or exclamation point?

UNIT 2
Description

READING:
Description

Reading Strategies: Reading for Controlling Ideas

Training yourself to find the main or controlling idea of a paragraph or essay is a major step in learning to comprehend your reading assignments, whether in this book or in other college textbooks. To find these main ideas you must, of course, understand the meaning of *individual* sentences. But even more important for total comprehension, you must learn to see the relationships between ideas.

A basic step in learning to recognize relationships is to become aware of the differences between statements of large general ideas and statements of either smaller particular ideas or specific details. In this Reading Strategy section you will first practice identifying levels of generality and specificity in *words*, the smallest units of meaning. Next, you will examine larger units of meaning, *sentences*. Then you will be ready to find the large, general, controlling ideas in *paragraphs*. Finally, you should be able to recognize the controlling ideas of entire *essays*.

Words

Look at the following pairs of words and identify the differences or similarities between them. In *some* of the word pairs you will find one word that is general and one that is more specific.

Examples
spider   (*specific* — a type of insect)
insect   (*general* — a category)
furniture   (*general* — a category)
chair   (*specific* — a type of furniture)

In other pairs both words seem to be at the same level of generality or specificity.

Examples
honesty   (*equal* levels of generality —
generosity both are character qualities)
fork   (*equal* levels of specificity —
spoon   both are types of eating utensils)

EXERCISE 1

In the following word pairs, mark G for general, S for specific, or E for equal levels of generality or specificity.

1. mother
   parent
2. wood
   cord
3. car
   truck
4. house
   building
5. toe
   foot
6. love
   hate
7. city
   New York
8. religion
   Catholicism
9. soldier
   corporal
10. angry
    happy
11. instrument
    tool
12. axe
    tool
13. vehicle
    bicycle
14. disgust
    emotion

Sentences

Now consider the differences or similarities between some *sentences*. In some cases, one will seem more general and the other more specific in the sense of either supporting the general idea or expanding on it. To find the more specific statement, look for certain *key words*, perhaps a pronoun, indicating that the statement cannot stand alone. These key words seem to refer back to a more general statement or word(s).

Example
There was an *increase in* homebuilding *jobs* during the last six months. (*general*)
Most of *these new jobs* were held by young nonunion men. (*specific*)

Notice that the word *these* needs something to refer back to; it is a signal or key word showing that the sentence is not the main or general statement.

In other cases, two sentences will seem equal in levels of either generality or specificity. Here again, key words are important: words like *also, another*, or coordinating conjunctions such as *and* or *or* may signal similar levels.

Example
The *lambs were jumping* about in the meadow.
Meanwhile, goats were butting their heads in the barnyard. (*equal* levels of details)

Notice above that the word *meanwhile* signals or emphasizes the similar level of specificity.

EXERCISE 1

For each of the following pairs of sentences:

a. *Mark* the more general sentence *G* and underline key word(s).

b. Underline the word or words in the second sentence that helps you make your choice.

c. If the pair seems equally general or equally specific, *mark* them *E* and underline twice the word(s) that helped you make this choice.

1. My mother is a terrible housekeeper.
   She dusts my room about once a month.

2. A cord measures eight feet long by four feet high by four feet wide.
   It is the volume and weight of wood that the average nineteenth-century horse was expected to pull on a crude sledge over snow.

3. They changed all the locks on their doors.
   They also removed their window screens.

4. She had to go.
   I was delighted to watch the demise of the supermother.

5. Lack of money is one reason he didn't go to college.
   And lack of self-discipline is another.

Paragraphs

Now that you can distinguish between general and specific words and sentences, you can read entire paragraphs with better comprehension. In the texts or essays you read, a main idea may be stated anywhere in a paragraph; however, there are several positions where the main idea is most likely to be located. Your increased awareness of these locations not only can help you to improve your comprehension by giving you a sense of control, but also can increase your reading speed. In other words, if you have a clear idea of possible locations for main ideas, you will find yourself searching them out quickly.

The following list identifies the most common positions for main ideas of paragraphs.

1. *In the first sentence.*

    The most common placement of the main idea is the first sentence of the paragraph (sometimes it is given in the form of a question). In this type of paragraph, the author makes his or her most general statement first and then supports that general statement with details, examples, or explanations.

    Example

    Fisherman's Wharf in San Francisco is a symphony of discordant sounds. Angry claws snap as lobsters and crabs fight in their glass prison. Fish, destined for the evening meal, splash noisily as they flop from side to side in crowded tanks. The loud rasps of the scaling knife and the splattering of ice onto hard pavement crash against the chorus of shoppers bickering over prices and gulls shrilling their presence. Beyond, the sea pounds a rhythmic beat.

2. *In the last sentence.*

    The second most common placement of the main idea is at the end of a paragraph. Details, examples, or discussions come first, building up to the main idea.

    Example

    Siamese cats eat when and as much as they want. They roam around the house or outside without answering to anyone. In fact, they come to people only when the urge moves them, sometimes responding to an agreed-upon name but more often acting on some far-off call of the wild impelling them to race madly away. Sometimes they skitter quietly about the room on their own private hunt; other times they pound heavily across the carpet, dashing over the back of the couch and down, demanding attention. *The most independent of all cats, the Siamese insist on personal freedom.*

3. *In the first and last sentence.*

    Sometimes the author uses both the first and last sentences to show the *complete* main idea. That is, the first sentence is only part of the main idea and needs the additional information of the last sentence to form the complete controlling idea. At other times, the author states the same idea *twice* in the same paragraph, using the repetition for emphasis.

Example

   Several recently developed appliances are already being widely used in the home. In the kitchen, men and women use microwave ovens to cook, defrost, or reheat their food. In the bathroom, some people now have showerheads that can be adjusted to give a hydro-massage. And in some homes, people have both trash compacters and garbage disposals. *For their users, these appliances are viewed as technological advantages as well as advancements.*

4. *In the middle of the paragraph.*
   Another common location of the main idea is in the middle of the paragraph. In this type of paragraph, some details lead up to the main idea, and some additional details follow it. A variation on this pattern is the placement of the main idea in the second sentence, preceded by a sentence of detail or introduction and followed by the rest of the paragraph's details or discussion.

Example

   College students using this text prepare for close readings of the selection assigned. They examine in advance the vocabulary list, read the headnote and Ideas to Think About, and then skim the selection. *In other words, effective student readers follow specific steps to gain a clear understanding of a reading selection assigned for class discussion.* After the preparatory steps, the students read the discussion questions and then read the selection closely to find the main ideas and the vocabulary words that require a dictionary search. Next, students check the discussion questions again, making sure they will be able to take part in a class discussion. Finally, if there is any doubt about the last step, students reread the selection.

5. *Implied controlling idea.*
   Sometimes the main idea of the paragraph is implied rather than stated explicitly. But since all effectively developed paragraphs *must* have a controlling idea, the reader must infer it from the paragraph's details. As a reader, you must ask, "What is the *central focus* of this paragraph?"

Example

   I can easily walk ten, fifteen, twenty, any number of miles, commencing at my own door, without going by any house, without crossing a road except where the fox and the mink do. Concord is the oldest inland town in New England, perhaps in the States, and the walker is peculiarly favored here. There are square miles in my vicinity which have no inhabitant. First along by the river, and then the brook, and then the meadow and the woodside. Such solitude! From a hundred hills I can see civilization and abodes of man afar. These farmers and their works are scarcely more obvious than woodchucks.

— Henry David Thoreau, *My Journal*

In the above example, the central focus is found in the details describing the areas around the author's house that are suitable for solitary walks. The controlling idea is that Thoreau finds pleasure in nature, away from civilization.

EXERCISE 1

Indicate the controlling idea in each of the following paragraphs from essays in this unit.

> Now personally, I was never able to get my radish flower to blossom even in cold water. And the place mats I made from a magazine pattern ended up costing $4.65 a piece (they were also excruciatingly ugly). Furthermore — bad person that I am — when I am carpooling children on a July day in my unairconditioned car, my strongest desire is not to lead a wholesome chorus of "Ninety-nine Bottles of Beer on the Wall." I am more likely to be fantasizing about an impenetrable soundproof plastic chauffeur's barrier around my seat.
>
> — Goodman, *"Your Better Basic Supermother"*

> Pleasant warmth and fine food are not the only pleasures to be had by cutting firewood. The woodcutter soon learns a great deal about trees and woods. He has to in order to select the best firewood, and this can be a real puzzle in the jumble left by land-clearing operations. If the woodcutter also encounters some of the fine woods used in carpentry and joinery and is willing to read dendrological literature, he learns about a myriad of forest products and how they were and still are being used by some rural people.
>
> — Haas, *"Confessions of a City Woodcutter"*

Essays and Extended Passages

Just as a controlling idea governs the development of a paragraph, a controlling idea governs an essay or an entire section of a book. Finding these ideas is a very important reading strategy; it forces you to see the relationships in the passage you read. In a sense, by expressing the controlling idea, an author shows a purpose in writing, whereas by *finding* the controlling idea, you develop a purpose in reading — comprehension.

Training yourself to find the controlling idea of an essay or extended passage from a textbook should be easy for you after having worked with the main ideas of paragraphs. You now have a good understanding of the difference between general and specific and between general and supporting ideas. Even though there is no set formula for locating these main ideas, some questions can guide your reading. Ask yourself the following questions.

1. Is the controlling idea stated in the title in a shortened form?
2. What one basic idea is the author trying to impart about the subject in general? What words state or express that one thing? Are these words echoed or restated somewhere as a reinforcement of the controlling idea?
3. What seems to be the author's main purpose in writing the essay? The controlling idea is often presented in a *direct* statement of purpose.

4. Is the controlling idea stated at the beginning of the essay? Sometimes it is found at the end of the first paragraph or at the beginning of the second. One or more of the initial paragraphs may be an introduction. Try to find the separation between the introduction and the main discussion. Later we will deal specifically with types of introductions, but here, with your new-found awareness of general and particular as well as your skimming skills, you can deal with these things by trial and not so much error.
5. Is the controlling idea near the end of the essay? In the last paragraph(s)? Here too, skimming skills can help you to spot the overall controlling idea, which appears as a kind of summing up.

EXERCISE 1

Find the controlling idea in your assigned selection for this unit. Mark any place or places where the thesis is *restated* in some form. Which questions or hints from the list above helped you find the thesis?

Words and the Language: Words in Context — Restatement and Example

All writers, especially those treating highly technical or complex materials, frequently define words for their readers. More often, however, they indicate their meaning through restatement and example. In other words, they may rephrase an idea or concept in a less complex way or cite examples that clarify its meaning. For example, if an author states that "there are no true synonyms in the English language," she might explain this statement by adding "that is, even words considered to be alike have slightly different meanings and overtones." Or if a writer states that "no family can have financial security if it relies on *deficit spending*," he might clarify his comment by offering this example: "For once a family forms the habit of buying on credit, becoming addicted to the convenience of Visa and Master Card, it soons creates a quicksand of debt and sinks lower and lower without hope of rescue."

Careful reading will enable you to spot such restatements and examples, but there is a reading strategy that will help you to focus on these passages with ease. Authors often *signal* that they are about to restate an idea or cite an example by using certain phrases or punctuation marks. In the following sample sentences, some of these signals are underlined so you can become familiar with their use. Note how these phrases and punctuation marks help to focus your attention and to clarify words that are not familiar to you.

Examples

1. The criminal showed signs of being a *sociopath*. For example, he showed no remorse for his actions, could not conform to the cultural ethics of the community, lacked an ability to delay fulfillment

of his desires, and saw no wrong in any action that brought him pleasure.

2. Huckleberry Finn, like Don Quixote, is a *picaro*. <u>For instance</u>, he is an outcast who wanders through the countryside interacting with people who exemplify the sins, foibles, and follies of society.

3. The Wall Street analyst projects a *bull* market for the coming months. <u>In other words</u>, he anticipates prices of stocks to rise in the near future.

4. During the English *Renaissance*, writers often looked to classical Greek and Roman authors for inspiration. <u>To illustrate</u>, there was a rebirth of the epic, a rebirth of poetic forms, and a rebirth of dramatic techniques.

5. The miser, fearful of attorneys, did not foresee that his *holographic* will would lead to legal confusion, <u>that is</u>, contradictory opinions as to the validity of his handwriting.

6. I do not eat *red meat* <u>(</u>beef, pork, and lamb<u>)</u>.

7. In spite of my pain, I refuse to take *narcotics* <u>such as</u> codeine, phenobarbital, and morphine.

8. With the rapid increase in the price of oil, a corresponding increase will soon develop for oil-derivative *synthetic* materials: nylon, plastic, polyethylene, and urethane.

9. You must check the patient carefully for the major sign of *hyperventilation*—excessive deep breaths, a condition that causes an excess of carbon dioxide in the blood.

EXERCISE 1
Make a list of all the signals for restatements and examples: *for example, for instance*.

EXERCISE 2
For each of the nine examples above, write a definition of the underlined words.

EXERCISE 3
Skim the explanatory sections of this unit to look for five *signals* of restatements and examples. Write in your notebook how each of the five leads directly to a clarification of the discussion.

Reading Descriptions

In the Reading Strategies section of this unit, the focus shifted from *skimming*, the strategy in Unit 1 for a first reading, to strategies for a later close or in-depth reading. Finding the main or controlling idea was discussed in connection with a paragraph or an essay, the type of composition already identified as *exposition*. And just as skimming was shown to be helpful in reading exposition and *narration*, reading closely is helpful in dealing with narration, exposition, and description, the type of writing that dominates the three reading selections in this unit. However, when you understand the purpose and makeup of description, you will also understand how and why close reading of description differs somewhat from close reading of exposition.

The purpose of description is to present the reader with a picture of a person, subject, or setting. Although description is sometimes used alone, it more often appears in connection with one of the other types of writing — exposition, narration, or persuasion. *Descriptive writing, then, should be read and understood for its relationship to an author's purpose and attitudes* and for its levels of generality or specificity. These levels can reveal an author's purpose and attitude. Therefore, as a reader of description, you should note carefully the following elements of description (notice that some categories overlap).

1. *Concrete details.* A concrete detail is a specific description that supports, reflects, or expands a writer's attitude or purpose.

    Example
    The modern math student, using a calculator instead of a slide rule, makes speedy and accurate calculations.

2. *Images.* An image is a concrete, literal (real, actual) description of a person, physical object, or sensory experience that can be known through one of the five senses (sight, sound, taste, touch, and smell).

    Examples
    Lightning crackled and sizzled across the darkened sky. (sound and sight)

    The orange calico kitten's bristled tongue scratched its way across my cheek. (sight and touch; concrete details)

3. *Similes.* A simile is a comparison, using *like* or *as*, between two objects. The comparison is between two things essentially different yet similar in one aspect.

    Examples
    Anger heated up in me like water about to boil.

    The lecturer was as exciting and informative as stale beer.

4. *Metaphors.* A metaphor is an *implied* (indirect) comparison between two things without the use of *like* or *as*.

   Examples
   Neil's ugly words shredded the fabric of their friendship.

   Suddenly a woman's voice sirened throughout the hospital-like silence of the sleeping campground.

5. *Connotative language.* Connotative words or phrases imply or suggest meanings different from their dictionary definition; they may carry a positive (favorable, good) or a negative (unfavorable, bad) meaning. Some words, standing alone, may seem neutral (neither good nor bad), but in context with other words, or in a sentence, take on a connotative meaning. For example, the word *drugs* to an elderly person suffering the pains of age-related disease is positive, but, to parents with a son hooked on heroin, *drugs* is negative. Denotative language, on the other hand, means words that don't carry any emotional overtones or value judgments.

   Examples
   thin   lean   slender   scrawny   slim   skinny

   Which of the above words do you consider positive, negative, or neutral? You may find that because of a difference in values, your classmates differ with you.

EXERCISE 1

In the reading selection assigned to you in this unit, mark the descriptive passages. Underline the descriptive elements and note their type (details, images — similes, metaphors, connotation).

READINGS: SELECTION ONE
from My Journal
by Henry David Thoreau

Ideas to Think About
1. Many animals look very similar yet on close examination differ in small details. What, for example, is the difference between a frog and a toad? a butterfly and a moth? a grasshopper and a cricket?
2. Thoreau captures the sights and sounds of toads through careful observation. As you read the following paragraph, mark the places where he makes you see and hear what he sees and hears.

Vocabulary
Look at each word as it is used in the article. (The number in parentheses indicates the paragraph in which it appears.) First, try to understand the meaning from the way it is used in the sentence. Then, use the dictionary to clarify the meaning.

aquatic (1)
ludicrous (1)
quavered (1)
intermittent (1)

orifice (1)
monotonous (1)
lulling (1)
crevices (1)

from My Journal

Henry David Thoreau (1817–1862) was an American naturalist, philosopher, and poet. His works include *On Civil Disobedience, Walden,* and *A Week on the Concord and Merrimack Rivers.* The following excerpt comes from his journal in which he recorded his observations of nature and meditations on life.

My dream frog turns out to be a toad. I watched half a dozen a long time at 3:30 this afternoon in Hubbard's Pool, where they were frogging(?) lustily. They sat in the shade, either partly in the water, or on a stick; looked larger and narrower in proportion to their length than toads usually do, and moreover are aquatic.° I see them jump into the ditches as I walk. After an interval of silence, one appeared to be gulping the wind into his belly, inflating himself so that he was considerably expanded; then he discharged it all into his throat while his body or belly collapsed suddenly, expanding his throat to a remarkable size. [It] was nearly a minute inflating itself; then swelled out its sac, which is rounded and reminded me of the bag to the work-table, holding its head up [all] the while. It is whitish specked (the bag) on a dull bluish or slate ground, much bigger than all the rest of the head, and nearly an inch in diameter. It was a ludicrous° sight, with [the] so serious prominent eyes peering over it; and a deafening sound, when several were frogging at once, as I was leaning over them. The mouth [appeared] to be shut always, and perhaps the air was expelled through the nostrils. The strain appeared prolonged as long as the air lasted, and was sometimes quavered° or intermittent,° apparently by closing the orifice,° whatever it was, or the blast. . . . Their piping(?) was evidently connected with their loves. Close by, it is an unmusical monotonous° deafening sound, a steady blast — not a peep nor a croak, but a KIND of piping — but, far away, it is a dreamy, lulling° sound, and fills well the crevices° of nature.

Discussion

1. What does Thoreau reveal about the actions and sounds of toads? Why doesn't he describe all the physical features of the toads in full detail?
2. What does Thoreau mean by "the crevices of nature"? What is his attitude toward nature? Where do you think humans fit into his view of life?
3. Thoreau blends two descriptive techniques in this passage. At times he *shows* what he sees and hears; at other times he *tells* about his thoughts and experience. Point out where he *shows* and where he *tells* and then analyze the effectiveness of these techniques in this passage.

READINGS: SELECTION TWO
from Rain Song
by Frank Waters

Ideas to Think About

1. Have you ever had the opportunity to experience a ritual or ceremony of a different culture or religion? Did you feel critical? Excited? Comfortable? Like an outsider? Explain your reactions.
2. How have your attitudes toward Native Americans been influenced by history books? Other books? Movies? Have you ever known a Native American? How does this person differ from stereotypes found in books?
3. How do you feel about snakes? Do you think you could be persuaded to change your attitudes?
4. Think about any similarities you find between the ceremony discussed in "Rain Song" and a ritual in your own religion. What are the similarities and differences?
5. Find a passage where the author *shows* action in his descriptions and *tells* the meaning of the action as well.

Vocabulary

Look at each word as it is used in the article. (The number in parentheses indicates the paragraph in which it appears.) First, try to understand the meaning from the way it is used in the sentence. Then, use the dictionary to clarify the meaning.

stunted (1)	dexterously (7)
neolithic (3)	undulating (7)
esoteric (4)	consummation (8)
mandatory (4)	polarities (8)
latently (4)	cosmos (11)

from Rain Song

Frank Waters (1902–) is a distinguished Southwest author of more than forty books, both fiction and nonfiction. Born in Colorado Springs, Colorado, Waters has spent most of his life in the Southwest and as a boy lived on the Navaho reservation. He has written many books about Native American Indian life and culture, including *People of the Valley, The Woman at Otowi Crossing,* and *Masked Gods,* a book that deals with the mysticism, history, and meaning of Pueblo and Navaho ceremonies and legends. The following excerpt is from Waters' highly regarded *Book of the Hopi,* written with the help of his college-educated Hopi translator/illustrator, Oswald White Bear Fredericks.

It had been a summer of drought and despair. Niman Kachina brought no rain; for some reason the ceremony was improperly performed in some villages; in others another dance was substituted for the Home Dance. Nor did the Flute ceremony bring rain. The corn is stunted° in the fields. Old Chief Tawakwaptiwa died in April, and a successor is not yet appointed. An undercurrent of strife and evil runs through all the villages. This Snake-Antelope ceremony is the last hope, and it always brings rain. So, above as below, the sky reflects this battle between good and evil. And while the crowd, now shivering with cold, becomes restless with the long wait, the Hopis patiently watch the increasing tempo of the battle.

There comes a driving blast of sparse raindrops, each hard and cold as a pellet of ice. White Bear patiently squeezes out from the packed rows of Navajos, climbs down the ladder, and goes to the car. Down in a narrow street one can see him listening to a group of older Hopis. All are looking upward. The black storm clouds are being driven northward past the village. The rain does not come. Instead, the sky gets blacker, the air colder. White Bear returns with a coat to wrap around my thin shirt. The Navajos begin to smell, so closely we are packed together. Still we sit wordlessly watching the storm clouds turn west across the desert.

Then suddenly they file into the plaza — two rows of twelve men, each like a pair of prayer sticks for each of the six directions, the Antelopes ash-gray and white, the Snakes reddish-brown and black. The appearance of the Snake chief strikes the keynote of the somber scene. There is something neolithic° about his heavy, powerful build, his long arms, his loose black hair hanging to his massive shoulders. At the end of the line trudges a small boy. Silently they encircle the plaza four times — a strange silence accentuated by the slight rattle of gourds and seashells. As each passes in front of the *kisi*[1] he bends forward and with the right foot stomps powerfully upon the *pochta*, the sounding board over the *sipapuni*[2]. In the thick, somber silence the dull, resonant[3] stamp sounds like a faint rumble from underground echoed a moment later, like thunder from the distant storm clouds.

This is the supreme moment of mystery in the Snake Dance, the thaumaturgical[4] climax of the whole Snake-Antelope ceremony. Never elsewhere does one hear such a sound, so deep and powerful it is. It assures those below that those above are dutifully carrying on the ceremony. It awakens the vibratory centers deep within the earth to resound along the world axis the same vibration. And to the four corners it carries to the long-lost white brother the message that he is not forgotten and that

---

[1] Evergreen shelter that houses snakes during snake dance.
[2] The underground ceremonial chamber.
[3] Continuing to resound, reechoing.
[4] Magical.

he must come. There is no mistaking its esoteric° summons. For this is the mandatory° call to the creative life force known elsewhere as Kundalini, latently° coiled like a serpent in the lowest centers of the dual bodies of earth and man, to awaken and ascend to the throne of her Lord for the final consummation of their mystic marriage.

The power does come up. You can see it in the Antelopes standing now in one long line extending from the *kisi*. They are swaying slightly to the left and right like snakes, singing softly and shaking their antelope-testicle-skin-covered gourds as the power makes its slow ascent. Then their bodies straighten, their voices rise.

The Snake chief at the same moment stoops in front of the *kisi*, then straightens up with a snake in his mouth. He holds it gently but firmly between his teeth, just below the head. With his left hand he holds the upper part of the snake's body level with his chest, and with the right hand the lower length of the snake level with his waist. This is said to be the proper manner of handling a snake during the dance. Immediately a second Snake priest steps up with a *kwawiki* or feathered snake whip in his right hand, with which to stroke the snake. He is commonly known as the guide, for his duty is to conduct the dancer in a circle around the plaza. As they move away from the *kisi* another dancer and his guide pause to pick out a snake, and so on, until even the small boy at the end is dancing with a snake in his mouth for the first time. It is a large rattlesnake, its flat bird-like head flattened against his cheek. All show the same easy familiarity with the snakes as they had with the squash vines the day before.

After dancing around the plaza the dancer removes the snake from his mouth and places it gently on the ground. Then he and his guide stop at the *kisi* for another snake. A third man, the snake-gatherer, now approaches the loose snake. It has coiled and is ready to strike. The gatherer watches it carefully, making no move until it uncoils and begins to wriggle quickly across the plaza. Then he dexterously° picks it up, holds it aloft to show that it has not escaped into the crowd, and hands it to one of the Antelopes singing in the long line. The Antelope, smoothing its undulating° body with his right hand, continues to sing.

So it goes on in a kind of mesmeric[5] enchantment in the darkening afternoon. There is nothing exciting about these men dancing with snakes in their mouths — only a queer dignity that reveals how deeply they are immersed in the mystery, and a strange sense of power that seems to envelop them. The seashells with their slight, odd sound are calling to their mother water to come and replenish the earth. The song of the Antelopes is describing the clouds coming from the four directions, describing the rain falling. All the Hopis know that if it does not rain during the Home Dance of Niman Kachina rain will come with the Snake Dance.

---

[5] Hypnotic.

For this is the consummation° of the union of the two universal polarities,° the release of that mystic rain which recharges all the psychic centers of the body and renews the whole stream of life in man and earth alike.

It is dusk now. The battle between the elements is over, and the sky is covered by low-hanging clouds. Out of them fall a few drops of rain. It is enough. The last of the snakes has been danced with and a group of women are making a circle of cornmeal beside the *kisi*. All the Antelopes bring their armloads of snakes to deposit within the circle. Then quickly the Snake members grab up as many snakes as they can carry and take them out on the desert, some each to the west, the south, the east, the north. Here they are blessed again and released to carry to the four corners of the earth the message of the renewal of all life, as it is known that snakes migrate back and forth across the land.

When the men come back each drinks a bowl of strong emetic[6] called *nanayo'ya*. The men then stand on the edge of the cliff to retch. Otherwise their bellies would swell up with the power like clouds and burst. The women help them clean off the paint on their bodies, after which they return to the kiva for purification.

The Snake-Antelope ceremony is the last major ceremony in the annual cycle which began with Wuwuchim, Soyal, and Powamu and carried through Niman Kachina and the Flute ceremony. It is a great ceremony and a subtle one. For if the first three symbolize the three phases of Creation and the next two carry through in some manner the evolutionary progress on the Road of Life, the Snake-Antelope ceremony cuts through the past to the ever-living now, and its stage is not the externalized universe but the subjective cosmos° of man's own psyche. Whatever its meanings, and they are many to many students, it shows how the interplay of universal forces within man can be controlled and made manifest in the physical world. That this is accomplished within the framework of what is commonly regarded as a primitive and animistic[7] rite is a great achievement.

Discussion

1. Notice the verb tenses in the first three sentences of this selection. Notice also that the author changes tense in the fourth sentence. What effect does he create by this shift to the present tense?
2. Waters calls the Snake-Antelope ceremony a "battle between good and evil." What is shown to be evil? What is the relationship of rain to this battle?
3. Where does Waters state the main idea of the essay?
4. Underline some words or phrases that appeal to your sense of sound, sight,

---

[6] Causing vomiting.
[7] Concerning a belief that all objects possess souls.

taste, smell, or touch (texture). Note the words that describe action and those that describe people or environment. Which type is found most often? How does this type of description relate to the author's focus?
5. Can you find specific words that connect one action to another? How does Waters' use of the present tense help to move the action forward in time?
6. Why do you think the snakes "are blessed . . . and released"? In what ways do the snakes in the Hopi ritual seem to have meanings different from the snake in the Garden of Eden?

UNIT 2 DESCRIPTION

READINGS: SELECTION THREE

from The Other Side of the Bull Mountains
by John Heminway

Ideas to Think About

1. Have you ever tried to talk somebody out of doing something you thought he or she was *not* qualified to do? How did you feel when that person was successful? When that person failed? Do people have a right to fail? Explain.
2. In this essay, the author makes a change in the way he lives. How do you feel when a friend or relative changes his or her lifestyle? Why? Have you ever made a rather drastic change in your own lifestyle? Explain.
3. As you read, look for some of the specific ways the author changes. Notice especially some of the things he observes, for example, his impressions of his environment.

Vocabulary

Look at each word as it is used in the article. (The number in parentheses indicates the paragraph in which it appears.) First, try to understand the meaning from the way it is used in the sentence. Then, use the dictionary to clarify the meaning.

talisman (1)	goaded (13)
neophyte (2)	ominous (15)
arcane (3)	nomenclature (18)
pauper (6)	hallowed (20)
effete (10)	precipitously (21)

from The Other Side of the Bull Mountains

John Heminway is a television writer and producer, and a cattle rancher in the Bull Mountains. He is also the author of *The Imminent Rains: A Visit Among the Last Pioneers in Africa* as well as articles in *Town & Country, Reader's Digest,* and various travel magazines. The following article appeared in *Quest/80.*

Most Montana ranchers chew a brand of tobacco called Old Copenhagen. They drop a thumbful of it behind their lip and punctuate conversation with gritty streams of spit. Copenhagen is as much a talisman° of raw-boned life in the modern West as the Tony Lama boots and the Stetsons.

I have plunged into the West as deep as any neophyte° should dare, but I am not ready for Old Copenhagen. My father, a cousin, and I bought a working cattle ranch two summers ago. We made our decision against the well-meant counsel of fellow Easterners and the quizzical stares of our neighboring Westerners. Financially I am about as deep in cattle manure as I can possibly sink. Every month there are new demands on our strained budget and, according to the accountant, another two years will pass before the seesaw of expenses and income settles onto the horizontal.

For nearly a year and a half we had studied every ranch for sale in Colorado, Wyoming, northern Idaho, and Montana, subscribed to agriculture journals, delved into such arcane° references as *Cowboy Economics*. I learned a new language: "animal units," "bangs," "acre feet," "blackleg," and, in one 10-day span, I traveled 6,000 miles through the northern Rockies.

Finally, in August 1978, after countless trips through Montana, I saw the Bull Mountain Ranch, one hour north of Billings. It encompassed about five and a half thousand acres, most of it deeded. There were no attractive rivers or buildings on it to inflate the price. The fences, corrals, and barns needed immediate attention and the hay meadows would have to be redeveloped. For a comparatively small dry-land ranch the price seemed realistic.

Talk about country that was both wild and productive — here was the place I had been looking for all the time. To the east the land was open and flat with views of distant cliffs. In the middle it consisted of choppy hills, studded with sandstone, rimrock and stands of black and yellow pine. And in the north, one section was so isolated that it could only be reached on horseback in winter.

My cousin, older and wiser, embarrassed me into the final decision. "Let's strike," he said, "when the iron is hot." With a sweep of the pen we became the owners of the Bull Mountain Ranch and almost immediately I realized that I would have to change. My cousin would look to the business side of the ranch, I to the cattle operation. I felt as strange as the pauper° who became the prince. Basically, I was still an Easterner. For me corrals were still paddocks, a jog on horseback still a trot, "drouths" a mispronunciation of "droughts," and "outfit" an outlandish word for a car. Further, the Westerner had a remote personality, still to be plumbed. Binding oral contracts in the West were almost twice as good as those on paper. The cowboy, it seemed, had been educated at the school of hard bargains. Robbery may be frowned upon but getting the best of a sucker was good sport. In the end, my neighbors seemed to blend horse sense and frontier courtesy in a carefully considered recipe.

Floyd Cowles and his wife, Ruby, came to work for us almost immediately. Floyd was in his sixties and had had a lifetime of experience running dry-land ranches in Montana. Knowing nothing about public relations, he was unable to crow about his achievements or his abilities. "Will you need any extra help?" I asked, testing him.

"Naaah, any help I need, Ruby can do."

"How about if I signed on as your assistant from time to time? For unskilled labor I'm pretty good for a day's work."

He studied me carefully, and for a moment I wondered if he was going to turn me down. Finally, in a tone suggestive of one who would do as he was told, he said, "Okay." Floyd evidently was inclined toward action, not toward words. His true devotion was to ranches, not to formalities.

Soon my language underwent a prairie change. Instead of "Yes" I began to say "You bet." Herefords lost their second "e," and one time I found myself improvising a Western metaphor to describe a multicolored herd of cattle. "Them cows resemble my grandmother's stew," I said. In fact, my grandmother never made stew.

By the time autumn had plucked the leaves from our three lone cottonwoods, I was still riding bareheaded. Nor did I have boots with pointed toes and fancy tool work. When I yearned for tobacco it was not for Copenhagen but for a brand called Walnut packed into the bowl of an effete° pipe. I was not even a fledgling cowboy. I was merely a transplant, still to be blooded.

Winter in the northern Rockies is the blooding time. What lay in store were four months that would be compared to the notorious cold and snow of 1886–87, when an estimated 70 percent of all Montana cattle starved. Admittedly, range management had improved during the intervening years and this winter's death loss would be marginal, thanks to fencing and feed. Still, the weather was clearly determined to humble every Montana rancher.

Autumn had been seductive. During October and part of November the crested wheat grass was the color of a lion's mane. Clouds raced above the buttes. Occasionally a herd of antelope grazed our meadow, drawn by the abundance of grass.

On November 9 the first snow fell. It settled heavily and even when the sun timidly reappeared the next day, patches clung to the ground. Two days later, more snow, and this time a wind goaded° it from behind, forming drifts along the lee on the rimrock. Every morning after dawn, in the two highest sections where our 37 heifers and 117 cows were pastured, Floyd and I would chop an inch and a half of ice from the water tanks. By November 16 the cows had what Floyd called a please-don't-snow look in their eyes. He decided to move them to lower pastures where the grass still broke through the snow. The next morning we saddled horses and drove the cows and heifers nearer to the ranch house. "Sometimes," Floyd noted, "you get a storm like this and a few weeks later the weather does a turn-about and once again it's fall." But the snows continued and Thanksgiving was white.

Weather had come to dominate our conversations. In the evenings when we sat around the kitchen table, Floyd might ring up one of his daughters and open conversation with, "That horse of yours died of winterkill yet?" If November was bad, December was sure to be worse. All development projects on the ranch had ceased. Our big hay shed, scheduled for completion in November, would now not be ready for use until April.

Hay. The word now had an ominous° sound. In October Floyd had vowed that 80 tons (half a ton for each cow and heifer) would see us through winter. "Last year was the first time I ever needed to feed a cow more than half a ton. But don't worry, you'll never see another winter like that again." By the end of November, thinking that we might be acquiring more land and cattle, I purchased additional hay. We never bought the land, but in December we could see that my misjudgment would save us. And it did — until mid-January, when we had to start hunting once again for more hay, this time at inflated prices. From November 16 until the end of March our cattle survived exclusively on purchased hay. Had there been a blade of grass protruding through the snow the cows would have found it, but for nearly five months our fortune in grazing land lay totally buried, while we paid over a dollar a bale for somebody else's grass. Throughout the winter I vowed to myself that the No. 1 priority during the coming summer would be the development of our own hay meadows, that someday we would become self-sufficient.

By the beginning of January the drifts were large enough to bury a truck and Floyd was admitting that this winter was certainly as bad as the previous one, possibly worse. Old-timers were quoted in the *Billings Gazette* saying that the winters of neither 1917–18 nor 1935–36 had begun so early, nor had the snows been so continuous. For weeks the temperature never rose above 20 degrees Fahrenheit, and on a few nights it dropped to −30 degrees. "Sometimes," Floyd deadpanned, "you get a January thaw. But then again, it often doesn't get here until March." . . .

Our cows, bought in September, had allegedly been bred to calve in February, having come from a part of the state where winters are mild. Conversely, ranchers in the Bull Mountains generally time their calving to the warming trends in late March and early April. Our calving was therefore two months premature, coinciding with winter's lowest temperatures. What kind of calf could possibly survive when the mercury stayed below −20? . . .

For the next month our corrals resembled a hospital emergency room after a train wreck. Ruby and Floyd practiced a form of folk veterinary medicine, heavy on hunches, short on nomenclature.° When a heifer tried to kill her calf, we adopted it and fed it from a bottle. When an afterbirth remained lodged in the uterus of a cow, we put her in the steel "squeeze" and removed it ourselves. Another time, a cow's udder became gummed up; her calf might have starved had we not massaged her teats until the milk began to flow. Floyd's horse and mine fought one day, opening an ugly gash on my horse's shoulder. By lantern light we dressed the wound and, without an anesthetic, bound the flesh with four stitches. In the event of a breech birth, we were prepared with chains, pulley, and poles to pull the calf. During all this, the only bill from the professional vet was for a $2 bottle of scarlet oil.

Neither Ruby nor Floyd had been able to leave the ranch since before Christmas. All their food had been stockpiled during the fall and stored in the freezer. The mail and newspapers arrived about once every two weeks, and over 90 percent of the ranch was snowbound, inaccessible even to a man on horseback. All our energies were concentrated within a short radius of the ranch house. The corral, deep in manure, had become little more than a feedlot. After we had fed the cattle in the early morning, our work became a mathematical job of juggling bunches of cows in varying stages of pregnancy and motherhood, opening gates, closing gates, cleaning sheds, keeping our eyes peeled for abnormal behavior, and making sure that the horses were on constant alert to help cut cattle. . . .

By mid-February, I had discovered a drab brown jumpsuit as protection against the cold, mud, and loose hay. Floyd disapproved. Ranchers did not wear coveralls, according to him. "You look like one of them beet farmers," he insisted. But I had begun to enjoy upsetting the time-honored traditions of the cowboy. Frankly, most of a cowboy's winter work is feeding his cattle — a numbingly dull task that bears little resemblance to the hallowed° legends. The 70-pound bale of alfalfa, not the horse, is the true symbol of the Montana cow-puncher. Every morning, before anything else, we would load a ton of hay on the pickup, call the cattle with singsong "kabobs," and then scatter the hay in long snaking lines through the west pasture. Floyd in particular resented his dependence on the pickup. "Machines, machines," he often muttered. He had his heart set on a team of mules that he felt sure would simplify our feeding operation. "We won't have to make a lot of unnecessary trips back and forth to the stacks. A wagon can carry up to 100 bales, and then if a guy gets a good team, he doesn't need an assistant to off-load. He ties up the reins, calls to his team to 'gideyap' or 'whoa,' and throws off the bales himself. It makes a lot of sense."

It did make a lot of sense. Energy Secretary James Schlesinger had just announced on television that the price of gasoline would increase precipitously° by the end of the year. A team of mules might be a sensible way of cutting our future costs. At the first break in the weather, Floyd would drive to South Dakota for an evenly matched pair.

On the road up from town there is a dangerous corner known throughout the country as "Mildred's," in honor of the widow whose cow camp is set in the valley nearby. Everyone knows her and treats her with respect. She keeps her own counsel, speaks her own mind, and nothing, not even the cantankerous cow that broke her shoulder and several ribs last year, can slow her down. On February 12 I knocked at her door, ostensibly to inquire about a pony I had bought from her son-in-law. "How're your calves doing?" she asked me almost immediately.

"Pretty good for calves born in January," I said. "We've got some scours [an intestinal infection], but I suspect we'll have that under control in a few days."

Before I could stop her, she was ferreting through the refrigerator, comfortably located in the center of the living room. "Got just the thing here," she said. She handed me a $2 packet of pills for the calves.

"Kind of awkward," I said. "I don't have any money on me."

She fixed me with plowshare eyes. "I don't know if back East you people think being neighborly is weird or something, but it's the way we do things around here."

Stung but refreshed, I soon found myself using the word *neighbor* as a verb. When George Snider one day deposited a posthole digger at our barn without being asked, I thanked him for "neighboring." When another neighbor's car broke down and he walked four miles through the night without bothering to wake up Floyd for help, it was considered very unneighborly, even insulting.

In part thanks to Mildred's barb, human society in the Bull Mountains soon came to be very important to me. Previously, I had always boasted of being uncomfortable with crowds. I tried to depend on no one. Now I began to revel in chance encounters with neighbors. Two pickups stopping on a lonely road would often initiate a landmark friendship. And one Sunday a meeting with Haven Marsh, another neighbor, became a highlight. He was driving his tractor along our road, pulling his two young daughters, seated on trays, through the snow. When he saw me he stopped and we discussed the issues of the day: the sight of a well-fed herd of mule deer on our mutual boundary, the mailman's conspicuous absence during the blizzards of the last two weeks. Small talk admittedly, but in the end we had assured each other that although the world might be going to the dogs, all was right in the Bull Mountains.

By the end of February, with the calves now numbering 70, the much-touted thaw finally reached the Bull Mountains. Floyd took advantage of the break to go down to Rapid City in search of a mule team, leaving the calving to Ruby and me. But no sooner had he gone than a mantle of gray slid across the distant hills, and the weather made one of those dramatic reversals for which Montana is famous. From 40 degrees, it plunged to −12 in just two hours. The snows began. "Got a calf out in the pasture," Ruby announced, peering through the kitchen window with binoculars. "We'd better bring him in or he'll freeze up." I saddled her horse. Bundled against the cold, Ruby rode out into the drifts; I followed on foot.

Newborn calves are confused by horses. So while Ruby led the cow, I prodded the calf to follow. It did not. At last I picked it up in frustration and stumbled forward until it slithered through my arms. The cow, dazed by the shrieking snow, then retraced her steps to double-check that this spidery creature was indeed hers. So we advanced — 20 feet forward, 10 feet back, while my ears, toes, and fingers slowly became numb. Finally I was able to drop the 70-pound package inside a shed, just in time to return to the coulee to move all the rest of the "heavies" to corrals. That way, any newborns would at least be safe from the ice and wind. Some were born and they survived.

By dawn our storm was in Nebraska, and the skies were clear. Floyd returned, looked over all the newborns, and made no comment apart from a nod that was my first and greatest compliment.

Now that March has arrived at last, the snow has turned to mud and our calf crop numbers 110, with another 30 still to go. The roads are totally impassable and at times the only way to move through the country is on our hay wagon, pulled by the new team of mules. But the grass is beginning to "green up" and at almost any time of day I can take heart in a sight of unimaginable beauty — the cows with heads lowered, grazing for the first time in five months on the real thing. We ended winter with a gambler's margin — a dozen uneaten bales of hay.

I tried some Copenhagen yesterday and I have decided forever that I never will be ready for it. It seems likely I will always remain an Easterner. But when I rode my gelding yesterday to renew acquaintance with some of the northern sections of our land, I noticed I was beginning to ride more like a Westerner — seat glued to the saddle, slight slouch, the reins in my left hand, my right arm down by my side. For most of the way I rode along the base of the rimrocks, my eyes searching for deer in the woods, eagle pinpricks in the sky. All I saw were tracks, and a Western meadowlark singing for a mate. Whatever change had come over me during the winter was not through the birth of a new spirit but through the discovery of an ancient instinct, sensed like the pleasure and pain of a long-neglected muscle. My joy in having good neighbors and fat calves was proof that I was irreversibly in the business of letting things grow. Spring has been as good as its word.

Discussion

1. Find examples of physical descriptions of people or the environment in the story. Underline the words or phrases that make you see, hear, smell, taste, or feel (texture).
2. Now find examples of descriptions of actions. Underline any words or phrases that make these actions vivid.
3. Examine the first and last paragraphs. Why do you think Heminway begins and ends with these descriptions? Look at them for both the ideas (content) and the writing techniques (form).

4. How well did Heminway prepare for his new life? How much has he changed? Mark specific passages that show such changes.
5. Even though Heminway bought the ranch with his father and cousin, he makes only brief references to them, concentrating instead on Floyd and Ruby Cowles and Mildred, the widow. How does this deliberate selection of details by the author help him to focus on his main idea?

WRITING: Description

Writing Assignment: A One-Paragraph Descriptive Essay

The writing assignment in this unit again offers many choices of topics for you to develop into a one-paragraph essay through a set pattern of organization. This new *F-D* pattern, *F* (focus), *D* (details), will enable you to transform your perception of a person, object, action, or scene into a *word picture,* a vivid presentation that will allow your readers to take part in your experience. In other words, if you offer your readers sufficient details and focus their attention carefully, they will be able to see, hear, feel, taste, or smell what you describe and will react to your picture as you want them to.

In general, writers have two possible approaches available to them: they can *tell* or *show* what they want to communicate. To tell means to relate information efficiently, that is, to sketch a word outline; to show, in contrast, means to describe fully, that is, to paint a complete word picture. Both approaches or techniques of writing are used by all good writers, but at different times and for different purposes. For example, if a sportswriter wants to offer a quick summary of a baseball game, he might say, "Rod Carew hit a low, outside fast ball into left field." However, if the same writer wants to give his readers a sense of the excitement of the game, he might say, "With eyes squinted into slits, cleats clutching the dirt, arms and legs contracted to spring, Rod Carew watched as the fast ball dipped down and away, and then he lunged, his bat swatting the ball into deep left field." Notice that in the first sentence, the reader is told who the batter is, what type of ball was thrown by the pitcher, and where the ball was hit. But in the second sentence, the reader is not only given the same information, but also can "see" the batter, "feel" the excitement of the moment, and "sense" the cat-like ability of the athlete.

Before beginning to write your descriptive essay, think of the details you could use to show your readers what you have experienced through one or more of your senses. As you write your first draft, follow the assigned pattern closely, offering first a strong focus and then filling in the paragraph with vivid sensory details. Although the assigned pattern is but one of the many possible organizations that can be used to describe something or someone, it offers an easy introduction to description and a basis for further variation and expansion. Perhaps you might want to experiment with some variation of this pattern in sections of your assigned three- or five-paragraph essays later in this semester or in your other college papers.

Assignment

Select one of the following topics based on the reading selections in this unit and write a descriptive one-paragraph essay of at least eight to ten sentences. To organize your material, use the *F-D* pattern.

F — *Focus*, setting the scene or telescoping in on a dominant feature of a person or object. (one to three sentences)

D — *Details*, describing shapes, sizes, colors, odors, tastes, textures, feelings, heat, sounds, and tones. (seven to nine sentences)

As mentioned above, the *F* part of the pattern can either set the scene or focus on a dominant feature. For example, in paragraph 12 of "The Other Side of the Bull Mountains," Heminway sets the scene for his description of the onslaught of winter (paragraph 13).

> Autumn had been seductive. During October and part of November, the crested wheat grass was the color of a lion's mane. Clouds raced above the buttes. Occasionally a herd of antelope grazed our meadows, drawn by the abundance of grass.

In contrast, Thoreau introduces a toad, that he first thought was a frog, before he adds detail.

> My dream frog turns out to be a toad.

The *D* section offers the necessary details to finish your picture. For example, Heminway goes on to describe the snow, wind, ice, pasture, and animals. Thoreau goes on to describe the actions and sounds of toads before he implies the unity of all nature. Yet neither writer mentions everything he sees — details are chosen carefully. Only those details that give depth to the impressions the author wishes to convey to the reader are shown. Remember, you will be writing a word picture, not a word photograph. Don't feel you must describe everything or crowd your picture with details that cannot contribute to the overall image you want to offer your reader.

TOPICS

THOREAU

1. Observe something in nature, such as a bluejay, butterfly, or grasshopper, for ten minutes. Describe what you see and hear using words that allow your readers to share your experience.
2. For five to ten minutes, observe a singer performing on television or at a concert. Describe the singer's actions and sounds so that your readers can share your experience.

WATERS

1. Describe part of a ceremony that you witnessed or took part in, such as a wedding, a religious rite, or a graduation. Make certain that the event has

special meaning to you and focus in on one part that spotlights the essence of the event. Don't try to describe the entire ceremony in one paragraph.
2. Describe an action of one person, perhaps a basketball player making a left-handed hook shot, a tennis player serving the ball, a dancer performing an intricate step, or a baker frosting a large cake.

HEMINWAY

1. Every now and then we are faced with violent or frightening natural events such as tornadoes, earthquakes, torrential rains, blizzards, droughts, or floods. Describe either the situation itself or the environment immediately after the occurrence. Again, don't *tell* your readers how frightening the event was or how your home, city, or surrounding area looked. *Show* them!
2. Describe a situation in which you had to perform an act for which you weren't prepared or trained. Perhaps you had to change a tire, cook dinner, or change a baby's diaper. Let the humor or frustration of the situation evolve from your description.

Brainstorming and Shaping

Brainstorming ideas, even though they may begin only as vague fragments, helps focus on your subject and is the first step in writing a rough draft. Finding your focus is not always easy, but a good brainstorming session in which you examine ideas and the raw data of your experience can help you to develop a focal point for your discussion. Before you begin to brainstorm, however, reread the writing assignment carefully. Choose the topic that appeals to you most. Be sure you have a pencil and paper for sketching ideas. Remember that, whether you are working in a group or individually, asking questions is vital to a good brainstorming session.

EXERCISE 1

1. Form groups according to the choice of assignments. The groups may have to be adjusted if too many have chosen one topic; the groups should be no larger than four or five. For example, everyone interested in question 2 based on Henry David Thoreau's description should form a group. Try to help each other as much as possible by listening carefully, jotting down notes, and asking questions.
2. One by one, all group members should recreate the scenes and/or people they have chosen for their descriptions as fully as possible, always including all the details that come to mind. This step is important because it helps you accumulate your raw data. For example, if you have chosen a person who has affected you deeply, perhaps a math teacher whom you disliked intensely because he embarrassed you and made you hate algebra, you might describe the teacher, the classroom, and the incident for your group. Perhaps you remember a small, windowless, mint-green room with messy

equation-filled chalkboards. Perhaps the teacher wore a dull, tan, wrinkled suit and had hair and skin to match. His wrinkled tan face might have been accented by faded gray eyes that peeked at you from behind his glasses. All this could have combined to create the sense of gloom you felt at the knell of the 11:00 bell that made your mind go a kind of blank tan as well. Try to make the group see, feel, taste, smell, and hear. Don't worry at this point if a detail doesn't seem to fit. For example, maybe the teacher kept a small vase of fresh flowers on his desk. The group should be taking brief notes as you describe.

3. Next comes the more difficult part. The group must decide which are the key details. Remember that the goal is a word picture not a word photograph, and you must decide upon a focus. For example, we would have to choose either the teacher, the classroom, or yourself. This choice determines all the details to be included. Your group may have a different dominant impression from the one you intend (this often happens), but the discussion will help form the focus for them and for you. You must be absolutely clear on the focus, or your paragraph may become more narration (telling) than description (showing). In addition, the group discussion will be useful in helping you isolate the key details. For example, perhaps the vase of flowers, although it did not seem to fit your negative feelings, works better than the equation detail because it provides contrast. Group discussion can help decide this. Here it becomes evident that subtraction is as important as addition in working with description. Make brief notes.

4. At this point, group members should ask the questions they have noted as they listened to you. There may be questions such as, "Did the class laugh?" "Did the teacher treat everyone the same way?" Ask yourself if the answers to any of these questions matter in showing your audience how traumatic the experience was. Remember, the group serves as the voice of the audience to whom you will write, so this step is important. For example, if the class did not laugh, perhaps the group might wonder why the experience was so painful. That might lead to a discussion of whether or not to include the class reaction at all. At this point, everyone should make a checklist of the key details that you have decided to include. Otherwise all those ideas have a way of getting lost.

5. After each key detail, the group can help with some word choices that will paint the picture for your reader. For example, what happens to your body when you are embarrassed? Are you suddenly more aware of your ears? Do they turn hot? Do they buzz? Maybe they scarcely hear. Try to help the author show both vividly and economically. Sometimes referring back to the reading selections helps here. Write down the specific word choices.

6. Collect everyone's notes on your experience.

7. Write a quick summary of your part of the session, using the collected notes and questions. So you won't forget what was said, write your summary as soon as possible after class. This can form the basis for your rough

draft. At the very least, the session should give you some more concrete ideas about the direction in which you want to move.

EXERCISE 2

Another way to find the focus of your paragraph and the details that best reinforce it is through role playing. There are, of course, any number of ways to role play, but the primary task of this assignment is sharing your dominant impression with your reader by appealing to his or her senses. A way to do this is by asking yourself specific questions. For example, "How can I make my reader see, hear, taste, feel, and smell how I felt changing that tire for the first time in my life?"

1. Choose a time when you can be alone and quiet. Close your eyes and recreate the event. Perhaps you were driving on a busy freeway or lonely road. What lane are you in? What do you see? What do you hear? Is it day or night? Step out of the car and walk around to examine what remains of the tire. What does it look like? Write down all that you see, hear, taste, smell, and feel after you have replayed the scene. Recreate the whole experience from beginning to end in sequence. Sketch the results as quickly as you can. Don't worry about grammar, sentence variation, or fine detail at this point.
2. Now return to the scene and check off all the details that seem to best build the impression you want to give. For example, perhaps the mangled and split tire reinforces your feeling of fear and relief at having escaped death. Perhaps this doesn't fit at all. Perhaps getting the jack in place is more central. Make a list of the key details adding or subtracting as you sketch them.
3. Reexamine the details you have isolated and try to choose sensory words that best fit them. For example, perhaps being in the lane closest to the center divider on a freeway serves as a key detail. Here a simile (a comparison using *like* or *as*) can be very useful in showing that terrible experience to your reader. Try to pick a noun or noun phrase that shows what you felt. Maybe you felt *like a feather in a hurricane*. Perhaps your car, which minutes ago seemed like such a powerful machine, strong and safe *as a battleship*, now seems more *like a canoe caught on a tidal wave of onrushing cars*. Similes *show* what you want to convey without *telling*. Try a list of nouns or noun phrases to compare. You may not use everything on your list, but the game will help you with specific detail, and, when you are through, you will have ample raw data with which to begin your rough draft.

Writing the First Draft

Now you are ready to write your rough draft. Reread the writing assignment carefully and be sure you have all your brainstorming notes together. Reread them as well. Remember, this is only a first draft so don't worry too much about fine detail. Start by getting the first three or four sentences down on paper. Beginning an essay or paragraph is much like getting into a swimming pool. Some people dive in and some walk slowly, but all people have a few moments of shock when they first get wet, no matter how hot they are. But after this first shock, the water begins to feel good — even warm. Even the "toes-first" swimmer usually gets in all the way. The rough draft is called rough for a reason. It will be full of cross-outs and margin notes. Just start with your *F-D* pattern, beginning by setting the scene or telescoping in on a dominant feature of a person or object. The following sentences will probably be easier to write once your focus sentences are established. Be sure you have a finished rough draft of at least eight sentences.

Revising the One-Paragraph Descriptive Essay

As you reread your rough draft, you must ask certain basic revision questions just as you did in Unit 1.

Basic Revision Questions

1. Do I have a clear, unified focus? Does my paragraph telescope in on one major theme?
2. Do I offer sufficient details, examples, or explanation so that my reader gains a complete understanding of what I am trying to say?
3. Is all my information accurate? Appropriate?
4. Is this information organized so that my reader can understand what I have said? Could I reorganize my paragraph so that it would be more effective?

Those questions are basic to all revision, but the *F-D* pattern requires some additional questions.

Additional Questions

1. Is my focus clear? Does it prepare my reader for the details that follow?
2. Do all my details fit the focus (the scene, or the dominant impression of the person)?
3. Do I have enough detail to show my readers without telling them? Is there any detail I should add to increase understanding?
4. Have I bored my readers with more detailed description than I need? Could I make better comparisons?

Now make the changes suggested by your answers to these questions.

EXERCISE 1

The assignment asks you to follow the *F-D* pattern (on page 59) closely even though the description could be done in other ways.

Reread your paragraph and see if you can outline it according to the *F-D* pattern.

Example

Focus: The math teacher was drab enough to set the tone of the class.

Detail: He wore beige, had beige skin and eyes, and made mathematics beige.

If you cannot outline your paragraph clearly into two parts, some reshaping and reorganizing are necessary. Be patient with yourself; all writers have to do some reorganizing in almost every paragraph they write.

EXERCISE 2

Exchange paragraphs with a classmate. Read one another's papers carefully. Pose the same questions that you did of your own papers. For example, are the details clear and the comparisons effective? Are all of them necessary? Can you suggest any alternative word choices that might improve either the focus or the description? Is the organization clear? Discuss your findings with the writer.

EXERCISE 3

When your paragraph is returned, read it over once more. Make any changes you feel will improve it based on your classmate's evaluation and your own further evaluation. At this point you may want to recopy the paragraph so that it is ready for the next step, editing. Your paragraph may be difficult to read by now, but sometimes during the copying process, changes in wording will occur to you.

Editing

Word Choice: Abstract and Concrete Nouns; Relative and Specific Adjectives

Writing at times can be very frustrating. Sometimes you can sit at your desk for hours writing a letter to a friend or relative, trying to express your thoughts and feelings accurately only to have this friend or relative misinterpret what you have written. Other times, you can struggle with ideas and facts every evening for a week to prepare an essay or term paper for class and have your teacher only comment that parts of your work are not clear. Such frustration in writing can never be completely overcome, but a certain awareness can assist your ongoing effort to achieve clear, precise discussions.

As we said in Unit 1, the first elements of written language are words. Although little communication can occur if single, unattached, unrelated words are merely dropped onto a page, they carry the essence of meaning to the reader when joined together according to the rules of language. For example, if you were to open a book and read the following, you would not understand what the author intends to say.

                man   chicken
a   for   woman Sunday
    dinner   roasting a
her
        a   dinner   sold.

But if the writer organizes the words according to language rules, you have: "A man sold a roasting chicken to a woman for her Sunday dinner." Yet not all words communicate concisely even when organized carefully into a sentence. Two such types of words that might confuse a reader are *abstract nouns* and *relative adjectives*. Nouns are words that give *names* to things: *man, freedom, rose, love, hatred, mountain, geography, Wisconsin, dish, democracy,* and *theory.* Adjectives are words that *modify* nouns, that is, they describe them: *pretty, small, red, various, many, dirty,* and *sad.* Notice how nouns and adjectives work together in the following examples:

    adj.   noun   adj.   noun   adj.   noun   adj.   noun
beautiful women, dirty clothes, many hours, modern history,

    adj.   noun
complex theory.

Nouns such as those cited above can be divided into two types: *concrete* and *abstract.* Concrete nouns are those nouns that name things we can see, hear, taste, smell, or touch, that is, things accessible to our five senses. Abstract nouns, however, usually refer to ideas or concepts or to things we feel emotionally. For example, if you read the word *car*, you can relate that word to the machine moving on the street; you can see it, hear it, touch it, smell its fumes, or even, if you are silly enough, taste it with your tongue. But can you do any of these things to freedom, love, or beauty? In other words, abstract nouns have no physical reality — they belong to our world of thought, feeling, and judgment. Because of this characteristic of abstract nouns, no two people ever agree fully as to their meaning.

If a friend tells you that she feels deep love for her uncle, does she feel the same way you do when you claim you love popcorn? Love backpacking? Love your boyfriend or girlfriend? Probably not. If you write a term paper in which you advocate democracy, do you mean the same type of government followed by the Soviets? Again, probably not, although the USSR claims to follow democratic principles. And if you promote "freedom for all," do you mean freedom to vote, freedom under the law, freedom to slander, freedom to kill, or limited freedoms?

From these examples, you can see how abstract words can cause confusion or can allow your readers to misinterpret what you say. Yet you need these abstract words to communicate, so what can you do to transmit your ideas and feelings clearly to your readers? The answer is *explain, describe,* or *define* your term fully. Don't say, "I advocate democracy." Say, instead, "I advocate the American democratic system as outlined in the Constitution." And don't say, "Frustration overcame me." Say, perhaps, "Frustration overcame me; I wanted to dance all night but sat in a corner with blistered feet."

A second type of word that needs expanded discussion is the *relative adjective*. If you say that your suit is woolen, your reader knows exactly what material was used to make your outfit. But if you say that your brother is tall, can your reader know your brother's height? If all men in your family measure at least six feet, your tall brother might be six feet eight inches. But if the average man in your family is five feet eight inches, your tall brother might be five feet ten inches. Tall, then, is a relative term, a word whose meaning depends on the writer's point of view. For example, the words *pretty, small, ugly, many,* and *fat* can mean different things to different people. So when you use such words, always explain your meaning carefully. As you write, ask yourself the following questions.

1. Does my reader know exactly what I mean by these words?
2. Does my reader use these words in the same way I do?

If your answer is either "No" or "I don't know," expand your idea and explain your terms.

EXERCISE 1

Look over the following lists of nouns and adjectives. Underline all abstract nouns and relative adjectives.

Nouns	Adjectives
baby	fat
Canada	red
love	two
table	ugly
boat	several
liberty	tiny
pencil	lovely
originality	wooden
cat	transparent
anger	British

EXERCISE 2

Choose two of the nouns and two of the adjectives you have underlined and write sentences in which you *use* and *explain* the words.

Examples

socialism: John believes in socialism, a form of government in which the state owns all major industries.

short: The desk is so short that I have to double over to write on it.

As you have worked on the above exercises, you might have had difficulty explaining your ideas fully. Don't feel discouraged, because all writers must struggle at times to translate their ideas into words. This is especially true when you are trying to express feelings or to describe a situation. One way to ease the burden of relating your emotions or of making your ideas more vivid is to use figures of speech, especially *similes* and *metaphors*. A simile is a comparison between two or more things using the words *like* or *as*. For example:

My car sounded *like* a frog with the whooping cough.

Anger is *like* a clogged-up chimney, filling the room with smoke.

A metaphor, in contrast, is a comparison between two or more things without using *like* or *as*. For example:

My life is a junk yard of broken parts.

Anger is a clogged-up chimney, filling the room with smoke.

Notice particularly the simile and metaphor describing anger. By comparing an abstract noun, *anger*, to a concrete noun, *chimney*, the simile brings physical reality to an emotion. The readers can now approach anger through their senses — seeing, smelling, hearing, and even tasting the fumes enveloping them. Notice also that the metaphor makes a tighter, more positive relationship. In the metaphor, anger is not *like* a clogged-up chimney; it *is* the clogged-up chimney; it is solid, destructive, dangerous, dirty, and burning. Or notice the difference in intensity between "I eat like a pig" and "I am a pig." Finally, when writing similes and metaphors, remember to create new, original comparisons that are accessible to your readers' backgrounds. Most people know what sloppy eaters pigs are, but do they know how ducks eat? Would they understand the meaning of "I eat like a duck?"

EXERCISE 3

Choose three of the following nouns and write similes with them.

Example
Love is like a lemon drop, both sweet and sour.

1. depression
2. anxiety
3. madness
4. happiness
5. bitterness
6. frustration
7. music
8. fat
9. horror
10. home

EXERCISE 4

Change your similes to metaphors. Explain the differences in meaning and intensity between the comparisons.

Example
Love is a lemon drop.

EXERCISE 5

Evaluate the following sentences. Do they communicate exactly? Do they need more specific information? Would the use of similes or metaphors assist understanding? Make any changes in the sentences that you feel would help communicate more clearly or more vividly.

Example
A tall tree stands in front of the house.

Revision
A twelve-foot elm tree forms shadows across the front of my house.

Example
That music is too loud.

Revision
Listening to that music is like sticking your head inside the bell of a blaring tuba.

1. The baby is small for his age.
2. My pants are too short.
3. That movie was terrible.
4. My parents purchased a large house in New England.
5. The sour apples upset my stomach.

EXERCISE 6

Check over your one-paragraph descriptive essay and underline all abstract nouns and relative adjectives. Now evaluate those words. Do you need to explain them? Would similes or metaphors make the paragraph more lively and interesting? Make the necessary changes.

Sentence Structure: Coordination

In Unit 1, we discussed kernel sentences and then expanded them by adding modification both to the noun or subject part of the sentence and to the verb part. You found that all kernel sentences could grow in this way.

COORDINATING PARTS OF SENTENCES

Another way in which kernel sentences can be expanded is by compounding or connecting together parts of sentences or two or more complete sentences. Consider the following two sentences.

The icy rain continues.

The snow continues.

We can contract the first sentence by eliminating the repeated word *continues* and joining the remaining words *the icy rain* to the second sentence.

The snow and icy rain continue.

Notice that now the verb must agree with the new compound subject. Since the subject is now plural, the verb must change to *continue*.

We have reduced these two short, somewhat repetitive sentences into one expanded sentence by compounding or connecting the subject, and we have done so with a coordinator, in this case *and*. Notice also that compounding does exactly what its name implies; it yokes together two or more equal sentence parts — subjects, verbs, objects, phrases or clauses — and makes them work together as a unit. Compound (often called *coordinated*) elements within the sentence can be joined with one of the following coordinators: *and, but, or, for, nor, so,* and *yet*. Each, however, has a different meaning.

Consider these two sentences.

Ranchers often chew tobacco.

Ranchers often smoke tobacco.

Again these sentences are necessarily repetitive and would be more effective written in one statement. Contracting the first sentence eliminates those words that are repeated in the second sentence (*ranchers* and *tobacco*), and adds the word *chew* to the second sentence.

Ranchers often chew or smoke tobacco.

Here two sentences have been made into one expanded sentence by compounding the verbs *chew* and *smoke* with an appropriate coordinator, *or*.

Finally, consider two more short, repetitive sentences.

It had been a summer of drought.

It had been a summer of despair.

Again, a more effective sentence is produced by using only one of the repeated phrases *it had been a summer of* and joining the remaining words *drought* and *despair*.

It had been a summer of drought and despair.

In this sentence, objects of the preposition *of* have been joined by the coordinator *and*.

EXERCISE 1

Combine the following sets of sentences by eliminating repetition and adding an appropriate coordinator.

    1. The new queen bee emerged from the hive.
       Several drones emerged from the hive.

2. The queen flew above the hive.
   The queen mated with one of the drones.
3. The workers flew toward the honeysuckle.
   The workers flew toward the rosemary.
4. Returning workers carried nectar back to the hive.
   Returning workers carried pollen back to the hive.
5. Small black ants were climbing the legs of the hive.
   Small black ants were entering the doorway.
   Small black ants were crawling between the supers.
   The bees were buzzing angrily.
6. We found five fully capped frames of honey in the second super.
   We found only four fully capped frames of honey in the third super.
7. We could eat the extracted, strained honey.
   We could eat the honey right in the comb.
8. I liked the comb honey on toast.
   I liked the comb honey on muffins.
   I liked the comb honey on hotcakes.
   I liked the extracted honey on plain bread.
9. After the extraction, honey was all over the cupboard.
   After the extraction, honey was all over the floor.
   After the extraction, honey was all over the door.
   After the extraction, honey was all over every member of the family.

COORDINATING WHOLE SENTENCES

Sentence expansion works not only by compounding words within a sentence but also by compounding whole sentences. Whole sentences can be joined by coordinators or by a semicolon; each has its own special function. (See Table 2-1.) Again, the purpose of joining sentences with coordinators is to express their relationship accurately. Consider the following two sentences.

The battle between the elements is over.

The sky is covered by low-hanging clouds.

In this example, one sentence follows the other as though no relationship existed between them. Yet your reader needs to know the connection you intend between these two thoughts by coordinating them and showing their meaning more precisely.

The battle between the elements is over, and the sky is covered by low-hanging clouds.

Table 2-1 Coordinators

Function	Coordinator	Example
addition	and	the gopher and the mole
alternative	(either . . .) or	the desk or the chair
negative alternative	(neither . . .) nor	Neither Gary nor Tom wanted to study.
exception	yet	He came yet he talked to no one.
cause	for	They went for they had no choice.
opposition	but	They studied but felt uneasy about their exams anyway.
effect	so	They studied well so they passed their exams.
close relationship between sentences	; (semicolon)	My sister was home crying; I sat gloomily on the park bench.

In other words, not only is the battle over, but those low clouds are hanging in the sky as a sign that the battle waged in the course of the Rain Dance ceremony is over and rain is indeed on the way. A similar lack of coordination of ideas occurs in the following sentence.

> I have plunged into the West as deep as any neophyte should dare.
>
> I am not ready for Old Copenhagen.

Again, the intended meaning of the writer is lost unless these two thoughts are connected.

> I have plunged into the West as deep as any neophyte should dare, but I am not ready for Old Copenhagen.

As you can see, the compound sentence yokes together two or more sentences. Each sentence within the compound sentence balances the other and uses the coordinator as a kind of fulcrum, the balancing point of a teeter-totter.

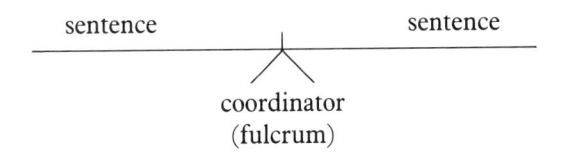

```
       sentence              sentence
    ─────────────────┬─────────────────
                    ╱ ╲
                 coordinator
                  (fulcrum)
```

Notice that in both these compound sentences a comma precedes the coordinator. As will be discussed in the next section on punctuation, compound sentences are generally formed by placing commas before the coordinators.

Another means of forming compound sentences is through the use of a *semicolon* (;). Like the coordinator, the semicolon acts as a fulcrum between balanced sentences:

> Niman Kachina brought no rain; for some reason the ceremony was improperly performed in some villages; in others another dance was substituted for the Home Dance.

A semicolon, however, is stronger, more dramatic, and more forceful than a coordinator and as such should be reserved for special emphasis or indicate cause or subsequent action or explanation.

> I rowed back early before the others; I couldn't wait to show the fish to my parents.
>
> Upon graduating from college, we put our books back on the shelf; then next fall we took them down again when we realized that our college degrees were not enough.

Whether you combine with coordinators or semicolons, remember that when you coordinate you are joining together two or more related ideas.

EXERCISE 2

Review the coordinator diagram and then form compound sentences out of the sentences that follow. Use a semicolon or the most appropriate coordinator. More than one answer is possible, so be prepared to discuss the reasons for your choice.

1. We read by the electric lamp.
   We wash our dishes in the electric dishwasher.
2. The gardener trimmed the oleander hedge.
   He did not mow the lawn.
3. San Francisco attracts thousands of fine food lovers each year.
   That city has many two- and three-star restaurants.
4. She felt uneasy and frightened.
   It was her first morning on the job.
5. Invest your money in stocks.
   Put it in the bank.

USING TRANSITIONAL ADVERBS WITH COORDINATION

The transitional adverb also shows relationships between sentences. Transitional adverbs, such as *therefore, however, moreover, consequently,* and *then* are also called conjunctive adverbs since they not only join ideas in a particular relationship but also function as adverbs to add extra meaning. However, these words can only yoke together ideas, not parts of sentences. That is, when you indicate a particular relationship between two sentences by means of a conjunctive adverb, you still need to indicate the grammatical relationship with a semicolon, a period and capital, or a comma and coordinator.

> The Native Americans of the Northwest Coast believed in personal guardian spirits; therefore, each person called for help from his guardian spirit before going fishing or hunting.

Unlike coordinators, transitional adverbs frequently can be moved to different positions within the sentence. In fact, positioning the conjunctive adverb after a key word or phrase often serves to pull your reader along with the flow of your ideas.

> The Native Americans of the Northwest Coast believed in personal guardian spirits; each person, therefore, called for help from his guardian spirit before going fishing or hunting.

Study the following list of common transitional adverbs.

1. *To express addition or similarity:* again, besides, also, similarly, moreover, in addition, furthermore.
2. *To express cause and effect:* therefore, hence, consequently, thus, as a result, then.
3. *To show sequence:* first, second, third, next, later, finally, then, in conclusion, in summary.
4. *To show contrast:* however, nevertheless, on the other hand.
5. *To emphasize:* in fact, indeed, to be sure.

EXERCISE 3

Go back over each sentence in Exercise 2. Substitute a transitional adverb for the coordinator in each sentence. Do they work equally well? Is there a difference in effect? Do you need to adjust your punctuation?

EXERCISE 4

Look over your writing assignment carefully. Have you formed compound sentences when such connections would express the intended relationship between two sentences more precisely? Have you used appropriate coordinators or semicolons? Have you used appropriate transitional adverbs? Have you eliminated needless repetition by contracting some sentences and expanding others through coordination?

Punctuation: The Compound Sentence

As mentioned previously, compound sentences can be formed by using either conjunctions or semicolons. When forming compound sentences with conjunctions, the writer generally places a comma *before* the conjunction.

Example
Jeremy practiced the intricate guitar solo all day long, but he still had difficulty with the third bar of the introduction.

Yet all compound sentences are not this long; many, in fact, are quite short:

Example
I turned on the key but the engine wouldn't start.

Would a comma before *but* in this short sentence serve any purpose? Think of a comma as a separator; it establishes sections of a sentence and thus aids a reader in seeing large or independent phrases and in grasping units of meaning. In the first example, the two sentences in the compound sentence are rather long, and so the reader might need help in recognizing the two equal parts of the whole statement. In the second example, however, the two parts of the statement are easy to grasp without help from a comma.

There is another reason for placing a comma before a conjunction in a compound sentence. A comma separates elements of a sentence, forcing the reader to make a brief pause before continuing reading. This enforced pause throws a minor emphasis onto the conjunction and the words that follow it. So if you were to read, "I turned on the key but the engine wouldn't start," you would probably have a slight stress on *I turned on the key* and little stress on *but the engine wouldn't start*. Now if you put a comma before *but*, your stress would change; now *but* gains stronger emphasis. The sentence without the comma might be used as part of a general discussion on the problems with your car, but the sentence with the comma might be used in dialogue, relating your shock that the engine wouldn't turn over (*but!*). Which of the two ways to punctuate the sentence is correct? Both. As the writer, you must make a *conscious choice*, deciding whether you wish to stress the first part of the sentence or both parts.

A second option you have in forming compound sentences is to substitute a semicolon for the conjunction or the conjunction and comma.

1. At the last minute, Mitch took his eyes off the target and the dart chipped into the wall.
2. At the last minute, Mitch took his eyes off the target, and the dart chipped into the wall.
3. At the last minute, Mitch took his eyes off the target; the dart chipped into the wall.

Again you might ask which sentence is correct. And again the answer is all of them. The writer must make conscious choices. Using a semicolon allows two ideas to yoke tightly together, almost making one thought out of two — forcing the reader to grasp the entire statement as a whole, as one interrelated idea. Reread the three examples above and note the following.

1. Example 1, using a conjunction without a comma, emphasizes the first part of the sentence slightly more than the second part.
2. Example 2, using a conjunction and comma, forces added stress onto *and the dart.*
3. Example 3, using a semicolon, unifies the two ideas expressed in each sentence and adds, because of the semicolon, extra stress on the second half.

All in all, the choice is yours to make whether to use a semicolon, conjunction, or conjunction and comma. Be sure, however, to control your choices consciously. Know why you form and punctuate your compound sentences as you do and understand the effect of your choices on your reader.

EXERCISE 1

Write three compound sentences for each of the following sets. Form one with a conjunction without a comma, one with a conjunction with a comma, and one with a semicolon. Then evaluate each group of sentences for effectiveness and emphasis.

1. The boys raced their sled down the hill.
   Benjamin won the race.
2. No teacher enjoys giving tests.
   No teacher enjoys failing students.
3. Yesterday morning the sky was bright blue.
   By afternoon, the storm shook the city.
4. Today the stock market plunged to new lows.
   The bond market maintained its value.
5. With the recent rise in the price of gold, earrings for pierced ears have doubled in cost.
   Wedding bands have tripled in cost.

EXERCISE 2

Add commas before the conjunctions wherever you think they are necessary. Be prepared to defend your decision.

1. Agatha, a funny little Persian kitten, tangled her paw in a ball of yarn so, after many frantic leaps and spins, she meowed for help.
2. I hate spinach and I loathe carrots.
3. I have never known anyone as clumsy as you and, if I ever do, I hope I never have to dance with him.
4. The team has moved to Anaheim yet it has maintained its old name, the Los Angeles Rams.
5. Nobody wanted to see the school carnival fail yet nobody wanted to work to make it a success.

EXERCISE 3

Check over your one-paragraph descriptive essay. Are there any places where commas might go before a conjunction? Are there any commas before conjunctions that should be erased? Are there any compound sentences formed with conjunctions that would be more effective if semicolons were to be substituted? Make any changes you feel would strengthen your discussion.

Preparing the Final Copy and Proofreading

In preparing your final copy, follow the manuscript conventions listed under the section on proofreading in Unit 1. Use one side of the paper only. Check for correct margins and double spacing; center a title at the top of the page; indent the first sentence of each paragraph; and correct any errors neatly with correction fluid, clean erasures, or lines drawn through mistakes.

Now you are ready to proofread. Read your final copy aloud, slowly and carefully. Ask yourself the following questions.

1. Are the words spelled correctly? Are hyphens at the ends of lines placed correctly between the syllables of divided words? If you are uncertain about either your spelling of certain words or the division of any word, check your dictionary.
2. Have you made any accidental changes in your text or omitted any words?
3. Is the punctuation correct?
   a. Are there capitals and periods to indicate complete sentences?
   b. Are compound sentences accurately punctuated?

UNIT 3
Exposition: The Development of Ideas

READING:
Exposition: The Development of Ideas

Reading Strategies: Comprehension through Supporting Ideas; Recognition of Levels of Generality

In the reading lesson in Unit 2, you first developed your awareness of the difference between main or controlling ideas and specific ideas. Next, while keeping in mind the important difference between general and specific, you practiced finding the most general, or controlling, idea in a paragraph or in an essay. In this unit, we will concentrate on the specific ideas that support a paragraph's controlling idea. Such supporting materials explain, prove, extend, or substantiate — that is, back up — a writer's general statement. Learning to recognize these types of materials will help you read effectively in three ways.

1. This kind of recognition helps you to better understand controlling ideas.
2. This kind of recognition helps you become a good, *critical* reader, one who can evaluate supporting materials and who can decide whether or not a writer has presented a well-developed, logical discussion.
3. This kind of recognition reinforces your understanding of the relationships among ideas.

Types of Supporting Ideas

Many different types of supporting materials are used to develop paragraphs. Some materials that you will find most frequently in your reading are similar to the following examples. Notice carefully the relationships between the italicized controlling ideas and the support.

1. *Examples.*
   Examples, one of the most commonly used types of supporting material, generally consist of verifiable (provable) information, statistics, or models of items introduced in the controlling ideas:

   Several kinds of fuels must be considered for our purpose. Oil, for example, has been widely used in the United States during the past fifty years. (model)

   The Constitution places specific restrictions on many federal officeholders. The president, for example, must be native born and at least thirty-five years old. (verifiable information)

   A reliable estimate based on past experience can be made. Ninety percent of the students who fulfill their assignments will receive grades of C or better. (statistics)

2. *Extended examples.*
   Extended examples are examples that have been fully developed:

   We are running out of energy sources. To illustrate, oil, a fuel that has been widely and even carelessly used in the United States, is now recognized as finite and may no longer be available for the use of our children's children. As yet, however, we have no other available source of energy as versatile and efficient.

3. *Comparison.*
   A comparison is the statement of explicit similarities between two things or ideas:

   Young and old alike need love. Babies need the caressing touch of their parents, and old people need the reassuring hugs of their children.

   Note: *Analogy* is a type of comparison in which two things or ideas that are not usually considered to be alike are shown to be similar in some way:

   The human circulatory system, with its heart and arteries, is like an electrically powered pump forcing water through a plumbing system.

4. *Contrast.*
   A contrast is a statement of explicit differences between two things or ideas:

   Skilled and unskilled readers are different in one important way. A skilled reader has a plan of attack, but an unskilled reader has only a wish for victory.

5. *Graphic aids.*
   Graphic aids include charts, drawings, graphs, and diagrams. They are often used to clarify a point of discussion:

When you take notes, try to follow some of the suggestions given in this discussion. Figures 1–8 show the relationships among these suggestions and explain how these suggestions can be used efficiently.

6. *Quotations and indirect quotations.*
   Direct quotations use the exact words of another writer or speaker and are enclosed in quotation marks. Indirect quotations are a rephrasing of another person's statement and are not placed within quotation marks. Many indirect quotations begin with the word "that":

   Dr. Jones feels strongly about the use of specific details to support an assertion: "You must give concrete evidence for your claims." (direct quotation)

   Dr. Jones insists that we must supply our readers with specific information in support of every claim. (indirect quotation)

7. *Concrete description.*
   Concrete description uses details to show what has happened or how something looks, sounds, tastes, or feels:

   The boy was shocked. Droplets beaded his forehead and harsh gasps chugged painfully from his tightened throat.

8. *Parts of the whole.*
   Parts of the whole are the component parts of a thing or idea:

   Professional football has become a game for specialists. Each team now has at least three distinct squads. First there is the offensive squad, which plays when the team has possession of the ball.

9. *Cause or effects.*
   Causes are the things, people, or events that bring about a situation. Effects are the results of an action or situation:

   The divorce rate in California has tripled in recent years. Appalled at this increase, many people blame the situation on working wives. (cause)

   The divorce rate in California has tripled in recent years. As a result, many children are now raised by a single parent. (effect)

10. *Steps in a process.*
    Steps in a process are chronological steps taken while performing a task:

    Tuning an acoustical guitar requires seven steps. First, the sixth, or E, string is tuned to the appropriate note on a pitch pipe.

11. *Statements of opinions.*
    Statements of opinions are expressions of a writer's beliefs:

To me, all strenuous physical exercise is a violation of the body. Jogging at six o'clock in the morning shocks the brain, cramps the muscles, and drenches the body with sweat.

12. *Definitions.*
    Definitions serve as types of explanations clarifying the controlling idea. They are often used in highly technical discussions:

The American Textile Company recently installed a malimo and a dobby loom. The malimo, a textile machine developed in East Germany, stitches together three sets of yarn at a very high speed.

EXERCISE 1

Choose 5 paragraphs from your reading assignment in this unit. Underline the controlling idea of each and note in the margin of your text which type of support is used to develop the paragraphs. Don't be hesitant about writing in your text — it, like most books, is a source of interaction. The text provides you with information and you provide responses. Remember: Only through such interaction can learning take place.

Words and the Language: Words in Context — Contrast and Negation

Other clues that writers give to help their readers unravel the meanings of words are *negation* or *contrast*. In other words, writers often clarify their discussions by telling what something is *not* or by showing how one thing *differs* from another. Look at the following examples carefully to see if you can guess the meanings of the italicized words from their context.

John, who wears very thick glasses, is *myopic*, not far-sighted.

Mary was once *diabetic* but now has a low blood sugar count.

Reading these sentences carefully, you can guess what *myopic* and *diabetic* mean, even if these words are unfamiliar to you. For if John is not far-sighted, he is probably near-sighted; and if Mary now has a low blood sugar count, she probably once had a high blood sugar count.

As you read your college assignments, newspapers, and magazines, you should look for the negations and contrasts that help explain the meanings of words. A simple strategy that will help you focus on these clarifications is to watch for signals that indicate an author is about to explain his or her terminology through negation or contrast. Some of these signals are the following words and phrases: *but, while, now . . . then, on the other hand, however, not, yet.* Examine the following sample sentences, noting how the meanings of the italicized words are explained and how the underlined words serve as signals to the reader.

Examples

1. My brother was sure that I would *default* on his loan to me, but I repaid him within two weeks.

2. My parents joined an *interdenominational* church, while I maintained my membership in an orthodox Protestant chapel.

3. I now feel quite *pessimistic* about my future; yesterday, before my final exam, I thought I could conquer the world.

4. At times, especially when I lie around the house watching TV all day, my mother thinks I am a confirmed *laggard*. On the other hand, after I spend the entire afternoon cutting the lawn, she tells all her friends that I am an industrious, energetic young man.

5. My railroad stocks declared a good *dividend* this year; last year, however, they paid nothing.

6. The orator is an expert in *circumlocution*, not brevity of speech.

7. I find the misuse of energy an *abomination*, yet I often waste energy, especially when I'm in a hurry and forget to turn off lights as I leave for work.

EXERCISE 1

For each of the italicized words in the above examples, write the definition that the contrasting phrase seems to suggest. Compare your definition with that of your classmates.

EXERCISE 2

As you read through the following sentences, see if you can guess at the meanings of the italicized words. Check your answers in a dictionary.

1. My blind date claimed that he knew immediately that we were *kindred* souls, whereas I knew as soon as I saw him that we had nothing in common.

2. My sister thought the rock concert was rather *scintillating*, but I thought it was very dull.

3. On the one hand, my teacher claims my sentence contained a *dangling modifier;* on the other hand, I insisted my adjectives were properly placed.

4. My first reaction to the demands of the drill sergeant was *defiance*, but after peeling ten pecks of potatoes, I learned the art of obedience.

5. I ordered a *brogan* to wear at work, not a loafer or oxford.

Reading Exposition: Information

The reading selections in Units 1 and 2 present specialized strategies for reading narration and description. A third type of composition, exposition, was introduced in the Reading Strategies section of Unit 1. Now, in this section, you will practice applying these strategies as you read the following essays.

The purpose of exposition is to explain a thesis (the general or main topic of a discussion). Exposition sometimes appears alone, but often two or more composition types are combined — for example, description to enhance and support exposition, or narration to reinforce exposition. And just as the types of *composition* may appear alone or in combination, the *methods* used in exposition may also appear singly or in various combinations. In the Reading Strategies for this unit, these methods, shown in relationship to textbook reading, have already been discussed as *supporting ideas*. When reading essays, review the same methods of exposition: example, illustration (expanded example), comparison, contrast, quotations, parts of the whole, cause, effect, steps in a process, statements of opinion, and definition (this method will be discussed fully in the next unit).

EXERCISE 1

In your assigned essay for this unit, find two or more examples of the above methods of exposition; mark them in the text, and explain their relationship to the main idea of their paragraphs.

READINGS: SELECTION ONE

from The Magic of Memory
by Laurence Cherry

Ideas to Think About

1. Can you remember some things more easily than others? What is easy for you to remember? Faces? School work? Names? Skills? Movies? Books? Why do you think this is so?
2. The author claims that "our memories are probably our most cherished possession." What do you consider your most cherished possession? Why? What value do you place on your memory?
3. This article discusses some theories about memory. Look for the main theories; where in the paragraphs do you find most of them?

Vocabulary

Look at each word as it is used in the article. (The number in parentheses indicates the paragraph in which it appears.) First, try to understand the meaning from the way it is used in the sentence. Then, use the dictionary to clarify the meaning.

extract (2)   perception (5)
electrode (3)   decrement (10)
senile (5)   implication (11)

from The Magic of Memory

A National Media Award winner, Laurence Cherry is a widely published science writer. The following article first appeared in the summer 1980 edition of *Science Digest*.

Our memories are probably our most cherished possessions. More than anything else we own, they belong uniquely to us, defining our personalities and our views of the world. Each of us can summon thousands of memories at will: our first day at school, a favorite family pet, a summer house we loved. And yet the marvel of memory continues to be a tantalizing mystery. Nevertheless, within the past few years great advances have been made in understanding what memory is, how it works, and how it may possibly be improved. "We're standing at the brink of a whole new era in memory research," says Dr. Steven Ferris, a psychologist at the Millhauser Geriatric Clinic. "For the first time, there's a general feeling that we're really on the right track."

For years, the prevailing theory was that remembering was somehow connected to electrical activity inside the brain. But within the past decade, it's become clear that chemical changes must also be involved, otherwise our memories could never survive deep-freeze, coma, anesthesia and other events that radically disrupt the brain's electrical activity. Ingenious[1] research over the past few years has demonstrated that biochemical changes do indeed accompany learning and remembering. In one dramatic experiment, mice, who usually prefer the safety of darkness, were taught to fear the dark and were then killed. Extracts° of their brains were injected into untrained mice, and they then began to shun the dark. Other experimenters have shown that the amounts of certain chemicals, such as RNA, radically increase with learning, as do the amounts of certain neurotransmitters — chemicals released by brain cells that help conduct nerve impulses from one brain cell to another. Memory, then, is also chemical in nature, although exactly in what way remains a mystery. . . .

3   Almost all memory researchers now agree that our brains record — and on some level remember — everything that ever happens to us. Many people who've narrowly escaped sudden death, such as soldiers and mountain climbers, have reported that in the few seconds that seemed left to them a stream of long-lost memories flashed before them. The first experimental confirmation that the brain does record every experience in this minute way came some years ago from Dr. Wilder Penfield of the Montreal Neurological Institute. He hoped to cure epileptics by stimulating a part of their brains called the temporal cortex with a mild electric current. Because the brain is immune to pain, Penfield was able to operate with his patients fully awake. To his astonishment, simply by touching the brains of some patients with the tip of his wire-thin electrode,° he was able to evoke astonishingly precise and vivid memories. "I see a guy coming through the fence at the baseball game," exclaimed one patient, whenever Penfield touched the upper part of his left temporal lobe. "It's the middle of the game, and I'm back there watching him!" Another woman reported being back at a concert she had once attended and could even hum along with the orchestra whenever her brain was stimulated.

4   Investigators using hypnosis have been as astonished as Penfield at the amazing capacity of our memories. Once in a trance, good hypnotic subjects can report detailed recollections of events that took place days, months, even decades ago — which, when checked against old records and diaries, turn out to be accurate. "Everything, absolutely everything, is remembered," says one hypnotist.

5   Even senile° patients, who can hardly remember recent events at all, retain the ability to remember new experiences, but only very briefly. "Give them a list of nonsense syllables to memorize, and for a few seconds they do almost as well as healthy young people in remembering," says one expert. But apparently the brains of senile subjects cannot elec-

---

[1] Clever.

trochemically translate the new information and shift it into long-term storage. It seems rather as if our perceptions,° in order to be remembered for more than a few seconds, must be sorted out and slid into place like folders into file cabinets. Some of the cabinets are easily opened, their contents readily available to us. Others, thanks to still unknown processes, are locked away, only to be retrieved if the files are jarred open by hypnosis or a researcher's electrode.

For years, scientists hunted for the brain's elusive "memory center," where long-term memories might be processed and stored. Above all, the hippocampi, small, seahorse-shaped structures about three centimeters long, deep within each half of the brain, were targeted as the possible center. If one hippocampus is injured, memory is temporarily affected, then eventually returns. But if both are damaged, the loss of memory is final. Patients who have lost their hippocampi live in a strange, twilight world. If they meet you, they will shake your hand and five minutes later greet you as a complete stranger. Although they can still perform well enough on IQ tests and speak quite intelligently, it's as if some crucial memory system had been cruelly short-circuited. Often they're aware something is wrong and try to hold on to their memories. But the attempt is usually useless, and even when they forget the reason for their sadness, they remain depressed.

Is it possible to improve your memory?

The surprising answer appears to be yes. Dr. Richard J. Wurtman, professor of endocrinology at the Massachusetts Institute of Technology, recently discovered that the food we eat can affect the amount of neurotransmitters in our brains and — by implication — how well we can remember.

In 1975, Wurtman and his colleagues learned that choline, a common food substance found in large quantities in egg yolks (and to some degree in meat and fish as well), has a pronounced effect on the brain's ability to make an important neurochemical called acetylcholine, almost certainly involved in memory. . . .

Meanwhile, new information is being gathered about memory loss among older people. With the exception of an unfortunate minority (possibly about 10 percent of those over 60) who suffer from Alzheimer's disease, a progressive ailment that leads to almost total memory loss, the news is good. "I think the most crucial thing we've learned is that it simply isn't true that you lose your memory as you get older," says Dr. James Ninninger of the Payne Whitney Psychiatric Clinic. "That's simply one of the self-fulfilling prophecies that should be dropped." At Johns Hopkins University, studies of men over many years as they grow older confirm this belief. "There are some subjects sixty-five to ninety who are just not showing any decrements,°" says Dr. Nathan Shock, who admits that the findings surprised him.

Although some brain changes do seem to come with age, in most cases their effect on memory is not nearly as serious as once thought. Even the idea that we begin to lose hundreds of thousands of brain cells each day past the age of 30 — with the usual grim implication° that our brainpower must diminish — has recently been hotly disputed. "As a neuroanatomist, I've been intrigued by this myth of disappearing brain cells, because it lends a spurious air of scientific validity to our practice of relegating old people to empty lives," Dr. Marian C. Diamond, professor of anatomy at the University of California at Berkeley, has said. As she points out, almost no studies of brain loss have been done in humans and only a few haphazard ones in animals. "In fact," she insists, "there is only a trivial decrease in the number of brain cells — right up through old age."

Another recent finding is that intellectual stimulation keeps memory at its peak — just as physical exercise does for our muscles. In the Johns Hopkins' studies, the people who showed the least memory impairment as they aged were those who had made problem-solving a way of life. Studies in monkeys and rats have shown the same thing: constant mental activity preserves memory. And at least until we reach the outer limits of old age, the continuous amount of new information we are always storing should help us to remember, not cause us to forget. Dr. Patricia Siple, a psychologist at the University of Rochester, has found that a large store of information helps our memories. We remember not so much words and sounds as concepts, which form a kind of indexed system to recall information.

Recent research indicates that, unlike a container that can be filled, our memory far more resembles an ever-growing tree, continually putting out new roots and connections, memory building on memory, rivaled in complexity only by the mysterious, ever-challenging brain itself.

Discussion

1. Most of us have been told by our mothers that some kind of food will improve our brains or eyesight or curl our hair. We are told, "Eat your carrots. They will make you see better." "Fish is brain food." What does the author report the relationship to be between food and memory? What other reports have you read concerning food and increased mental or physical capacity?
2. Memory researchers agree that our brains record — and remember at some level — everything that happens to us. What do you suppose would happen if you suddenly remembered everything on a conscious level all at once?
3. What are the main ways in which we now may be able to improve our memories? What are some of the myths concerning memory that research has exposed?
4. In his title, Laurence Cherry calls memory "magic" and in the first para-

graph "a tantalizing mystery." What three important aspects of memory does he state as his focus? Underline the places in the essay where he discusses each of these aspects. If the divisions do not seem clear, try to see if some ideas overlap.
5. Mark the important theories Cherry lists. What types of supports does he use to discuss the theories? How valid are these supports?
6. Find two analogies. Why do you think the author uses them? How are they helpful to you?
7. This article is basically a report or explanatory essay. At what point does the essay become somewhat persuasive? In other words, where does it begin to try to encourage you to act in a certain way?
8. Why are you or why are you not convinced by the evidence about food substances and intellectual stimulation?

UNIT 3 EXPOSITION: THE DEVELOPMENT OF IDEAS

READINGS: SELECTION TWO
Mankind's Better Moments
by Barbara Tuchman

Ideas to Think About
1. Have you ever felt a little discouraged about the world situation? Why?
2. Do you ever wish you could hide from evidence that shows this is not the best of all possible worlds? Why? Have you been able to hide the truth from yourself?
3. What recent world events or inventions made you glad to be part of humanity?
4. After you have skimmed the article, read it carefully and underline the main ideas. Then underline the supporting ideas that substantiate the main or controlling ideas.

Vocabulary

Look at each word as it is used in the article. (The number in parentheses indicates the paragraph in which it appears.) First, try to understand the meaning from the way it is used in the sentence. Then, use the dictionary to clarify the meaning.

ignoble (2)	tenacity (10)
decadent (2)	ribaldry (16)
altruism (3, 18)	phenomenon (20)
endeavor (4)	despondent (24)
extrapolations (7)	paradox (25)
heresies (7)	abeyance (25)

Mankind's Better Moments

Barbara Tuchman is a Pulitzer Prize-winning historian who has written a number of books including *Guns in August* and *A Distant Mirror*. This article was adapted from her Thomas Jefferson lecture delivered in Washington and sponsored by the National Endowment for the Humanities, the highest honor the federal government confers for distinguished intellectual achievement outside the world of science.

In this troubled world of ours, pessimism seems to have won the day. But we would do well to recall some of the positive and even admirable capacities of the human race. We hear very little of them lately. 1

Ours is not a time of self-esteem or self-confidence as was, for instance, the 19th Century, whose self-esteem may be seen oozing from its portraits. Victorians, especially the men, pictured themselves as erect, 2 noble and splendidly handsome. Our self-image looks more like Woody Allen or a character from Samuel Beckett. Amid a mass of worldwide troubles and a poor record for the 20th Century, we see our species — with cause — as functioning very badly, as blunderers when not knaves, as violent, ignoble,° corrupt, inept, incapable of mastering the forces that threaten us, weakly subject to our worst instincts; in short, decadent.°

The catalogue is familiar and valid but it is growing tiresome. A study of history reminds one that mankind has its ups and downs and during the ups has accomplished many brave and beautiful things, exerted stupendous endeavors, explored and conquered oceans and wildernesses, achieved marvels of beauty in the creative arts and marvels of science and social progress, loved liberty with a passion that throughout history has led men to fight and die for it over and over again, pursued knowledge, exercised reason, enjoyed laughter and pleasures, played games with zest, shown courage, heroism, altruism,° honor and decency; experienced love, known comfort, contentment, and, occasionally, happiness. All these qualities have been part of human experience and if they have not had as important notice as the negatives nor exerted as wide and persistent an influence as the evils we do, they nevertheless deserve attention, for they currently are all but forgotten.

Among the great endeavors, we have in our time carried men to the moon and brought them back safely — surely one of the most remarkable achievements in history. Some may disapprove of the effort as unproductive, as too costly, and a wrong choice of priorities in relation to greater needs, all of which may be true but does not, as I see it, diminish the achievement. If you look carefully, all positives have a negative underside, sometimes more, sometimes less, and not all admirable endeavors° have admirable motives.

Great endeavor requires vision and some kind of compelling impulse, as in the case of the Gothic cathedrals of the Middle Ages. The architectural explosion that produced this multitude of soaring vaults, arched, ribbed, pierced with jeweled light, studded with thousands of figures of the stone-carvers' art, represents in size, splendor and numbers one of the great, permanent artistic achievements of human hands.

What accounts for it? Not religious fervor alone. Although a cathedral was the diocesan seat of a bishop, the decision to build did not come from the Catholic Church alone, which by itself could not finance the operation, but from the whole community. Only the common will shared by nobles, merchants, guilds, artisans, and commissioners in general could command the resources and labor to sustain such an undertaking. Each group contributed donations, especially the magnates of commerce who felt relieved thereby from the guilt of money-making. Collections were made from the public in towns and countryside, and indulgences granted in return for gifts. Voluntary work programs involved all classes. "Who has ever seen or heard tell in times past," wrote an observer, "that powerful princes of the world, that men brought up in honors and wealth, that nobles — men and women — have bent their haughty necks to the harness of carts and like beasts of burden have dragged to the abode of Christ these wagons loaded with wines, grains, oil, stones, timber and all that is necessary for the construction of the church?"

The higher and lighter grew the buildings and slenderer the columns, the more new expedients and techniques had to be devised to hold them up. Buttresses flew like angels' wings against the exterior. It was a period of innovation and audacity. In a single century, from 1170 to 1260, 600 cathedrals and major churches were built in France alone. In England in that period, the cathedral of Salisbury with the tallest spire in the country was completed in thirty-eight years. The spire of Freiburg in Germany was constructed entirely of filigree in stone as if spun by some supernatural spider. In the Sainte Chapelle in Paris the fifteen miraculous windows swallow the walls; they have become the whole.

Explanations of the extraordinary burst that produced the cathedrals are several. Art historians will tell you that it was the invention of the ribbed vault, permitting subdivision, independence of parts, replacement of solid walls by columns, multiplication of windows and all the extrapolations° that followed. But this does not explain the energies that took hold of and developed the rib. Religious historians say these were the product of an age of faith that believed that with God's favor anything was possible. In fact, it was not a period of untroubled faith but of heresies° and Inquisition. Rather, one can only say that conditions were right. Social order under monarchy and the towns was replacing the anarchy of the barons so that existence was no longer merely a struggle to stay alive but allowed a surplus of goods and energies and greater opportunity for mutual effort. Banking and commerce were producing capital, roads making possible wheeled transport, universities nourishing ideas and communication. It was one of history's high tides, an age of vigor, confidence and forces converging to quicken the blood.

Even when the general tide was low, a particular group of doers could emerge in exploits that still inspire awe. What of the founding of our own country? We take the Mayflower for granted, yet think of the boldness, the enterprise, the determined independence, the sheer grit it took to leave the known and set out across the sea for the unknown where no houses or food, no stores, no cleared land, no crops or livestock, none of the equipment or settlement of organized living awaited.

Equally bold was the enterprise of the French in the northern forests who throughout the 17th Century explored and opened the land from the St. Lawrence to the Mississippi, from the Great Lakes to the Gulf of Mexico. They came not for liberty like the Pilgrims, but for gain and dominion, and rarely in history have men willingly embraced such hardship, such daunting adventure and persisted with tenacity° and endurance.

Happily, man has a capacity for pleasure too, and in contriving ways to entertain and amuse himself, has created brilliance and delight. Pageants, carnivals, festivals, fireworks, music, dancing and drama, parties and picnics, sports and games, the comic spirit and its gift of laughter, all the range of enjoyment from grand ceremonial to the quiet solitude of a day's fishing has helped to balance the world's infelicity. Homo ludens, man at play, is surely as significant a figure as man at war or at work. No matter what else is happening, the newspapers today give more space to the sports pages than to any other single activity. (I do not cite this as necessarily admirable, merely indicative.) In human activity the invention of the ball may be said to rank with the invention of the wheel. Imagine America without baseball, Europe without soccer, England without cricket, the Italians without bocci, China without ping pong and tennis for no one.

But mankind's most enduring achievement is art. At its best, it reveals the nobility that coexists in human nature along with flaws and evils, and the beauty and truth it can perceive. Whether in music or architecture, literature, painting or sculpture, art opens our eyes and ears and feelings to something beyond ourselves, something we cannot experience without the artist's vision and the genius of his craft. The placing of Greek temples like the Temple of Poseidon on the promontory at Sunion outlined against the piercing blue of the Aegean Sea, Poseidon's home; the majesty of Michelangelo's sculptured figures in stone; Shakespeare's command of language and knowledge of the human soul; the intricate order of Bach, the enchantment of Mozart; the purity of Chinese monochrome pottery with the lovely names — celadon, oxblood, peach blossom, claire de lune; the exuberance of Tiepolo's ceiling where, without the picture frames to limit movement, a whole world in exquisitely beautiful colors lives and moves in the sky; the prose and poetry of all the writers from Homer to Cervantes to Jane Austen and John Keats to Dostoevsky and Chekov — who made all these things? We — our species — did.

If we have lost beauty and elegance in the modern world, we have gained much, through science and technology and democratic pressures in the material well-being of the masses. The change in the lives of, and society's attitude toward, the working class marks the great divide between the modern world and the old regime.

It is true, of course, that the underside of the scientific progress is prominent and dark. The weaponry of war in its ever-widening capacity to kill is an obvious negative, and who is prepared to state with confidence that the overall effect of the automobile, airplane, telephone, television, and computer has been on balance beneficent?[1]

Pursuit of knowledge for its own sake has been a more certain good. There was a springtime in the 18th Century when, through knowledge and

---

[1] Doing good.

reason, everything seemed possible; when reason was expected to break through religious dogma like the sun breaking through fog, and man armed with knowledge and reason would be able at last to control his own fate and construct a good society. The theory that because it exists, this is the best of all possible worlds, spread outward from Leibniz; the word "optimism" was used for the first time in 1737.

16   What a burst of intellectual energies shook these decades! In the 20 years, 1735–55, Linnaeus named and classified all of known botany; Buffon systematized Natural History in 36 volumes; the American, John Bartram, scoured the wilderness for plants to send to correspondents in Europe; Voltaire, Montesquieu and Hume investigated the nature of man and the moral foundations of law and society; Benjamin Franklin demonstrated electricity from lightning; Dr. Johnson by himself compiled the first dictionary of the English language; Diderot and the Encyclopedists of France undertook to present all knowledge in enlightened terms; the secret of making porcelain having just previously been discovered in Europe through intensive experiments, its manufacture in a thousand forms flourished at Meissen and Dresden; clearing for the Place de la Concorde, to be the most majestic in Europe, was begun in Paris, and the fantastic cascades of Caserta constructed for the Bourbons of Naples; 150 newspapers and journals circulated in England; Henry Fielding wrote *Tom Jones*; Thomas Jefferson was born; Tiepolo painted his gorgeous masterpiece, the Four Continents, on the archducal ceilings at Wurzburg; Chardin, no less supreme, painted his gentle and affectionate domestic scenes; Hogarth, seeing a different creature in the species, exposed the underside in all its ribaldry° and squalor. It was an age of enthusiasm: At the first London performance of Handel's Messiah in 1743, George II was so carried away by the Hallelujah Chorus that he rose to his feet, causing the whole audience to stand with him. A custom was thereby established, still sometimes followed by Messiah audiences.

17   If the twenty-year period is stretched by another ten, it includes the reverberatory voice of Rousseau's "Social Contract," Beccaria's groundbreaking study on "Crime and Punishment," Gibbon's beginning of the "Decline and Fall," and despite the Lisbon earthquake and Voltaire's "Candide," the admission of "optimism" into the Dictionnaire de l'Académie Française.

18   Although the Enlightenment may have overestimated the power of reason to guide human conduct, it nevertheless opened to men and women a more humane view of their fellow passengers. Slowly the harshest habits gave way to reform — in treatment of the insane, reduction of death penalties, mitigation of the fierce laws against debtors and poachers, and in the passionately fought cause for abolition of slave trade. The humanitarian movement was not charity, which always carries an overtone of being done in the donor's interest, but a more disinterested benev-

olence — altruism,° that is to say, motivated by conscience. Through recent unpleasant experiences, we have learned to expect ambition, greed or corruption to reveal itself behind every public act, but it is not invariably so. Human beings do possess better impulses, and occasionally act upon them, even in the 20th Century. Occupied Denmark, during World War II, outraged by Nazi orders for deportation of its Jewish fellow citizens, summoned the courage of defiance and transformed itself into a united underground railway to smuggle virtually all 8,000 Danish Jews out to Sweden. Far away and unconnected, a village in southern France, Le Chamben-sur-Lignon, devoted itself to rescuing Jews and other victims of the Nazis at the risk of the inhabitants' own lives and freedom. "Saving lives became a hobby of the people of Le Chamben," said one of them. The larger record of the time was admittedly collaboration, passive or active. We cannot reckon on the better impulses predominating in the world; only that they will always appear.

The strongest of these in history, summoner of the best in men, has been zeal for liberty. Time after time, in some spot somewhere on the globe, people have risen in what Swinburne called the "divine right of insurrection" — to overthrow despots, repel alien conquerors, achieve independence — and so it will be until the day power ceases to corrupt, which, I think, is not a near expectation.

The phenomenon° continues today in various forms, by Algerians, Irish, Vietnamese, peoples of Africa and the Middle East. Seen at close quarters and more often than not manipulated by outsiders, contemporary movements seem less pure and heroic than those polished by history's gloss, for instance the Scots of the Middle Ages against the English, the Swiss against the Hapsburgs, Joan of Arc arousing a dispirited people against the occupier, the Albanian Scanderbeg against the Turks, the American colonies against the mother country.

So far I have considered qualities of the group rather than of the individual, except for art which is always a product of the single spirit. Happiness too is a matter of individual capacity. It springs up here or there, haphazard, random, without origin or explanation. It resists study, laughs at sociology, flourishes, vanishes, reappears somewhere else. Take Izaak Walton, author of *The Compleat Angler,* that guide to contentment as well as fishing of which Charles Lamb said, "It would sweeten any man's temper at any time to read it." Although Walton lived in distracted times of revolution and regicide, though he adhered to the losing side in the Civil War, though he lost in their infancy all seven children by his first wife and the eldest son of his second marriage, though he was twice a widower, his misfortunes could not sour an essentially buoyant nature. "He passes through turmoil," in the words of a biographer, "ever accompanied by content."

Walton's secret was friendship. Born to a yeoman family and apprenticed in youth as an ironmonger, he managed to gain an education and through sweetness of disposition and a cheerful religious faith, became a friend on equal terms of various learned clergymen and poets whose lives he wrote and works he prefaced. John Donne, vicar of the parish in Chancery Lane where Walton worked, was his mentor and his friend. Others were Archbishop Sheldon of Canterbury, George Morley, Bishop of Winchester, Richard Hooker, Sir Henry Wotton, George Herbert, Michael Drayton and the Royalist, Charles Cotton.

The Compleat Angler, published when the author was 60, glows in the sunshine of his character. In it are humor and piety, grave advice on the idiosyncracies of fish and the niceties of landing them, delight in nature and in music. Walton saw five editions reprinted in his lifetime while innumerable later editions secured him immortality. The surviving son by his second wife became a clergyman; the surviving daughter married one and gave her father a home among grandchildren. He wrote his last work, a life of his friend Robert Sanderson, at eighty-five and died at ninety after being celebrated in verse by one of his circle as a "happy old man" whose life "showed how to compass true felicity." Let us think of him when we grumble.

Is anything to be learned from my survey? I raise the question only because most people want history to teach them lessons, which I believe it can do, although I am less sure we can use them when needed. I gathered these examples not to teach but merely to remind people in a despondent° era that the good in mankind operates even if the bad secures more attention. I am aware that selecting out the better moments does not result in a realistic picture. Turn them over and there is likely to be a darker side, as when Project Apollo, our journey to the moon, was authorized because its glamor could obtain subsidies for rocket and missile development that otherwise might not have been forthcoming. That is the way things are.

It is a paradox° of our time that never have so many people been so relatively well off and never has society been more troubled. Yet I suspect that humanity's virtues have not vanished, although the experiences of our century seem to suggest they are in abeyance.° A century that took shape in the disillusion that followed the enormous effort and hopes of World War I, that saw revolution in Russia congeal into the same tyranny it overthrew, saw a supposedly civilized nation revert under the Nazis into organized and unparalleled savagery, saw the craven appeasement by the democracies, is understandably suspicious of human nature. A literary historian, Van Wyck Brooks, discussing the 1920s and '30s, spoke of "an eschatological despair of the world." Whereas Whitman and Emerson, he wrote, "had been impressed by the worth and good sense of the people, writers of the new time" were struck by their lusts, cupidity[2] and violence,

---

[2] Desire for wealth.

and had come to dislike their fellow men. The same theme reappeared a few months ago when a drama critic, Walter Kerr, described a mother in a play who had a problem with her two "pitilessly contemptuous" children. The problem was that "she wants them to be happy and they don't want to be." They prefer to freak out or watch horrors on television. In essence, this is our epoch. It keeps turning to look on Sodom and Gomorrah; it has no view of the Delectable Mountains.

Discussion
1. In paragraph 9, Tuchman opens with the controlling idea that man has a capacity for pleasure and then claims that in seeking and making up ways to amuse ourselves, we have also created "brilliance and delight," for man is as significant "at play . . . as man at war or at work." The author then lists a number of supports for this belief. In what ways would you agree that people are as significant at play as they are at work or war? List some supports of your own. In what ways would you find it defensible that we give more newspaper space to the sports pages than we do anything else?
2. In what ways are you suspicious of human nature as, Tuchman suggests, most of us are? What national and international events in the recent past have made you feel this way? Why?
3. Tuchman says the quest for liberty has been the strongest reason for people to give their best. She says this will be true as long as power corrupts. What does she mean by this? What is the historical evidence you have to support this? In what ways do you agree?
4. In what ways do you agree or disagree that, in an age when we have so much, we do not have social ease? What evidence exists to support the idea that we do not want to be happy?

READINGS: SELECTION THREE

Symbol of Success: The Real Horatio Alger
by Anthony Brandt

Ideas to Think About

1. How do you react to success stories portrayed in the movies? Do you feel pleasure when someone you know or read about becomes successful? Why or why not?
2. What type of success do you most admire? Financial? Victory over a physical handicap? Over a bully? Over fear or shyness? Discuss why.
3. Many people believe in the "American Dream." What do you think the American Dream is? As you read the following article, see how the author debunks this concept.

Vocabulary

Look at each word as it is used in the article. (The number in parentheses indicates the paragraph in which it appears.) First, try to understand the meaning from the way it is used in the sentence. Then, use the dictionary to clarify the meaning.

saga (3)
elaboration (3)
crass (3)
benefactor (7)
ineffectual (10)
mediocrity (10)

debunk (12)
imprudent (14)
tedious (15)
phenomenon (16)
perseverance (16)

Symbol of Success: The Real Horatio Alger

Anthony Brandt is a freelance writer. The following article appeared in the April 1980 edition of *Quest/80's*.

No other people in the world have been as preoccupied with the idea of success as Americans. The early Puritans were much concerned with the best means of getting on in the world, and wrote about it. They set a tradition. To this day books devoted to the hows and wherefores of success continue to appear, and they are consistent best-sellers.

None of them sell, however, the way Horatio Alger's books sold. This bald, pudgy, mild-mannered, more or less unknown little man, who by the time he died at the age of 67 in 1899 had written 106 books, almost all for boys, may have been the best-selling author of all time. The most *conservative* estimate of sales of his books stands at 15 million copies; other guesses have gone as high as 300 million — which is probably stretching things by a couple of hundred million. But the meaning is clear: Alger was an extraordinarily popular writer, without question the most successful of all those who have written about success.

One consequence of Alger's popularity was that his name became identified with the very idea of success in America, at least insofar as that idea can be equated with making money. When we hear Alger's name, we generally think of "rags to riches" — the saga° of the poor but ambitious kid from the streets who makes a million, or the office boy who becomes chairman of the board. It's such a common theme in American life that it needs no further elaboration,° and we take its connection with Alger for granted. For years the American Schools and Colleges Association gave out annual "Horatio Alger Awards" to men who had "climbed the ladder of success," who had risen, through a combination of hard work, ambition, and brains, from obscure origins to the top. Social critics since the 1920's have crucified Alger as the archspokesman for this crass,° materialistic side of the dream of success. As everyone knows, that's what Alger's books are about: the Ragged Dicks and Tattered Toms from the slums who, Brave and Bold, indefatigably[1] Struggling Upward, wanted nothing but Fame and Fortune, and got it.

What's so curious about this identification of Alger with the rags-to-riches myth is that Alger's novels do not support it at all. Some 10 to 15 years ago scholars began actually reading Alger again, and they found to their surprise that the boys in them did not rise to the top, but only to a clerkship or perhaps, at best, to a junior partnership in a small or medium-size enterprise; that they usually came from middle-class families fallen on hard times and seldom from the slums; and that their success, such as it was, was almost entirely dependent on luck.

Struggling Upward, first published in 1886, is typical. The hero, Luke Larkin, is the son of a widow who has had to resort to dressmaking to make ends meet. Luke contributes to the family's income by working as a janitor at the village school. Luke is honest and works very hard, but he's clearly going nowhere. Worse, the Larkins have an enemy in town, the local banker, Prince Duncan, who contrives to make it appear that Luke has stolen a tin box containing $25,000 in bonds from the bank.

Luke does, in fact, have a tin box, given to him for safekeeping one dark night by a mysterious stranger. Luke is arrested, but at his trial, at which Prince Duncan, as the local magistrate, presides, the mysterious stranger comes forward at the last minute and, producing the key, opens Luke's box. It contains not the bonds, but miscellaneous papers which the stranger identifies as his own. Luke is freed and the stranger rewards his honesty by taking him to New York and buying him two new suits and a watch; he also gives him a part-time job. Shortly thereafter Luke happens

---

[1] Incapable of being tired.

to meet the owner of the missing box of bonds, an important man of business named Mr. Armstrong, who immediately recognizes, just as the mysterious stranger had, Luke's sterling qualities. He employs Luke to look for his former clerk, the only man who knows the numbers of the bonds, the original list having been lost. The story goes on in this vein, proceeding from one improbability to the next, until Luke returns with the list of numbers. The thief is revealed to be none other than Prince Duncan, and the mysterious stranger turns out to be a cousin of his father's who in gratitude for Luke's help and in appreciation of his honesty, makes over $10,000 to Luke to start him on his way. Mr. Armstrong then takes Luke into the firm as an office boy at what Alger describes as a "liberal" salary — perhaps as much as $10 a week.

This may be high melodrama — or low, as one prefers — but it's plainly not a "rags-to-riches" story as we usually conceive one. Luke works hard, he's smart and ambitious, but his success has little to do with industriousness and ambition; success emerges, rather, from an unlikely chain of coincidences only the most desperate of writers might conceive. Yet Alger, it's clear, was not desperate. He *liked* this story — so much that he duplicated it time and time again. A boy is honest, upstanding, and industrious, plays the game absolutely straight, and gets nowhere in particular until he saves a merchant's son from drowning, stops a runaway horse and carriage and rescues the wonderfully rich woman inside, or otherwise finds himself in the right place at the right time. This might be called "finding the benefactor°"; the benefactor then rewards our hero with a modest stake (Alger was fond of the figure $10,000) and a modest job, usually in a clerkship, in a modest enterprise. So consistent is this story that it ought to be capitalized: it's Alger's Story, the only one he ever told.

It remains something of a mystery how this simple but unlikely story became what we think of in connection with Alger: the myth of rags-to-riches, the epic of ragged boot-blacks climbing through sheer will and effort to the top. One critic has suggested that the story is true to life, that many successful men did get their start through a lucky break and were taken in hand by a benefactor. More likely, the myth became connected with Alger after people stopped reading his books, some 15 or 20 years after his death in 1899. The titles of Alger's novels are deceiving; people may have forgotten that in *Fame and Fortune* the fame consists of the hero being admitted to polite society on Madison Avenue, and the fortune is a quite comfortable, but still modest, salary of $1,400 a year.

But even more curious than the transformation of Alger's story into the rags-to-riches myth is what happened to the story of Alger's life. One would expect that somebody so successful would be well-known as a man, that people would be interested in him. Not so. Alger may have been one of the best-selling authors in American history, but his contemporaries ignored this human phenomenon. Almost nothing was written about him while he was alive, and not until 1928, nearly 30 years after his death, when his books were long since out of fashion, did a biography of Alger appear.

The author was Herbert R. Mayes, then a young journalist just getting started, later the editor of *McCall's*. According to Mayes, the author of *Strive and Succeed, Risen from the Ranks,* and the other epics of success was himself a miserable failure, an ineffectual° man who spent his life wanting to write a Great American Novel, a silly mediocrity° who ran away from a domineering father to live *la vie bohème* in Paris; ran away from that to the ministry, ran away from that to take refuge in New York boardinghouses and cheap novels for teenage boys. Mayes quoted from diary entries detailing Alger's first experience with sex ("I was a fool to have waited so long. It is not vile as I thought"); his romance with a pure-hearted New England girl, which his cruel father broke up; his life-long despair over his inability to write serious fiction; his disgust with his actual success. As Mayes told it, it was a rather scandalous, deeply ironic life. The public took no notice and Mayes's book did not sell, but the critics adored the irony. The man whose name was practically synonymous with success was himself a failure. Poetic justice strikes again.

For the next 40 years or so, almost all critical comment on Alger's work was based on Mayes's biography. Distinguished literary critics made profound psychological observations on the origins of Alger's Story in his life as Mayes told it, while social scientists drew interesting conclusions about the meaning of success from the same source. A few critics suspected that something was wrong: Alger's diary could not be found where Mayes said he found it, in the Harvard University library, Mayes was consistently wrong about dates, and other facts seemed to be awry. But for the most part the authorities accepted Mayes's book at face value. The *Dictionary of American Biography*'s account of Alger's life is based almost entirely on Mayes. In 1963 the writer John Tebbel published a book on Alger the biographical portion of which was heavily indebted to Mayes. For most writers, Mayes's version of Alger was too neat, too useful, to question: Alger's own story belied his Story. It was ironic. It was fascinating.

But it wasn't true. In 1974, in letters to an editor at Doubleday published in the newsletter of the Horatio Alger Society, Mayes revealed that he had made the whole thing up. He had written, he explained, a takeoff on the debunking° biographies that were popular in the 1920's. Neither he nor his publishers had expected the book to be taken seriously; when even influential critics accepted it, they were afraid to expose the critics to ridicule by revealing the truth.

The net result is that we know practically nothing of value about Horatio Alger. The surviving facts are few and, with one major exception, unrevealing. Alger was born on January 15, 1832, the son of a minister of the same name who at one time was elected to the Massachusetts state legislature. He attended Harvard College, graduating in 1852. He wrote extensively for magazines, attended Harvard Divinity School, tutored private students and taught at several boarding schools, served a congregation in Brewster, Massachusetts for a few years, was briefly an assistant editor on a newspaper, and moved to New York in 1866 and lived there, in boardinghouses, most of the rest of his life. He made two trips to Europe, both, apparently, wholly uneventful. He also made a great deal of money, but seems to have given most of it away to needy boys and their families. He never married. Several years before he died he moved back to Massachusetts, where his sister, also a writer, took care of him. His correspondence has for the most part not survived. His sister reportedly burned his manuscripts. That's all we know.

With that one exception. Alger's most recent biographer, Edwin P. Hoyt, whose book on Alger was published in 1974 but who found out about Mayes's hoax beforehand, discovered the reason why Alger left the ministry in 1866, after serving the parish in Brewster for several years. He was accused of "unnatural familiarity with boys," as the report of the parish committee put it — in short, of pederasty. Alger didn't deny the charge, according to Hoyt; his only response was that he had been "imprudent°." He left Brewster the same day the committee report appeared and soon made his home in New York. So there's a surprise in the story after all.

But does it make any difference? Do we know any more about Alger now than we did before? There isn't a hint in any of his 106 books of any kind of sex at all. Only once does an Alger hero kiss a girl, and then reluctantly. Nor is there any evidence whatever that Alger abused his friendships with all the boys he helped in New York. So hard put is Hoyt to find anything interesting to report about Alger's life, in fact, that he tells the Brewster story twice and devotes most of his book to tedious° recountings of the plots of Alger's novels. Who was Horatio Alger? We still don't know.

Yet the identity of the man, in the final analysis, is clearly less important than the phenomenon° of his remarkable success. No one sells millions of copies of the same Story told over and over again unless that Story means something special, unless it touches something profound in people's minds. The heart of Alger's books is always that moment when the young hero finds his benefactor, when at last his qualities as a *person* — his courage, his perseverance,° his honesty — are recognized by a kindly authority figure and he is rewarded, not so much for what he's done, but for what he is. Perhaps the millions of people who made Alger himself so successful didn't want success just in simple material terms, but what success implied: recognition. The reward, the job are not significant in themselves in Alger's story; rather, they are a kind of stamp of approval, an acknowledgment of worth. Our hero has come through. In the face of all kinds of difficulty — numerous enemies, endlessly malign circumstances — he has established his value as a human being. It is still possible to read an Alger novel and be touched by this message, a message that survives Alger's wooden style and the improbabilities of his plots. Struggle — it is, at bottom, the struggle to maintain one's integrity — does have its reward. Hang on, and the world will eventually believe in you. That may be what success really means for most people.

Discussion
1. Brandt claims that Horatio Alger's stories do not fit the rags-to-riches myth even though Alger himself is identified with it.
    a. Does Brandt define his use of the term *myth?* What does he mean?
    b. Look at paragraphs 7 and 8. How does a "lucky break" contradict the myth? Discuss why you agree or disagree with Brandt's viewpoint.
2. Mayes's biography was written in 1928, thirty years after Alger's death, but was revealed as false only recently (1974). According to Brandt, why was the biography accepted as true for so long?
3. In paragraph 13, Brandt introduces, but does not discuss, the "one major exception" to all the unrevealing facts about Alger. What is the effect of not discussing this fact until the next paragraph? How does Brandt feel about this surprise? How do you know?
4. What is the main idea of this essay? In how many places do you find variations on this main idea? Underline them.

WRITING:
Exposition: Information

Writing Assignment: A One-Paragraph Topic, Restriction, Illustration Essay

In the first two writing assignments, you followed specific paragraph patterns*. These patterns not only helped you organize your ideas and materials, but also assisted you in establishing contact with your readers. Organization and adjustment to the needs of an audience are interrelated aspects of writing, that is, two strings manipulated by the writer-puppeteer. For example, if a puppeteer fails to coordinate all his actions, his strings will tangle and his marionette will flop about without purpose. Likewise, if a writer neglects adjusting her organization to the needs of the audience, the communication will become a jumbled collection of facts and ideas. The writer might understand what is said, but the reader will be confused. A necessary first step in writing, then, is to identify your reading audience and to estimate its needs.

Like a puppeteer, you have to consider the total effect of your work and make certain that the audience is capable of responding as you wish. Consider these questions. Would an adult audience in Paris fully appreciate a marionette performance of "Hamlet" presented in English? Would an audience of three- and four-year-old children fully understand a performance of "The Mikado"? Would a college sophomore majoring in history fully understand a detailed, scientific explanation of black holes? And would the average American adult be able to respond to a humorous article that relies on British slang and includes many references to London restaurants, shops, and bus routes? Probably not, so what adjustments would have to be made in each instance? Less detail? A change in vocabulary? More description? Different references? A different focus? The following questions should aid you in understanding your readers' needs and allow you to adjust the scope of your topic to them.

1. What do my readers probably *know* about my topic?
2. What do my readers *need to know* about my topic?
3. What do my readers probably *need to have reviewed* about my topic?

Once you have evaluated your readers' needs and have considered appropriate adjustments of your materials and ideas, you are ready to consider your

---

*Adapted from theories outlined in Richard E. Young, Alton L. Becker, and Kenneth L. Pike, *Rhetoric: Discovery and Change* (New York: Harcourt, Brace, and World, 1970).

essay's organization. In this unit and in Units 4–10, you will focus upon the presentation of ideas, facts, and opinions and expand upon them. An expository essay requires that you state your controlling idea very clearly so that your audience will be preset to evaluate your points of discussion. Yet using an explicit or clearly stated controlling idea is not a new concept for you, since you practiced seeking out such statements by other writers in the reading lesson of Unit 2 and in the reading discussion of this unit. In addition, you incorporated such controlling ideas in each of your writing assignments so far this semester. For example, the *S* in the *S-N-E* one-paragraph essay of Unit 1 was a formal statement that established the focal point of your narration and the *F* in the *F-D* one-paragraph essay of Unit 2 was a statement of focus that allowed you to describe a person, place, or thing using sensory details; both opening statements could be called *topic sentences*.

A topic sentence, then, is an explicit statement of a paragraph's controlling idea. It is a contractual agreement established by the writer, promising not only that a certain topic will be discussed, but also that all information offered in the paragraph will relate to this topic. This promise should not be broken any more than a business contract should be violated. As the writer, you set up the terms of your contract and fulfill its stated obligations. If you fail to do so, your readers will consider their relationship with you to be "null and void," that is, broken and without value. They can respond to this broken agreement by refusing to accept your views, by denying their full attention to your discussion, or by stopping reading.

In the following assignment, you will write a one-paragraph essay in which you offer both a clearly stated topic sentence and an expanded discussion. Your topic sentence may be a statement of fact, a personal opinion, or a hypothesis (an assumption, based upon established facts, that an idea or situation is probably true). As you work on your essay, remember that your topic sentence is your contract with your readers, so be sure everything you write relates directly to it and that no extra information slips into your paragraph to block reader comprehension.

To insure that your contract with your readers is fully understood by them, your topic must be *limited, unified, precise,* and *clear*. A *limited* topic sentence means that you promise your readers no more than you can discuss fully in one paragraph. No audience wants to read a string of generalizations or can learn much from undeveloped, unexplained ideas. For example, if you were to write only one paragraph on black holes, you could not fully explain their origin, physical properties, effect on the universe, or role in future explorations of space. You might, however, define the term *black holes* or describe their gravitational force. Of course, with such a difficult subject, the limitations you put on your topic must also be based on the background of your readers. Likewise, you could not discuss your relationship with your parents in one paragraph, but you might be able to tell how you and your father disagree on the merits of a four-cylinder engine or what you dislike about such an engine. A limited topic sentence thus means a controlling statement that promises a limited discussion, one that can be developed adequately within one paragraph.

A *unified* topic sentence means that only one primary idea is expressed. In other words, you must focus tightly on one controlling idea and eliminate all secondary thoughts on the matter. Note the following topic sentences.

> Americans must develop efficient energy sources and stop building dangerous nuclear reactors.
>
> In 1980, Mount St. Helens once again became an active volcano, and many earthquakes shook the state of Washington.

The first topic sentence offers two ideas — the development of efficient energy sources and the prohibition of nuclear reactors. In the second topic sentence, two ideas are again present — the eruptions of the volcano and the earthquakes. Left as they are, these topic sentences will confuse the audience since they lack focus. Yet the first topic sentence could be unified by simply tightening up the controlling idea.

> America must develop safe, efficient energy sources.

The second topic sentence could be unified by simply eliminating the statement about earthquakes, saving that information for inclusion within the paragraph.

> In 1980, Mount St. Helens once again became an active volcano.

A *precise* topic sentence means that all ideas are exact or specific rather than general. For example, consider the following topic sentences.

> Chicago is an interesting city.
>
> America is a great nation.
>
> The president has many jobs.

Each of these sentences is vague. In the first sentence, does *interesting* mean that Chicago differs from other cities in its physical appearance or that it has many interesting museums and parks? In the second sentence, does *great* mean that America is powerful? Large? Free? In the third sentence, does *many jobs* mean that the president has many responsibilities or that the president holds several jobs in addition to being president? Notice how precise the following topic sentences are in contrast to these first three examples. Here the writer offers exact contractual agreements so the readers can now focus their attention and evaluate the writer's comments fairly.

> Chicago offers its tourists a choice of many recreational attractions.
>
> America has the largest Gross National Product (GNP) of any nation in the world.
>
> One of the president's responsibilities is to act as commander-in-chief of the armed forces.

Finally, a *clear* topic sentence means that there are no ambiguities in the controlling idea. Ambiguities here refers to confusing phrases, groups of words that could be misread or misinterpreted. For example, in the sentence "John hates terrifying old men," does John hate old men who terrify him or does John hate to terrify these old men? In the sentence "The butcher sold chickens and geese that are frozen," does the butcher sell fresh chickens and frozen geese or are both the chickens and geese frozen? Both sentences need clarification.

EXERCISE 1

As we mentioned earlier, topic sentences must be *limited, unified, precise,* and *clear*. As they serve as your contractual agreement with your readers, they must establish specific guidelines for you to follow as you develop your ideas. Furthermore, they must prepare your readers for your discussion. Once your readers know what topic you are about to develop, they can focus their attention and read quickly and effectively.

Evaluate the following topic sentences. Rewrite those that are not *limited, unified, precise,* or *clear*.

1. President Truman had many difficult decisions to make during his first term of office.
2. Professional football is a violent sport and requires many strategic plays.
3. Farmers in Wisconsin specialize in poultry and dairy products that are shipped throughout the country.
4. The devaluation of the American dollar might create complex problems for the European Common Market nations.
5. The Supreme Court has assumed many roles since its establishment in the late eighteenth century.
6. Nuclear reactors produce cheap electrical energy but they also create problems with their radioactive by-products.
7. The modern 35-millimeter cameras have revolutionized amateur photography.
8. Michelangelo was a leading Renaissance painter.
9. Freud established the bases for psychoanalysis.
10. European cars are better than American cars.

Assignment

Write a one-paragraph essay using either a *T-R-I-I-I* or an *I-I-I-R-T* pattern. The paragraph should contain at least 150 words.

T — Topic sentence.

R — Restatement or restriction of the topic sentence.

I — Illustration.

The *T*, or topic sentence, must be *limited, unified, precise,* and *clear.* Remember to adjust your topic and topic sentence to your readers' needs.

The *R* of the paragraph can be either a *restatement* of the topic sentence or a further *restriction* of it. A restatement clarifies the topic sentence through explanations or rewording. For example, look at the first two sentences in paragraph 13 of "Symbol of Success." In this paragraph, the first sentence is the topic sentence: "The net result is that we know practically nothing of value about Horatio Alger." The second sentence clarifies the first through an explanation of the phrase "practically nothing of value": "The surviving facts are few and, with one major exception, unrevealing." In contrast to a *restatement*, a *restriction* of the topic sentence narrows the topic of the paragraph to a more specific area. For example, in paragraph 6 of "The Magic of Memory," the topic sentence is again the first sentence: "For years, scientists hunted for the brain's elusive 'memory center,' where long-term memories might be processed and stored." The second sentence of the paragraph, the *R*, restricts the paragraph to one area of concentration, the hippocampi: "Above all, the hippocampi, small, seahorse-shaped structures about three centimeters long, deep within each half of the brain, were targeted as the possible center." Both types of *R*'s, the *restatement* and the *restriction*, work as focusing agents for the future development of your topic.

The *I*'s, or *illustrations*, of the paragraph can be any of the following means of development. (Review the Reading Strategies section of this unit.)

1. *Details or facts.* That is, descriptive details or concrete facts that explain or clarify the topic sentence.
2. *Examples.* That is, models that represent types of things mentioned in the topic sentence. For example, if the topic sentence focuses on American sports, examples could be baseball, football, and basketball.
3. *Parts of the whole.* That is, elements that make up the topic. For example, if the topic sentence focuses on a football team, the *I*'s could be the offensive team, the defensive team, and the kicking team.
4. *Causes or effects.* That is, causes or effects of the situation mentioned in the topic sentence.
5. *Points of comparison or contrast.* That is, the similarities or differences between two or more things mentioned in the topic sentence.
6. *Statements of opinions.* That is, expressions of the writer's beliefs about the topic.
7. *Definitions.* That is, a clarification of the topic sentence by defining terms.
8. *Steps in a process.* That is, a chronological description of the steps to be taken in completing a task mentioned in the topic sentence.

Each *I* can involve more than one sentence, but each must focus on only one facet of discussion. For example, an *I* in a paragraph focusing on the dangers of smoking might read like the following sentences.

> Another peril for smokers is cancer of the mouth cavity. This situation is especially true for pipe and cigar smokers, since they keep the inhaled smoke in their mouths rather than breathe it into their lungs. As a consequence, the delicate tissues of their gums and tongues have increased contact with the tars of the tobacco.

In writing your assignment, you have two alternative organizational patterns from which to choose. You can begin your paragraph with your topic sentence and then proceed to write your *R* and *I*'s, or you can reverse this order by introducing your *I*'s first and work toward your *R* and *T* (*I-I-I-R-T*). The *T-R-I-I-I* pattern is valuable at any time, whether as a one-paragraph essay or as one of many paragraphs in a longer work. It is also very useful as an introductory paragraph to an essay or an essay examination.

Example

(*T*) In recent years, television has been blamed for almost all behavioral problems of children. (*R*) In fact, psychologists, doctors, educators, and parents have cited television as an important cause of emotional and intellectual difficulties in children. (*I*) TV is accused of teaching violence as a normal, exciting way of life through cartoons, war movies, and crime stories. It seems that every time an emotionally disturbed child commits an aggressive act, someone recalls a similar act portrayed on a recent TV program. (*I*) Television is also accused of teaching poor eating habits through commercials promoting junk foods, that is, foods with high sugar contents. Since a new medical theory claims that excessive sugar in a diet can lead to hyperactivity, doctors and parents are now blaming TV not only for decayed teeth but also for unruly behavior. (*I*) And finally, television is accused of hindering education. Citing recent statistical studies, psychologists and educators claim that the average school age child watches 4–7 hours of television daily. These are the hours that should be devoted to homework and reading.

Like the *T-R-I-I-I* pattern, the *I-I-I-R-T* pattern is very useful as a one-paragraph essay, as one of many paragraphs in an essay, and as an introductory paragraph. It is also especially useful as a conclusion to a lengthy discussion. Care must be taken, however, in writing an *I-I-I-R-T* paragraph. Be sure your paragraph is coherent, that is, make certain your ideas flow naturally one to another. Don't drop isolated points of discussion next to each other.

Example

(*I*) In recent years, television has been accused of hindering the education of American children. Citing recent statistical studies, psychologists and educators claim that the average school age child watches 4–7 hours of TV each day. These are the same hours that should be devoted to reading and homework. (*I*) Television has also been accused of teaching poor eating habits through commercials promoting junk food, that is, food with a high sugar content. Since a new medical theory claims that excessive sugar in a diet can cause hyperactivity, doctors and parents blame TV for not only dental cavities but also unruly behavior. (*I*) Finally, television has been accused of teaching violence as a normal, exciting way of life through cartoons, war movies, and crime stories. It seems that every time an emotionally disturbed child commits a violent act, someone recalls a similar act portrayed on a recent program. (*R*) Whatever the truth of the situation, psychologists, doctors, educators, and parents cite television as a major cause of many childhood emotional and intellectual difficulties. (*T*) In fact, television has become the scapegoat for most behavioral problems of today's American children.

TOPICS

BRANDT

1. Discuss your attitude towards wealth. Be sure to explain what the word *wealth* means to you. Your audience is your grandparents or an elderly relative.
2. Introduce a person who has influenced your life. This influence may have been either positive or negative. Your audience is your classmates.

CHERRY

1. Explain an experiment you attempted or read about in one of your textbooks. Your audience is your English teacher.
2. Explain why you changed an opinion you held until recently. For example, once you might have thought that women should be drafted but now feel they should be exempt from the draft. Perhaps you once believed that college students should not work during the school year but now believe that job experience complements school learning. Your audience is your parents.

TUCHMAN

1. Discuss one characteristic of the American people. Perhaps you might evaluate the generosity of Americans or their work ethic. Your audience is the foreign students attending your school.

2. Discuss a belief held by one group of people about another group. Perhaps you might wish to comment upon the views held by your classmates about college teachers; the views held by science or business majors about history, art, or music majors; or the views held by athletes about people who don't participate in sports. Your audience is college-educated adults.

Brainstorming and Shaping

Identifying Your Audience

1. Choose your topic and audience.
2. Prepare a data sheet similar to Data Sheet 3-1. Notice how Sample Data Sheet 3-1 is filled out.

Choosing the Illustration

Select two of your sample topic sentences for possible use in your writing assignment. Write a brief outline for a *T-R-I-I-I* paragraph for each. These same outlines can be reversed for *I-I-I-R-T* paragraphs.

Examples
1. *T* — TV commercials that promote junk foods threaten the health of young children.

    R — Junk food, those foods with high sugar content, can cause both physical and behavioral problems.

    I — Foods with high sugar content can damage teeth.

    I — Excessive sugar in a child's diet can lead to hyperactivity.

    I — Junk food ruins appetites for nutritional meals.

2. *T* — Most American children spend more time each week watching television than they do attending school and doing homework.

    R — They stare at the TV set before breakfast, after school, after dinner, and on and off throughout the weekend.

    I — The average child watches television 3–5 hours each weekday.

    I — The average child watches television 6–8 hours per day on weekends.

    I — The average child spends 20 hours per week in school and 5 hours per week on homework.

Data Sheet 3-1   Audience

A. Topic: _____

B. Audience: _____

C. General Characteristics of the Audience:
   1.
   2.
   3.
   4.
   5.
   6.

D. Probable Knowledge of Reading Audience on Topic:
   1. What do my readers probably know about my topic?
      _____
      _____

   2. What do my readers need to know about my topic?
      _____
      _____

   3. What do my readers need to have reviewed on my topic?
      _____
      _____

E. Probable Opinions Held by Reading Audience on Topic:
   1.
   2.
   3.

F. Five Possible Topic Sentences:
   1.

   2.

   3.

   4.

   5.

A. Topic: Television.
B. Audience: Parents who are active members of an elementary school PTA.
C. General Characteristics of the Audience:
   1. Age: between 25 and 40.
   2. Sex: more women than men.
   3. Education level: high school graduates; some college graduates.
   4. Work: most men work full time; some women do not work out of the home, some work full time, and some work part time.
   5. Concerns related to topic: children's education, health, and behavior.
   6. Other pertinent information: probably have 2 television sets in home; fathers watch TV sports events in evenings and weekends; two or more children in family.
D. Probable Knowledge of Reading Audience on Topic:
   1. What do my readers probably know about my topic?
      Sports, cartoons, and old movies dominate Saturday TV. Violence and sex are often portrayed on TV. Commercials on children's programs promote toys and food. Public Broadcasting UHF stations have better-quality children's programming.
   2. What do my readers need to know about my topic?
      Which programs on commercial TV are best suited for children. Which programs on commercial TV are least suitable for children. Commercials are often sexist and racist. Most foods advertised on TV have high sugar contents. Commercials indoctrinate children to want specific products.
   3. What do my readers need to have reviewed on my topic?
      TV is not a responsible babysitter. Parents must supervise all TV watching. Children make heroes out of TV characters.
E. Probable Opinions Held by Reading Audience on Topic:
   1. TV portrays too much violence and sex.
   2. Children watch too much TV.
   3. TV stations should take responsibility for what they present, especially before 9 P.M.
F. Five Possible Topic Sentences:
   1. Most American children spend more time each week watching television than they do attending school and doing homework.
   2. TV commercials that promote junk foods threaten the health of young children.
   3. TV commercials portray women as sex objects.
   4. TV sports programs fail to encourage children to participate in athletics.
   5. Parents must assume responsibility for their children's television activities.

Writing the First Draft

Choose one of your outlines as the basis for your writing assignment, a 150-word, one-paragraph essay following either the *TRIII* pattern or the *IIIRT* pattern. As you write your first draft, be sure you develop each of your illustrations sufficiently so that your readers fully understand your points of discussion. *Do not discard your data sheet and outlines; they must be submitted with your final draft.*

Revising the One-Paragraph Topic, Restriction, Illustration Essay

Your assignment requires that you follow either the *T-R-I-I-I* or *I-I-I-R-T* pattern of organization. Look over your first draft, outline, and data sheet and then review the basic revision questions.

Basic Revision Questions

1. *Is all my information accurate? Appropriate?*
   Have you bored your readers by repeating information they already know? Have you misinformed your readers by giving them false information? Have you offered all the information needed by your readers?
2. *Is this information organized so that my reader can comprehend what I have said? Could I organize my paper so that it would be more effective?*
   Does your outline follow either the *T-R-I-I-I* or *I-I-I-R-T* pattern of development? Does your one-paragraph essay follow your outline?
3. *Do I have a clear, unified focus, that is, does my paragraph telescope in on one major theme?*
   Do your *R* and *I*'s relate directly to your topic sentence? In developing your illustrations, have you added any information that does not relate to your topic?
4. *Do I offer sufficient details, examples, or explanations so that my reader gains a complete understanding of what I am trying to say?*
   Are your *I*'s fully explained? Do your readers need any additional clarification?

   For this assignment, two additional questions should be added.

Additional Questions

5. *Is my topic sentence limited, unified, precise, and clear?*
6. *Do my illustrations follow one of the formats suggested in the Assignment section of this unit?*
   Refer back to the list of types of illustrations. For this assignment, all *I*'s must be parallel, that is, of the same type.

EXERCISE 1
1. Check over your first draft and evaluate your topic sentence. Is it limited, unified, precise, and clear? If not, revise it so it fulfills all four requirements and can serve as an effective contractual agreement between you and your audience.
2. Evaluate your one-paragraph essay by asking the six revision questions posed in this section. If you answer either "No" or "I don't know" to any question, you probably need to revise your work. If you are not sure your information is accurate, check your facts in your school library. If you are not sure you have met your readers' needs, review both your data sheet and your essay to see if your discussion concentrates on what your readers need to know and what they need to have reviewed. Make all necessary adjustments to your essay.
3. Exchange papers with a classmate. Read each other's essay, role playing as the specified audience. For example, if your audience is a foreign student, have your classmate pretend to be from another country. Comment on each other's adjustments to the specified audiences. Jot down all of your classmate's suggestions and evaluate them. Remember: you don't have to agree with your classmate's comments; your development of ideas might be effective without any adjustment. Assume responsibility for all final decisions, revising as you believe necessary.
4. Complete all revisions and write a clean draft in preparation for editing.

Editing

Word Choice: Denotation and Connotation

Careful word choice is vital to all good writing, but precise word choice is imperative, that is, absolutely necessary, in writing definitions. As we said earlier, each of us is different and each of us brings different experiences to what we read and write. Because of our varied backgrounds and individuality, we often assign subtle differences in meaning to words we read and write. Although we can agree on the *denotation* of a word, that is, its dictionary definition or literal meaning, we frequently adopt personal *connotations* of a word, that is, associative or suggestive meaning. All words have literal meanings, but their additional meanings, those implied meanings we give through association, are often emotionally charged, some positive and some negative. Even colors have developed associative meanings; for example, many of us think of "pink" as youthful and girlish but consider "gray" as dull, bland, or old.

As writers, we must always be conscious of the connotative meanings of the words we choose so that we are clearly understood. But in order to achieve this effectiveness, we need to understand how connotation works. Consider, for a moment, the two words *assertive* and *passive*. The dictionary defines assertive as a positive trait that means "to state or express strongly; affirm. To defend or maintain one's rights." Using the literal meaning in the sentences "He asserted himself" or "She asserted the statement to be true" seems clear and without any emotional overtones. However, if you write "She is an assertive woman," some readers might consider the sentence to be an insult to the woman discussed, suggesting that she is rather aggressive. Another reader might take the statement as a complimentary comment on the woman's independence. Some prospective employers might even read this sentence to mean that the woman is an undesirable prospective employee, for they might associate *assertive* with *pushy* or *troublesome*. In other words, assertiveness in a woman has been and still is often considered an unfeminine characteristic. In contrast, the denotation for *passive* is "accepting without responding or initiating an action in return." But if you say, "He is passive," you may have, depending on the context, created a negative response in some readers. The traditional American male role is usually thought of as aggressive. Thus calling a man passive might suggest that he is less than male or that he is weak. This suggestion may not be your intention at all, but unless your description is expanded and explained, this may be what you communicate.

Misunderstanding, confusion, and hostility are certainly not the desired results of writing, but they are all too easy to create if you are not careful to make the right word choices and surround them with appropriate and adequate context. For example, the woman in the first illustration could be prevented from getting a job solely on the basis of a careless word choice. In fact, even the dictionary must be consulted with care because connotative language is frequently used in its definitions and lists of synonyms.

Yet connotation also affords us the opportunity to paint, shade, and expand meaning. Like simile and metaphor, it gives our language richness and has enormous power to communicate and create responses. It is the writer's responsibility, his contract with his readers, then, to put this richness to work by treating the issue of connotation with care. Any advertising copywriter would attest to this issue. Consider for a moment the word *new*. We see it stamped boldly on every product from computers to toothpaste. In our society this word seems to suggest *better, improved,* and *superior,* yet its dictionary definition is "Of recent origin; having existed only a short time, lately made . . . not yet old; fresh, recent . . . Freshly introduced. . . ." Nowhere does the literal definition say *new* is better, improved, or superior. But its connotative meaning does. Otherwise advertisers would certainly not invest the millions of dollars they do to sell us their products on the basis of this small word. That *new* can elicit such a response is an interesting comment on American society and certainly illustrates the power of connotative language.

Abstract words such as *freedom* and *democracy* also have connotative meanings that create emotional responses. For example, calling someone a liberal at a Republican convention would certainly draw a reaction that reading the dictionary definition of *liberal* would not suggest. Here the context and audience are keys to the reaction. In the 1940s and 1950s, the sentence, "His patriotism is obvious," would have elicited a positive response if it were written for any campus newspaper in the country. The same sentence would have created a strong negative response in the 1960s and early 1970s because of Vietnam and Watergate. The word *student* has also gone through connotative changes due to politics. For example, before 1960, "He is an involved student" would have suggested something positive about the person. In the late 1960s that same sentence would have been met with suspicion and hostility in many conservative neighborhoods due to the riot at Kent State, Vietnam demonstrations, and the 1968 Democratic convention. What are the attitudes toward patriotism and students today?

EXERCISE 1

Following is a list of five incomplete sentences with an italicized word. Each incomplete sentence can be completed to create a statement that has either a positive or a negative connotation.

Example
He is so *liberal* that

Positive connotation: He is so *liberal* that his students feel free to express themselves.

Negative connotation: He is so *liberal* that the committee would not hire him.

Complete each incomplete sentence in two ways. First complete each sentence to produce a positive connotation of the italicized word and then rewrite the sentence to produce a negative connotation of the word.

1. The typical *consumer* is
2. He is such an *activist* that
3. Her *dogged* pursuit made
4. Her *artful* answer was
5. The *politician* tried

EXERCISE 2

Write five sentences using the following modifiers with the word *man*. Then write five sentences using the same modifiers with the word *woman*. Evaluate how the words may have changed connotations.

Examples
The assertive *woman* slowly entered the room.
The assertive *man* slowly entered the room.

Would both of these have been positive in the past? Today?

pretty
cute
handsome
lovely
attractive   +   man
weathered   woman
tough
soft

EXERCISE 3

Make your own list of five abstract nouns that could have a positive or negative connotation depending on their use. Some interesting abstract nouns are *intelligence, creativity, dictatorship, liberty, equality, originality, duty, honesty, independence, integrity* and *responsibility*. Write five sentences in which the words you choose have a negative connotation. Then write five sentences in which your abstract nouns have a positive connotation. Use the same abstract nouns for both.

EXERCISE 4

Go over your one-paragraph definition essay and check it for connotative language. If any undesirable connotative words have crept in, be sure to eliminate them.

Sentence Structure: Subordination

In Unit 2, we studied the kernel sentence and its expansion through addition of simple modifiers and through the compounding of kernels with coordinators or semicolons. Everyone feels comfortable with these types of sentence expansion, which are learned very early in life; but as people mature, they gain the ability to form even more complex sentences and have more choices in expressing their ideas. A choice similar to coordination that adds complexity to the sentence is subordination. *Coordination* and *subordination* are relatively simple means of joining two independent sentences by means of a word such as *and, but, although*, or *because*. (See Table 3-1.)

Coordinating conjunctions, or coordinators, as the *co-* suggests, join two grammatically equal structures; in contrast, subordinating conjunctions, or subordinators, form expanded sentences by creating main structures and substructures. A substructure, a statement headed by a subordinator, cannot stand alone for it no longer contains a completed thought.

Table 3-1 Coordinators and Subordinators

Coordinators	Subordinators
and	because
but	if, as if
or, nor	though, although, even though
for	as though
yet	since
so	so that, in order that, in that
	provided that
	after
	before
	until
	when, whenever
	as
	unless
	in spite of
	whether
	while
	where, wherever

The following two sentences are equal structures that can be joined by either a coordinator or a subordinator.

The human population in Southern California is increasing.
The condor population in Southern California is decreasing.

The condor population in Southern California is decreasing *and* the human population is increasing.

The condor population in Southern California is decreasing *because* the human population is increasing.

The writer chooses the alternative that best fits the purpose and context of the larger paragraph.

Student writers sometimes confuse these three choices with three other structures that do not usually work — the fused sentence, the comma splice, and the fragment. First, sentences pushed together without a conjunction or a semicolon form a *fused sentence*. Note the following example.

Two sentences pushed together without a conjunction form a fused sentence such a structure can confuse the reader.

Second, two sentences held together only by a comma form a *comma splice*. Note the following example.

Two sentences pushed together with only a comma forms a comma splice, such a structure can confuse the reader.

Reading the sentence aloud clearly indicates the inadequacy of the comma and the necessity for a period, semicolon, or conjunction. Always remember: the comma is a separator; it cannot yoke sentences together. Finally, a period after a clause introduced by a subordinator creates a *sentence fragment*. Note the following example.

> When a writer puts a period after a clause introduced by a subordinator.

This kind of faulty sentence is easy to write because only one word, the subordinator, creates the fragment. This kind of sentence fragment is also easy to correct by simply adding a sentence to it.

> Although fragments occasionally work in casual or narrative writing, they detract from more formal writing.

Or the subordinator could be changed to a coordinator to make the sentence structurally complete.

> Fragments occasionally work in casual or narrative writing, but they detract from more formal writing.

As with fused sentences and comma splices, you can identify fragments through either grammatical analysis (Is the first word a subordinator? A coordinator?) or through reading the sentence aloud. If you have a fragment, you will probably not drop your voice to the low pitch that normally occurs at the end of English sentences.

EXERCISE 1

Identify whether each of the following statements is a fragment (*F*), a fused sentence (*f*), a comma splice (*CS*), or an independent sentence (*IS*). Correct the fragments by either eliminating the subordinator or by adding an independent clause. Correct fused sentences and comma splices by either (1) adding correct punctuation, i.e., a period and capital or a semicolon, or (2) joining the clauses by adding a coordinator or a subordinator. Use all the options.

> *Examples*
> FRAGMENT CORRECTED
> After I read *The Tyrrany of Greece over Germany.*
>
> I felt ambiguous about the influence of ancient Greece after I read *The Tyranny of Greece over Germany.*
>
> FUSED CORRECTED
> The senator could not refute the charges against him the evidence clearly proved him guilty of taking bribes.
>
> The senator could not refuge the charges against him; the evidence clearly proved him guilty of taking bribes.

INDEPENDENT

Although he examined the man's skin carefully, the dermatologist could not diagnose the cause of the rash.

1. Because the winter storms did irreparable damage to the barn.
2. The family members relentlessly pursued their own pleasures there was nothing lethargic about their actions.
3. The demise of the dictator left the country without leadership, for they had no established means of appointing a successor.
4. The inaugural ceremony took place on the west side of the capitol, it had always previously been held on the east side.
5. After he dismantled the engine and cleaned all its parts.
6. Cigarettes can be harmful to your health, much evidence has been amassed to link cigarettes to cancer.
7. Yesterday, when I learned about the fire at the hotel.
8. Mark Twain liked individuals but not people he referred to them as the damned human race.
9. With the death of John Lennon, all Beatles fans lost part of their youth.
10. She loved onions, especially on hamburgers and liver the onions hated her.

So far, then, we have identified three kinds of words and one mark of punctuation with which we can combine sentences. To review, the simplest and most common type of word to use to combine sentences is a coordinator. A more complex type of word to use to join sentences is the subordinator, which sets up a clear relationship between two thoughts. Both the subordinator and the coordinator function grammatically to join sentences. A third type of connector, the *transitional adverb* (see Table 3-2), also shows relationships between the ideas expressed in two sentences but has no grammatical function; sentences must be punctuated as two separate sentences just as if the transitional adverb were not there. Finally, if two sentences have a closer relationship to one another than to other sentences in a paragraph, a *semicolon* rather than a period and capital may be used. Semicolons often work well in pairing sentences whose relationship is indicated with a transitional adverb such as *however*.

After dieting, starving, and denying myself pleasure for three weeks, I finally lost some weight; however, after eating, feasting, and enjoying myself for three days, I gained all the weight back again.

EXERCISE 2

The following paragraph lacks coherence because words that serve to connect sentences have been omitted. Add appropriate coordinators, subordinators, and transitional adverbs to make the paragraph clear and smooth. Use appropriate punctuation.

We wondered whether the predatory skills of coyotes improve with age. We compared the time that nine young coyotes from three to six months old and 15 adults spent in the activities of searching, orienting and stalking. They

Table 3-2 Options for Joining Sentences

Purpose or Function	Coordinators	Transitional Adverb	Subordinators
Addition Similarity	and ;	again also besides furthermore in addition moreover similarly	as . . . as
Cause and Effect	for so	as a result consequently hence than therefore thus	because in as much in order that since so that when
Time Sequence	;	first, second later next then	after as before since when whenever while until
Conclusion	;	finally in conclusion in summary	
Contrast or Alternative	but or (nor) yet ;	however nevertheless on the other hand	although even though though whereas
Condition	;		if provided that unless
Manner	;		as, as if as though

were hunting mice or ground squirrels. The adults, it turned out, spent less time searching and orienting. The times adults devoted to these activities were much less variable than those of the pups. There was no difference in the time spent stalking. The coyotes in both age groups devoted an average of about 5.5 seconds. It would appear that the pups are less effective than the adults in locating their prey. Once the prey has been located coyotes in either age group will stalk briefly and then go in for the kill. Studies of coyotes in captivity reveal that pups only 30 days old are capable of carrying out a successful predatory sequence on a mouse. Coyotes of that age rarely have an opportunity to kill small rodents in the wild. They clearly have the ability.

— from Marc Bekoff and Michael C. Wells, *"The Social Ecology of Coyotes," Scientific American,* April 1980, p. 144

Punctuation: Commas with Subordinators

As mentioned in Unit 2, commas function as separators, sectioning off parts of a sentence. They help readers to see large phrases and to grasp distinct units of meaning. Commas also force readers to make brief pauses before continuing on. These pauses place extra stress on words immediately following the commas. Look at the following two sentences, which differ only in that one has a comma sectioning off a word and the other has no comma.

Yet, I hate studying for exams.

Yet I hate studying for exams.

The first example puts stress on both the word *yet* and the word *I,* making the sentence read as a vehement expression of displeasure. The second example stresses only *yet,* so the sentence reads as a simple statement of fact. With these awarenesses of the *function* and *effect* of commas, we can investigate the use of this punctuation mark on the left and right branches of a sentence.

A fully developed sentence can be divided into three parts: *left branch, midbranch,* and *right branch.*

	base or kernel sentence	
left branch	midbranch	right branch

The midbranch includes the kernel or base sentence and its modifiers. The left branch, that part of a sentence that *precedes* the complete subject of the sentence, can be one of the following sentence components.

1. A single word.

Now	I want to sleep.	
left	midbranch	right

Yesterday	my father sold his car.	
left	midbranch	right

2. A phrase.

In the morning,	the church bells will toll his death.	
left	midbranch	right

Following the discussion,	the president made his decision.	
left	midbranch	right

3. A subordinate clause.

If she won't admit her error,	she will lose my respect.	
left	midbranch	right

After Carlos recovered from his illness,	he could only work part time.	
left	midbranch	right

The right branch, that part of a sentence that *follows* the midbranch base sentence, can also be a word, a phrase, or a subordinate clause.

1. A single word.

	This is my favorite color,	blue.
left	midbranch	right

	She ordered coffee,	black.
left	midbranch	right

2. A phrase.

	The photographer enlarged the 35-mm negative	to 11" x 13".
left	midbranch	right

	Sally's favorite book is Moby Dick,	an allegorical story of evil.
left	midbranch	right

3. A clause.

	The airplane limped through the air	although two of its four engines were dead.
left	midbranch	right

With an understanding of the three branches of a sentence and the function and effects of commas in a sentence, you can understand how to use this punctuation mark effectively. In this unit, we will focus on two uses of the comma — before and after the midbranch of a sentence. The following simple rules will enable you to use the comma in these positions with ease.

1. Section off all left-branch subordinate clauses from the midbranch.

   Because he could not change a tire, he had to wait for a tow truck.

2. Section off all long phrases on the left branch from the midbranch.

   Tripping over my own feet, I nose-dived into a stack of garbage cans.

3. Section off short phrases and single words on the left branch from the midbranch if you wish to adjust your emphasis.

   In the morning he rode to school.

   In the morning, he rode to school.

   No I won't do that.

   No, I won't do that.

4. Section off any left-branch words or phrases from the midbranch if these words or phrases might otherwise cause confusion or misreading.

   Shooting the hunter killed the attacking lion.

   Shooting, the hunter killed the attacking lion.

   (Notice that in the first example, the reader is apt to read *shooting the hunter* as a unit of meaning.)

5. Section off a right-branch word or phrase that describes or renames the final noun of the midbranch base sentence.

   Mary sold her car, *a 1975 Pontiac.*

   (*A 1975 Pontiac* renames *car,* the final noun of the midbranch sentence *Mary sold her car.*)

   The young student crammed for the test, *the final examination in chemistry.*

   (*The final examination in chemistry* describes *test,* the final noun of the midbranch sentence *The young student crammed for the test.*)

6. Section off right-branch subordinate clauses from the midbranch if you want to adjust emphasis. You must make conscious choices in these cases.

   I quit my job *because I wanted a chance* to experiment with life.

   I quit my job, *because I wanted a chance to experiment with life.*

EXERCISE 1

Add commas to the following sentences where necessary. Be prepared to justify your decisions.

1. After falling asleep in front of the TV I dreamed I was a crew member of the spaceship Enterprise.
2. Tomorrow I will call home.
3. The exterminator sprayed the house a nursery for hungry termites.
4. Sitting down the fat baby laughed with self-satisfaction.
5. My history teacher specialized in the Italian Renaissance a period beginning in the early fourteenth century.
6. A farm boy Ruben felt lost and alone in New York.
7. According to many scholars the Roman Empire fell because of its decadence.
8. The gardener planted rose bushes in the front yard.
9. Although the army was well trained for battle it could not resist the overpowering forces of the enemy.
10. I often wondered if you are worthy of holding office.

EXERCISE 2

Check over your one-paragraph essay to see if all right- and left-branch commas are used correctly and effectively. Make any necessary changes.

Preparing the Final Copy and Proofreading

In preparing your final copy, follow the manuscript conventions listed under the section on proofreading in Unit 1. Use one side of the paper only. Check for correct margins and double spacing; center a title at the top of the page; indent the first sentence of each paragraph; and correct any errors neatly with correction fluid, clean erasures, or lines drawn neatly through the mistakes.

Now you are ready to proofread. Read your final copy aloud, slowly and carefully. Ask yourself the following questions.

1. Are the words spelled correctly? Are hyphens at the ends of lines placed correctly between the syllables of divided words? If you are uncertain about either your spelling of certain words or the division of any word, check your dictionary.
2. Have you made any accidental changes in your text or omitted any words?
3. Is the punctuation correct?
   a. Are compound sentences accurately punctuated?
   b. Is the comma placed after an introductory subordinate clause?
   c. Are the commas correctly placed with the right-branch subordination?

UNIT 4
Exposition: Definition

READING:
Exposition: Definition

Reading Strategies: Phrase Reading

Efficient readers read much more quickly when they read silently than when they read aloud. When reading silently, their eyes move forward by taking in clusters or groups of words rather than by looking separately at each individual word, as they do when pronouncing words for oral reading. In contrast, inefficient readers tend to read silently the same way they read orally — word by word — and in doing so they tend to regress, frequently rereading because they often miss a meaning. Now, as a college student you need to become an efficient reader, increasing both your comprehension and your speed by training yourself to focus on word clusters.

Eye movement, eye span, and regression are three terms that describe what happens to your eyes when you read. You read from left to right and from top to bottom; but, rather than moving smoothly and evenly, your eyes move through a series of fixations, pausing at one place, then moving on to another, and then to another. Your *eye span* encompasses the number of letters or words you can see at one glance, or *fixation*. Although you may not be able to see as much at one glance as Willie Mays, whose superior peripheral vision enabled him to set batting records, you can train your eyes and brain to work together to select clusters of meaning or phrases for each eye fixation.

These clusters of meaning grow out of the kernel sentence, so if you can recognize the subject and verb of a sentence and can connect these words with their modifiers, you will be able to fixate on clusters of meaning rather than on individual words. For example, notice the following sentence.

The experienced *carpenter drove each* long *nail* into the roof with only one blow, forcing the grooved boards into position.

In this sentence, *The carpenter drove each nail,* which includes a subject, verb, and direct object, serves as the kernel of the complete thought. Now examine the complete sentence once again, this time observing how modifiers are attached to the kernel to enrich and expand its message. The sentence might be read effectively through a series of eye movements that pause at phrases clustering around key words.

> The experienced *carpenter*
> *drove* each long *nail*
> into the *roof*
> with only one *blow,*
> *forcing* the groved *boards*
> into *position.*

An even more efficient reader might cluster this sentence into only three sections, as opposed to the six above. Can you see what the most meaningful groupings would be?

> The experienced carpenter drove each long nail
> into the roof with only one blow,
> forcing the grooved boards into position.

EXERCISE 1

In the following paragraph, indicate reading phrases in each sentence with slash marks. The first two sentences have already been broken into fairly short phrases. If you already have a larger eye span, your phrases might be longer.

On November 9 / the first snow fell. / It settled heavily / and even when the sun / timidly reappeared / the next day, / patches clung / to the ground. Two days later, more snow, and this time a wind goaded it from behind, forming drifts along the lee of the rimrock. Every morning after dawn, in the two highest sections where our 37 heifers and 117 cows were pastured, Floyd and I would chop an inch and a half of ice from the water tanks. By November 16, the cows had what Floyd called a please-don't-snow look in their eyes. He decided to move them to lower pastures where the grass still broke through the snow. The next morning we saddled horses and drove the cows and heifers nearer to the ranch house. "Sometimes," Floyd noted, "you get a storm like this and a few weeks later the weather does a turn-about and once again it's fall." But the snows continued and Thanksgiving was white.
— Heminway, *"The Other Side of the Bull Mountains"*

EXERCISE 2

Underline the one phrase of the five phrases listed on the right side of the paper that is the same as the one phrase on the left. Work quickly, moving your eye forward constantly, taking in each whole phrase at a glance.

Example

        the modern miracle   • a mighty miracle   • a wooden warrior

                                • the modest vehicle   ~~the modern miracle~~

                                            • the modern mirage

1. a car's interior   • an inferior car   • interior corners

                              • a roaring inferno   • a car's interior

                                      • inside a car

2. another area   • a mother ant   • another's area

                           • another area   • an area

                               • and other area

3. in large measure   • a large treasure   • in large letters

                            • in measured laps   • in long meters

                               • in large measure

4. close at hand   • a closed hand   • close at hand

                         • a handy closet   • clothes at home

                             • clothes on hand

5. the electric lamp   • the electric harp   • the lamp selection

                          • the electric lamp   • the lamplighter's song

                               • the energy slump

When you finish, record your time in seconds and then check for errors.

EXERCISE 3

Make up exercises that are similar to Exercise 2. Exchange papers with a classmate and do each other's exercises according to the instructions in Exercise 2.

Cloze Exercise

Your mind grasps meaning more effectively when you read by phrases. Forcing your eyes to move forward by fixating on sequential, meaningful phrases communicates ideas to you more easily than by reading word by word. This improved comprehension occurs because as your mind grasps ideas, it tends to *anticipate* what will come next. In other words, you don't need to look slowly and carefully at individual letters or words. As soon as your eyes see part of a meaningful phrase in its context, your mind will fill in missing words or ideas and you can push quickly on to fixate briefly on the next phrase. This type of reading helps you reduce regression or rereading, a habit that interferes with the forward flow of ideas.

One of the most effective exercises for training you in phrase reading and anticipating what will come next is the Cloze exercise. In such an exercise, blanks indicate that words have been omitted from a reading. The reader must fill in the blanks with words that make sense in the whole context. Sometimes the omitted words are connector words (coordinators like *and* or *but*, or prepositions like *in* or *before*); sometimes the omitted words are key nouns and verbs that control the meaning of the passage. Often there is no single right answer and so readers may select words that they feel are best suited to the passage. For example, note the blanks in the following sentence.

I __(a)__ the cut wood into __(b)__ trunk of my car __(c)__ waved __(d)__ to my helper.

For slots (b) and (c), *the* and *and* are the obvious choices, but for slot (a) there are several choices — *loaded, put, piled, pushed*. Which do you think is best? Can you think of more than one choice for slot (d)? Haas's original sentence was, "I loaded the cut wood into the trunk of my car and waved good-bye to my helper."

Now do the following Cloze exercise. Such an exercise will appear in many of the units; by the time you finish this book, you should be more adept at reading by phrases and at anticipating what words and ideas will be coming up next in your reading. These exercises should usually be timed so that you force yourself to move ahead quickly. Afterwards, as a class or in groups, discuss the answers, considering the various possibilities and the signals within each sentence that guided your decisions.

The farm my family _____ I visit each _____ looks still _____ calm from a distance, nestled in a peaceful valley. But_____ everything there is in turbulent motion. The farm is located on a river that moves rapidly over rocks _____ boulders and constantly carves a wider _____ deeper trough for itself between the hills. Brown, scarred mountains rise _____ the ripening cornfields, _____ from high in

_____ crags, blackbirds swoop _____ over the vegetable gardens _____ apple orchards. Tractors _____ steadily over the outlying fields, their blades tearing up the red earth _____ throwing small _____ in the tractors' wakes. Serenity _____ only an illusion.

Words and the Language: Using Context to Infer Meaning

In the first three units you learned to recognize three fairly obvious signals to meaning — definition; restatement and example; and contrast and negation. These are easily recognizable because all involve some form of redundancy, that is, repetition of meaning or negative repetition.

Other kinds of contextual clues are not so clearly recognizable because they do not have clear signals. Often we must *infer* (unravel or determine) the meaning of an unknown word by its relationship to familiar words or by the established mood or situation in a passage. You probably already use this method without realizing it, but you can expand your reading vocabulary more easily by letting the context help you make inferences about the meaning of unknown words. Before stopping to look up a word in the dictionary, take some chances; keep on reading to see whether or not clues to a word's meaning can be found in a subsequent sentence. For example, notice the italicized word in the following passage.

> His *tenacity* eventually brought him success. Even though many publishers rejected his manuscript, he continued to send it out until, finally, one company accepted it enthusiastically.

Even if the meaning of *tenacity* is unknown to you, its use in the context of the passage probably suggests the meaning of "sticking to it," stubbornness, or persistence.

EXERCISE 1

Look at the following sentences and try to infer the meaning of the italicized words.

1. Because the only eyewitness to the accident reacted so emotionally, the policeman could not get an *objective* report.
2. The student's sentence was so *ambiguous* that half the class thought it meant one thing while the rest believed it meant the opposite.
3. Some people complain about student *apathy* yet students show great enthusiasm for their off-campus activities.
4. Jeff's work progress was *impeded* by his lack of skills and motivation.

5. Although Armando is usually very loving toward his sister, he *inadvertently* hurt her feelings when he ignored her at the party.

EXERCISE 2

Open one of your textbooks to a chapter that has been assigned but not yet covered. Read the material, find a word you don't know, and place a wavy line under it. Try to infer the meaning from the context. Write your guess on a card or sheet of paper. Then check the definition in the dictionary to see how close you were; if you were wrong, try to evaluate why. Repeat the process for other assigned readings until the method becomes almost automatic.

READINGS: SELECTION ONE

Your Better Basic Supermother
by Ellen Goodman

Ideas to Think About

1. "Your Better Basic Supermother" discusses the myth of the Supermother who does everything possible for her children. What myths of perfection influence your life and your own expectations of yourself? Do you often feel obliged to be a Superdaughter or a Superperson? A Superbrother or a Supersister? A Supergirlfriend or a Superboyfriend? A Superworker or a Superstudent? Why? Have you succeeded? What price did you pay?
2. Have you observed any differences in atittudes about being a parent? Have you noticed such differences between your parents' generation and your grandparents'?
3. This article first defines an image of perfection and then goes on to show that the author does not live up to it herself. Where does this shift occur?

Vocabulary

Look at each word as it is used in the article. (The number in parentheses indicates the paragraph in which it appears.) First, try to understand the meaning from the way it is used in the sentence. Then, use the dictionary to clarify the meaning.

tyrannies (1)
relentlessly (4)
impenetrable (6)
demise (7)

transitional (8, 12)
overcompensating (13)
jettison (14)

Your Better Basic Supermother

Columnist Ellen Goodman writes about social change with humor and honesty. Her topics, ranging from parenthood to politics and business, examine human foibles and follies. Goodman, a graduate of Radcliffe and a Nieman Fellow at Harvard University, appears frequently on television and radio. Her *Boston Globe* column, syndicated by *The Washington Post* Writers Group, appears in more than 200 newspapers. Her books include *Turning Points* and *Close to Home*.

1 I have now been through two generations of Mother's Days, which is odd, considering that my daughter is only eight. But it seems like we've passed through time zones in our notions of mothering and especially in the tyrannies° of supermothering.

2 The Supermother, for those of you who haven't met her, is that Perfect Person against whom we compare ourselves in order to fully experience

failure, not to mention self-loathing, and a complex labeled inferiority. She is the lady we carry around in our heads just for the guilt of it.

Now the Supermother who was reigning when I first got into the family business was your better basic, devoted, selfless Total Mother whose children never had runny noses because she was right behind them, wiping. Her children were the ones in the school lunchroom with sandwiches cut in the shapes of turkeys at Thanksgiving and bunnies at Easter.

She was the one who made Halloween costumes out of potato sacks and decorated dinner with parsley, and once — following the instructions in a woman's magazine — made a bookcase out of used popsicle sticks. She was relentlessly° cheerful and was actually known to have initiated and completed an entire game of Monopoly with two six-year-olds. She loved car games.

Even on Mother's Day, she was delighted to clean up the kitchen after those helpless urchins — daddy and the kiddies — had made her breakfast in bed. Weren't they cute, after all?

Now, personally, I was never able to get my radish flowers to blossom even in cold water. And the place mats I made from a magazine pattern ended up costing $4.65 apiece (they were also excruciatingly ugly). Furthermore — bad person that I am — when I am carpooling children on a July day in my unairconditioned car, my strongest desire is not to lead a wholesome chorus of "Ninety-nine Bottles of Beer on the Wall." I am more likely to be fantasizing about an impenetrable° sound-proof plastic chauffeur's barrier around my seat.

So, you can see why I was delighted to watch the demise° of the Supermother. She had to go. At a time when nearly half the mothers in the country were also employed outside the home, the Supermother wasn't going to get the right amount of worship time.

But the problem is that Supermother I has reappeared as Supermother II, a new, revised, updated model — from traditional to transitional°. She is now "Supermom at Home and on the Job."

The All-Around Supermom rises, dresses in her chic pants suit, oversees breakfast and the search for the sneakers and then goes off to her glamorous high-paying job at an advertising agency, where she seeks Personal Fulfillment and the kids' college tuition. She has, of course, previously found a Mary Poppins figure to take care of the kids after school. Mary Poppins loves them as if they were her own, works for a mere pittance and is utterly reliable.

Supermom II comes home from work at 5:30, just as fresh as a daisy, and then spends a truly creative hour with the children. After all, it's not the quantity of the time, but the quality. She catches up on their day, soothes their disputes and helps with their homework while creating something imaginative in her Cuisinart (with her left hand tied behind her back). Her children never eat at McDonald's.

After dinner — during which she teaches them about the checks and balances of our system of government — she bathes and reads to them, and puts the clothes in the dryer. She then turns to her husband and eagerly suggests that they explore some vaguely kinky sexual fantasy.

The transitional° Supermother does not ask for help, by the way, because she has "chosen to work" and therefore, she reasons, it's her problem. Besides, she can do it all. Up, up and away . . . As for me, I wish her the best of luck and I truly hope she has paid up her health insurance.

Supermom II, you see, is still overcompensating° like mad for not being Supermom I. She probably is anxious because she doesn't put raisin faces in the kids' oatmeal. She is making up for her guilt trip to the office.

But the time has come — why not, it's Mother's Day, isn't it? — to jettison° all the accumulated Kryptonite, and dump the Supermothers of today and yesterday overboard.

No Supermothers need apply.

Discussion

1. Using one or more adjectives, describe Goodman's tone or attitude toward her subject matter. For example, is it serious or playful? Honest or insincere? Formal or informal? Find the specific words or phrases in the essay that support your opinion.
    a. Would the essay be just as effective if Goodman had used a different tone? Why or why not?
    b. How do you account for the short, apparently undeveloped paragraphs?
2. Locate three main assertions or controlling ideas and then decide what types of support Goodman uses to develop those assertions and to define "Supermother."
3. To what kind of audience is Goodman directing her essay? How can you tell? What other audiences would be interested? Why? Why might some readers object to or be bored by this essay?
4. By using "Supermom," Goodman avoids some repetition of "Supermother." What other effect does she gain by this shift?
5. In paragraph 1 of this essay, the author suggests that we have gone through many changes in our thinking about motherhood. What changes does she go on to note and to suggest?
6. Goodman disagrees with the image of Supermother. Describe both Supermother I and Supermother II. Are they mythical beings or do they exist? Have you seen them on television or read about them? Do you know them personally? Why does Goodman take issue with this image of perfection?
7. Writing students are often warned against using clichés, that is, lifeless, overused expressions, and yet this article contains many. Look for the clichés here and try to decide whether they add to or detract from the effect of the article.

READINGS: SELECTION TWO
Why Man Explores (1)
by Philip Morrison

Ideas to Think About
1. Have you ever felt a need to explore a place you had never been before? For example, have you ever explored a new road for no special reason?
2. Morrison defines human nature and internal models and then expands on both definitions. Why does he devote so much time to these two definitions?
3. As you read the following essay, note the ways the author expands his definitions.

Vocabulary
Look at each word as it is used in the article. (The number in parentheses indicates the paragraph in which it appears.) First, try to understand the meaning from the way it is used in the sentence. Then, use the dictionary to clarify the meaning.

diverse (1)
ethnography (1)
artifacts (1)
tawdry (1)

impoverished (2)
conjecture (2)
genetics (9)
analogy (Discussion)

Why Man Explores (1)

Philip Morrison is Institute Professor and professor of physics at Massachusetts Institute of Technology. His contributions to astrophysics include physical descriptions of such celestial phenomena as supernovae, cosmic X-rays, and quasars. But here he writes of more humble, earthly things: termites.

If you should ask, "Why do human beings explore?" I would answer, as I think the Greeks would have answered, "Because it is our nature." Now I am anxious to avoid the mistake of thinking that the term *human nature* is self-explanatory. It covers every activity of our species, the most diverse° ethnographies,° all the artifacts° that grace the museums, and even the often-tawdry° publications that pack the newsstands of Los Angeles.

"Human nature" is an impoverished° description of all that diversity. But there is one feature — for me, it is perhaps the only feature — that does define human nature. We are beings who construct — singly and collectively — internal models of all that happens, of all we see, find, feel, guess, and conjecture° about our experience in the world. For me, exploration is filling in the blank margins of that inner model.

I was struck by the work reported by some French entomologists in South Africa who studied the work of certain species of large termites. Termites, of course, are social animals of considerable power and prowess. The structures they build are large and enduring architecture, 15 and 20 feet high on some occasions. They dot the landscape like so many termite skyscrapers.

Layer upon layer, hidden within this termitary, which rises out of the ground, are true arches, curved arches that support the next floor, and then more arches for the next, and so on, exactly like the crypts of a building somewhere in Italy.

No great architect has designed where the termites' arches will be. No one has counted them. No one has decided on them. The work overall is adaptive and improves the termitary, providing it its strength and its ventilation. So the termites go on building arches; they will do so for tens of millions of years on end. There is no internal model within any termite for how those arches should be built. There are in the DNA some kinds of simple rules that tell them how to make arches in a general way. These instructions do not include the making of the arch itself, but rather the instructions needed to achieve the construction of an arch.

There is never an arch present until one appears by chance; whereas when we build arches, or anything else, the arch is in some sense present before it ever exists. That is what I mean by an internal model. The need to complete that internal model — to extend and fill in its fringes — is, I think, what we mean by exploration.

I recognize that this deep need to complete the internal models is certainly expressed differently in different cultures. Sometimes it lies quiet. The pioneer alpinists who in the early nineteenth century went to Switzerland found villagers who had lived there all their lives and had never searched their mountaintops. But once the visitors raised the idea that it might be worthwhile, it turned out that among the villagers there were a few young men who had silently ventured up to the peaks even before the English gentlemen arrived to hire them. They became the first mountain guides. Climbing wasn't celebrated; it didn't butter any parsnips or feed any goats. It was needed somehow to complete the model.

I believe those cultures that manage to show some public concern for filling in the edges of a model, for extending the margin of the map, are those in which we now live and those in which we shall live for most of the time of human history.

For me, humans explore because time after time, when we wish to adapt to the world as our inner nature has evolved, both by genetics° and by culture, we can do nothing else.

Discussion

1. Describe a time when you just had to explore a new trail or place you have never been before. Explain your reasons for your action.

2. How does Morrison define human nature? How do you define human nature?
3. What is the purpose of the discussion of termites in an essay on human exploration?
4. How does Morrison define internal models?
5. Morrison uses analogy to link the definitions that reveal his thesis. What is that analogy° and how does it link his definitions of human nature and internal models?
6. Name two analogies aside from the termite reference and discuss their function and importance to Morrison's thesis.

READINGS: SELECTION THREE

from Confessions of a City Woodcutter
by George H. Haas

Ideas to Think About

1. What activities do you enjoy and believe in but often need to justify to others? Perhaps hunting, spending money on a hobby or a trip? Daydreaming? How do you justify these interests? Do you ever find yourself getting angry at your accusers?
2. What comes to mind when you hear the phrase "city woodcutter"? Why would he have "confessions" to make and want to publish these confessions in a magazine? Why should a woodcutter need to confess and justify himself and to whom?
3. This article relies on many definitions to clarify some unfamiliar terms. Look for them as you read. Notice how they often differ from one another in length and content.

Vocabulary

Look at each word as it is used in the article. (The number in parentheses indicates the paragraph in which it appears.) First, try to understand the meaning from the way it is used in the sentence. Then, use the dictionary to clarify the meaning.

myriad (13)	condemnation (26)
stealthy (19)	averting (30)
phenomenal (26)	devoid (30)
regeneration (26)	obstinately (35)

from Confessions of a City Woodcutter

George H. Haas is a senior editor of *Outdoor Life* magazine.

1 My muscle-powered four-and-a-half-foot bucking saw was eating nicely into the sweet-gum log when I sensed that someone was standing behind me. An eight-year-old boy who lived nearby was watching me with sad disapproval. I guessed what he was about to say. Almost everyone deplores the destruction of trees.

2 "Mister," he asked, "why do you cut the trees down?"

I had been through it before, and my answer was ready. "Sonny," I answered, "I don't cut trees down; I cut them up."

3 His puzzled look gave me the chance to say that bulldozers had knocked the trees down the day before, as evidenced by the upturned roots, and that I was merely getting some firewood before the builder

trucked the trees to the city dump. I told the youngster that houses much like his own were to be built where the woods had stood and I asked if he thought that was wrong.

"No, mister," he allowed and proved it by picking up branches for me while I made the last cut through the big log.

I loaded the cut wood into the trunk of my car and waved good-bye to my helper, but the boy didn't wave back. He stood and stared at the fallen trees. A haphazard tree house in the old maple lay smashed under a big oak. That last bit of forest where cowboys and Indians pursued each other was gone, and where the squirrels were hiding was a mystery. Forty years ago, my own childhood woods disappeared in a like manner. The site now lies under the parking lot at Aqueduct Race Track.

In the distance across upper New York Bay, the tall buildings of Lower Manhattan, dwarfed by the twin towers of the World Trade center, loomed above the gray-green water. The boy and I were only nine-and-a-half miles from Wall Street.

I'm a city woodcutter. Every year I stack five cords of hardwood for my fireplace, and all of it is cut on Staten Island — one of New York City's five boroughs. Woodcutting here is much like woodcutting anywhere except for confrontations with people who recently escaped the concrete and steel of Brooklyn and Manhattan. These people are particularly horrified by the destruction of nature in any form.

When I first started cutting wood 15 years ago, fireplace wood sold here for $30 a cord; today the price is $100, as it was for a short time during the 1973 oil shortage. At an average price of $60 a cord, let's say, I have cut approximately $4,500 worth of fuel — a worthwhile sum.

A cord measures eight feet long by four feet high and four feet wide. It is the volume and weight of wood that the average 19th-century horse was expected to pull on a crude sledge over snow. The load was usually held together from front to back by a single cord and so "cord" became the name of the measure.

According to the U.S. Forest Service, the available heat from one cord of mixed dry hardwood comes to about 20 million British Thermal Units. It would take about 200 gallons of heating oil to produce the same heat. In most cities, heating oil has lately sold for 80 cents a gallon, so a cord of good wood currently equals the value of $160 worth of oil. In terms of natural gas, good firewood is worth even more, and in terms of electric heat, a cord of hardwood should be kept locked in a shed guarded by a Doberman pinscher.

Economics is a dull science, but I do enjoy watching the bewildered oil man when he comes to fill our tank in midwinter. I peek at him from the kitchen window while he stands in the snow over the intake pipe, astonished when it overflows so quickly. And then there is the cooking. Broiling steaks and short ribs over open coals is a pleasure and an art.

A canny[1] reader might say that the pleasure of heating and cooking with wood does cost something because I must buy gasoline and oil for my chain saw. I don't. The noise of a chain saw on a weekend, particularly on Sunday morning, arouses neighbors to frenzied resentment. My hand tools do the work, and it is surprising how quickly a good, sharp saw cuts. The trick is to have your own sharpening and settling tools. I use an ax, a hatchet, a bolo (heavy-duty machete), two saws, a sledge, a maul, wedges, and a sawhorse. All my tools were bought years ago or inherited, so their original cost is no concern, and I doubt any of them will need replacement during my lifetime. Of course, if my woodcutting time was debited, say at a common laborer's rate, my wood would cost a great deal, but on that basis, playing golf or tennis costs even more. If one values time only according to its monetary worth, nothing is worthwhile except working for money.

Pleasant warmth and fine food are not the only pleasures to be had by cutting firewood. The woodcutter soon learns a great deal about trees and woods. He has to in order to select the best firewood, and this can be a real puzzle in the jumble left by landclearing operations. If the woodcutter also encounters some of the fine woods used in carpentry and joinery and is willing to read dendrological literature, he learns about a myriad° of forest products and how they were and still are being used for some rural people.

Staten Island is one of the very best places in North America to cut wood — the variety of trees here could not be greater. On the north side of the island lies the hilly terminal moraine of the great North American glacier, on the south is the runoff plain, and in between are slopes and creeks with fertile banks. The island's climate is warm enough for many trees that are normally not found outside Southern states; it is also cold enough on the uplands here to nurture more Northern species. In fact, New York City is one of the few places in this country where the ranges of some Southern and Northern trees overlap. This small overlap zone includes southern Connecticut, central New Jersey, eastern Pennsylvania, and southern New York. One reason for the original quick growth of this area as a population center was the availability of a wide variety of timber and forest products.

Writing in 1930, William T. Davis, a fine local naturalist, listed 112 different tree species growing on Staten Island — most of them native, but some "adventives" (ornamental, fruit, or nut trees brought here from Europe and the Orient to adorn country estates). I have found all but four of the species listed by Davis, plus approximately 40 "new" exotics.

Identifying exotic trees is often puzzling. A neighbor once asked me to cut a 60-foot tree that grew in his yard. By tree-ring count I later

---
[1] Clever.

determined that the tree was much older than the house — the first structure built on that site — or any other nearby building. Therefore, it was a true wild tree and I'd never seen anything like it. The bark of the trunk was a strange dead black and the heart-shaped leaves were as long as 12 inches. My friend wanted the tree cut because it produced an annoying number of seeds that rattled in brittle empty pods and kept his wife awake at night.

17   Using a manual I finally identified the tree as a royal Paulownia, named in honor of Grand Duchess Anna Paulovna Romanov. Native to China and eastern Asia, this startling tree was brought to European Russia by botanists and was widely planted as an ornamental because of its extravagant clusters of fragrant violet blooms. Seedlings were presented to foreigners and some were planted on estates in the Eastern U.S., mostly in the South. In some places it has become a pest tree because it grows rapidly and crowds out native trees.

18   That a Chinese tree should make its way to my neighbor's yard in New York City by way of Russia and the Atlantic intrigued me so much that I pleaded with its owner not to cut it. I explained the tree's origin and told him he should be pleased to have it. But the tree's history made no difference — a dirty tree, much less a noisy one, has no place in modern living. I cut it, and the wood burned with a clear yellow flame. . . .

19   Cutting one Norway maple taught me that trees are sometimes the victims of stealthy° murders rather than noisy slaughter. A maple tree grew in front of a neighbor's house between the sidewalk and the curb. I knew the man who had planted it shortly after he had moved into the new house. But in its 10th year, the tree put out very little leaf, and in its 11th spring, only one branch bore leaves. The tree's owner asked me to cut the tree and remove the wood.

20   I cut the maple close to the ground in order to leave a short stump that would soon rot away. When the butt log was quartered, the normally white wood displayed beautiful blue-green stains, differentiated according to the varying density of the wood's grain. The staining was so beautiful that I called my wife to see it. Since the color did not fade when exposed to the air, I knew it must have been in the fiber of the wood itself and I soon found out how it got there. A six-inch hole had been drilled into the tree almost at ground level. Someone had placed a copper rod in that hole and closed it with a wooden plug to conceal his crime. The chemicals in the growing tree turned much of the rod into blue-green copper sulphate, which was carried up the trunk by the rising sap. A little reading told me that copper sulphate kills trees if taken internally. Merely standing where the tree had stood told me who the killer was. He lived in a house up the street and his picture window view of the Manhattan skylines was being cut off by the growing tree. . . .

21   Cutting firewood has taught me a great deal about trees and wood,

but I have also learned much about people while swinging an ax or jerking a saw back and forth.

Most of my Staten Island neighbors are tradesmen, workmen, or minor civil service employees. Many times I have been visited by one or the other of them while cutting wood. The visitor is often walking the family dog. "Hello," he says and watches while I sway back and forth to cut a log with my big saw. "Takes a long time, don't it," is the usual remark, but by the time he says it, I'm often through the log and starting a new cut. Finally, the visitor shakes his head and says something like: "You should buy a chain saw."

To explain why I do not, I say that I need the exercise, that I don't want to disturb people with a chain saw's noise, and, finally, I hold up my left hand to show two stumps of amputated fingers, which I explain were lost to a power saw many years ago. Power saws terrify me.

My visitor usually shakes his head and walks away, muttering something about wasted time. It took me a while to understand this downright hostility to physical labor and hand tools. Most city-bred Americans hate "inefficiency" and find it difficult to understand why anyone would do handwork when a suitable machine can be bought to accomplish the task. They use machines in their daily work, and they buy machines for the work they do on their own time. Most of them own $250 power mowers, even though all the grass on their small city lots could be cut with a handmower in less than half an hour. Without knowing why, they feel uneasy about a person who eschews "labor-saving" machines. This dislike, common among native Americans, seems to be rare among older people born of European peasant stock.

No one actively enforces New York City's laws against cutting live trees. The enforcement agency is the New York City Police Department, but most policemen are completely ignorant of the laws' existence. Even if an ordinary policeman knows about these laws, how can he tell if a man is cutting trees legally on his own land or not? Each construction job and every bulldozer operator or woodcutter would have to be investigated. It simply isn't possible. Fortunately, most people like trees enough not to murder them wantonly and some love trees enough to come to their defense.

Several times enthusiastic conservationists and protectionists have discussed this with me, and they always deplore the continuing elimination of woodland within the city and in the suburbs. I always try to cheer them by explaining that woodland is being regenerated at a phenomenal° rate in Eastern rural areas, but they see destruction close to home and are more affected by it than by regeneration° elsewhere. I sympathize, but sometimes I am included in their condemnations° of bulldozer operators, land developers, and road builders because of the all-too-obvious presence of a big woodpile in my yard. I resent the accusations, and I sometimes fight back with a little venom. The nonconsumerist is really telling me that he is holier than I am. I am not very holy, but neither is he.

After listening quietly for a while, I ask where my accuser lives and the reply is often "Oak Park," "Dongan Hills," "Westerleigh," or some other part of Staten Island. I then point out that to build a house almost anywhere on the island, except in the swamps, requires the destruction of trees and many seedlings to clear the land. I also note that houses contain thousands of feet of lumber.

The only American houses that are built largely without the destruction of trees are concrete and stucco bungalows on desert sites, mostly in Arizona and Nevada. And even with them, wood scaffolding and forms for poured concrete are often used. If you live in a house, you are responsible for the destruction of trees because of your need for shelter. The same applies also to those who live in apartment houses, although the guilt is more removed. Aside from a few hermits who live in natural shelters such as caves, all of us are responsible for the cutting of many trees.

To lessen the shock, I always point out that trees and other living things cannot be preserved. Natural death overtakes them, and wise use before that event is largely guiltless, provided other trees or living things are allowed to replace them through natural growth or artificial generation such as forestation. Burning wood as fuel is perhaps the least harmful form of consumption since trees replace themselves very rapidly if allowed to do so. And wood fires create only the pollution that nature herself produces. The products of wood oxidation are the same as those generated by a tree that rots away unused by man. Oil, coal, and gas, on the other hand, are fossil fuels that can never be replaced, and burning them produces pollution.

I almost always win this argument, but pursuing it has been a study in extremism. Many people who believe in averting° the destruction of life are vegetarians. Their attitude is admirable in some ways, but I confess that I have often amused myself by noting that many vegetarians wear leather shoes and leather belts and carry leather wallets. And cloth for clothing is produced largely from vegetable sources such as flax, which must be cut to make cloth. Few things destroy animals and birds more effectively than a big cotton field, which is devoid° of anything for them to eat, but many protectionists wear cotton clothing. Wool is produced by sheep that feed avidly[2] on vegetarian growth. Overgrazing by sheep created many deserts.

Ecologically sensitive Americans are commonly well-educated and well-read. Strictly speaking, they should feel guilty whenever they consume yet another book or magazine. Paper is made from wood pulp,

---

[2] Eagerly.

which in turn is made from trees. By reading this magazine [*Quest*], you are helping to consume at least one tree and if you consider the volume of your lifetime reading, the total destruction wrought by you alone is almost impossible to calculate.

Extreme nonconsumerists frequently become fruitarians. A fruitarian avoids all foods except fruits and nuts. In primitive societies, these fruits and nuts are gathered in natural forests, and the fruitarian theoretically takes only a small number of fruit from each tree or bush so that it is never deprived of the opportunity to reseed itself.

This is probably the highest degree of nonconsumerism, but in modern society, nuts and fruits purchased at the market are almost always the result of intensive agriculture. To grow walnuts, pecans, litchi nuts, blueberries, strawberries, or currants, an agriculturalist must clear land for his trees or bushes or he must purchase or lease cleared land for the purpose. In doing so, the grower is responsible for the destruction of the natural flora and the birds, animals, and insects that live in it.

The modern American fruitarian who buys fruit and nuts in the market is just as responsible for the destruction of nature as the agrocorporation that produces his food.

Wise use of natural resources and replacement or at least natural regeneration whenever possible seems a much better way of life to me, provided we can eventually limit population to zero growth or cause it to decline. To my obstinately° realistic mind, to be alive is to consume, and in an interdependent economy, it doesn't matter much which items one eats and uses. I believe this most enthusiastically on a winter night when my family sits down to a broiled steak. Even our innocent dog consumes the scraps with murderous teeth that have never killed.

Discussion

1. Haas defines some of his terms by:
    a. telling the function.
    b. using examples.
    c. describing physical qualities.
    d. showing historical evolution or development.
    e. making an analogy.
   Find examples of each of these types of definitions.
2. List three pleasures Haas finds in cutting firewood. How and where does he develop these assertions? What is puzzling to the woodcutter?
3. Haas states, "I have also learned much about people while swinging an ax or jerking a saw back and forth." What generalizations or observations does he make about people, based on his experiences as a woodcutter? Are you convinced that his generalizations are valid? Why or why not?
4. The author defines many terms apparently without emotion. But where in the essay do you find ideas or language that either express the writer's

emotions or appeal to the reader's emotions? Underline these words. What does Haas gain or lose by limiting his use of emotional appeals?
5. The author's "confessions" are a defense of woodcutting in the city. Why does he defend this activity? How does he defend it?
6. This essay employs much narrative and descriptive writing. Remembering the discussions of these two kinds of writing from Units 1 and 2, find examples of each type and discuss their contributions to the essay.

WRITING:
Exposition: Definition

Writing Assignment: A Three-Paragraph Definition Essay

The writing assignment in this unit asks you to *define* a word, *explain* your definition, and then *expand* your definition through discussion. This procedure insures that your reader fully understands your use of a term. For example, if you were to write a paper on the techniques of volleyball, you would need to define and explain the term *spike* (to slam a ball down into the opponent's court). If you don't, most readers, particularly those new to the game, will not only lose interest in what you say but will also be unable to understand the volleyball technique. Likewise, if George Haas, in "Confessions of a City Woodcutter," failed to define *cord*, *adventives*, and *fruitarians*, would you have been able to follow his discussion? Would you have lost interest? Definitions, then, are often vital parts of written communication, because writers cannot always use words from their own vocabularies and expect their readers to understand what they mean. Nor can writers expect readers to look up words in a dictionary or even to find all technical terms in every dictionary.

If you were to explain how to make lasagna, you might use the following terms: *sauté, ricotta, medium heat, reduce,* and *mince*. Which terms would probably need definitions for an eighteen-year-old reader? An eight-year-old child? Your grandfather? A group of people of all ages? In making the appropriate decision, you would first have to consider your "intended audience," the readers for whom you write, and then make some general assumptions about their knowledge on your subject. You could assume that most eight-year-old children would not be familiar with most of your terms; that the eighteen-year-old might not know *mince* and *reduce;* and that your grandfather, whose hobby is cooking, would know all the terms. Although every assumption you make might not be correct, you would now be able to define most of the words that might cause problems for your readers.

All writing situations are not as easy to solve as the one above, for cooking is an activity in our daily lives. We all have spent time in the kitchen, either cooking or watching others cook, so most audiences should be familiar with most recipe terminology. But few activities are as familiar as cooking to so many people. One of you might be a photographer, another a stamp collector, and yet another a skin-diver. And one of you might be studying to be a doctor, another a chemist, and a third an accountant. Consequently, each of you probably knows certain technical terms that are unknown to others, and each may have specialized meanings for certain common words we all use. These are the words that need to be defined.

With an awareness of these differences in the knowledge of all people, you need to evaluate the words you employ in your writing and ask yourself the following questions.

1. *Is this a common word for a common, concrete thing?* For example, when you say "dog," do you refer to your family pet, a canine? If so, you have no need to define your term.
2. *Is this a common word with an unusual meaning?* For example, if you were a show salesperson, you might refer to the "dogs" in the store. In this case, you would not be speaking about your family pet but about the ugly, unsalable shoes on sale on Dollar Day. You must define this type of usage.
3. *Is this an abstract term?* For example, if you discuss freedom, will your reader know the type of freedom you mean? Probably not, so define or explain the term.
4. *Is this an unfamiliar word for a common, concrete thing?* For example, if you call your grandmother's illness "atherosclerosis," would your reader know you mean hardening of the arteries? Probably not, so either define the term or make the meaning apparent through its context.
5. *Is this an unfamiliar term for an unfamiliar thing?* For example, to a person who has never studied chemistry, both the term "colloid" and the type of mixture to which it refers are unknown. Define the term carefully.

An even more important question to ask is whether to give a short definition or an extended definition. Sometimes you may not need to give a full definition for every troublesome word. Other times you will need to supply your readers with extended discussions, ranging in length from one to three paragraphs to many pages. The decision on how extensively to define a word depends on the importance of that word to your discussion. Notice, for example, Haas's different approaches to definition in his essay. He defines *cord* fully, offering an extended two-paragraph explanation, since much of his discussion on the value and use of wood pivots around this word. But notice his brief definition of *adventives* placed within parentheses. Here Haas offers an interesting piece of information; but this information is not central to his focus; it is merely complementary. You as the writer, then, must decide which words to define, how to define them, and how extended your definitions must be. When you conclude that you need an extended definition, you give your reader the *denotation* of the word (a dictionary-type definition), an *explanation* of that denotation, and an *expansion* of your discussion to insure full understanding by your reader.

Assignment

Write a three-paragraph essay in which you define a term that needs an extended definition. Such a word might be a *word with a special meaning*, a *technical word*, or an *abstract word*. Use the following pattern of organization.

Paragraph number 1 $\begin{cases} D - \text{Denotation. (1 sentence)} \\ E - \text{Explanation. (2–6 sentences)} \end{cases}$

Paragraph number 2   *e* — Expansion. (5–10 sentences)

Paragraph number 3   *e* — Expansion. (5–10 sentences)

In writing the denotation (*D*), you need to include three pieces of information: the term to be defined; the class or group to which the term belongs; and any special characteristics that set off this term from others of the class or group.

Examples
A pencil (word to be defined)
is a writing tool (class)
made of a graphite cylinder encased by wood. (distinct characteristic)

Larceny (word to be defined)
is a crime (class)
in which personal property or money is stolen without the use of violence. (distinct characteristic)

The explanation (*E*) sections of the extended definition either explain the denotation or restate it in simpler terms.

Example
D — Ecology is a branch of biology that investigates the relationships between living organisms and their environments.

E — It traces such things as physiological mutations, changes in life cycles, and behavioral adjustments caused by variations in the organisms' surroundings. For example, as tidal waters change in composition and temperature, some sea life may die out, others may develop, and others may make adaptations to permit the continuance of life.

The expansion (*e*) sections of your extended definition add supplementary materials to assist your reader in gaining a firm grasp of your meaning. This expansion can be accomplished in many ways.

1. *Comparison and contrast,* that is, showing how two things are alike and different. For example, a pencil could be compared and contrasted to a pen. Both are used to write on paper but are constructed with different materials and produce different types of writing.
2. *Cause and effect,* that is, showing how one situation has brought about another. For example, polluted waters, lacking a sufficient supply of oxygen and containing chemicals poisonous to sea plants, eventually bring about the death of certain fish and crustaceans. These animals would lack adequate food and oxygen for survival.
3. *Details,* that is, offering full descriptions or supplying additional information. For example, in defining a guitar, you might give the dimensions of

the instrument, describe the sounding board, differentiate between the six strings, or outline the tuning process.
4. *Background information,* that is, offering the history of a thing. For example, in defining the same guitar, you might choose to discuss how the instrument was developed, explain its relationship to similar instruments that were in use before its development, or explain how variations on the first guitar were made.
5. *Division by parts,* that is, telling about the various parts that make up the thing being defined and explaining their functions. For example, in defining a television set you might want to describe the various parts of the set such as the tuner, picture tubes, transformer, and transistors. If you do a division by parts, you should also explain how all parts interact with each other.
6. *Analogy,* that is, comparing an unfamiliar thing to a familiar thing. For example, in trying to explain the workings of a computer, you might wish to relate the computer to a bank of electrical switches. Each switch has only two positions — on and off. But if you had a wall of one hundred switches, each controlling one light, you could create many, many combinations of lights. After fully describing how this bank of lights could work, you could show how the operations of a computer are similar in operation, although different in function.

These are just some of the ways you can extend your formal definitions, but you must make conscious choices as to which types of expansion would best suit your particular purpose. In making your choices, concentrate on your intended readers, seeking to relate your discussion to their personal backgrounds. For example, of what value would an analogy of a computer to a calculator be if your readers have never used either machine? You may use a different type of expansion in each of your *e* paragraphs, but you must try to keep your discussion coherent, with one idea leading clearly to the next idea. Perhaps you should review Haas's essay to see how he unifies his essay and connects one definition to another.

Topics

1. Define a technical term used in one of your hobbies. Assume your reader has no experience in this field.
2. Define a common word that you use in an unusual way. Assume your reader has never heard the word used in this way. Perhaps you might want to use a slang word and assume your readers are your parents.
3. Define one of the following: *superfather, superperson, superdaughter, superstudent.* Assume your readers are your classmates.
4. Define an abstract term, such as *liberty, honesty, freedom.* Assume your readers are your classmates.

Brainstorming and Shaping

Group Work

1. Divide into groups of two. Try to pair off with a member of the opposite sex or a classmate with an academic major different from yours.
2. Each of you should list five terms used in your major or in your hobby. Exchange lists and ask your partner to choose the word or words that are the most confusing, difficult, or foreign to him or her.
3. Tell your partner the denotation (*D*) of the word he or she has chosen and offer a two- to six-sentence explanation (*E*). Have your partner ask questions about the term. For example, you might say, "A carbohydrate is an organic compound containing carbon, hydrogen, and oxygen. Found in the form of sugar, starch, and cellulose, it is a vital nutrient for life. In fact, no life on earth could have developed without an adequate supply of carbohydrates." Your partner then might ask, "What is an organic compound? Why is it necessary for life? What are its specific properties? What is its formula?" Jot down all questions and then reverse roles, with your partner now offering a definition and explanation for the word you have chosen and with you asking questions.
4. Work separately for ten to fifteen minutes. During this time, you should review your partner's questions and plan out the expansions (*e*) to your definition, using one or two of the methods listed in the assignment section of this unit.
5. Repeat your definition (*D*) and explanation (*E*) to your partner but now add your planned expansions (*e*). Again, your partner should ask questions that you jot down for further reference. Reverse roles, with your partner offering a fully expanded definition and you asking appropriate questions. When you have completed this group work, you may still need to consider new approaches because your partner has wanted to know more about your topic. Don't be overly concerned if this happens. Evaluate your partner's questions while you are preparing your assignment at home. Do all questions really need to be answered? Remember that you cannot tell everything you know in three paragraphs. Choose the most valid, meaningful questions and try to incorporate their answers into your expansion sections. Perhaps you might need to change your techniques. In other words, perhaps an analogy would be more effective than a comparison or a discussion of background material.

Individual Work

1. Choose an intended audience and list its major characteristics. For example, you might name high school math teachers as your readers, and so the list of characteristics might include *logical, educated with a master's degree, middle-aged, interested in science, middle-income,* and *disciplined.* List as many characteristics of your audience as possible.

2. Choose one of the suggested writing topics and a particular word to define.
3. Evaluate what needs to be explained and what types of expansions would best suit your chosen audience. Select two types of expansions and try them out on the audience. Pretend that you are this audience and challenge any confusion or lack of explanation. Decide on the most effective approach.

Writing the First Draft

Your writing assignment and brainstorming session should have given you sufficient material for most of your essay. Review everything you have written to date and write your first draft. Again, remember that it is a first draft. What is important at this point is getting everything together and forming a workable unit of ideas. You can always revise and edit, but you must have this base to work with.

Revising the Three-Paragraph Definition Essay

Your assignment asked that you write a three-paragraph definition essay following the *DE-e-e* pattern of organization. Read over your first draft and then study the basic review questions presented in Unit 1 and the special questions for this assignment.

Basic Revision Questions

1. *Is all my information accurate? Appropriate?*
   Have you misinformed your readers by giving them false information? Have you offered all the information needed by your readers?
2. *Is this information organized so that my reader can comprehend what I have said? Could I organize my paper so that it could be more effective?*
   Does your essay have three paragraphs — a definition and explanation paragraph and two expansion paragraphs?
3. *Do I have a clear, unified focus; that is, does my paragraph telescope in on one major theme?*
   Do your explanation and expansions relate directly to your definition? Have you added any information that does not relate to your topic?
4. *Do I offer sufficient details, examples, or explanations so that my reader gains a complete understanding of what I am trying to say?*
   Is your definition clarified sufficiently? Are your expansions developed sufficiently?

Special Questions for a Three-Paragraph Essay

1. Have I used appropriate common words for common concrete things?
2. Is my denotation clear?
3. In my expansions, have I used any abstract terms? Are their meanings clear to my audience?

4. In my expansion, have I used any common words with unusual meanings? If so, does my audience need to have them explained?
5. In my expansion, have I used any unfamiliar terms for common, concrete things? If so, have I made my meaning clear to my readers?
6. In my expansion, have I used any unfamiliar terms for things unfamiliar to my audience? If so, have I fully explained what my audience needs to know?

Remember to consider your audience when you answer these questions so that you can offer them enough information and explanations to insure their full comprehension of your term.

EXERCISE 1
1. Analyze your three-paragraph essay according to the review questions previously listed. If you have answered "No" or "I'm not sure" to any question, you probably need some revision. Make any changes necessary.
2. Exchange papers with a classmate. Read through each other's papers carefully. Then make a checklist of answers to all revision questions just as you did on your own papers. Try to outline the essay. When you have finished, go over the results of both evaluations with your partner. This activity is important because it provides an opportunity to get a direct response from a member of your reading audience. Finally, make any changes suggested by your discussion.
3. Make a clean copy of your revised essay in preparation for editing.

Editing

Word Choice: Strong and Weak Verbs (2)
Because verbs determine most of what happens in sentences, choosing the right ones is crucial to effective writing. You already know how verbs function to express a state of being or to bring action to a communication. The exercises you did in Unit 1, which reduced excessive use of *have, do,* and *be,* illustrated the precision and energy that action verbs add to writing. But we need to examine strong and weak verbs further. Strong verbs, the action verbs, generally make things move in a sentence; weak verbs, the nonaction verbs, often create static, immobile sentences. Consider these two sentences: "That picture flatters her" and "The picture of her is a flattering one." In the first sentence, we have the direct action verb *flatters*. In the second sentence, one must switch *flatters* to the adjective *flattering* because the weak linking verb *is* replaces the action verb. This change also requires the addition of the preposition *of*. So the weak linking verb *is* creates the need to add words but subtracts power.

Eliminating *there is* and *there are* from writing is another way to avoid weak verbs. These constructions are frequently wordy and can make awkward sentences. To change these sentences, move their subjects to the beginning of the sentences and substitute strong verbs for *is* or *are*.

Examples
There are several things that happen when mother visits us.
Several things happen when mother visits us.

There is nothing that I can do for him.
I can do nothing for him.

Notice the economy of words in the revised sentences.

Get is another weak verb to avoid. The colloquial use of *get* instead of *be* as an auxiliary should be eliminated from college writing. Perhaps it may be used in speech or informal writing, but even then strong verbs are preferable. Notice how much more effective the first example is than the second.

John took Jim's watch.

Jim's watch got taken by John.

Get is easy to overuse because it is a part of so many slang and colloquial expressions. For example, we say *get with it, get going, get lost, get your act together*. Notice the reduction in words when *get* is removed.

1. We got over it.
   We recovered.

2. I am getting better.
   I am improving.

3. We are getting together tomorrow.
   We are meeting tomorrow.

In every case fewer words and a cleaner, more accurate sentence is the result of eliminating *get*.

Strong verbs are usually more effective if they appear in an active rather than a passive form in the sentence. With an active form, the subject does the action. With the passive form, the subject receives the action. Consequently the passive form usually weakens the strong verb.

Example

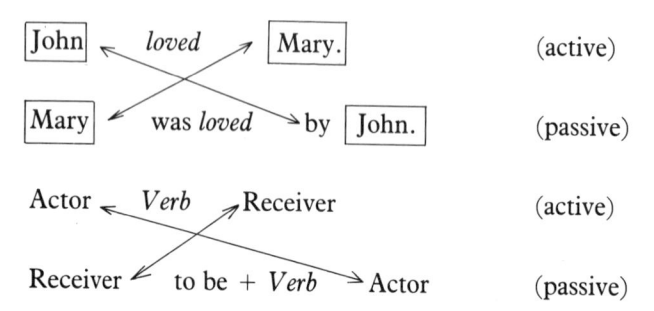

| John | *loved* | Mary. | (active) |

| Mary | was *loved* by | John. | (passive) |

Actor — *Verb* — Receiver   (active)

Receiver — to be + *Verb* — Actor   (passive)

The diagram illustrates the shifts in word order between active and passive verbs; the passive obviously requires more words. So most of the time, active verbs are certainly preferable for both power and economy.

But the passive is the best construction to use on certain occasions. Consider the difference in meaning between the following sentences.

My car hit a truck.

My car was hit by a truck.

My car had an accident with a truck.

Which sentence would make the insurance company happiest?

The coffin was lowered into the ground.

The coffin lowered itself into the ground.

The coffin dropped into the ground.

The first sentence is the only reasonable choice unless an unusual phenomenon or a terrible accident occurred.

The passive also serves to explain a process to someone who will have to perform it. For example, "The mechanic holds the wrench in his left hand" might not be as clear as "The wrench is held in the left hand." However, if you were describing the process to someone merely reading about it without intending to perform it, perhaps the first sentence would be a better choice. It depends on where you want your focus of attention.

In choosing between active and passive constructions, your decision must consider focus and emphasis. Sometimes the passive verb will be more emphatic than the active verb. For example, the sentence "A bus ran over the little boy" emphasizes the bus. In contrast, using the passive verb to form "That little boy was hit by a bus" puts the emphasis where it belongs, on the child. Another reason for choosing the passive verb is to emphasize the results of an action rather than the action itself.

Examples

Her homework was finished, and her room was cleaned.

His laundry was done, and his clothing was packed.

You must make conscious choices on this matter. Remember that the verb forms you choose affect emphasis and focus.

EXERCISE 1

Eliminate *there is* and *there are* from the following sentences by shifting the subject to the beginning of the sentence.

1. There are a number of reasons that I do not want to do this.
2. There is nothing that he can do about her debts.

3. There are always a thousand reasons he gives for being late.
4. There are serious problems facing this country.
5. There are limits that one can reach by overdoing a good thing.

EXERCISE 2

Revise the following sentences by eliminating all forms of *get* and replacing them with appropriate verbs.

1. We got taken to school every morning.
2. We are getting a new car today.
3. John is getting older-looking rapidly.
4. We got done very early.
5. Cracking knuckles really gets me.

EXERCISE 3

Change the following sentences from passive to active.

1. Laurie was chosen by the teacher.
2. Steve was hurt by Fred's remark.
3. His actions were observed by a whole team.
4. His mistakes were caused by exhaustion.
5. She was pleased by his attention.

EXERCISE 4

Change the following sentences from active to passive.

1. Larry slugged Laurie on the chin.
2. Julie drives the car too fast.
3. They tell us fibs everyday.
4. The movie shows too much violence.
5. John helped Jean every day.

After you change these sentences from active to passive, discuss under what circumstances they might be more effective in the passive. In other words, what is emphasized by changing from active to passive?

EXERCISE 5

Go back to your definition essay and examine your verb choices carefully to be sure they are the strongest for your purposes. Make any necessary changes.

Sentence Structure: Combining for Style

The most common structures of sentences are those we have already studied: the simple sentence used alone or combined through coordination or subordination.

Examples

SIMPLE SENTENCES

The voters recognized the self-serving attitude of the senator.

The senator claimed to be interested in helping others.

SENTENCES COMBINED THROUGH COORDINATION

The senator claimed to be interested in helping others, but the voters recognized his self-serving attitude.

SENTENCES COMBINED THROUGH SUBORDINATION

Although the senator claimed to be interested in helping others, the voters recognized his self-serving attitude.

You are familiar with each of these structures. You started using the first as soon as you learned to talk, the second probably in the elementary grades, and the third probably between fifth and tenth grade. You first used these structures orally at school; later wrote them; and then probably studied them at school, learning to identify and to create them consciously. Theoretically, such study helps you write clear, grammatical sentences without fragments or run-ons. But a far more important reason for studying sentence structure is to gain conscious control over your writing style (how you present your materials to your readers).

Good style attracts your reader's attention; poor style blocks it. Indeed, badly written pieces bore your readers, for only a strongly motivated audience that is fascinated with your subject (or with you) will continue reading poorly written pieces. Well-written pieces, on the other hand, involve your readers in what you are saying and promote good responses toward your views. Consider books or articles you have picked up recently. If the subject matter and the style engaged your interest, you kept reading; if the subject matter and the style bored you, you read on only if you had to. Think of the textbooks you have to read. Are some interestingly and clearly written? Are some dull and confusing? Gaining conscious control over your sentence structure, then, will help you develop an interesting and clear style that will capture your readers' interest and won't bore or confuse them.

After you have written and revised a draft of your paper, you need to edit it, looking for improvements in word choice and, in what concerns us here — sentence structure. Reading each paragraph aloud will help you spot repetitious, monotonous sentence patterns or effectively structured sentences.

EXERCISE 1 Combining Sentences for Variety and Fluency

The following draft of a paragraph describing university education in China during the Cultural Revolution needs editing. Though informative and well organized, it is ineffective because it is composed entirely of simple sentences. The effect is a boring monotony. You can improve the style of this paragraph by combining some of the sentences through coordination or subordination, although you will probably want to leave some of the sentences as they appear. Your final draft should contain a pleasing variety of structures that brings out and adds to the meaning of the paragraph. As you edit, you may want to skim through the list of subordinators and coordinators on page 116. You will also want to read the paragraph aloud.

>   The Cultural Revolution emphasized the correctness of social attitudes more than the attainment of academic knowledge. Mao taught that correct social attitudes could be learned through manual labor. Two years of work with good recommendations were required before admission to a university. There was no standard national examination. Many unqualified students attended the universities. They were good communists. They had to take remedial classes. At the university they continued to get work experience. Basic theory was slighted. As a result, this period of Chinese history produced few intellectual leaders.

In the above exercise, you decided which type of sentence structures would best convey the given information. Such sentence-combining exercises will help you to gain control over sentence structure, to understand your writing options, and to acquire fluency and judgment in writing. Another such exercise is imitation, a standard practice often performed by generations of students of writing. In this exercise, you will duplicate the structure of a well-written model but change the subject. The object of this exercise is to help you become familiar with various kinds of structures that you may not otherwise try on your own.

EXERCISE 2 Imitation, Stressing Coordination and Subordination

Write new sentences on new topics by imitating the structure of the following models.

Example

MODEL
To this day books devoted to the hows and wherefores of success continue to appear, and they are consistent best-sellers.

— Brandt, *"Symbol of Success: The Real Horatio Alger"*

IMITATION
In the Renaissance, songs devoted to the causes and effects of love flourished among aristocrats, but most were trite redundancies.

1. Distinguished literary critics made profound psychological observations on the origins of Alger's Story in his life as Mayes told it, while social scientists drew interesting conclusions about the meaning of success from the same source.
— Brandt

2. Memory, then, is also chemical in nature, although exactly in what way remains a mystery.
— Cherry, *"The Magic of Memory"*

3. If one hippocampus is injured, memory is temporarily affected, then eventually returns.
— Cherry

4. We were seeing memory, and it was spreading throughout the entire brain.
— Cherry

5. Memory researchers have found that we remember best when we introduce short rest intervals between periods of study or practice.
— Cherry

6. The catalogue is familiar and valid but it is growing tiresome.
— Tuchman, *"Mankind's Better Moments"*

7. Even when the general tide was low, a particular group of doers could emerge in exploits that still inspire awe.
— Tuchman

8. Although the Enlightenment may have overestimated the power of reason to guide human conduct, it nevertheless opened to men and women a more humane view of their fellow passengers.
— Tuchman

A third kind of sentence-combining exercise that will help you gain fluency asks that you decide in which order to put your ideas and structures within a sentence. Will you put your main idea first or last? Will you put modifiers at the beginning, middle, or end of a sentence? You should select the order that best conveys your meaning to your reader.

Do you want to say "the agile, muscular athlete" or "the athlete, agile and muscular"? Through such choices you control emphasis, rhythm, and flow and relationship of ideas in your paragraph. Therefore, throughout this text, you will be asked to consider the possible sentence positions for modification units such as words, phrases, and clauses. Here you will consider the options in positioning clauses. In the last paragraph of the article on Horatio Alger, Brandt writes the following sentence.

> No one sells millions of copies of the same Story told over and over again unless that Story means something special, unless it touches something profound in people's minds.

Yet, Brandt could put the two "unless" clauses first.

> *Unless* a story told over and over again means something special, *unless* it touches something profound in people's minds, no one could sell millions of copies of it.

By selecting the first pattern, Brandt creates momentum in his paragraph, linking the first part of the sentence, "millions of copies," with the "success" of the previous sentence and leads into the next sentence with the last part of the sentence, "something profound in people's minds." Also by selecting the first pattern, Brandt uses the normal, usual sentence pattern for the English language in which the main subject and verb come first in a sentence, with modifiers appearing at the end. A change in the normal sentence order calls attention to the part that is out of its normal position and places extra emphasis on it. Thus by moving the "unless" clauses to the right side of the sentence, we place extra emphasis on them.

Another factor to consider in deciding on sentence structure concerns the emphatic beginning and end positions. These positions in a sentence are the strongest, receiving the most emphasis by the reader. Consider the following options (adapted from a sentence on memory by Cherry).

Normal word order:

> Almost all memory researchers now agree that our brains record everything that ever happens to us unless the process of remembering is artificially interrupted.

A clause at the beginning:

> Unless the process of remembering is artificially interrupted, almost all memory researchers now agree that our brains record everything that ever happens to us.

A clause in the middle:

> Almost all memory researchers now agree that, unless the process of remembering is artificially interrupted, our brains record everything that ever happens to us.

Can you see the difference in emphasis and effect of each option?

EXERCISE 3   Options in the Position of Subordinate Clauses

Combine the following sentences in two or, if possible, three different ways: first with the subordinate clause at the end of the sentence; second, with the subordinate clause at the beginning of the sentence; and third, with the subordinate clause in the middle of the sentence. The third option will not be possible in all sentences. With each option, be prepared to discuss the difference in effect. Note that, as in the Horatio Alger example above, you may need to change the wording if you change the order.

1. Main Clause (*MC*): untrained mice began to shun the dark
   Subordinate Clause (*SC*): when extracts of the brains of fearful mice were injected into the brains of untrained mice

2. *MC:* memory is temporarily affected, then eventually returns
   SC: if one hippocampus is injured

3. *MC:* patients who have lost both hippocampi will shake the hand of a friend
   SC: as if she is a complete stranger

4. *MC:* neuroscientists think that memory involves the whole brain
   SC: although the hippocampi may be important to remembering

5. *MC:* a beginning chess player will likely remember only six or seven pieces of a chess position
   SC: if a chess position is shown to a beginning chess player for five seconds

Punctuation: Commas with Items in a Series; Comma Review

One of the most important uses of the comma is as a separator of items in a series. These series consist of any of the following parts of a sentence.

1. *A series of words.*

   Examples
   the big, fat, ugly mule
   a red, white, and blue flag

2. *A series of phrases.*

   Examples
   in the valley, on the plains, or on the mountain top
   broke the door, shattered the windows, and crumbled the gate

3. *A series of clauses.*

   Example
   after he wrote his book, after he sold it to a publisher, but before he sold it to a movie studio

4. *A series of sentences.*

   Example
   He yelled, he screamed, and he cried.

Notice that in each series, commas are used to separate the individual items. Notice also that a comma is *always* placed before the conjunction.

Example

The president, the vice president, the cabinet, and the executive staff appeared before the convention.

EXERCISE 1

Separate items of a series with a comma in the following sentences.

1. Whenever I fly to New York whenever I sail to Catalina Island and whenever I ride a train through the Rockies I thrill at the diversity of this nation.
2. The clown's suit was pink purple orchid and yellow.
3. The lightning sparked the thunder roared and the rains pelted the city.
4. Yesterday morning, the candidate reaffirmed his belief in a country of the people by the people and for the people.
5. The small toothless baby cooed at her father smiled at her grandmother and screamed at her mother.

EXERCISE 2

Review the rules governing the use of commas that are explained in Units 2 and 3 in the Editing and Punctuation sections. Place commas in the following sentences wherever you believe they are necessary. Be prepared to explain your decision.

1. After cramming for the test for three days I forgot all the dates I memorized.
2. Whatever the reason he gives for his behavior I can't believe him since he often lies to protect himself.
3. The photographer developed five rolls of film but one roll was underdeveloped one was overdeveloped and one was spotted by chemicals.
4. No cocker spaniels are not smarter than poodles.
5. If she were to tune her guitar it might not sound so sour.
6. When we asked the dentist why our bill was so high she replied that inflation has doubled her overhead.
7. History may offer lessons from the past but it can't force people to learn from them.
8. Rents have gone up food prices have gone up and clothing prices have gone up but my salary stands still.

9. Since the beginning of April the daily temperature has never fallen below 75°F.
10. After inheriting money from his grandfather Harry bought a new car a Camaro with an automatic transmission a tape deck and air conditioning.

EXERCISE 3

Review your three-paragraph essay to see if you have used commas correctly and effectively. Make any changes necessary.

Preparing the Final Copy and Proofreading

In preparing the final copy of your three-paragraph definition essay, be sure to follow the manuscript conventions listed under the section on proofreading at the end of Unit 1. Use one side of the paper only. Check for correct margins and double spacing; center the title, in this case the term to be defined, at the top of the page; indent the first sentence of each paragraph; and correct any errors neatly with correction fluid, clean erasures, or lines drawn neatly through the mistakes.

Now you are ready to proofread. Read your final copy aloud, slowly and carefully. Ask yourself the following questions.

1. Are all the words spelled correctly? Are hyphens at the ends of lines placed correctly between the syllables of divided words? If you are uncertain about either your spelling of certain words or the division of any word, check your dictionary.
2. Have you made any accidental changes in your text or omitted any words?
3. Is the punctuation correct?
    a. Are compound sentences accurately punctuated?
    b. Are subordinate sentences accurately punctuated?
    c. Do commas divide all items in a series?
    d. Do all sentences end with either a period, question mark, or exclamation point?

UNIT 5

Exposition: Problems and Solutions; Questions and Answers

READING:
Exposition: Problems and Solutions; Questions and Answers

Reading Strategies: Scanning

Scanning means to survey a printed page with a specific purpose, stopping when you find what you are looking for to focus on the information you need. In other words, scanning entails selectively acquiring information. For example, suppose you need a full definition of the word *jog*. You would follow these four basic steps.

1. Scan the dictionary until you find the *J* section.
2. Scan from *ja* to *jo*, glancing at the upper corner of each page for the first and last words found on each page.
3. When you find the right page, glance down the page to *jog*, skipping over all other words.
4. Focus on *jog* and write down the definition.

Such a procedure is rather simple, for it is scanning in its most fundamental form. But scanning can also be more complex. The important thing to remember is that scanning is a vital part of information gathering at every level of the learning process, whether it involves reading a college catalog, finding information in the yellow pages of the telephone book, searching through want ads, or reading a card catalog. Although scanning is a skill you already possess, you probably need to learn to scan at a greater speed and with more efficiency in order to gather information from textbooks and to research topics for term papers. The following exercises, then, are designed to increase your speed and efficiency and are given in their order of difficulty. Record the time you start and end each exercise. Repeat the exercise each day, striving to reduce the time required to extract the sought-after information.

EXERCISE 1

1. In your weekly television guide, find the oldest movie to be shown on a particular day.
2. Choose a movie you know is playing in a theatre in your city. Search the entertainment section of your local paper for the theatres presenting the movie and check the times the movie starts.

EXERCISE 2

Go to the classified section of your daily paper to find and check all of the following information.

1. Three houses for sale between $50,000 and $100,000.
2. Two used sofas for sale.
3. One secretarial job opening.
4. One typewriter for sale.

EXERCISE 3

1. In your college catalog, find three courses required for graduation with a B.A. in history.
2. In the yellow pages find the following and note them.

   The names of car painters.
   A housecleaning service.
   The names of car stereo installers.

EXERCISE 4

In this text, find the following information, jotting it down on a note pad as fast and neatly as possible.

1. A definition for the creative process.
2. A definition for a fruitarian.
3. A definition of the "rags-to-riches" myth.

Cloze Exercise: Focus on Nouns and Coordinators

In the last unit, you practiced reading by phrases and anticipating what comes next in a discussion. Much of your ability to fixate your eyes on a meaningful phrase and to anticipate the next segment of a sentence or paragraph came from an understanding of the context of this phrase. In other words, if you first read "Philip, falling against the garage window, broke the glass and cut his arm," you are prepared to fill in the missing words in the following sentence.

"His mother rushed __a__ to the emergency __b__ where a doctor stitched up his __c__."

As Philip is a masculine name, space *a* cannot be filled in with *her*, only *him*. Space *b* must obviously be either *hospital, room,* or *ward,* since "emergency hospital," "emergency room," and "emergency ward" are not only common terms, but also the obvious places for a mother to rush an injured child. Space *c* must be *arm,* since this is the injured part of Philip's body.

Anticipating meaning from context, then, is an important technique that assists you in reading quickly and effectively. Yet something else also helps you to fixate on meaningful phrases in a sentence. This other clue to phrase perception is an understanding of the grammar of the English language. Unfortunately, the word *grammar* often evokes unpleasant memories of grammar lessons, exercises, and drills throughout school years. Yet grammar does not have to be boring, difficult, or even frightening. Grammar simply means the *rules* of a language that govern sentence structure. These are the *rules* applied and recognized by all users of a language, even very young children.

Young children first learn to understand simple words, but, by the time they are two or three, they can understand full sentences. Have you considered how they are able to do this? Generally, a two-year-old cannot generate a sentence of more than two or three words: "No night-night," "Me want milk," "Pick me up." But this child can not only understand long sentences, but also can often understand so well that his or her parents have to start spelling out messages they don't want the child to hear. The only reasonable answer as to how children can understand sentences that they can't produce is that they have an intuitive knowledge of the rules governing sentence formation. They don't know that they know these rules; they can't actively generate many grammatical sentences; and they don't even know what the word *grammar* means. They do, however, understand the roles played by different parts of speech and know how words combine to form meaningful statements.

You, as adults and as fluent users of the English language, also know the grammar of the language and actively employ this knowledge every time you listen to another person speak, read a book, or write a college assignment. For example, without much thought, you realized that space *a* in the example above could not be filled in by *he* or *his*. You also realized that spaces *b* and *c* required nouns, not verbs or adjectives. This knowledge of grammar, then, helps you to anticipate meaning by providing you with clues or signals that indicate which type of word belongs within a particular part of a sentence.

One type of word you reviewed in Unit 2 was the coordinator, a word that functions as a fulcrum between parts of a sentence. These coordinators are *and, but, or, nor, for, so,* and *yet.* Remember, however, that each of these coordinators has a slightly different function. "And" functions as a sign of equality:

Mary *and* James were cousins.

"But" functions as a sign of opposition:

Mary studied every night, *but* James studied only on Saturday.

Another type of word used to form sentences is the noun, a word that gives names to things. In Unit 4 you practiced recognizing concrete and abstract nouns. Now, to help you fixate your eyes on meaningful phrases, you need to review the *functions* of nouns. Nouns can function in the following ways.

1. As a subject (S) of a verb (V):

        S   V
    The mayor *ran* for reelection.

2. As an object (O) of a verb (V):

            V   O
    The dog *bit* the mailman.

3. As an indirect object (IO) answering the questions "to or for whom" and "to or for which":

      V   IO
    I *gave* Pedro a present.

4. As an object of a preposition (P):

          P   O
    I went *into* the house.

As you work through the following Cloze exercise, keep in mind how nouns and coordinators function and where they are apt to appear in a sentence. This awareness will aid you in anticipating what comes next in a discussion and in choosing correct words to fill in the blanks. When you finish, be ready to explain what type of words you used for each blank space and how these words function within the sentence.

EXERCISE 1

Writing can often be very frustrating. You sit at your _____ for hours, writing a _____ to a close friend _____ you spend hours and _____ preparing a difficult homework _____ for an English Composition _____. And after all this _____ spent struggling with words _____ ideas, your friend or _____ fails to understand your _____. Because of these frustrating _____, you fear you lack

_____. Don't! Be patient! All _____, whether they are amateurs _____ professionals, often feel this _____. Yet, for every moment of frustration, there is a moment of joy and feeling of accomplishment when words and ideas join to form a clear communication.

Words and the Language: The Structure of Words — Roots

Now that you have gained experience finding contextual clues, the most important strategy for adding words to your vocabulary, you are ready to study the structure of words. Since you will not always be able to grasp the meaning of unfamiliar words through an author's context, or indeed be able to "sound out" a word when you use it in writing, you need to acquire skill in analyzing words, seeking out their meanings, and spelling through a recognition of their component parts. To know, for example, that *psyche* is a Greek word meaning *mind* or *soul* helps you not only to grasp the meaning of words such as *psychology* and *psychotic* but also to spell correctly. (An Old English word for *psyche* would probably be spelled *sike*, and thus we would get *sikology* and *sikotic*.)

The most important part of the structure of English words is the *root*, or the base of the word. The root, which could be either an independent word or a base or word element to which *prefixes* (parts before the root) and *suffixes* (parts after the root) are added, carries the basic meaning of the word. *Tract*, for example, a root that means to pull or draw, can stand alone, but more often it is seen with added prefixes, suffixes, or both.

1. detract, contract, attract
    Prefixes added before the root.
2. tractor, tractable, traction
    Suffixes added after the root.
3. distraction, contractor, attractive
    Prefixes added before and suffixes added after the root.

English has many, many roots. Some of the most common come from Old English (*lord, believe*), but since English is a language that loves to borrow, many roots commonly used today have been borrowed from other languages, especially Latin (*duc* — meaning to lead: *duct, introduce, deduction*) and Greek (*micro* — meaning small: *microscope, microphone, microcomputer*). Most of the Old English roots you probably already know because they are our everyday words. Now is the time, however, to become more familiar with Greek and Latin roots, the bases of many new words that you will meet in your college classes. Begin by learning the twenty roots listed in Table 5-1. (Additional roots are listed in Appendix D.) As you meet other roots in your textbooks, you can add to this list, checking for their meaning in your dictionary or in Appendix D.

Table 5-1: Important Greek and Latin Roots and Their Meanings

Root	Meaning	Example	Definition
act, ag	to do, act	activate	to set in motion, make active
aud, audit	hear	auditorium	place to hear and see a performance
auto	self, from within	automobile	self-propelled land vehicle
bene, bon	good	beneficial	advantageous
biblio	book	bibliography	alphabetized list of books
bio	life	biography	written account of a person's life
cap, capt, cep	head	capital	official seat of government
corpor	body	corporation	group acting as one body
cred, credit	to believe	credible	believable
derm	skin	dermatology	study of the skin and its diseases
domin	to rule	dominate	to have power over
fac, fic, fec	make	factory	plant where goods are manufactured
frater	brother	fraternal	brotherly (organization)
graph	writing	autograph	a person's signature
mitt, miss	send	transmit	to send across
omni	entire, all	omnivorous	eating both animal and vegetable matter
port, portat	to carry	portable	easily carried or moved
scrib, script	to write	scribble	to write hurriedly, carelessly
ten, tent	to hold	tenacity	quality of holding firmly, stubborn
vid, vis	to see	visual	capable of being seen
voc, vocat	to call	vocal	pertaining to the voice

EXERCISE 1

From your reading assignment in this unit, find five words containing any of the roots shown in the above list. Check a dictionary to find accurate meanings to write down for each word.

EXERCISE 2

Choose a word formed from one of the following roots to fill in each blank.

voc   audit, aud
domin   cred
frater   vis
derm

Example
The moon was barely *visible* because of the thick layer of clouds.

1. I wasn't sure I wanted to join a _____ my first year at college.
2. When Jim's face began to peel, he went to a _____.
3. Karen was astounded; she thought the discovery of oil in her backyard was _____.
4. The concert music was barely _____ because of the noisy, rude crowd.
5. Cathy always wants to be the leader; she likes to _____ every activity.
6. Even though I'm usually quiet, I had to _____ my objection at that meeting!

READINGS: SELECTION ONE

Reflections on My Brother's Murder
by David Finn

Ideas to Think About

1. How many times have you been so bored that you were desperate for something to do? Describe one such situation to your classmates. What did you do to end your boredom?
2. What senseless act of violence that stands out as especially shocking have you either personally witnessed or heard about in the news? Can you suggest possible causes for this behavior?
3. In the following essay, Finn first narrates a moment of horror and then poses a problem facing society and offers his own solution. As you read, note these three sections of the essay.

Vocabulary

Look at each word as it is used in the article. (The number in parentheses indicates the paragraph in which it appears.) First, try to understand the meaning from the way it is used in the sentence. Second, use any clues to meaning through the structure of the word. Then, use the dictionary to clarify the meaning.

retrieve (1)
interrogation (2)
desperation (2)
irony (6)

assumption (6)
deterioration (8)
innovative (9)
futile (10)

Reflections on My Brother's Murder

David Finn is chairman of the board of Ruder and Finn. The following article appeared in Saturday Review, *May 1980.*

1 Several months ago, my brother, Herbert Finn, a prominent civil rights lawyer from Phoenix, Arizona, was shot and killed while visiting my family in New York. We had been to the opera — Herbert, his wife, my wife, my sister, my daughter, and I — and the six of us drove to the quiet residential neighborhood of Riverdale, where my daughter lives. I left the car for a few minutes to take her to her apartment. While I was gone, several young black men held up the rest of the family, taking pocketbooks from my wife and sister and grabbing my brother's wallet as he took out his money for them. Although no one is quite sure what happened, we think my brother reached out to retrieve° the credit cards in his wallet

because he was planning to leave the next day on a trip to Egypt and Israel. One impatient robber fired a single .22-caliber bullet, and all of them fled. A moment later I arrived on the scene to find the women screaming and my brother dead.

All that night I repeated four words — *I can't believe it* — so often that they must be imprinted on my brain. The murder took place just after midnight, and we finished with the police interrogation° at 5:30 the next morning. My wife and I had a couple of drinks to try to calm our nerves, but the alcohol didn't work. I couldn't stop myself from shivering (although I wasn't cold) and repeating the four words endlessly. In desperation,° I took a pad from the drawer next to my bed and wrote "I can't believe it" 26 times, as if writing it out would serve as a cathartic[1] for disbelief. But it was no help. I truly could *not* believe it. I went on repeating the words to myself all through the next day as I sat with my wife, sister, and sister-in-law in three different police stations, going through hundreds of mug shots and answering questions posed by various teams of detectives. While I could not absorb the reality of what had happened, neither could I get the sight of it — the sight of my brother slumped in the back seat — out of my mind.

About two weeks later, four suspects were arrested. Their ages were 19, 17, 17, and 15. Newspaper accounts stated that three of them came from middle-class homes in Mt. Vernon, New York.

Two of the youths confessed. The story they told deepened the crease of incredulity[2] in my brain. It went something like this: One boy borrowed his mother's car to go to a high-school dance. He changed his mind and instead picked up three friends, drove to a pizzeria, then to a disco, and finally went for a ride in Riverdale. As they were cruising, the four boys thought of sticking up an ice-cream store, but by the time they got there it was closed. Later, they passed our car, saw the people in it, and thought it looked like an interesting target. They pulled into a driveway, and three of them said they'd check our car and be right back. The fourth boy waited, listening to his car radio. A minute later he heard a noise and the three ran back screaming, "Get out of here, get out of here." As they sped away, one of the boys kept asking another, "Why did you do it? Why did you shoot him?" "I had to," he answered, and then said reassuringly, "Don't worry about it." They argued for a while. Finally, one of them distributed $44 to each of the others. "You shot (this guy) for less than $200? That's stupid," one of the boys remarked. "Don't worry," the murderer insisted.

As told by the two who confessed, the casualness of the whole incident — taking my brother's life to get some money for fun — makes the

---
[1] A method of riddance.
[2] Disbelief.

tragedy all the more unbearable. It was apparently just a matter of going after easy pickings and striking down a victim who might have been trying to hold out. It was like swatting a fly. That was all there was to it.

In the months that followed, the shock waves of what we initially took to be a private nightmare radiated farther than any of us could have imagined. People from all over the world called and wrote to give some expression to the pain they felt. I could almost hear the whispers echoing in the atmosphere as anybody who had the slightest connection to us passed the story on. What dumbfounded acquaintances was the senselessness, the chilling irony,° of Herbert's death. Dying from an illness is no better than dying from a robber's bullet, but we learn to accept death from disease as fate, while murder threatens to undermine the assumption° that man can control societal forces.

A friend who served for many years as Chief of Police in the Bronx, Anthony Bouza, has likened the unchecked spread of crime to a cancer that will destroy our society unless we attack its cause — poverty and unemployment. People who can't speak the language, can't get jobs, and can't find decent places to live are excluded from society. They come to feel that robbing and killing are the only ways they can survive. Desperation, Chief Bouza believes, overwhelms morality and the law. What is worse, he says, is the more recent development. As the poor increasingly resort to their desperate solutions, more fortunate youths adopt the same measures to accomplish their own ends. Robbing and killing fill the emptiness caused, not by hunger, but by boredom and a lack of purpose in their lives. The cancer that begins in the burned-out buildings of our cities metastasizes[3] to the rest of society.

A number of people, reacting to my brother's death, are seeking cures for the disease Bouza describes. Some say they will work for stricter gun-control laws. Others want tougher sentences for convicted criminals. Still others want to reinstate the death penalty. And some want to work for a stronger and better equipped police force. But it seems to me that these efforts, many of which are clearly necessary, are unlikely to rid us of the cancer; they treat the symptoms, not the disease. The cancer itself can be arrested, I believe, only if we minister to its root cause. We must stop the decay in our cities and the deterioration° to exercise that power.

The shock of my brother's death has in itself given rise to some innovative° ideas that illustrate the kind of determination called for. While talking about Herbert's death, for example, a friend who heads an influential foundation raised the question of relating education to work opportunities. He proposed an unusual plan for a pilot project: if a small group of underprivileged students would promise to finish their college education, he would arrange jobs for them in advance, guaranteeing them po-

---

[3] Spreads.

sitions on graduation. The companies for which they would work would pay only half their salaries, and his foundation would pay the rest. If the project succeeds, he would encourage other foundations to do the same thing for thousands of young people. His idea could be the small beginning of a major accomplishment.

My brother's death was cruel, inhuman, personally devastating; but I do not want to believe it was futile.° Taking initiative to cope with the disease rather than despairing at its ravages is the only sane response to our tragedy. If we who have been subjected to such horrors can show the world that we have not lost our faith, if out of our pain we can help to awaken the forces within our society that are capable of curing the disease, his death and the deaths of other martyrs of the streets will not have been in vain.

10

Discussion

1. This essay treats a problem and solution. Finn suggests that his terrible experience points to a serious social problem. What is the problem? What are some of the proposed solutions?
2. According to the article, robbing and killing are results of the emptiness caused by boredom. Although boredom does not always cause crime, it can have serious effects on our lives. What are some of the effects boredom has had on your life? On the lives of your friends? Has boredom ever caused you to do something you might not otherwise have done?
3. Finn places his greatest emphasis on teenage boredom and poverty as the causes of urban crime. What do you believe are other reasons why violence and crime have increased in American cities? Explain. What solutions to these situations can you propose?

READINGS: SELECTION TWO

We'd Better Not Make Book on U.S. Literacy
by Robert C. Solomon

Ideas to Think About

1. Which issues do you enjoy debating? Why? With whom do you debate? Why?
2. When was the last time you were so angered or excited by something you read that you talked back to the author? When? Why?
3. How often do you read for the pleasure of examining ideas that are entirely new to you? Explain.
4. In the following essay, Solomon first defines "the new illiteracy" and then discusses the problems brought about by a lack of reading books, essays, and informative articles. As you read this essay, evaluate both the author's definition and explanation of the problem. Does he offer a solution?

Vocabulary

Look at each word as it is used in the article. (The number in parentheses indicates the paragraph in which it appears.) First, try to understand the meaning from the way it is used in the sentence. Second, use any clues to meaning through the structure of the word. Then, use the dictionary to clarify the meaning.

illiterate (1)
elitism (1)
futile (1)
voraciously (2)
obsessively (2)

pathos (4)
plausibility (10)
impotence (10)
dissident (10)

We'd Better Not Make Book on U.S. Literacy

Robert C. Solomon teaches philosophy at the University of Texas at Austin. He is the author of *The Passions* and *History and Human Nature*.

Recently, when Isaac Asimov said in *Newsweek* that we are a nation of illiterates,° he was answered by a flood of mail accusing him of elitism° and, of course, self-interest, since he is one of the few writers who actually make a living off those who read. But his point was overlooked — that democracy is futile,° no matter how "free" the press, if nobody reads or debates the issues.

The new illiteracy is new because it is a form of intellectual starvation that affects people who in fact read voraciously,° even obsessively° — food-can labels, sports headlines, *People* magazine captions and at least the cover of the *National Enquirer*. But they don't read books. Or essays. Or any magazine article without pictures or with a "cont'd on p. 37."

Some would argue that what Asimov calls "illiteracy" is in fact only the replacement of the linear-print medium by more exciting audio-visual media. That all-too-familiar claim is dangerously false.

A television documentary can indeed convey the pathos° of a family in need, the brutality of a battle or the look of a guilty congressman in far more detail and with far greater accuracy than print can hope to do. But even if TV programming were uniformly excellent and informative, it lacks something that only print can provide: time to *think*.

No matter how many ideas there might be in a television show or movie, they become *our* ideas only when we stop to reflect on them. And that takes leisure, effort, and practice — the kind that reading requires. We sometimes say that a good book is one that "you can't put down," but I would argue the contrary, that the best books are those that force you to stop and think at every turn. (Asimov's own books are an excellent example.) Our concentration on what Marshall McLuhan once called the "cool" (non-participatory) media deprives us of ideas just as thoroughly as food processing deprives us of nutrition.

The mind is like a muscle, which no good American would admit neglecting — it must be exercised, stretched until it hurts a little, every day. In return it becomes stronger, more flexible and more enjoyable to use. The new illiteracy is a form of atrophy and deprivation.

We have come to believe that information — facts, facts, and more facts — is all there is to knowledge. But, even if we could get all of our facts from television, it is books that give us ideas.

We are afraid of ideas — afraid to think, afraid of appearing clumsy or stupid. Even our intellectuals retreat to the tangible and easily demonstrable — biographies, concrete experiments and specific anecdotes. We retreat to clichés, once-powerful ideas that have since been dried and strung like beads on our secular rosary — clichés about democracy, freedom, selfishness, human rights, the right to life, human nature, looking out for No. 1 and getting in touch with one's true feelings. They look like objects of thought, but are in fact just the opposite: replacements for thinking. Which renders reading and thinking unnecessary.

The paradox of all of this is that ours is the most idea-based nation on earth. One would be hard-pressed to name another nation so thoroughly founded on ideas — and books. Our founding fathers were all philosophers and social theorists — well-read, and proud of it. Other societies treasure their customs, traditions and rituals; we revere our principles. Yet the myth persists that we are an "anti-intellectual" society. We shun abstract theories, perhaps, but has not the basis of our conception of society always been the need to argue conflicting ideas?

One could argue with some plausibility° that the reason some people believe in free speech is that they also believe in the impotence° of mere ideas. "It's only an idea" is a way of denying seriousness. We have a schizoid view of ideas, thinking and thinkers: they are on the one hand powerful, essential and sometimes dangerous, and on the other hand abstract, useless and foolish. We try to sail through this confusion by treating ideas as oddities, but this is another way of dismissing them. Can one imagine a Russian dissident,° for example, who could be sent to prison for his ideas if they were truly only "interesting"? And, indeed, the experience of everyone who has ever given a lecture in a Communist-bloc country has been the awesome realization of the importance of ideas — not mere conclusions reduced to catechism[1] but the debate and the thinking themselves. Perhaps if certain ideas were forbidden to us, instead of being simply ignored or edited out of our informational diet, then we, too, would come to appreciate them.

Reading is a form of thinking. Perhaps, in some distinguished company, conversation could supply the same sort of stimulation (but one cannot imagine that such company could be ill-read). The new illiteracy is not so much a matter of ignorance — indeed, we are probably the best-informed society on Earth — but something just as damaging: the deprivation of ideas. The Buddha, perhaps, could have reached profound revelations while looking at a flower, but most of us need more input. Sentences. Books. Arguments to make us angry. Descriptions that spur our imagination. Fabrications to set our minds wandering. That is the argument for literacy — above the need for information, the necessity of reading fine print on contracts and understanding the few public notices that have not yet been reduced to pictures.

"Man is a thinking reed," wrote Blaise Pascal, but in the days when reading was unchallenged as a source of mental power. Nowadays, the formula would have to be "those who think read." However spectacular the media revolution, that truth will probably be with us for a long time.

Discussion

1. Solomon contends that the best books are those we can put down, ". . . those that force you to stop and think at every turn." Explain what you think he means by this statement and name at least one book that you reacted to in such a way. What caused your reaction?
2. Solomon says that treating ideas as oddities or as "interesting" is a way of dismissing them. What does he mean by this? What evidence can you think of which might support his notion that we are intellectually starved? Are

---

[1] Principles taught by questions and answers.

we afraid to think? Do you see evidence of intellectual starvation in your classes? Explain. Are students afraid to take risks? If so, why?
3. Solomon poses a problem, "those who think read," but they must read about ideas and believe in the power of ideas. The problem is that we don't often read this way. We don't often take chances or try to form new ideas. For that reason, we risk a terrible kind of illiteracy. Does Solomon pose a solution to the problem? Explain. What other solutions to the problem are possible?

READINGS: SELECTION THREE

from Vegetarianism: Can You Get by Without Meat?
from Consumer Reports

Ideas to Think About

1. Do you follow a vegetarian diet? Why? If not, what judgments have you made about friends who refuse to eat meat? What images does the word "vegetarian" create in your mind?
2. In what ways do you think a vegetarian might be healthier than a meat eater?
3. Notice the careful use of definition in the essay. Look for definitions of words you have wondered about. Look also for definitions that might change your mind about vegetarianism.

Vocabulary

Look at each word as it is used in the article. (The number in parentheses indicates the paragraph in which it appears.) First, try to understand the meaning from the way it is used in the sentence. Second, use any clues to meaning through the structure of the word. Then, use the dictionary to clarify the meaning.

proscribe (2)   monotonous (25)
disseminate (4)   leached (29)
regimen (5)   ameliorated (35)
synthesize (20)   tenuous (35)

from Vegetarianism: Can You Get by Without Meat?

A growing number of Americans don't eat meat. According to a recent survey, some seven million people in the U.S. now consider themselves vegetarians — nearly three times the number estimated a generation ago.

They eschew[1] meat for a variety of reasons. Some vegetarians don't eat meat because it's too expensive. Others consider it wrong to kill animals for food. Some think that feeding grain to cattle and hogs is a wasteful use of a precious commodity. Others belong to a religion that proscribes° eating meat. And for some, it's a matter of personal taste; they can't stomach the idea, as George Bernard Shaw put it, of "eating corpses."

---

[1] Avoid.

But the reason most often cited by U.S. vegetarians is health. They believe that forgoing meat is better for them.

Through the years, though, physicians and nutritionists have often questioned whether people could be adequately nourished without eating animal protein. Nutrition textbooks sometimes included the section on vegetarianism in the chapter on food fads. Knowledge of the nutritional status of vegetarians in the U.S. and elsewhere was not well disseminated,° and the practice was often associated with the diets of people in poor countries who didn't have enough food — let alone enough meat — to eat. Vegetarianism may seem novel in the U.S., where so much meat is eaten, but it's commonplace in other parts of the world — because of the culture, the religion, or the food supply. Research begun initially to improve the diets of those with a limited food supply is now answering many of the questions about the adequacy of vegetarian diets. And most American vegetarians eat far better than a peasant in southern India or rural Guatemala.

Accordingly, the perception of vegetarianism is changing in the U.S. No longer condemned out of hand as a faddish way of eating or a starvation regimen,° vegetarianism can be an alternative way of achieving a healthful diet.

What Do Vegetarians Eat?

Vegetarians don't necessarily limit themselves to so-called natural or organic foods, though the desire to eat such foods has led some people to become vegetarians. Many vegetarians buy all their food in an ordinary supermarket; they simply skip the meat counter.

Neither do vegetarians eat only vegetables. Most of the seven million Americans who describe themselves as vegetarians eat everything but "red" meat (beef, pork, and lamb). Some also avoid poultry or fish. Some eat no meat but Thanksgiving turkey or Christmas ham. In the strict sense of the word, those people are not vegetarians, because they still eat some animal flesh.

The word "vegetarian" was coined by English vegetarians in 1842 to describe people, such as themselves, who ate no meat, fish, or fowl. Since some used milk, eggs, and cheese and some didn't, more terminology came into use. Vegetarians who do eat dairy products and eggs became known as "ovolacto-vegetarians" (eggs and milk vegetarians, in Latin). Others eat milk products but not eggs; they're known as "lacto-vegetarians."

The total vegetarian, a rarity in the U.S., eats no animal products at all. Some total vegetarians, called "vegans," also refuse to use fur, leather, wool, and other inedible animal products, because they believe it wrong to exploit animals for any reason. To them, vegetarianism means more than what's for dinner.

Another philosophy that can lead to a vegetarian regimen is Zen macrobiotics, a system devised by a writer named George Ohsawa in the 1960's. Ohsawa prescribed a series of 10 diets, a progression from meals that include some animal protein, such as fish, to a very restricted diet consisting mainly of brown rice (the perfectly balanced food, according to Ohsawa). The "higher" macrobiotic diets have become notorious for sometimes causing severe malnutrition and even death. They are especially dangerous for children.

The consequences of the macrobiotic progression illustrate a basic nutritional fact: The fewer kinds of foods you eat, the harder it is to be well nourished. The reverse is also true: It's easier to be well nourished when you're eating many kinds of food. Ovolacto-vegetarian diets, which can include a wide variety of foods, differ little from typical Western fare in nutritional adequacy. Total vegetarians must take greater care, but they too can be well nourished.

In 1974, a committee of the National Academy of Sciences National Research Council, which publishes the Recommended Daily Allowances for the U.S., evaluated vegetarian diets. It concluded that all but the most restricted ones are nutritionally safe. "The most important safeguard for average (vegetarian) consumers," said the report, "is great variety in the diet" — advice that's equally sound for people who eat meat.

All four basic food groups are open to ovolacto-vegetarians: milk (milk, cheese, yogurt, ice-cream, and other dairy foods); vegetable-fruit; bread (bread, pasta, rice, cornmeal, breakfast cereal, and other grains); and meat alternatives in the meat group (eggs, dried beans and peas, peanut butter, lentils, soybeans, nuts, seed).

Ovolacto-vegetarians drop meat, poultry, and fish from the meat group. (Lacto-vegetarians would also forgo eggs.) But that still leaves quite a few protein-rich foods in the meat category, and protein is also to be found in the other groups.

The total vegetarian drops the milk group and has thus cut out most obvious sources of protein. Yet adequate and even generous amounts of protein can be obtained from the remaining groups.

How Much Protein?

Most American adults eat about twice the Recommended Daily Allowance (RDA) for protein, and protein deficiency diseases are rare in the U.S. Analyses of the diets of ovolacto-vegetarians and total vegetarians by nutritionists show that, although they tend to eat less protein than those who eat meat, they still eat more protein than they need. . . .

Protein has assumed an almost religious importance in the American diet. Some people still believe that eating protein makes you stronger and that strenuous exercise requires eating extra protein, though those notions were disproved long ago. Protein's primary function in the body is the creation and repair of tissue — from skin, muscles, and bones to hair and toenails. The amount of protein you need, therefore, depends more on your size and age than on your activity.

An average man's RDA for protein is 56 grams; a woman's is 44 grams. The RDA for children is proportionally more for their weight than the RDA for adults, because children are growing. The following table shows how the RDA's change with the age and sex: 18

	Age	Protein RDA
Children	1–3 years	23 grams
	4–6	30
	7–10	34
Females	11–18	46
	19+	44
Males	11–14	45
	15+ . . .	56

Besides eating enough protein, you have to eat enough *high-quality* protein. The quality of a protein is determined by its amino acids. 19

Steak vs. Soy Protein

Proteins are large molecules composed of various combinations of 22 smaller compounds called amino acids. The human body, if it has enough raw material, can synthesize° most of those amino acids. But eight or nine — called the essential amino acids — cannot be synthesized. They must be supplied in food, and they are needed in certain proportions. 20

Other animals produce proteins whose amino acids are in roughly the same proportion as those required by humans, so protein from animal flesh, milk, and eggs is called complete, or high-quality, protein. Wheat germ, dried yeast, and soybeans approach animal protein in quality. But most plant proteins are low in one or more essential amino acids; the deficient (or limiting) amino acid varies from plant to plant. 21

The body doesn't care where its amino acids come from, and few vegetarians eat just one plant food. Most of them eat some animal protein, and most animal protein is complete. Animal protein also improves the quality of plant protein when the two are eaten together — an effect known as protein complementation. Thus, the limiting amino acids in macaroni, shredded wheat, or rye bread are filled in when those foods are eaten as macaroni and cheese, shredded wheat and milk, or an egg-salad sandwich on rye. So ovolacto-vegetarians needn't worry about getting enough good quality protein. 22

It's also possible to improve the quality of plant protein by combining 23 foods with different limiting amino acids. And because the limiting amino acids of similar plant foods tend to be similar, you don't have to memorize an amino-acid table to complement plant protein.

Beans and rice, for example, are a food combination common throughout the world. The limiting amino acid of the beans (methionine) is supplied by the rice, and the limiting amino acid of the rice (lysine) is supplied by the beans. Grains (such as rice, oats, wheat, and corn) and legumes (such as beans, lentils, and peas) complement each other effectively. Combinations can be as mundane as peanut-butter sandwiches or as exotic as tabouli, the cracked wheat and chick-pea salad of the Middle East. Other plant proteins don't complement the protein in grains and legumes quite as well but are still useful as protein sources.

Protein malnutrition usually occurs only when you don't get enough food to eat. The person most vulnerable is the young child eating a monotonous° all-plant diet. Plant foods are generally bulky and have a low protein content (cooked rice, for example, is only about 2 percent protein). It's therefore sometimes hard for small children to eat enough to meet their protein needs. Even a small amount of animal protein, such as milk, can significantly improve the quality of protein a child eats. Fortified soy milk can also be useful in helping a child get enough high-quality protein.

Besides protein for the total vegetarian, there are a few nutrients that a vegetarian must seek out with some care. They are the vitamins and minerals supplied mainly by meat, milk, and eggs in the typical American diet. One of them, vitamin B-12, is found almost exclusively in food of animal origin.

Meat Minerals: Iron, Zinc

Because the iron in plants is not as readily absorbed as the iron in meat, vegetarians, particularly children and menstruating women, have a greater chance of becoming deficient in iron.

Legumes (notably soybeans), whole grains, leafy green vegetables, and dried fruit are good plant sources of iron. Milk and eggs are poor sources. Total vegetarians, whose main protein sources are legumes and grains, may be ingesting more iron than ovolacto-vegetarians, who rely on dairy products and eggs. . . .

An excellent source of dietary iron, largely lost in modern kitchens, is the iron leached° into food from uncoated cast-iron pots. Some nutritionists recommend that vegetarians cook at least two meals a week in a cast-iron pot.

Like iron, zinc from plant sources is less available than that from animal foods. Zinc is found in several plant foods, including legumes and whole grains. Zinc is also found in milk and eggs. . . .

Mainly from Milk

When the milk group is abandoned, so is the usual major dietary source of calcium, riboflavin, and vitamin D. Calcium and riboflavin are contained in green leafy vegetables. . . . Collard greens, kale, and broccoli all provide good amounts of riboflavin and calcium without the interference of oxalic acid. Whole-grain and enriched breads and cereals are another source of riboflavin. Calcium is also found in soybeans, almonds, and sesame seeds. . . .

Under ideal conditions, vitamin D is probably not required in the diet. A form of the vitamin is produced by exposure of skin to the ultraviolet rays of the sun. Again, reports of vitamin D deficiency diseases in adults are rare, but several cases of nutritional rickets among children eating macrobiotic or total vegetarian diets have been reported in the U.S. and in Britain. Limited exposure to sunlight, especially in winter, may increase the risk of vitamin-D deficiency. There are no good plant sources of vitamin D, but supplements or fortified soy milk can fill the RDA.

The Tables Turned

While some family doctors and parents worry over possible nutritional deficiencies in a meatless diet, most vegetarians are convinced that their way of eating is healthier than the way Americans eat. Claims for the superior health of vegetarians abound, beginning with the beguiling and blunt statement that vegetarians live longer. More specifically, vegetarianism is credited with protecting its practitioners from the "degenerative diseases of civilization" — coronary heart disease, cancer, high blood pressure, and diabetes, among others.

There is little evidence as yet to support those claims. Stories of long-lived vegetarian tribes in mountain retreats don't count. The life of a Hunza or a Vilcabamban differs in too many ways other than diet from the life of a vegetarian in Cincinnati or San Francisco.

Some health problems, though, may be ameliorated° by a vegetarian diet, because it's often a low-calorie diet. Several studies have found that vegetarians tend to have lower weight for their height than nonvegetarians. Since obesity may be a risk factor in several diseases, including gall bladder disease, high blood pressure, and adult-onset diabetes, a tenuous° connection can be made between being a vegetarian and having a lower risk of developing those diseases. But you have to be a trim vegetarian. . . .

Studies comparing populations that have different eating habits offer similarly contradictory hints about the effects of a vegetarian diet. Seventh Day Adventists, half of whom are ovolacto-vegetarians, are a group often compared with the rest of meat-eating America. Seventh Day Adventists have lower serum cholesterol levels than other people. A high serum cholesterol level is one of the risk factors in coronary heart disease. Seventh Day Adventists are older when they have their first heart attack. Yet one study found that Seventh Day Adventist women who were total vegetarians had a risk of death from coronary heart disease not much different from that of the general population.

Seventh Day Adventists also have lower incidences of several kinds of cancer, including some cancers that may be diet-related. Yet Mormons, who do eat meat, have similarly low incidences of those cancers. So something else may be making the two groups less vulnerable — such as their overall life style, which includes abstinence from tobacco and alcohol.

Human lives and human diets are so complex that to pin complicated and poorly understood diseases on a certain way of eating is virtually impossible, especially when done in retrospect. Observation of factors that might contribute to disease and death is more reliable when a group of people is selected, evaluated, and then followed for 15 or 25 years — a prospective study, in other words. Such studies looking for differences in the long-term health of vegetarians and nonvegetarians have been started, but the results won't be known for a long time. "Until then, we can only guess," says Dr. Noel Solomons, associate professor of clinical nutrition at the Massachusetts Institute of Technology and an ovolacto-vegetarian. "We may never get an answer, even from the prospective studies," he added, "because of the possibility that other great changes might occur in society over such a long period of time."

Discussion

1. This essay poses a question and offers an answer. What is the major question it seeks to answer? What is the answer?
2. What are some of the main categories of vegetarians? Which seems to be the most sensible category? Why? Which one seems to be the healthiest choice in view of the information on nutrition you now possess? Even if you would not consider vegetarianism, what evidence seems solid enough to make you consider diet modification? Explain.
3. Many definitions are included in this essay. What type of definitions are employed (review Vocabulary in Units 1 and 4)? Are all of these definitions necessary? Why? Should the author have offered definitions for any other terms?

WRITING:
Exposition: Problems and Solutions; Questions and Answers

Writing Assignment: A Three-Paragraph Problem/Solution or Question/Answer Essay

Working through the first four units of this text, you practiced writing different types of essays. These writing assignments helped make you aware of the need to develop controlling ideas for your essays, to organize materials clearly, and to define abstract and difficult words*. Above all, these assignments taught you to select, focus, and manipulate your content in order to communicate effectively with your readers. You learned to make conscious choices as you wrote, always aware of the needs and possible reactions of your audience.

Yet a single paragraph and an extended definition provide only limited communication. They can, for example, introduce or conclude a larger essay, explain terms or minor concepts, describe a small scene or one object, narrate a brief episode, or develop a very restricted point of discussion. Writers, however, must often develop more extensive discussions, narrate longer episodes, or describe more details. In this unit, then, you will learn to expand your communication into a three-paragraph expository essay that includes an introductory paragraph and two explanatory paragraphs. This type of essay can often be used for your weekly college assignments in your other classes, for business letters, and for small professional reports or memos.

The Thesis Statement

One major difference between an informative paragraph and an expository essay lies in the introduction to the discussions. A paragraph's controlling idea is generally introduced by means of an explicit *topic sentence,* while an essay's controlling idea is usually introduced by means of an explicit *thesis statement.* Both types of statements must be unified, clear, precise, and limited; but, since a thesis statement controls the development of an entire essay, it must present a broader topic than does a topic sentence.

> *Examples:*
> *Thesis Statement:*
> The 1980 presidential campaign involved three major candidates.

---

* Adapted from theories outlined in Richard E. Young, Alton L. Becker, and Kenneth L. Pike, *Rhetoric: Discovery and Change* (New York: Harcourt, Brace, and World, 1970).

Topic Sentence:
The Democratic candidate was the incumbent president, Jimmy Carter.

Thesis Statement:
Within the past thirty years, computers have become a major tool of business, science, and education.

Topic Sentence:
Computers have recently been introduced to literary research.

Thesis Statement:
A major focus of geological study involves earthquake prediction.

Topic Sentence:
Research into the cause of earthquakes also includes the observation of animal behavior immediately preceding a seismic event.

Although thesis statements cover larger areas of discussion than topic sentences, you must take special care to limit their scope to an area of discussion that can be handled fully. In other words, make a contractual agreement with your readers that you can fulfill in the space allotted for the discussion.

EXERCISE 1

Evaluate the following sentences. Which are appropriate as thesis statements for a three-paragraph essay? Which are appropriate for topic sentences? Which are *not* appropriate for either? Be prepared to defend your decisions.

1. Three distinct climates occur in France: the Atlantic type, the Mediterranean type, and the Central European type.
2. Qualitative inorganic analysis involves the detection of all acid radicals, all metallic ions, and all elements.
3. Bentonite is volcanic ash deposited by the wind.
4. Silk is the only natural fiber that occurs in a filament form.
5. Women operatic singers are classified as dramatic sopranos, lyric sopranos, and coloratura sopranos.

In this unit you will write an expository essay that focuses on one of two types of situations that often challenge writers. Sometimes writers, as you have seen in one reading selection in this unit, want to suggest *solutions* to *problems* that confront their readers; and at other times, they want to suggest *answers* to *questions* asked by their readers. For example, the dean of your college might be faced with a problem of student apathy, that is, students showing little interest in serving as student government officers, in supporting the school's athletic program, or in joining school organizations and clubs. Or perhaps a group of middle-aged adults might ask why some college students show little confidence in the American government. Having opinions and information on these topics, you could express your point of view and inform your readers by following a problem/solution or question/answer organizational pattern in your writing.

In using either of these two organizational patterns, you must keep tight control over three aspects of your writing: an awareness of your readers' needs, your thesis statement, and the information to be used in the development of your essay. Most important of these is, of course, your awareness of your readers' needs, for this awareness enables you to formulate your thesis statement and to select appropriate ideas, information, and examples in support of it. Not all readers need or can use the same information. Some require full, detailed discussions; some need brief, simplified discussions; and some want full, nontechnical discussions. And not all readers are psychologically prepared for the same argument or explanation. Some people may want to read about the writer's viewpoints, even if they do not agree with these opinions, while other people may be unwilling to face unpleasant ideas or facts. Because of these reader differences, you must carefully evaluate your particular readers' possible needs and abilities and then adjust your topic sentence accordingly.

Your thesis statement, as in all exposition, must be *limited, unified, precise,* and *clear* so it can serve as a contractual agreement with your readers. In a problem/solution (P/S) three-paragraph essay, however, your thesis must state a problem for which you have a possible solution.

Examples:
Many Americans are no longer able to afford adequate medical care.
Citizens of Los Angeles fear that the 1984 Olympics will force a tax increase.

In contrast, your thesis statement in a question/answer (Q/A) three-paragraph essay asks an indirect question, that is, a question couched within a sentence.

Examples:
The audience asked the candidate about his views on a tax deduction.
Physicians and nutritionists have often questioned whether people could be adequately nourished without eating animal protein.

Direct questions can sometimes be used in question/answer essays, but they often cause problems, especially when they are directed at the readers. For example, if your thesis asks, "Have *you* ever had a dream that came true?" readers who answer "no" might stop reading. But if your thesis reads, "Psychologists have often questioned whether or not dreams can predict the future," your readers can read without personal involvement. The question no longer is directed at their personal past experiences and now treats a topic of general scientific interest. In other words, indirect questions offer more objective generalizations than do direct questions and tend to avoid personal biases and involvement. Even if the indirect question employs the pronoun "I," as in "I have often been asked if I believe in miracles," readers are not forced to relate to their own experiences and are capable of evaluating your statements fairly.

EXERCISE 2

Thesis statements serve as your contractual agreement with your readers and establish guidelines for you to follow as you develop your ideas. The thesis statement in a P/S essay must present a problem that is of interest to your readers. If this problem is not relevant to your readers' lives, they will probably not continue reading.

Evaluate the following thesis statements. Rewrite those that are not limited, unified, precise, and clear.

1. Americans will face problems in the future.
2. Great Britain has a high rate of inflation and a serious immigration problem.
3. The city police and the Highway Patrol officers who ride motorcycles often are faced with problems of belligerent drunk drivers.
4. American manufacturers can't compete with many foreign companies in price and quality.
5. Senior citizens are neglected.

EXERCISE 3

Evaluate the following thesis statements for Q/A essays. Rewrite those that are not asked indirectly or that address the reader directly.

1. Why do most parents have difficulty in communicating with their teenagers?
2. Have you ever attempted to backpack in the Rockies?
3. The students asked why you have to write so many term papers.
4. People often ask why you attend college.
5. Can the Pirates win the pennant?

Finally, to keep your readers' interest, confidence, and good faith, you must present them with up-to-date, accurate, and appropriate information. First, you must offer your readers the latest information possible, since ten-year-old scientific theories, five-year-old statistics, and last Monday's weather forecast for last Tuesday have little value today. Second, you must provide accurate information, because misinformation not only violates your ethical responsibility to enlighten your readers, but also might anger them if they discover your errors. And third, you must offer your readers information that is neither too difficult nor too simplified, or you might bore or confuse them. Remember that bored, confused, or angry readers will not respond as you want them to and are apt to quit reading.

Assignment
Write a three-paragraph essay employing either the P/S or Q/A organizational pattern. The essay should contain at least 400 words.

Problem/Solution:
   Paragraph 1: Statement and explanation of the problem
   Paragraphs 2 and 3: Proposed solution

Question/Anjswer:
   Paragraph 1: Indirect question and explanation of the situation
   Paragraphs 2 and 3: Proposed answer to the question

A P/S essay contains two interrelated sections. The first paragraph, the P, presents a *limited, unified, precise,* and *clear* topic sentence that introduces the problem to be discussed. This problem is then explained fully so that the readers can understand the proposed situation. For example, note the expansion of the thesis statement in the following example, which treats the problem of financing a college education. The intended readers are college students.

   (P) Many of today's college students face severe financial difficulties. With the rising costs of tuition, books, and living expenses, a bachelor's degree costs between $15,000 and $40,000 and threatens to become an impossible dream for young people from lower- and middle-class families. Even those students who once thought that they had saved sufficient money for four years of schooling now must seek ways to earn or borrow additional funds.

The second and third paragraphs of the essay, the S, offer one or two possible solutions to the stated problem. These solutions must be workable and precisely stated because idealistic and vague solutions seldom convince readers. For example, to suggest that the unemployment rate could be reduced by providing jobs for every citizen sounds logical and humane, but could this solution actually be implemented and would it work? Who would fund these jobs? Where would the money come from? What types of jobs would they be? Would every unemployed person be willing to take one of these jobs? And to say that the solution to air pollution is to put a stop to all violators of the local Clean Air Law fails to name the violators or to offer concrete means of implementing the law. In other words, in order to convince your readers to accept your solution, you must offer them one that is possible, precise, and fully developed.

   (S) Yet no serious student need quit school because of a lack of money. First, many students can apply for scholarship grants that cover tuition and book costs. Such scholarships are offered by state and local governments, service organizations such as the Kiwanis Club, large corporations, alumni societies, and the schools themselves. Second, students can apply for educational loans from their schools or local banks. These bank loans do not require collateral because they are guaranteed by the federal government. Finally, students can earn money by working on campus at work-study jobs established by their schools. Information on these scholarships, grants, and work-study jobs can be obtained at most colleges' financial aid departments.

(S) Other possible, but perhaps less attractive, options available to students faced with severe financial problems involve changing schools or attending school on a part-time basis. Since many students do not qualify for either scholarship grants or loans and often have difficulty keeping up with full class loads while working twenty to thirty hours per week, they may need to adjust their original educational plans. For example, they could transfer to low-tuition state or city colleges that charge little or no tuition. If such transfers are not possible, they may have to take fewer classes each semester so they can work enough hours to support themselves and still pay tuition. Such a step will, of course, postpone their graduation, but they can eventually complete their schooling. For some students, then, education requires sacrifice and determination, but it is available to those who persevere.

By putting together the P and S, we can form an integrated essay that not only states and explains a problem facing the readers, but also offers a possible solution.

Many of today's college students face severe financial difficulties. With the rising costs of tuition, books, and living expenses, a bachelor's degree costs between $15,000 and $40,000 and threatens to become an impossible dream for young people from lower- and middle-class families. Even those students who once thought that they had saved sufficient money for four years of schooling now must seek ways to earn or borrow additional funds.

Yet no serious student need quit school because of a lack of money. First, many students can apply for scholarship grants that cover tuition and book costs. Such scholarships are offered by state and local governments, service organizations such as the Kiwanis Club, large corporations, alumni societies, and the schools themselves. Second, students can apply for educational loans from their schools or local banks. These bank loans do not require collateral because they are guaranteed by the federal government. Finally, students can earn money by working on campus at work-study jobs established by their schools. Information on these scholarships, grants, and work-study jobs can be obtained at most college financial aid departments.

Other possible, but perhaps less attractive, options available to students faced with severe financial problems involve changing schools or attending school on a part-time basis. Since many students do not qualify for either scholarship grants or loans and often have difficulty keeping up with full class loads while working twenty to thirty hours per week, they need to adjust their original educational plans. For example, they could transfer to low-tuition state or city colleges that charge little or no tuition. If such transfers are not possible, they may have to take fewer classes each semester so they can work enough hours to support themselves and still pay tuition. Such a step will, of course, postpone their graduation, but they can eventually complete their schooling. For some students, then, education requires sacrifice and determination, but it is available to those who persevere.

Like the P/S essay, a Q/A essay has two parts. In this format, however, the first paragraph of the essay states a question (the thesis) and explains it fully. For this assignment, the question should be an indirect question such as, "College students often ask why so many term papers are assigned." Remember, do not speak directly to your reader when presenting the question; that is, do not use the word "you." Instead, state the issue objectively, offering a contractual agreement or thesis statement that promises to treat your topic fairly and impersonally. Notice in the following example that the audience, a group of college students, is not addressed directly and that the question is explained in detail.

(Q)   College students often ask why so many term papers are assigned. Students, especially those in their junior and senior years, must often submit two to five papers a semester. Preparing these term papers generally involves considerable library research and takes between ten and forty hours to write. In addition, the grades on these papers often make up 25 percent of the final grade for a class. For students who have difficulty writing these term papers, the assignments seem to be unnecessary burdens.

The second and third paragraphs of your Q/A three-paragraph essay answer the question posed in the thesis statement. Special attention must be taken, however, to meet your readers' needs. In other words, offer as much information as your readers need, use words understood by them or define your terms, and avoid unnecessary technical explanations. Don't tell all you know; *tell only what your readers need to know.*

(A)   But term papers are not meant to be busywork or punishment for college students. Rather, they are intended to be meaningful teaching activities, helping students to investigate topics more thoroughly than presented in the textbooks. These texts can neither treat all topics equally or with full details, nor answer all questions that students might want answered. For example, a student in a history class who hopes one day to study law might want to learn as much as possible about the establishment of the English judicial system, yet the assigned text offers only brief discussions on the topic. Or a student in a sociology class who hopes to become a parole officer might want to investigate her home state's parole policies, but the text only generalizes on this topic as it pertains to the nation as a whole. Both students would have an opportunity to pursue their individual interests when researching a term paper.

(A) A second and perhaps more important benefit of writing term papers involves the development of analytical skills. Memorizing information for examinations can't train students to manipulate and evaluate ideas and facts. But by researching a topic and then selecting and organizing materials for an extended discussion, students can develop their abilities to integrate concepts and information to form their own conclusions. For example, a student of literature, researching the influence of Roman drama on Shakespeare, would need to read widely in Roman and Shakespearean drama, compare and contrast techniques used in both types of plays, and be prepared to justify any conclusions drawn. As a result of this work, the student, like any writer of term papers, would not only have a better understanding of the topic, but also a more developed analytical ability.

Putting these three paragraphs together, we have a fully developed essay that presents a question and its answer.

    College students often ask why so many term papers are assigned. Students, especially those in their junior and senior years, must often submit two to five papers a semester. Preparing these term papers generally involves considerable library research and takes between ten and forty hours to write. In addition, the grades on these papers often make up 25 percent of the final grade for a class. For students who have difficulty writing these term papers, the assignments seem to be unnecessary burdens.

    But term papers are not meant to be busywork or punishment for college students. Rather, they are intended to be meaningful teaching activities, helping students to investigate topics more thoroughly than presented in the textbooks. These texts can neither treat all topics equally or with full details, nor answer all questions that students might want answered. For example, a student in a history class who hopes one day to study law might want to learn as much as possible about the establishment of the English judicial system, yet the assigned text offers only brief discussions on the topic. Or a student in a sociology class who hopes to become a parole officer might want to investigate her home state's parole policies, but the text only generalizes on this topic as it pertains to the nation as a whole. Both students would have an opportunity to pursue their individual interests when researching a term paper.

A second and perhaps more important benefit of writing term papers involves the development of analytical skills. Memorizing information for examinations can't train students to manipulate and evaluate ideas and facts. But by researching a topic and then selecting and organizing materials for an extended discussion, students can develop their abilities to integrate concepts and information to form their own conclusions. For example, a student of literature, researching the influence of Roman drama on Shakespeare, would need to read widely in Roman and Shakespearean drama, compare and contrast techniques used in both types of plays, and be prepared to justify any conclusions drawn. As a result of this work, the student, like any writer of term papers, would not only have a better understanding of the topic, but also a more developed analytical ability.

TOPICS

FINN

1. Write a three-paragraph P/S essay on a problem confronting your community for which you have a workable solution. Be sure that the thesis statement is limited sufficiently so that you can explain it fully and discuss your solution in detail. Your audience is a community leader.
2. Write a three-paragraph P/S essay on a minor problem confronting your family for which you have a workable solution. Be sure that the thesis statement is limited, unified, precise, and clear. Your audience is an adult member of your family.

SOLOMON

1. In "We'd Better Not Make Book on U.S. Literacy," Professor Solomon discusses a problem concerning this nation for which he has no solution. Write a three-paragraph P/S essay in which you present the problem of the "new illiteracy" in America and offer your solution to the problem. Your audience is your teacher.
2. Professor Solomon asks why many Americans no longer read books, essays, and magazine articles without pictures. Write a three-paragraph Q/A essay in which you rephrase and explain this question and offer your own answer. Your audience is Professor Solomon.

"VEGETARIANISM"

1. Write a three-paragraph Q/A essay on a question often voiced by an adult to your generation. For example, many people ask college students about

the use of drugs on campus. State your question indirectly and do not use the word "you." Your audience is a middle-aged adult.
2. As individuals with different beliefs and preferences, we are often questioned about what we do or think. Write a three-paragraph Q/A essay on one question frequently asked you about one of your beliefs. Your audience is a friend.

Brainstorming and Shaping

1. Choose your topic and audience.
2. Prepare a data sheet similar to Data Sheet 5-1. Then look at Sample Data Sheet 5-1 to see how it can be filled in.

Data Sheet 5-1   Audience

A. Topic: _____
B. Audience: _____
C. General Characteristics of the Audience:
   1.
   2.
   3.
   4.
   5.
   6.
D. Probable Knowledge of Reading Audience on Topic:
   1. What do my readers probably know about my topic?
      _____
   2. What do my readers need to know about my topic?
      _____
   3. What do my readers need to have reviewed on my topic?
      _____
E. Probable Opinions of Reading Audience on Topic:
   1.
   2.
   3.
F. Five Possible Topic Sentences (a statement of a problem or an indirect question):
   1.
   2.
   3.
   4.
   5.

Sample Data Sheet 5-1 Audience

A. Topic: The high cost of a college education.
B. Audience: High school seniors.
C. General Characteristics of the Audience:
   1. Eager to begin college.
   2. Worried about college costs.
   3. Concerned about ability to succeed in college.
   4. Concerned about ability to work and go to school at the same time.
   5. Aware that parents can't offer much financial assistance.
   6. Concerned that school and work might prohibit much of a social life.
D. Probable Knowledge of Reading Audience on Topic:
   1. What do my readers probably know about my topic? Cost of tuition and books keeps going up. Part-time jobs are scarce. College work takes two or three times as much work as high school work.
   2. What do my readers need to know about my topic? Availability of scholarships. Availability of work-study jobs on campus. Availability of school and bank loans. Tuition costs. Other alternatives.
   3. What do my readers need to have reviewed on my topic? Nothing — they know little facts on the topic.
E. Possible Opinions of Reading Audience on Topic:
   1. A college degree is required for most professional and executive-level jobs.
   2. Only the rich and the poor who are eligible for scholarships can afford good universities.
   3. Only athletes and "A" students get scholarships.
F. Five Possible Topic Sentences (a statement of a problem or an indirect question):
   1. Many of today's college students face severe financial difficulties.
   2. Many universities provide on-campus jobs for their students.
   3. The federal government guarantees educational loans for college students.
   4. The cost of a college education has doubled within the past five years.
   5. Children of middle-class families are eligible for scholarship grants at most universities.

Choosing Materials for Your Solution or Answer Section

1. Choose one of your topic sentences for your three-paragraph P/S or Q/A essay.
2. Look over your answers in parts D and E of your data sheet. Select materials to be included in your essay on the basis of your audience's needs. If your readers hold beliefs different from yours, or if their beliefs are based on misinformation or personal bias, you must make certain that your essay explains your views clearly.
3. Write a brief outline for your essay. A sample outline follows.

Sample Outline
P — Thesis Statement:

Many of today's college students face severe financial difficulties.
1. A four-year degree costs between $15,000 and $40,000.
2. Low- and middle-class families can't afford to subsidize their children's college educations.
3. Savings are seldom adequate for college costs.

S — Summary of First Solution:

Funds are available for some serious students.
1. Scholarships are offered by schools, service clubs, corporations, and government agencies.
2. Loans are given to students by schools and banks.
3. Schools provide on-campus jobs for students.

S — Summary of Second Solution:

Other options are also available.
1. Students can transfer to less expensive schools.
2. Students can reduce their class loads and work part time.

Writing the First Draft

Using your outline as a guide, write your essay. Make certain that you develop each of the two sections of your three-paragraph essay sufficiently so that your readers can fully understand your points of discussion. *Save your data sheet and outline to submit with your final draft.*

Revising the Three-Paragraph Problem/Solution or Question/Answer Essay

Your assignment asked you to write a three-paragraph essay following either the P/S or Q/A pattern of organization. Look over your first draft, data sheet, and outline and then analyze your work according to the basic review questions presented in Unit 1 and the special questions for this assignment.

Basic Revision Questions

1. *Is all my information accurate? Appropriate?*
   Have you bored your readers by repeating information they already know? Have you misinformed your readers by giving them false information? Have you offered all the information needed by your readers?
2. *Is this information organized so that my reader can comprehend what I have said? Could I organize my paper so that it would be more effective?*
   Does your essay have either a "P" and an "S" or a "Q" and an "A"? Are your paragraphs organized clearly?
3. *Do I have a clear, unified focus; that is, does my paragraph telescope in on one major theme?*
   Do your S's or A's relate directly to your P or Q? In developing your essay, have you added any information that does not relate to your topic?
4. *Do I offer sufficient details, examples, or explanations so that my reader gains a complete understanding of what I am discussing?*
   Are all points of discussion fully explained? Do your readers need any additional clarification?

Additional Questions

1. Is my Problem stated as a limited, unified, precise, and clear topic sentence? Is my Question asked indirectly? Is this indirect question limited, unified, precise, and clear?
2. Is my Solution workable? Have I avoided idealistic and impractical solutions?
3. Have I avoided using the pronoun "you" in my indirect question?

EXERCISE 1

Check over your first draft and evaluate your thesis statement. Is it limited, unified, precise, and clear? If you have written a Q/A essay, is your question asked indirectly? Have you addressed your reader? Make any necessary changes in your thesis statement.

EXERCISE 2

Evaluate your three-paragraph essay by asking the review questions posed in this section. If you answered either "No" or "I don't know," you probably need some revision. If you are not sure your information is accurate, check your facts in your school library. If you are not sure you have met your readers' needs, review both your data sheet and your essay to see if your discussion concentrates on what your readers need to know and what they need to have reviewed. If your readers hold opinions based on misinformation or personal bias, you must check to see that you have informed them of the correct facts. Make all necessary adjustments to your essay.

EXERCISE 3

Put your assignment away for a day or two, then review it. You should be able to evaluate your work more accurately now that it is no longer fresh in your mind. Perhaps you could now role play, reading your assignment as if you were your designated readers. Make any revisions necessary.

EXERCISE 4

Write a clean draft of your revised paper in preparation for editing.

Editing

Word Choice: Appropriate Language — Levels of Usage; Clichés

In "We'd Better Not Make Book on U.S. Literacy," Robert Solomon explains his criteria for a good book. For some of us, a good book is one we cannot put down. Solomon disagrees. He feels a good book must make readers stop and think "at every turn." Yet good writing has some key ingredients upon which we can agree because, like a gourmet dish, good writing depends on a careful blending of ingredients. *Diction*, or word choice, is one of these ingredients. As you know, verbs are largely responsible for what happens in the sentence, but nouns share this responsibility. Nouns act as the actors and receivers of action, and adjectives and adverbs add modification to the sentence to enrich the product.

Because nouns, adjectives, and adverbs are the staples of written communication, they must be chosen carefully. But we are often careless about diction. We live in such a busy world that most of us often grab stock terms that cover a range of occasions instead of searching for exact words — the ones that best communicate our thoughts and ideas. How easy it is to say, "The concert was fantastic." But is it accurate to call a concert *fantastic?* After all, we refer to a pizza as fantastic — sometimes in the same sentence with the concert. Yet *fantastic* does not seem to describe either the concert or the pizza. A concert is full of vibrant sound; a pizza is full of succulent flavors. Each has special properties and unique sensory appeal. Using *fantastic* to describe a concert or a pizza is not wrong; it is, however, *colloquial*. Colloquial language uses the words and expressions that are acceptable and even appropriate in informal conversation. For example, to say "She is a crab, and her bad mood is driving me crazy" would be acceptable when talking to a close friend but not in an essay for an educated audience.

Slang, that is, novel, colorful expressions that reflect a group's special experience, is also inappropriate for formal writing. All groups have their slang. Impromptu speakers often *wing it* and vegetarians are *into health*. Yet slang is often inventive and vivid for those who understand it. For example, the Yiddish word *nebbish* means "poor thing," an unfortunate, mousey, little person. It is a word without an equivalent in English but whose sound somehow fits its meaning. However, one must understand Yiddish for the word to communicate. Another problem is that slang often does not stand the test of time. For example, in 1950, the word *cool* meant uninvolved or casual. Today, if this term is used at all, it means that everything is fine, or *mellow*. How many times have you heard a joke that depended on a slang word for its humor and you did not understand the joke because you did not understand the word? Comedians and audiences have suffered more than once because of this problem. Unless you are repeating conversation, slang should be used with care and restraint, for people tend to make judgments about a speaker who overdoes colloquial language and slang.

Jargon, another relative of colloquialism and slang, is the specialized vocabulary of any group, such as psychologists, educators, or engineers. Jargon is also vague, inflated, often meaningless language used to express relatively simple ideas, for example, "I loved his speech. His ideas are *cosmic* and *transcendent*" sounds impressive until one examines what a *cosmic* or *transcendent* idea is. The sentence is full of meaningless words, although we see such vague usage in all kinds of professional writing. The writer who indulges in such jargon runs the risk of saying nothing to an audience, or at least severely limiting the audience's reaction.

Another trap to avoid in your writing is *pompous diction*. Like jargon, this type of language is inflated, bloated with big words that say little. For example, "Juvenile delinquency is the natural concomitant of growing up, a result of a syndrome of symptoms" says nothing more than "Juvenile delinquency has many causes." This statement does not reveal a startling discovery and is not even meaningful, although in a lecture the often-inflated pronouncement sounds impressive. Yet the sentence is not "wrong" any more than jargon or slang is wrong; it is, however, imprecise, conveys little information, and makes writing dull.

Perhaps the most difficult trap to avoid in writing is the use of clichés — worn out, dull word combinations most of us have heard and read repeatedly. These word combinations are so familiar to us that we use them every day without even being aware of doing so. In fact, one way to answer "How do I recognize a cliché?" is to check your writing for these comfortable, pat little word combinations that come easily to you. In other words, if a combination of words comes quickly to mind and sounds familiar, it is probably a cliché. But you need not distort language or use exotic descriptions just to be original, since familiar combinations are sometimes useful. Most of the time, however, fresh, clear word choices make fresh, clear writing.

If you use the same words that hundreds of writers before you have chosen, would readers have any incentive to read your material? Of course not. This is one reason to avoid clichés as much as possible. For example, we have all heard people described as *tough as nails* or *slow as molasses*. And we have all probably at one time or another looked into a mirror and thought that we were getting *fat as a pig* or even *over the hill*. These phrases are comfortable, easy word clusters overused by thousands of people thousands of times. We use clichés because they are familiar and easy, but this same familiarity and ease can often make clichés difficult to recognize and, therefore, difficult to eliminate from our speech and writing. However, the elimination of clichés is vital to good writing because clichés bore your readers. For example, "The sun, a red ball of fire, sunk slowly into the sea" evokes a kind of plastic greeting-card response from an audience. How many bright, red sunsets have you read about? Subjects such as sunsets, the moon, the beach, flowers, and love have been written about so often that the danger of using clichés when describing these subjects is very great. Remember that certain subjects themselves are as overdone and overworked as the clichés that describe them.

Finally, remember that your diction should be consistent. Do not mix jargon or slang with formal language. Such a mixture jars the audience and seriously detracts from the effectiveness of your communication. Sometimes politicians, for example, will deliver a campaign speech decorated with slang, jargon, or colloquialisms that are specially directed to the particular group addressed. They do so to get closer to the audience, but this tactic rarely works; more often it causes the audience to laugh or mistrust the speaker's intentions.

EXERCISE 1

Colloquial phrases and words are italicized in the following sentences. Rewrite the sentences and substitute more formal diction.

1. I am *getting really mad*.
2. She is a *pretty terrific* person.
3. The promotion is *really fantastic* and she is *really into* her job.
4. There are *lots of* good friends to choose from.
5. He made a *really tremendous* breakfast, a late but *terrific* lunch, and a *fantastic* dinner.

EXERCISE 2

1. Change the tone of the following paragraph to a tone suitable for a note from a fifteen-year-old boy to a fifteen-year-old girl who scarcely knows him. Use your dictionary as you work through this exercise.
2. Change the tone of this paragraph to a tone suitable for a note written by a twenty-four-year-old man, a college graduate, to his twenty-four-year-old ex-fiancée, also a college graduate. Again, use your dictionary as you work through this exercise.

   I have been desirous of commencing communication with you but have endeavored to divert my attention to more profitable and intellectual pursuits. I have refrained from female companionship and have remained in my own safe edifice. But I have had a sufficient amount of punishment, and I am fearful that I am supplicating. In fact, I am all too cognizant of it. However, I can no longer disguise my emotional reactions.

EXERCISE 3

Substitute appropriate nouns, adjectives, or adverbs to make appropriate diction for an educated audience.

1. His ideas were *too heavy* for me to deal with.
2. My stereo is *really far out*.
3. Go *interface* with him so we can have some real *input* on the lack of *output* around here.
4. I wish you'd *hang out* with me. I am lonesome.
5. I dislike being with her because she is *really out to lunch*.
6. You are *nuts* to *buy what he says*.
7. John is *into* art and *needs his own space*.

EXERCISE 4

Revise any ten of the clichés in the following list and use your new phrases in a sentence.

Example
quiet as a mouse
quiet as hair growing
The audience grew as quiet as hair growing.

fat as a pig
thin as a rail
pale as a sheet
white as snow
old as the hills
smart as a whip
sharp as a tack
dead as a doornail
tough as nails
like putty in his hand
hard as a rock

fuzzy as a kitten
black as pitch
sticks like glue
clear as crystal
quick as a wink
slow as molasses
fit as a fiddle
innocent as a lamb
sick as a dog
nutty as a fruitcake
brown as a berry

EXERCISE 5

Both "The Magic of Memory" by Laurence Cherry and "Symbol of Success" by Anthony Brandt use clichés. Brandt uses clichés associated with the Horatio Alger myth ("rags to riches" and "climbed the ladder of success"). In the article on memory, there are such clichés as "on the right track" and "standing on the brink." In a few sentences, discuss whether or not these clichés are effectively used.

EXERCISE 6

Write a four- or five-sentence paragraph in which you use related clichés and platitudes. See how many you can make work together. Discuss the effectiveness of the paragraph.

EXERCISE 7 Edit Your Essay

Review your paragraph and check it for appropriate diction. Have you used colloquialisms? For example, have you used the intensive *really* incorrectly? Have you used slang? Jargon? Pompous diction? Make the necessary changes in nouns, adjectives, and adverbs to prepare for your final draft.

Sentence Structure: Combining through Relative Clauses

In addition to coordination and subordination, there is a third important sentence-combining technique that you learned early in your education — the *relative clause*.

> The fund *that* Fortune *Magazine rated highest last year* lost money this year.

Notice that this combined sentence is smoother and clearer than its two component sentences would be if set apart.

> *Fortune* Magazine rated a fund highest last year. The fund lost money this year.

Like the subordinate clause, the relative clause is produced by inserting one sentence into a second sentence. Introducing this inserted relative clause is a word that makes the clause dependent, that is, establishes it as a modifier of all or part of the second sentence. Note the introductory word and the modifying clause in each of the following sentences.

> *Examples*
> Sentences with Added Subordinate Clauses
>
> The student took beginning economics *because his uncle recommended it.*
> He thought he could get a "B" *if he studied hard.*
> He scheduled his time *so that he could study two hours after every class.*

Sentences with Added Relative Clauses

Unfortunately, he was often late to the class, *which started at 8:00 a.m.*

The class was taught by a professor *who was stimulating but disorganized.*

The class *that he liked best* turned out to be his economics class.

The first three sentences combine two simple sentences by means of subordinators, thereby producing modifier clauses that function as adverbs in the sentence. In other words, these clauses modify the verbs of the main sentence. The last three sentences, however, combine two simple sentences by substituting a relative pronoun — *which, who,* and *that* — for a noun in the inserted sentence, thereby producing modifier clauses that function as adjectives, the modifiers of nouns and pronouns. Note that a simple adverb can substitute for the whole subordinate clause and a simple adjective can substitute for the whole relative clause.

Example
Adverb Clause Replaced by Simple Adverb

He thought he could get a "B" *easily.*

He scheduled his time *well.*

The adverb simplifies the sentence, but the clause makes it more precise and interesting.

Example
Adjective Clause Replaced by Single Adjective

Unfortunately, he was often late to the *early* class.

The class was taught by a *stimulating, disorganized* professor.

In the first example, the single adjective simplifies the sentence, but the clause adds detail that makes the sentence more precise and interesting. In the second example, both sentences offer the same information, but they contrast in that the adjectives make the sentence more concise, while the clause makes the sentence more drawn out, dwelling more on the characteristics of the class. Both subordinate clauses and relative clauses, then, are products of sentence combining that make one sentence a modifier of another sentence; this modifier can be a clause or a single word.

EXERCISE 1

In the following sentences, substitute a subordinate clause for all italicized adverbs and a relative clause for all italicized adjectives. Make the clause give the same general idea but more specific detail than the single word.

Examples

SINGLE WORD ADVERB

The two murderers confessed casually.

ADVERB CLAUSE SUBSTITUTION

The two murderers confessed as if killing a human being were no different from walking across the street or drinking a cup of coffee.

1. We assume that man can control *atomic* forces. (adjective)

    We assume man can control forces *that* _____

2. The unchecked spread of crime is like a *destructive* cancer. (adjective)

    The unchecked spread of crime is like a cancer *that* _____

3. Vegetarianism is one way of eating a *nutritious* diet. (adjective)

    Vegetarianism is one way of eating a diet *that* _____

4. Some vegetarians *necessarily* refuse to use fur, leather, and wool. (adverb)

    Some vegetarians refuse to use fur, leather, and wool *because* _____
    _____

5. The human body can *usually* create most amino acids. (adverb)

    The human body can create most amino acids *if* _____

6. Americans seem to fear *abstract* theories. (adjective)

    Americans seem to fear theories *that* _____

7. The children sang *loudly*. (adverb)

    The children sang *as if* _____

8. Nobody likes to listen to a *scratchy* record. (adjective)

    Nobody likes to listen to a record *that* _____

9. College students *generally* study hard. (adverb)

    College students study hard *when* _____

10. A good book should be read *carefully*. (adverb)

    A good book should be read *as if* _____

The relative pronouns *who, which,* and *that* introduce relative clauses by substituting for a noun that is repeated in both sentences that are to be combined. *Who,* or *whom* (if the noun is an object), substitutes for people; *which* substitutes for animals, things, or objects; and *that* substitutes for either. Notice, however, that the relative pronoun must immediately follow the noun that it modifies.

Examples
1. *The History of Jazz* is the most popular music class at the college.

    The History of Jazz is taught only once a year.

The History of Jazz, which is taught only once a year, is the most popular music class at the college.

2. *Professor Bartly* teaches music.

   Professor Bartly will retire next year.

   Professor Bartly, who teaches music, will retire next year.

3. The college gave a teaching award to *Professor Bartly*.

   A national magazine wrote an article about *Professor Bartly*.

   The college gave a teaching award to Professor Bartly, about whom a national magazine wrote an article.

4. Professor Bartly had a cluttered *office*.

   Professor Bartly worked in his *office* every afternoon.

   Professor Bartly had a cluttered *office that* he worked in every afternoon.

EXERCISE 2

Select one of the relative pronouns (*who, whom, which,* or *that*) and use it to combine sentences. Substitute the correct word for the repeated noun in one of the following sentences:

Example
Isaac Asimov called the United States "a nation of illiterates."

Isaac Asimov received letters accusing him of being elitist.

Isaac Asimov, *who* called the United States "a nation of illiterates," received letters accusing him of being elitist.

1. *Television programs* can make us feel sorry for suffering persons.

   Television programs rarely make us think.

2. *People* think.

   People read.

3. *People* cannot easily absorb *iron* from plants.

   People can easily absorb *iron* from meat.

4. Many people eat a *combination of beans and rice*.

   The combination of beans and rice supplies needed amino acids.

5. *Vitamin B12* is stored in the liver.

   Vitamin B12 is water soluble.

6. *Total vegetarians* do not get enough Vitamin B12.

   Total vegetarians should take Vitamin B12 supplements.

7. *Football players* need to be in top condition.

   Football players exert a great deal of energy.

8. Some people never drink *coffee, tea, or Coca-Cola.*
   Coffee, tea, and Coca-Cola contain caffeine.
9. *The lady* sneezed all night.
   The lady was allergic to house dust.
10. *The senators* returned home to campaign for reelection.
    The senators gave many political speeches.

Another important characteristic of a relative clause is that one or more of its words can sometimes be omitted, making the sentence more concise yet still retaining its meaning. Because clarity and conciseness are elements of good writing, you may want to take advantage of this technique.

1. If a relative pronoun is followed by a noun or pronoun, it can often be deleted.

   The class [that] he liked best turned out to be his economics class.

2. If a relative pronoun serves as a subject and is followed by a *be* verb, both words can be omitted.

   Mrs. Ramsey is scolding her son, [who is] a football player.

   Our new Dodge Aries, [which is] brown and tan, needs some new paint on its left front fender.

3. If a relative pronoun serves as a subject and is followed by a *be* verb plus an action verb, both the pronoun and the *be* verb can be omitted.

   Max wants to sell the outboard motor [which is] lying on the garage floor.

   The speech [that was] delivered before the legislature condemned the governor.

EXERCISE 3

In the following sentences, eliminate the relative pronoun and, where appropriate, forms of *be*, in order to make more concise sentences.

1. Vitamin B12, which is deficient in vegetarian diets, is produced by microorganisms.
2. Atomic reactors, which are often considered dangerous, are capable of producing cheap energy.
3. The book that he read last year has been made into a movie.
4. The boy ran crying to his father, who was standing at the front door.
5. Yesterday, my pet chicken escaped from her coop, which is made of rusty wire and cardboard.

6. Jonathan, who was the friend of David, was the son of King Saul.

Both relative and subordinate clauses sometimes appear incorrectly in student papers as sentence fragments. However, reading the paper aloud and looking carefully at the structure can help you identify these kinds of fragments. Always remember that a relative clause and a subordinate clause cannot stand alone; they must be connected to full sentences.

EXERCISE 4

Most of the following are fragments of sentences. Identify which are complete sentences and which are fragments. Add a sentence to the fragments in order to make them complete.

Examples
Fragment: Which she resented.
    Her teacher gave her the lowest grade in the class, which she resented.

Complete: The copper calendar was made by the oldest monk, who had lived in the Tibetan Mountains for forty years.

1. Whom I liked the best.
2. I sold my car to the man who answered my ad.
3. That she knew would become dangerous.
4. Nobody loves her more than I do.
5. Which I felt was rather silly.

EXERCISE 5

Review your essay. Can any sentences be combined to create better focus, emphasis, or clarity? Make any changes you feel would improve your work.

Punctuation: Midbranch Commas

Now that you have practiced using commas to set off the left branch, the right branch, and words in a series, you are ready to focus on comma usage in the midbranch. As you know, the midbranch contains the kernel sentence and its modifiers.

	Tea contains tannic acid.	
left	midbranch	right
Yesterday,	my pet boa constrictor greeted my aunt	with a tight hug around her neck.
left	midbranch	right

	Mother, a lady of excellent taste, never wore slacks in public.	
left	midbranch	right

These midbranch modifiers, like left- and right-branch modifiers, can be single words, phrases, or clauses and are frequently set off by commas. In the midbranch, however, you have few punctuation choices to make; most comma usage is governed by specific rules. As these rules often confuse even very experienced writers, you should study the following discussion and examples most carefully before completing this unit's exercises.

To use commas correctly and effectively in the midbranch, you must always remember the difference between free and bound modifiers. *Free modifiers* describe, limit, explain, or rename the nouns, pronouns, and verbs of kernel sentences. They offer complementary information or details, that is, they expand a sentence but are not necessary parts of a sentence. In other words, these free modifiers can be taken out of a kernel sentence without damaging the sentence.

Example

John, *who is eighteen*, enrolled in college.

John enrolled in college.

Bound modifiers, in contrast, are necessary parts of a sentence. In other words, if you take a bound modifier out of a sentence, you change the intended meaning of the sentence.

Example

The man *in the black suit* witnessed the murder.

The man witnessed the murder.

Notice that in the first example "who is eighteen" is not necessary to the intended meaning of the sentence; the writer has simply given the reader some extra information. But in the second example, "in the black suit" is a vital part of the sentence's meaning. The writer apparently wishes to point out a specific person, not just any man.

> Rule 1. Set off all midbranch words in a series with commas. (Review Editing and Punctuation in Unit 4.)
>
> *Examples*
>
> The tubby, wooly sheepdog waddled into the wall.
>
> I sold my car, my stereo, and my skis to John.
>
> Rule 2. Set off all midbranch words, phrases, and clauses that act as free modifiers with commas.

Examples
1. Mary, a sophomore at Purdue University, changed her major for the third time.

2. The American cowboy's fame, a mixture of fact and fiction, has spread even to China.

3. You, Ellen, must clean your room!

4. My teacher gave me, a misunderstood and overworked student, an "F" in chemistry.

5. The boy ran, slipping and sliding, across the frozen pond.

6. Abraham Lincoln, who hoped for a peaceful reconstruction period, was killed soon after the end of the Civil War.

7. My father, a man who hates to reveal his emotions in public, squirmed throughout my wedding.

Notice that in all these examples, *two* commas are used — one *before* the free modifier and one *after* the free modifier. If only one comma were used, the meanings of the sentences would not be clear and many of the sentences would have been fragmented; that is, the subjects would have been cut off from their verbs.

Examples
John, a cello player joined the orchestra.

John a cello player, joined the orchestra.

Remember to always surround midbranch free modifiers with a *pair* of commas.

Rule 3. Do not set off bound modifiers with commas.

Examples
1. The car that clipped my left fender was a blue 1978 Celica.

2. Diets without adequate nutrients lead to physical deterioration of the body.

3. The reason for my anger is his refusal to pay back my loan.

4. The teenager found guilty of murder was given a life sentence.

EXERCISE 1
Examine the following sentences for comma errors. Add any commas needed and cross out any commas that do not belong. Be ready to defend your decisions.

1. Sleeping late, in the morning has become a bad habit.
2. The child sucking a red lollipop sat on her grandfather's lap throughout the flight.
3. Nobody, not even you should get something for nothing.
4. Carlos Dias a writer for the *Washington Post,* covers the Supreme Court.
5. My dog, a black, tan and white mixed-breed has the ears of a cocker, the tail of a collie and the snout of a boxer.
6. My friend whom I've known since kindergarten has just entered medical school.
7. The toad called out hoarsely and insistently to his fiancée.
8. Ron Cey diving in front of the third base bag tagged out the base runner.
9. Eating popcorn smothered in butter and sprinkled ever so lightly with salt is heaven.
10. The lawnmower eating its way across the grass, spit out sprays of grass pebbles and dust.
11. Jiro tried and tried to catch the mouse running throughout the house.
12. Changing a typewriter ribbon even for an expert typist can be a messy affair.
13. The salesman showed me, a doubting customer who always expects something to be overpriced the leather coat.
14. Jerry Dennis and Ken saw, or thought they saw a ghost flying through the attic.
15. Never never and never will I now then or ever drink sip or taste that smelly brew.

EXERCISE 2

Review your writing assignment to see if you have used commas correctly and effectively. Make all necessary changes.

Preparing the Final Copy and Proofreading

Follow the manuscript conventions listed under the section on proofreading at the end of Unit 1. Use one side of the page only. Check for correct margins and double spacing; center the title at the top of the page; indent the first sentence of each paragraph; and correct any errors neatly with correction fluid, clean erasures, or lines drawn neatly through the mistakes.

Now you are ready to proofread. Read the final copy aloud, slowly and carefully. This is an important step. Sometimes it is surprising the errors one can hear. Ask yourself the following questions.

1. Are all the words spelled correctly? Are hyphens at the ends of lines placed correctly between the syllables of divided words? If you are uncertain about either your spelling of certain words or the division of any word, check your dictionary.
2. Have you made any accidental changes in your text or omitted any words?
3. Is the punctuation correct?

UNIT 6
Exposition: Comparison and Contrast

READING:
Exposition: Comparison and Contrast

Reading Strategies: Reading and Recognizing Transitions

In Unit 2 you practiced finding the controlling idea in an individual paragraph, a passage, and an entire essay. Next, in Unit 3, you improved your reading comprehension by recognizing various types of supporting ideas. You may still, however, need to find some specific ways to follow the train of thought in a paragraph or an essay. For example, how can you recognize *specifically* when an author has finished stating a generalization and has begun to support, explain, or develop it? How can you know when an author has completed discussion of one main idea and moved on to another? And how can you tell when an author "shifts gears" to show a different or opposite idea? You need answers to all these questions, not only to help you locate the major ideas but also to see how the writer develops them.

Authors of expository writing use signals to indicate that they are moving from one idea or point to another. Such a signal is called a *transition*, a word that comes from the Latin verb *transire*, meaning "to go across." Writers use transitions to go across from one idea to another or to form a link of some kind between ideas. Once you become actively aware of transitions, either as single words or as phrases, you will find yourself more effectively locating main ideas and then understanding the flow or development of a discussion.

EXERCISE 1

Even before learning the specific types of transitions that authors use, you can find these signals; look closely at the previous paragraphs and mark any word or words that look like a transition as defined so far. Why did you mark them? What do they seem to do?

After doing Exercise 1, you probably realize that you already know a good deal about transitions. But now if you examine the various specific categories of transitions, you can become expert in the many ways transitions work, both for the author to make meaning clear and for you to comprehend that meaning. You can even speed up your textbook or other college reading once you are aware of these signals and know how they work, for you can then follow discussions more clearly and read through ideas more rapidly. Following are lists of some commonly used transitions, grouped according to the kinds of signals they give the reader. Be aware that these words can appear not only at the beginning of sentences but also within sentences. Note that the same words can be used for different purposes; therefore, some words fall into more than one category. Notice also that the coordinators, subordinators, and transitional adverbs listed in Unit 3 are some of the common transitions used. The main thing to remember is that these words signal an important change to the reader.

Another important point to remember is that the following lists are not all-inclusive; in your college reading you will find more signals to add to these lists. And a final point to keep in mind is that you may find these additional transitions because of their use in context; that is, some words will stand out as signals because of the way they are used in that particular discussion. Probably the most satisfying result of practicing this "signal word" reading strategy, as well as the strategies in previous units, is a growing awareness of how authors use language to communicate with their audience — you!

Signal Words

Among the most valuable transitions for you to locate are the *signal words* that tell you, the reader, that something is especially important.

this, that, these, those, one	and
-*est* forms of adjectives (safest, greatest, highest)	indeed
	despite
main	moreover
vital	even though
key	at any rate
significant	naturally
chief	above all
central	still
principal	of course

primary	especially
major	not only . . . but also
distinctive	should be (remembered, noted, observed)
finally	
just as	most (important, noteworthy, obvious)

Illustration Words

Illustration words signal that examples or illustrations will follow to clarify, define, explain, or develop an idea or a generalization.

that is (to say)	such as
for instance	as, as when
the following	to illustrate
for example	specifically

Order or Time Sequence Words

Sequence words indicate that the author is arranging things according to their order of importance or the order in which they happened.

first, second	soon, as soon as
next	when, whenever
then	subsequently
finally	presently
ultimately	here, there
most important	from . . . to, until
before, after	

Addition Words

Addition words tell you that the writer's idea will continue in the same direction, with more points or details added.

in addition	next (reason, quality, example, event)
also	
and	moreover
another	again
furthermore	other (reasons, qualities)

Comparison Words

Comparison words signal that two or more things are the same or similar.

similarly	and
likewise	just as . . . so

both
each
alike
also

comparatively
can be compared
same

Contrast Words

Contrast words signal that the writer will show an opposite view or change the direction of a previously stated idea. Or the writer may slightly alter or modify an earlier statement; the writer "shifts gears."

however
but
in contrast
instead
on the contrary
on the other hand
conversely
each
neither . . . nor
either . . . or
then . . . now
-er (forms of adjectives) than

still
yet
nevertheless
even though
although, though
despite
different from, than
whereas
while
more, less than
one . . . the other
some . . . others

Cause-Effect Words

Cause-effect words signal that one thing caused another to happen. Sometimes a cause-effect relationship is shown within a sentence that contains this kind of signal.

because
since
when, whenever
after
consequently
hence

then
if . . . then
thus
as a result
therefore
from . . . to, until

Summary Words

Summary words signal the conclusion of a topic. Sometimes they indicate the most important point within a paragraph or at the end of a longer discussion.

finally
last, last of all

in brief
again

therefore
hence
to summarize, to sum up
in conclusion, to conclude
to reiterate

to repeat
above all
most important
ultimately

Heading and Subheading Words

Heading and subheading words, often set apart from the text and printed in different types, are signals found in many textbooks. This transitional device, like all the others listed above, shows clearly that the author is moving from one idea to another. In addition, by presenting the heading in a different type, the author emphasizes the main or controlling idea of the ensuing section.

EXERCISE 1

Examine this unit and list the headings and subheadings. Mark the sections assigned to your class. In your own words summarize the main idea and supporting ideas of one section.

EXERCISE 2

Underline the transitional words in the following paragraphs. Identify the types of transitions used and describe how they help to clarify the ideas.

1. Rodeo grounds differ. Some are floodlit indoor arenas. Some are still dirt fields flanked by sun-bleached grandstands. But broncs with names like Midnight Black and Widow Maker create menacing echoes in Pendleton as in Oklahoma City when they rear and kick in imprisoning wooden chutes. Riders in big hats ease down on their backs with exactly the same fatalistic caution in Cheyenne as in Ellensburg or Calgary. And every crowd breathes tension: to be broken in seconds by disaster — as when a horse named Bay Beggar threw Deb Copenhaver in one celebrated spill and kicked him in the face as he hung from one stirrup — or by the kind of wild triumph a man reflects while surviving with grace on a beast gone mad.

    — O'Neil, *"Modernized Ritual of Rodeo"*

2. Early American engineers, then, reshaped the British railway and track structure. It should be noted that at the very time these developments were under way, other engineers modified and redesigned British locomotives and cars. Here again, the goal was to change only that which was necessary to adapt the mechanism to local needs. English inventors had developed the locomotive from the cumbersome steam carriage of 1804 to a fast and well proportioned unit of motive power of 1829. The general arrangement remained fixed from that date until the end of steam locomotion in 1960. The horizontal, multitubular boiler, separate firebox, power transmission by connecting rods (rather than gears), and blast-pipe

exhaust remained fundamental. Of course, the locomotive grew dramatically in size, and many auxiliary appliances were added over the years, but the basic plan stayed the same.

— White, *"Rails: From Old World to New"*

3. When I was a boy, my father's silence was one of the great mysteries of my life. Not only did he fail to answer when I spoke to him, he didn't even seem to hear me. There was no sign, no flicker in his face, to show that I had spoken, and I sometimes wondered whether I actually had. I used to stand there and listen, trying to catch the echo of my voice.

If I could have got my father's eye, could have looked him squarely in the face, I might have compelled him to answer me, or at least to acknowledge that I had spoken, but it was impossible to do this because he had a way of turning his head to one side, like a horse. I would walk around him, like someone circling a statue in a museum. Just as in medieval paintings people hold their heads to one side, so in my memory my father's face is always turned.

— Broyard, *"The Silent Generation: An Essay"*

EXERCISE 3

Choose a one-page selection from one of your college textbooks. Note the transitions you find and their type. If you find any transitions not listed here, write the entire sentence and then the transition type you think it is in your text or notebook.

Cloze Exercise — Focus on Adjectives

In Unit 5 you reviewed the functions of coordinators and nouns in a sentence. With these functions in mind, you were better able to fixate your eyes on meaningful phrases and to anticipate what comes next in a discussion. Another type of word that has a distinct function in a sentence is the *adjective*. Adjectives, as mentioned in Units 2 and 5, modify nouns; that is, they describe or limit nouns in the expansion of ideas in a sentence.

Adjectives are found in three positions in a sentence:

1. They appear *before* nouns:

    black ink, *funny* clown

2. They appear *after* nouns:

    a man, *fat* and *ugly*

    the girl, *laughing* at her puppy

3. They appear *after* a "to be" verb:

    The puppy is *silly*.

    The doctor is *puzzled*.

Recognizing the function and positions of adjectives in a sentence can assist you in reading effectively, for you can then quickly fixate on *noun phrases,* the units of meaning that include nouns and their modifiers.

In the following Cloze exercise, certain nouns, adjectives, and coordinators have been omitted. As you fill in the spaces, keep in mind both the functions and possible positions of these three types of words. On completion of the exercise, be prepared to justify your choices of words for each space.

EXERCISE 1

Definitions are often vital parts of written communication. Writers can't always use _____ from their own vocabularies _____ expect that their designated _____ understand. Technical words are _____ for many nonprofessional readers; _____ words can be very _____ for readers unfamiliar with _____, physics, or biology; and _____ nouns can mean different _____ to different people. In _____ words, good writers make _____ that all the specialized _____ they use in term _____, essays, letters, and magazine _____ have meaning to their _____.

Words and the Language: The Structure of Words — Prefixes

Your reading vocabulary can be further enlarged if you learn the most common prefixes, those parts of word structures that alter the meaning of roots, either through extending the meaning (*pre+judge* = *prejudge,* to judge beforehand without sufficient evidence) or through changing the meaning to its opposite (*dis+respect* = *disrespect,* a lack of respect). Learning to recognize prefixes is much easier than learning to recognize roots, because there are few prefixes in English and the same ones occur over and over.

Examine Table 6-1, which shows some commonly used prefixes, and then complete the following exercises.

EXERCISE 1

Using four or five of the prefixes listed in Table 6-1, list as many words as you can think of.

Example:
dis- disallow, disappear, disapprove, disbelieve, disjoin, disinterest

EXERCISE 2

From one of the reading selections, find five words that have prefixes for their first syllable. Check your dictionary; the first syllable *may* be part of the basic word form rather than a prefix.

Table 6-1   Some Commonly Used Prefixes

Prefix	Meaning	Example	Definition
a-	on	aboard	on board
ab-	from, down	aberration	a deviation from the proper or normal
ad- (also ac-, af-, ag-, al-, am-, an-, ap-, ar-, as-)	to	advise	to offer advice to
ante-	before	antebellum	before the war
anti-, ant-	against, opposite	antiseptic	pertaining to the destruction of disease-causing agents
bi-, bin-	two	bilateral	having two sides
com-, con-	with	convene	to meet formally
de-	from, down from, away, put down	deject	to destroy the spirit
dis-	not, away, lack, opposite	distrust	lack of trust
en-, em-	in, into, on	embark	to cause to board a vessel, set out on a venture
ex-	out (of, from), beyond	exalt	to raise in position
in-, im-	in, into, within	implant	to set in firmly
in-	not, without	inaction	lack of action
multi-	many, much	multicolored	of many colors
neo-	new, recent form	neophyte	a beginner, a new convert
pre-	earlier time, before	prearrange	to arrange in advance
pro-	forward, forth, in favor	proclaim	to announce publicly
re-	back, again	recall	to call back, order to return
semi-	partly, half, twice	semicircle	half a circle
sub-	under, inferior	submarine	under the sea
tri-	three, third	trident	three-pronged spear
un-	not	unattached	not attached
uni-	single, one	unicorn	fabled horse-like creature with one horn

EXERCISE 3

From the list at the left, add appropriate prefixes to the words on the right, checking your dictionary to be sure that the word form you have created is correct.

im-	content	act
sub-	annual	determine
pro-	tie	merge
bi-	pay	necessary
un-	standard	part
pre-	lighten	rate
re-	band	
dis-		
en-		

Define each word before adding the prefix and then again after adding it.

READINGS: SELECTION ONE

The Silent Generation: An Essay
by Anatole Broyard

Ideas to Think About

1. Do you like to talk or debate with your parents? Why? What do you discuss with them? Is there a generation gap blocking true communication? Explain.
2. Notice the many series of illustrations Broyard uses to prove his point that the generations are different.
3. As you read, note transitionals that signal contrasting ideas or new points of discussion.

Vocabulary

Look at each word as it is used in the article. (The number in parentheses indicates the paragraph in which it appears.) First, try to understand the meaning from the way it is used in the sentence. Second, use any clues to meaning through the structure of the word. Then, use the dictionary to clarify the meaning.

polemical (3)
dialectical (3)
hypothetical (3)
syllogistic (3)

incompatibility (7)
medieval (12)
credibility (19)
effusions (19)

The Silent Generation: An Essay

Anatole Broyard is a writer for the *New York Times*.

New York — I'm sandwiched in silence. My father was not a talker and neither is my son. Talking seems to be going out of style and this worries me, because I'm used to it. My generation talked all the time. We thought we would change the world with talk.

Talking shaped our faces, marked them around the eyes and mouth, sharpened, mobilized, grooved them. We licked our lips with speech.

You could parse[1] our faces. We had simple, declarative, interrogative, compound-sentence faces. Analytical, polemical,° dialectical,° hypothetical,° syllogistic° faces. Talk was our life sentence.

The books we read were talky: Dostoevsky, Lawrence, Mann, Joyce, Céline. We saw the world as an enormous question put to us and our first

---
[1] Analyze grammatically.

thought was to get a word in edgewise, to make ourselves heard. Later on, a few of us lay on Freudian couches and tried to talk ourselves free of talk.

Just as some people who are poor as children grow up with a lust for money, I grew up hungry for talk. My closest friends had immigrant parents who were uncomfortable with the language we learned in school and so there was not much talk in their homes either.

We were salesmen, my friends and I, talking up the world. We lived by description. There was less money around then and we furnished our lives with talk. In the Greenwich Village bar where we hung out, talk was free lunch.

We talked our women into loving us, and when we stopped talking to them they divorced us, calling it mental cruelty or incompatibility.°

Talk was our caste or class symbol. Certain words were like old school ties. Once when I was suffocating with loneliness on a boat in the Pacific, I met a man who used the word ontological[2] and I fell on him like a long-lost brother.

Because I yearned so long for it, talk has always meant too much to me. I have a terrible need to confide, to leap into intimacy. My eagerness in conversation startles people and they edge away, as if they are afraid I might kiss them.

My father's generation was secure in its convictions, and my son's has abandoned itself to ambiguities. I alone, it seems to me, am obliged to confront the palpable.

When I was a boy, my father's silence was one of the great mysteries of my life. Not only did he fail to answer when I spoke to him, he didn't even seem to hear me. There was no sign, no flicker in his face, to show that I had spoken, and I sometimes wondered whether I actually had. I used to stand there and listen, trying to catch the echo of my voice.

If I could have got my father's eye, could have looked him squarely in the face, I might have compelled him to answer me, or at least to acknowledge that I had spoken, but it was impossible to do this because he had a way of turning his head to one side, like a horse. I would walk around him, like someone circling a statue in a museum. Just as in medieval° paintings people hold their heads to one side, so in my memory my father's face is always turned.

There came a time at last when he couldn't look away. He was in a hospital bed and it would have been too painful to turn his head because the illness had spread to his bones. When I placed myself in his line of sight, he had to see me.

It was our last chance to talk and I felt all that I had to say thrilling my

---

[2] About the study of the nature of things.

nerves. I had a lifetime of small and large talk saved up. I took a great breath, opened my mouth like an opera singer, but only a sigh came out, because talk doesn't keep. Everything was concreted into lumps, like stuff left too long in the refrigerator. At the very end, I told my father that I would miss him. I did not say that I had always missed him.

My son, who is 15, has a silent face, like a cowboy or a sea captain, like a skier or a flyer. His face is smooth and idealized, like a sculpture. It looks airbrushed. If I were to ask him why he doesn't talk to me, he might answer, "About what."

In his school, on the soccer team, my son is taught to accept victory and defeat in silence, with what the Greeks called apatheia, a word rather like our understatement. My son is an athlete of understatement.

When he does speak, it reminds me of the way I learned to read in speedreading school. He takes words not singly, but in groups. His mind travels rapidly down the page of his speech without pleasure.

I suppose that, for his generation, too many words have been spoken. Talk lies over everything like dust. Fathers are nice guys who talk too much, who are nervous about definitions.

He makes me wonder whether talk has lost its credibility,° whether it has become devalued, like money and sex. It may be that talking was simply a fussy stage in our evolution, a talking age, like a stone age or a tool-using age. It seems to me that talking was rather like a pointillist or Impressionist period in the art of living, and we have moved on to an age of abstraction or action painting. And then history has edited away our effusions.°

I realize that I want to stuff my son with words, the way my mother tried to stuff me with food. Am I afraid he's going to starve, or that I will? I have a sense that he doesn't need talk; that, like the Oedipus complex, talk is a neurosis our culture no longer induces.

Discussion

1. You are already familiar with the use of simile and metaphor in description, but similes and metaphors are also an excellent way to show comparisons and contrasts. Notice the author's use of metaphor in the opening sentence of his thesis statement. "I'm sandwiched in silence." Find at least four other uses of figurative language that make a contrast clearer to the reader.
2. In discussing what his generation looked like, Broyard says, "You could parse our faces." "Parse" is an unusual verb to use in connection with examining faces. Discuss what you think he means by parsing faces. What is a compound-sentence face? What is a syllogistic face?
3. In what ways are you and your friends like Broyard's son? For example, do you feel that fathers and mothers talk too much and do you accept victory and defeat in silence? In what ways are you more like Broyard than his son? For example, do you feel the need to confide, to "leap into intimacy"?

4. Broyard says, "My son's generation has abandoned itself to ambiguity." Discuss what he might mean by that and why you agree or disagree with him.
5. This essay is clearly divided. Where is the division and what specific word choices does Broyard make to get from his generation to his father's, and from his father's to his son's?

READINGS: SELECTION TWO

Rails: From Old World to New
by John H. White, Jr.

Ideas to Think About

1. This essay emphasizes the ingenuity of the American railroad industry. Consider some recent railroad innovations that reveal such inventiveness. Discuss.
2. What American products reveal the "bigger is better" aspect of American technology?
3. As you read, think about other American technologies that refined foreign inventions so that increased capacity for greater productivity resulted (paragraph 1).
4. As you read, watch for transitions that signal contrasting ideas.

Vocabulary

Look at each word as it is used in the article. (The number in parentheses indicates the paragraph in which it appears.) First, try to understand the meaning from the way it is used in the sentence. Second, use any clues to meaning through the structure of the word. Then, use the dictionary to clarify the meaning.

viaducts (3)
visionaries (4)
pragmatic (5)
traverse (15)

innovations (16)
evolved (19)
modifying (19)

Rails: From Old World to New

John Hoxland White, Jr. is the curator of the Division of Transportation in the Natural Museum of History and Technology and the editor of *Railroad History*.

American railroad engineering practice illustrates several basic trends that seem characteristic of most United States technologies. These involve the adapting or refining of foreign inventions to our needs, cheapening the mechanism without impairing its effectiveness, and markedly increasing its capacity for greater productivity. We did not invent the railroad, but we did reshape it for our specific needs, devising ways to produce economical rolling stock, tracks, and structures to suit our small purse. And in time we greatly enlarged all elements of the railway on a scale rarely attempted elsewhere in the world.

There are factors involved in railroad engineering which can be found in other areas of the mechanical arts, factors so obvious that they tend to be overlooked in most histories of inventions. In art or science, invention can be done for its own sake. The individual's urge to create and explore is satisfied. The end can be an original theory, an imaginative formula, or simply a beautiful object. But in engineering, invention must have a practical end. It must not only work satisfactorily, it must work within a given cost range and yield a predictable profit.

It was this overriding concern with cost that forced American railway pioneers to modify radically England's greatest 19th-century invention, the steam railway. England possessed the technology and capital to do everything on a grand scale and so it is not surprising that her first public railways were engineering monuments. Imposing stone viaducts° spanned valleys, and magnificent, temple-like stations were erected in major cities. Locomotives and cars were highly finished and lavishly trimmed. Rails were solid wrought-iron bars fastened to stone block sleepers. It was all splendidly and expensively done, but it was necessary to build a first-class system if the British railway were to compete with the already established canal and highway networks.

The situation in North America differed greatly with that continent's vast area, small population, and few, widely scattered cities. Canals and roads were scarce, and no rivers connected the settled seacoast regions to the interior because of the mountain ranges stretching from Maine to Georgia. Thus the railway was viewed by some visionaries° as the best way to solve our transportation difficulties.

Naturally, the first American railroad builders turned to England for their models. The Boston and Lowell line was a near-perfect replica of the Liverpool and Manchester, while the Baltimore and Ohio began bravely building great stone viaducts and laying track after the British style. But climate and economics soon forced the pragmatic° Yankee engineers to find alternative ways to build a railway. They did not set out to produce a better railway than the British, but to fabricate a cheaper one, and the most direct way to lower costs was to lower standards. Level, direct lines involving excavations, fills, tunnels, and bridges were expensive, whereas meandering routes that followed rivers and ran around obstacles were, though less efficient, far cheaper to build. Scarce capital dictated the choice, and the lines could always be rebuilt later (as indeed they were, many times).

Americans proved masters of the art of building an inexpensive railway. Great forests offered excellent timber in seemingly inexhaustible abundance. Why build railways of stone and imported iron when so much wood was at hand? We turned quickly to the expediency of strap rail and wooden beam tracks, timber trestles, and wooden stations. Embankments and culverts[1] were framed or cribbed with log retaining walls. Wood was

---

[1] A channel under a road.

used for locomotive fuel and car construction. While the British boasted of their Iron Roads, we could only apologize for our seedy, frequently unsafe, but inexpensive Wooden Roads.

These construction techniques enabled us to build a provisional system of railways rapidly. And no one laid down track faster than Americans. Despite wars and depressions we averaged 2,500 miles of track a year between 1830 and 1890. By the beginning of the 20th century more than one-half of the world's rail mileage crisscrossed this country.

Track construction assumed its modern form during this period, with Robert L. Steven's introduction in the 1830's of T-section rails and wooden crossties. These replaced the older iron strap, wooden beam rails which, being weak, could support only light, slow locomotives and furthermore tended to peel up, causing numerous accidents. Steven's T-section rail and wooden crossties are now a worldwide standard.

Early American engineers, then, reshaped the British railway and track structure. It should be noted that at the very time these developments were under way, other engineers modified and redesigned British locomotives and cars. Here again, the goal was to change only that which was necessary to adapt the mechanism to local needs. English inventors had developed the locomotive from the cumbersome steam carriage of 1804 to a fast and well proportioned unit of motive power of 1829. The general arrangement remained fixed from that date until the end of steam locomotion in 1960. The horizontal, multitubular boiler, separate firebox, power transmission by connecting rods (rather than gears), and blast-pipe exhaust remained fundamental. Of course, the locomotive grew dramatically in size, and many auxiliary appliances were added over the years, but the basic plan stayed the same.

The first locomotives used in this country were imported from England in 1829. While they could perform admirably on the level, straight British lines, they were ill-suited to our crooked, feeble tracks. They had trouble negotiating the sharp curves and tended to derail frequently. An English engine on the Mohawk and Hudson Railroad was said to give "audible complaint of hard service" when passing through a curve. The line's chief engineer, a gifted man named John B. Jervis, found the British locomotive to be as near perfection as possible for a steam engine, but sadly lacking in the agility required for the makeshift American tracks. Jervis solved this problem in 1832 by designing an engine with a four-wheel carriage, or truck, attached under the front of the locomotive by a center pin so that the truck was free to swivel as it followed the track, thus guiding the locomotive around curves.

British regulations called for smokeless locomotives, and the only sure way to accomplish this was to burn coke, a distillate of bituminous coal. At the time, America mined very little coal and produced almost no coke; however, wood was our common fuel, and so deep, narrow fireboxes became the hallmark of American locomotives. Because of the need for more power to overcome grades, American engineers began to increase boiler pressure which subsequently increased the danger of explosion — much to the horror of overseas rail officials.

Because our operations differed so from those of the British, our locomotives were soon loaded with appurtenances.[2] Bells and steam whistles were added to warn pedestrians, cattle, and carriages to clear the tracks. Headlights were a necessity for night running, and the cowcatcher was introduced to cope with the foolhardy steer that would not yield the right-of-way to the train.

Climate, too, had its effect on locomotive design. Bitter winters, for example, necessitated shelters for the operating crews. The earliest engines provided a railing around the platform or the cab floor, and some enterprising engineers began to erect shelters as early as 1831. Gradually the cab became more common, particularly in New England, and by 1850 it was a standard fixture.

Less obvious than the addition of headlights, cabs, and cowcatchers was the substitution of materials used in American locomotive construction. Here is a fine example of innovative engineering at the shop level, one almost never reported in the histories of inventions that tend to dwell on inspired geniuses and great leaps forward, thus disregarding much of the real progress made by ordinary men in workaday situations. Our engineering ancestors discovered many ways to lower the cost of locomotives by using cheaper materials than those employed by European builders. Wrought iron was substituted for copper fireboxes with no loss of efficiency or safety, and we made wholesale use of cast-iron parts in place of iron forgings. Cast iron was often cheaper because iron castings required less machinery and skill than the manufacture of wrought-iron parts. Wheels, tires, and even such unlikely parts as crank axles were made of cast iron. In 1880 it was estimated that 33 percent of an American locomotive was cast iron.

Railroad car design also came to America from England, in the form of small, four-wheel cars with side doors, normally divided into three compartments like contemporary city omnibuses. This style proved unsatisfactory for American use, and so between 1831 and 1835, car builders invented a new style of railroad passenger car. The new body, a long, open, single compartment, held seats arranged on both sides of a center aisle. The entrance doors were positioned at the ends rather than on the sides of the body. Platforms at the end of the car permitted access to the doors. The car was carried by two wheel sets or trucks attached to the underframe by center pins, and so were free to swivel, permitting the car to traverse° sharp curves. The American coach had several advantages

---

[2] Apparatus.

over its European counterpart. The double-truck running gear did away with the galloping ride characteristic of four-wheel cars, while the elimination of multiple compartments made construction lighter, stronger, simpler, and less expensive. The basic soundness of this plan is demonstrated by its endurance. The most modern American rail cars, including the Metroliner, continue to be built on this old arrangement.

Inventiveness should not be thought of only as the discovery of a new device. It can also involve a new way of using existing tools. Straightline developments requiring no new machines often result in the greatest benefits to mankind. American railroad's efficiency and carrying capacity began to soar in the 1890's, not because of radical technical innovations° but because of a growth in all elements of the physical plant. Bigness became the essence of American railroading. Twenty-five and 30-ton locomotives gave way to 60- and 90-ton machines. And these were not just a few special monsters built for pusher service; they were commonplace engines built for standard use. Passenger cars, though still all wood, stretch out to 70 or even 80 feet in length. Freight cars grew from 10-to-30-ton capacity, and all-steel cars began to be produced commercially. Longer trains were being assembled and operated at higher and higher speeds. For many years 25 miles an hour was the best average one could expect, even aboard the fastest trains. In 1875, the New York Central's finest New York-to-Chicago train took 37 hours to make the trip. By 1938 the time was reduced to 16 hours.

Care must be taken not to ascribe these advances exclusively to better locomotives and cars. The whole railroad had to be upgraded. The steam locomotive, since the time of the *Rocket* (1829), had demonstrated its ability for fast running. But the tracks of the early period, as we have seen, were not built for such speeds. Only after traffic increased to provide larger earnings could the industry justify large-scale improvements in tracks and rolling stock. Greater traffic was, of course, directly tied to an increasing industrial output and population growth. As the American economy matured, so did the railroads. As tonnage and passenger mileage mounted, the railroads had no choice but to increase their capacity. At their peak in 1916 they were carrying 77 percent of the intercity freight traffic and 98 percent of the intercity passenger traffic. The nation at that time was more dependent on the railway than it is today on the highway.

What was true in 1916 is but a memory today. Passenger traffic has all but disappeared, and freight tonnage has slipped to less than 40 percent of the total goods moved in the U.S. The railroad has become essentially a bulk carrier, a new role which has generated new equipment and operating procedures. What is seen by some as a dying industry depends on the inventiveness process to stay alive. Since the Second World War, diesel-electric locomotives, introduced in 1924, have almost completely replaced steam locomotives, while freight cars have grown from 40 to 70 feet and have reached 100 tons in weight. A variety of special-purpose cars has emerged, such as the triple-deck automobile-carrying cars. The idea for these cars came from Europe but, typically, we greatly expanded the unit size and more fully capitalized on the carrying ability of such vehicles. As a result, the railroads are now carrying a major portion of the new automobiles shipped — a market they had almost entirely lost to motor trucks by 1960.

The American railroad has evolved° remarkably in the past several decades. While mileage, employment, and the number of locomotives and cars have declined significantly, its carrying capacity, based on ton-miles, has nearly doubled. This seeming paradox will not surprise anyone who has studied American railroad history and understands the industry's ability to survive by subtly modifying° its technology to meet new challenges.

19

Discussion

1. This essay is both a comparison and contrast of the English and American railway industries and a comparison between our early and present systems. In the essay, we are moved from England to America by the use of skillful writing techniques. The topic sentence, for example, in paragraph 5 mentions both English and American railroads. Then the contrast is introduced with "while" in the second sentence and "but," which is introduced as the first word of the third sentence. Point out as many other verbal connections between British and American railways as you can find in the essay. Point out the choices such as verb tense switches that White makes to lead the reader from what was before to what is now true of the industry.
2. White points out the American talent for fast production. He says no one laid tracks faster than we did. Point out another industry in which American speed in production was notable.
3. Consider some of the prices we have paid for our "bigger is better" philosophy. Discuss.
4. Are there any signs of a recent renewed vigor and interest in railroads? Explain.

READINGS: SELECTION THREE

from Modernized Ritual of Rodeo
by Paul O'Neil

Ideas to Think About

1. Consider your ideas about a cowboy. How did you develop them? Have movies and television helped shape your views?
2. What aspects of a rodeo contribute to its popularity? Which are your favorite events? Explain.
3. As you read, try to think about the first image that comes to your mind when you hear or see the word *cowboy*. Do you see the Hollywood/Las Vegas sequined version or the Hollywood John Wayne version?
4. As you read, watch for transitions that signal contrasting ideas.

Vocabulary

Look at each word as it is used in the article. (The number in parentheses indicates the paragraph in which it appears.) First, try to understand the way it is used in the sentence. Second, use any clues to meaning through the structure of the word. Then, use the dictionary to clarify the meaning.

fatalistic (1)   compensate (4)
contemptuous (2)   alacrity (7)
taciturn (2)   neophyte (15)
stoically (3)   entrepreneur (18, 26)

from Modernized Ritual of Rodeo

Paul O'Neil is the author of *The End and the Myth* and a frequent contributor to *Smithsonian* magazine.

Rodeo grounds differ. Some are floodlit indoor arenas. Some are still dirt fields flanked by sun-bleached grandstands. But broncs with names like Midnight Black and Widow Maker create menacing echoes in Pendleton as in Oklahoma City when they rear and kick in imprisoning wooden chutes. Riders in big hats ease down on their backs with exactly the same fatalistic° caution in Cheyenne as in Ellensburg or Calgary. And every crowd breathes tension: to be broken in seconds by disaster — as when a horse named Bay Beggar threw Deb Copenhaver in one celebrated spill and kicked him in the face as he hung from one stirrup — or by the kind of wild triumph a man reflects while surviving with grace on a beast gone mad.

Men who herded longhorns up the Chisholm Trail gave little thought to the future; by the same token, today's rodeo cowboys waste no time in contemplating the past folklore on which their profession is based. They cling stubbornly to this bruising and exhausting way of life for exactly the reasons the mountain men, prospectors and line riders of the Old West clung to theirs: pride in their own hardihood, a kind of veiled contempt for stay-at-homes with regular jobs and regular lives, the hope of striking it rich (though only a small percentage of performers make big money) and the stimulation of danger and suspense. They may dream of magenta-colored Cadillacs and use jet planes or campers to jump from arena to arena, but they are the same hard and hopeful breed of men for all that: footloose by necessity, reckless, ruefully philosophical, contemptuous° of pain, taciturn,° even shy.

Early rodeos seemed like home to men with such attitudes, and they happily risked their necks, often for little more than enough money to reach the next town, fairground, ball park, pasture or stockyard, wherever local merchants would put up the prize money. But in the last two decades the rodeo has emerged as a major national way of life. There were 618 rodeos in the United States during 1978 — shows blessed, at any rate, by the Professional Rodeo Cowboys Association — and scores of smaller, un-sanctioned exhibitions as well. They drew 16.5 million paying customers, distributed $7.2 million in prize money and made it possible for Tom Ferguson, a calf roper and steer wrestler, to become the first cowboy in history to earn more than $100,000 in 12 months — which he has done for the last three years. And feminist ferment has prompted a Girls Rodeo Association whose members risk their necks on broncs and bulls as stoically° as men: spectators at the Spring Creek, Nevada, Horse Palace saw cowgirl Sue Pirtle Hayes ride a bucking horse while eight months pregnant during a recent world's championship show, and saw Karen Christianson carried off unconscious with a broken cheekbone after being thrown by a Brahman bull. . . .

The modern rodeo subjects a performer to pressures the old working cowboy never knew. He must not only submit his body to constant abuse, since he must compete in as many shows as possible in pursuit of purses, but must also travel hundreds, even thousands, of miles in getting from arena to arena and must keep doing so for months at a time.

The cowboy compensates° for the aches, tension and sleeplessness of his life as best he can. He puts his faith in pills in many cases: keep-awake pills (hummers) on long drives, pain pills (Darvon or codeine if he can get them, aspirin if he cannot) to help him ignore bruises, torn ligaments or dislocated joints. Some gulp vitamin tablets and hope for magical results; some carry exercise equipment; some read books on positive thinking. They encase themselves in yards and yards of adhesive tape or vast wrappings of Ace bandage, partly to compensate for damage already suffered and partly as a kind of ritual calculated to protect them against bad luck or a bad ride as well as new wounds or broken bones.

But if most cowboys seek comfort in pills and portents, rodeo's superstars — and there have been very few of them — seem to have been men with a much more direct approach to the imponderables[1] of the arena. They have disregarded the tensions and risks of their calling and achieved a consistency of performance that could only have stemmed from some inner wells of unusual self-confidence. So has their lineal descendant, Tom Ferguson of Miami, Oklahoma, who burst into the news as professional rodeo's second biggest money winner while competing part-time as a college senior in 1973, became the first to top $100,000 (with a total of $114,110) in 1976, and has reigned since as the most brilliant of a new breed of cowboy.

Ferguson is a handsome young man — dark-haired, unassuming and now in his middle twenties — who sits a horse like a medieval prince: exactly the kind of target that attracts camp followers and fast-buck artists to the periphery of his world. But he has weathered adulation and sudden liquidity as well as the rigors of his calling with remarkable aplomb.[2] He is a gifted athlete, especially adept at steer wrestling in which a man on a horse bursts out after a racing horned beast, leaves the saddle and deposits his quarry motionless on the ground — in less than five seconds if he expects to share in the prize money. Most steer wrestlers are bigger than he — he is 5 feet, 11 inches tall and weighs 180 pounds — but he possesses reflexes which not only make him a marksman with a rope but allow him to upend a 700-pound steer with alacrity.° He puts his faith in method and conditioning rather than in heroics, seems too intent on his craft to be aware of temptation (he neither drinks nor smokes), sees no sensible reason for failure and accepts big purses like a banker stowing away returns on a loan.

The eminent roper and his wife, Debbie, a California girl he met in college, live simply when at home — they began with a house trailer and now rent a tiny bungalow for $100 a month. But Ferguson has spent $23,000 for a yachtlike, custom-built trailer in which to camp on the road, and another $9,000 for a dual-wheeled truck to provide it with high-speed motive power. This elegant conveyance not only boasts its own water supply (linked to a water purification system), a bathroom with shower, comfortable beds, air conditioning, a kitchen with refrigerator, and a generator which supplies its own electricity, but storage space for saddles, bridles and ropes and a rear stable area for three horses and their feed.

Ferguson drives 70,000 miles a year and lives the same, indescribably hectic life as his colleagues, trailer or not, once he sets out on the circuit. Most cowboys assume that they must enter at least 100 rodeos a year if they expect to make real money — Ferguson tries to hit 120 of them — and this involves competing simultaneously in two, or sometimes three,

---

[1] Things difficult to evaluate or measure.
[2] Poise.

rodeos if geography and the time factor make it possible. Ferguson was seldom able to sleep more than three or four hours in 24, for instance, in one recent assault on arenas in the Northwest.

He pulled out of Miami on Sunday of the week before Labor Day with his wife at his side and two horses in the trailer's rear compartment, and arrived in Salem, Oregon — more than 2,700 miles away — at five o'clock the next Tuesday morning, having stopped only for food and fuel. His prized roping horse wisely reclined in a stall on arrival at the Salem rodeo grounds, and Ferguson slept until noon. But not much thereafter: he was "up" at Salem that afternoon; at Walla Walla, Washington, on Thursday night; at Ellensburg, Washington, on Friday morning; at Pueblo, Colorado, that same night — and had to repeat at most of the same towns, plus another in Idaho, over the long weekend.

His wife was able to intercept him with the trailer a few times during this frantic game of leapfrog, but during most of it he was forced to abandon her and his horses while hitching rides with friends and using borrowed mounts at outlying arenas. He chartered planes twice to get to Seattle, caught commercial flights to Denver twice, and drove on to Pueblo in rented cars with two other cowboys who were also entered there: starting from Ellensburg on Friday (after competing there earlier in the day) and from Yakima, Washington, on Monday (after competing twice on Sunday), driving all night, and competing again shortly before taking off.

"We barely made it both times. We knew we were late Monday night; we left Denver driving 90 miles an hour and had a blowout. We got the car stopped but there were big pieces of rubber all over the road, and just as we got out another car came over a rise behind us and came screeching and sliding past us and slid off the road and crashed into a tree. We knew the guy was all right — he jumped out and came running over to write down our license number — so we put on another wheel and got out of there." Ferguson slept — at last — after the rodeo on Monday night, flew to Twin Falls the next day and ended the expedition with a last performance at Filer, Idaho, where his wife, having driven some 600 miles in the interim, awaited him.

This concentration and disregard of exhaustion paid him handsomely in the Northwest — $7,600 in just seven days — a figure interpreted as a measure of valor and worth as well as gain by the inhabitants of his violent and demanding world. . . .

Early bronc riders practiced on homemade "bucking barrels" — kegs hung from ceilings or tree limbs by rope or springs and yanked about by whooping colleagues or perspiring relatives and friends. Ex-rodeo champ Jim Shoulders improved on this rude concept by connecting an oil drum to the universal joint of a partially dismantled automobile, and activated it by throwing the car's gearshift lever from low to reverse and back again.

Today's young cowboys can improve their skills in seminars and schools that employ more sophisticated technology. One inventor, Joe D. Turner of Corrales, New Mexico, has sold hundreds of his electric bucking machines, known as the El Toro, to colleges, schools, and rodeo clubs across the country. And a tall Texan named Sam Reeves has duplicated the motions of a bucking horse or a rodeo bull in a machine he calls the Gold Nugget Rider Trainer: a fiberglass beast with walleyes and one satisfactory metal leg, which can unseat the aspiring bronc tamer as peremptorily as any rodeo outlaw of the fabled past. "Rodeo cowboys keep movies of their rides on different animals," he explains; "I looked at hundreds of them when I was developing the trainers, and I'm about to hook them to a computer which can be programmed to make them buck like any horse or bull you want to imitate. There's no point in getting on a machine that jumps one way and then getting on an animal that has different habits."

High school and college rodeoers have only to buy *Rodeo News*, the official publication of the International Rodeo Association, to find ads for clinics conducted by men who have won at Pendleton, Calgary and Cheyenne. Ex-all-around cowboy champion Larry Mahan puts students on real broncs — explaining, ominously, that the animal neither knows nor cares that the rider is a neophyte° — but prepares them for the subsequent rites of passage by shouting, "Positive mental attitude! PMA! Tell yourself there's no such thing as a negative thought!" Champion bull rider Gary Leffew — a student of Zen — sent one pair of aspirants into the California hills to commune with themselves for weeks, like young Indian braves, before consenting to instruct them in his dangerous trade. . . .

Modern cowboys take the punishment in stride. Here is Casey Tibbs, a rodeo champion of the 1950's, describing his peerless ability to commune with the plunging monsters which bore him — legs flailing, one arm high — into the arena: "You just fall into the rhythm and it's just like dancing with a girl."

There is no telling when the first rodeo — not then so formally named — was held, although one legend places it at Deer Trail, Colorado, some time in the late 1870's, and identifies the contestants as cowhands of the Hashknife, Campstool and Mill Iron ranches who matched their toughest horses and toughest men during a respite taken when their trail herds converged on a drive to the north.

But promoters, rather than cowboys, developed the format and dramatic potential of the rodeo, sold it on its own as an exciting amalgam of the spectacle and sport, and amplified the echoes it struck from the American past. Some of these sponsors were simply patriotic citizens, who nevertheless turned shows like Cheyenne's Frontier Days and the Pendleton Roundup into annual rites as unique and reflective of the national psyche as the World Series or Fourth of July parades. But if one man deserved credit for modernizing the rodeo, it was Guy Weadick, a 101 Ranch roper-turned-entrepreneur° who talked four rich Alberta cattlemen into lending him $100,000 in 1912, and used it to create the first Calgary Stampede. Weadick offered performers big money for the first time — a total of $20,000 in gold, with $1,000 guaranteed to every winner — and altered the concepts of all concerned in so doing.

Another high roller, Tex Austin, demonstrated beyond all doubt that rodeo was becoming a national rather than a Western phenomenon by drawing big crowds in Chicago (1919), Madison Square Garden (1922) and Yankee Stadium (1923). Promoters meanwhile organized themselves into a Rodeo Association of America and began naming national champions. And the cowboys themselves formed a union in 1936: the Cowboys Turtle Association ("We was slow as turtles in organizing"), which has since become the Professional Rodeo Cowboys Association.

This metamorphosis stemmed from rodeo's increasing acceptance as a big-time spectator sport — most dramatically as it punctuated its seasons with week-long exhibitions at New York's Madison Square Garden — and so coincided with the emergence of a reckless, outrageously handsome young bronc buster named Casey Tibbs, who lent the sport a kind of glamor it had never before achieved. . . .

While Tibbs was making headlines and fascinating audiences with his own particular brand of shamanism,[3] hundreds, then thousands, of college and high school students were caught up in a craze for parochial rodeo contests. This movement, which soon encompassed even grade school kids, began with student rodeo clubs and materialized in more than 50 Western colleges, providing rodeo's big time with a kind of self-energizing farm system. The college cowboys, forming their own Intercollegiate Rodeo Association, aped the professionals from the start: all contestants paid entrance fees, competed for cash, submitted to blackballing for failing to make a ride, and drove day and night during the weekends to escape this dreaded eventuality.

Many of today's college cowboys and, in fact, many professionals as well, have been performers since they were eight or ten — the National Little Britches Rodeo Association having been organized in 1961, and having attracted embryo cowboys and cowgirls by the increasing thousands in the West and Middle West ever since. A Little Britches rodeo is a complex phenomenon: there are junior and senior divisions for both girls and boys, and from five to six separate events for each of these categories. Contestants of both sexes array themselves in astonishing varieties of big hats, bright skirts, chaps, boots and spurs, do their best to beg, borrow or steal cans of fiery Skoal or Copenhagen snuff, which they tuck inside their

---

[3] Control of good and evil spirits by a witch doctor or medicine man.

lower lips, swagger about, sizing each other up, and doing their best to hide the fear and excitement which are part and parcel of rodeo at any level. . . .

This emulation of the dress, attitudes and skills of the Old West becomes something very like obsession with these amateur cowhands by the time they reach high school. They stand raptly at attention as an announcer intones something called the "Rodeo Prayer" at their annual national competition — which drew 1,131 of them from 29 states and two Canadian provinces when it was held at Helena, Montana, in 1977: "Help us, Lord, to live in such a manner that when we take the last inevitable ride to the country up there where grass grows lush green and stirrup high and the water runs cool, clear and deep, that You as our last judge will tell us that our entry fees are paid."

Today's reigning rodeo hero, Tom Ferguson, emerged from the ranks of schoolboys who competed as youngsters in the 1960's. Ferguson and his older brother, Larry (a top steer wrestler and roper in his own right), grew up at San Martin, California, after their father, Ira, trekked west from Oklahoma in the 1950's. They were riders — and were absorbing the lore of the arena — almost as soon as they could walk. Ira Ferguson had competed in rodeos in Oklahoma and Texas in the 1940's, and went on seeking prize money on the West Coast in the 1950's. "I told them to stay out of it," he says now. "I thought it was an awfully hard way to make a dollar." But the boys roped cats, dogs, fence posts and bales of hay for all that, dreamed of more glorious feats, and talked their mother into driving them around California with a roping horse named Ragmop to enter local events.

Tom Ferguson refused to be lured away into his high school's team sports; he needed weekends for amateur rodeos (the bush leagues — and not amateur at all — of professionalism) and every afternoon for practice in his father's back lot, where he tried to catch eight calves and jump 10 or 15 steers every night. He was the amateur (or California Cowboy Association) calf-roping champion as a senior in high school and won a scholarship to the California Polytechnic Institute at San Luis Obispo. He did not go alone. The institution's animal husbandry[4] department agreed to lend him stock pens, and he took six steers, ten calves and a roping horse when he set off to study agricultural business management, to go on with his punishing program of practice, and to pit himself against college cowboys from other Western schools. Not many, he discovered, were as well grounded as he, and he held his own with the best. Ferguson has made a great deal of money since he left college, breaking past records from his rookie year — and it is his earnings as well as his skills that make him an idol of the young.

---

[4] The controlled use of resources in agriculture.

This view of prizes as a reflection of hardihood and a reward for risk stems straight from the 19th century; the rodeo, for all its new trappings, has remained unchanged in attitude, essence and, largely, in procedure since it took shape at Pecos, Prescott and Miles City. But its time-honored format and a good deal of its individualism faces alteration by a syndicate of entrepreneurs° who have borrowed concepts from more stratified professional sports like football and baseball. In 1978 they launched "major league" rodeo with six teams (of 15 men and 3 women), a player draft, a league commissioner, and the prospect of future franchises in cities from coast to coast. The first six teams were organized into an Eastern Conference (Tulsa, Kansas City and San Antonio) and a Western Conference (Denver, Los Angeles and Salt Lake City). The season, from April 15 to September 15, culminated in a World Championship in which the Denver Stars defeated the Tulsa Twisters. The new league has not been sanctioned by the Professional Rodeo Cowboys Association, but the Star's owner, Guthrie Packard, believes most cowboys will come around. "People say the cowboy is a free-willed individual who wants no strings," he observes. "But team members have a rule book, dress code and curfew, and we've never had a curfew or dress-code violation."

Tom Ferguson, at least, would be surprised if the new order made much change in the cowboy himself. "We've still got to compete with broncs, bulls and steers," he says, "and *they* won't know the difference."

Discussion

1. The basic organization of this essay is comparison and contrast. Notice how skillfully the comparison between the rodeo of yesterday and today is made. For example, in the second paragraph, the bridge between then and now is made in the topic sentence by two techniques: a switch in verb tenses and the use of a semicolon to indicate coordinate independent clauses: "Men who *herded* longhorns up the Chisholm Trail gave little thought to the future; by the same token, today's rodeo cowboys *waste* no time in contemplating the past folklore on which their profession is based." Point out as many other places as possible in the essay where comparisons and contrasts are made with equal skill. For example, look for devices such as deliberate repetition, coordinators such as *and* and *but*, word choices such as *yesterday* or *today*, or items in a series that lead the reader back and forth in time.
2. What do you think is so captivating about rodeos that Tom Ferguson, who was an outstanding high school athlete, refused to participate in any other sport?
3. Why do you think the cowboy myth has such a firm hold on the imagination of people all over the world? In other words, are there any specific aspects of the image that have universal appeal?

WRITING:
Exposition: Comparison and Contrast

Writing Assignment: A Three-Paragraph Comparison and Contrast Essay

Your specific assignment in this unit involves comparing and contrasting two items, ideas, or events. In comparing two things, you will show their similarities; in contrasting them, you will point out their differences. In other words, to compare and contrast means to perform a special type of analysis — one that focuses upon particular characteristics of the things under examination. Because of their analytical nature, comparison and contrast questions are often asked in examinations since they reveal a student's understanding of an area. You should therefore train yourself to make comparisons and contrasts while studying, not only to prepare for future tests, but also to facilitate learning and to gain conceptual control of a subject.

Assignment

Write a three-paragraph comparison and contrast essay employing the following pattern of organization.

   Paragraph 1 — An introduction including an explicit thesis statement.

   Paragraph 2 — A comparison and contrast of point 1.

   Paragraph 3 — A comparison and contrast of point 2.

The first paragraph of your essay should act as an introduction to your essay's topic. Your thesis statement can appear at any point in the paragraph, but it must be limited, clear, precise, and unified. Yet the introductory paragraph must include more than a thesis statement. It should include any material necessary to set up your discussion and to develop reader interest. Possible ways to develop the paragraph include the following techniques.

1. A discussion of the historical background to your topic.
2. A discussion of the contemporary interest in your topic.
3. An introduction to your points of discussion with an explanation of the reasons these particular points have been chosen.
4. A discussion of the importance to the reader of an awareness of the similarities and differences between the two items under examination.

THESIS   1. The two largest cities in the United States, New York and Los Angeles, offer many career opportunities and recreational activities for their residents. As a result, young college graduates from throughout the United States often migrate to these urban centers in hopes of professional advancement and achieving fuller lives. Too often, however, some of these new arrivals have difficulty in adjusting to their new surroundings or in acquiring good jobs and then blame the cities for their unhappiness. Yet such situations need not occur if these young people understood the true character of large cities before moving away from their hometowns.

The next two paragraphs in your comparison and contrast essay should treat the two points of discussion mentioned in the introductory paragraph. For example, in the sample paragraph above, two characteristics of New York and Los Angeles, their career opportunities and recreational activities, are introduced. These two points, then, would serve as topics for the rest of the essay. These two points should be handled one at a time, with *one* point of discussion developed in *each* paragraph: the career opportunities of *both* cities would be compared and contrasted in the second paragraph, and their recreational activities would be compared and contrasted in the third paragraph. This organization of your essay allows your readers to understand the similarities and differences you discuss without having to remember details mentioned earlier and enables them to concentrate on each topic as it is presented.

2. For example, career opportunities in each of these cities differ greatly. Although both New York and Los Angeles have many types of businesses and large retail establishments that provide jobs for their citizens, these cities serve as the nation's headquarters for completely different types of industries. New York acts as the banking, investment, and publishing capital of the United States. In fact, most of the nation's major financial institutions and a large percentage of the nation's major book, magazine, and advertising companies are located in Manhattan. In contrast, the nation's aircraft, computer, and television and movie industries are centered in Los Angeles. Young college graduates in search of careers must therefore evaluate their educational preparation and career plans before choosing either city for their new home. For example, an electronics engineer would find more job opportunities in Los Angeles, while a writer would find more job openings in New York.

3. But these cities also differ in another major area that is important to individual lifestyle. Although both New York and Los Angeles offer many activities to enrich their citizens' lives, each city has its own recreational emphasis. New York provides the finest theatre and greatest museums in the country. In addition, almost every city block in Manhattan teems with restaurants, bars, and night clubs. In fact, New York is truly the nighttime capital of the entire continent and can compete with London, Paris, and Hong Kong in its cosmopolitan atmosphere. Los Angeles also offers these indoor recreations, al-

though with less richness and diversity, but it compensates for any lack in these areas by providing an enormous range of outdoor activities. Within the city limits, one can ski a mountain, surf in the Pacific Ocean, and develop a suntan lying by a backyard pool, all on the same day. With its semi-desert climate and its location on the coast, the city provides a year-round playground for adults and children alike. Los Angeles and New York thus provide some radically different opportunities and activities that can lead to either happiness or discontent for their new residents.

Notice that the sample essay has no extended conclusion. The last line in the third paragraph simply rounds out the discussion without summarizing the three paragraphs. Since your readers have not been asked to follow a very lengthy or complex analysis, they do not need any review of your major points or an extended final comment from you.

Thesis statements serve as your contractual agreement with your readers and establish guidelines for you to follow as you develop your essay. The thesis statement in a comparison and contrast essay must also present a discussion that is of interest to your readers, or they either will not pay close attention or will stop reading. Your thesis statement may state your areas of comparison and contrast or simply introduce your general topic; you must decide which would be most effective for your purpose in writing and which would help develop a smooth, clear introduction to your essay.

EXERCISE 1

Evaluate the following thesis statements, which are to control a three-paragraph comparison and contrast essay. Rewrite those that are not limited, unified, precise, and clear.

1. All immigrants to the United States have faced problems in adjusting to American customs.
2. Both senior citizens and college students face problems of affordable housing and part-time jobs.
3. Israel and Iran have serious problems of inflation, but the economic conditions of the world may soon change as a result of the discovery of new energy sources.
4. One can compare men and women.
5. The English railroad system differs from the American railroad system because it was adjusted to suit special needs.

EXERCISE 2

Write five thesis statements for a three-paragraph comparison and contrast essay. Do not indicate the specific points of comparison and contrast in these statements. Now rewrite these thesis statements, indicating the points of comparison and contrast. Which are more effective? In what situation? Why?

Although this assignment suggests that you write a three-paragraph essay, you could expand the comparison and contrast format to a much larger discussion. You could, for example, write a four- or five-paragraph essay by simply presenting one or two more points of discussion. Or, by substituting sections for paragraphs, you could produce an even longer paper.

Section 1 — Introduction.
Section 2 — First point of comparison or contrast.
Section 3 — Second point of comparison or contrast.
Section 4 — Additional point of comparison or contrast.

By considering your essay as a unified series of sections, you are able to develop each point of discussion more fully. In other words, some sections, like the introduction, might be one paragraph in length, while other sections might include two to five paragraphs. The length of each section would depend on the complexity of your points of discussion and the needs of your readers. The preceding sample essay, for example, offers an overview of the similarities and differences between New York and Los Angeles, but it could very easily be expanded to give an indepth picture of the two cities. For instance, the second paragraph could be expanded to three or four paragraphs by adding more details on job opportunities: specific companies could be named, the types of jobs available within these companies could be discussed, and the advancement potentials of each job could be evaluated.

Each of the following writing assignments is appropriate for a three-paragraph essay, but each one also could be expanded into a four- or five-page paper. Your instructor will explain how many points of discussion you should include in your essay and how fully developed each point of discussion should be.

TOPICS

BROYARD
1. Compare and contrast one of your attitudes toward life with that of your father or mother. Your audience is a relative over thirty-five.
2. Compare and contrast one of your worries or concerns with that of a friend or relative of another age group. Your audience is that friend or relative.

WHITE
1. Compare and contrast the role of the automobile in your community with its role in another city or country. Your audience is your teacher.
2. Compare and contrast the design of one brand of electronic equipment (radio, hi-fi, tape recorder) with the design of another brand. Your audience is a person planning to buy electronic equipment.

O'NEIL
1. Compare and contrast today's professional athletes in a particular sport with athletes in this sport during a previous period. Your audience is your teacher.

2. Compare and contrast a folk hero of today with a folk hero of a previous time period. Your audience is your classmates.

Brainstorming and Shaping

1. Choose your topic and audience.
2. Prepare a data sheet on your audience that is similar to Data Sheet 6-1.

Data Sheet 6-1

A. Topic: _____
B. Audience: _____
C. General Characteristics of the Audience:
   1.
   2.
   3.
   4.
   5.
   6.
   7.
   8.
   9.
   10.
D. Probable Knowledge of Reading Audience on Topic:
   1. What do my readers probably know about my topic? _____
      _____
   2. What do my readers need to know about my topic? _____
      _____
   3. What do my readers need to have reviewed on my topic? ____
      _____
E. Probable Opinions of Reading Audience on Topic:
   1.
   2.
   3.
   4.
   5.

As you have probably noticed, the data sheet for this unit has *not* asked you to construct a thesis statement. Since a comparison and contrast essay requires you to analyze your topic, not simply to report information that fulfills your audience's needs, you need to make some conscious choices before formulating your thesis; that is, you need to decide not only how two things are similar and different, but also which points of comparison and contrast are most meaningful to both you and your readers. For example, if your readers are considering applying either to Ohio State University or to Reed College in Oregon and they plan on majoring in political science, which of the following topics would interest them most?

Campus location.
Size of student body.
Political science course work.
Faculty-student ratio.
University reputation.
Football and basketball success.
Costs.
Housing availability.
Campus activities.
Political science faculty reputation.
Weather.
Campus architecture.

To write an effective comparison and contrast essay, then, you must evaluate three things before forming your thesis statement: the audience, the similarities and differences between the two items under consideration, and the relative importance between these similarities and differences.

Data Sheet 6-2 will assist you in recognizing the similarities and differences between the items under consideration for your essay. But before you begin filling out the form, be sure to spend time thinking about your topic. This time spent reviewing what you already know about your topic need not take place at your desk; some of the best ideas that writers develop often occur while driving, watching television, lying on the beach, walking across campus, or lying in bed waiting for sleep. Perhaps you should carry a small notebook with you at all times, so that, when an idea occurs to you, you can jot it down for future use.

3. Prepare a data sheet similar to Data Sheet 6-2. Then take a look at Sample Data Sheet 6-2 to see how it can be filled in.

Certain aspects of the sample data sheet should be especially noted. First, the order of importance of the characteristics was selected on the basis of the information assembled in Data Sheet 6-1. For example, a data sheet on college students who are planning a European vacation would probably indicate little interest in quality of food, lodgings, and shopping. Most students would be more interested in things they could do and people they could meet.

Second, characteristics 1–4 could either be combined into one section entitled "Things to Do," or they could be handled as separate topics. Since the assignment asks for only three paragraphs and since these items are interrelated, they have been combined for reader interest. However, if the assignment had

Data Sheet 6-2 Comparison and Contrast

A. Topic: _____
B. Characteristics of Item 1:   Characteristics of Item 2:
   1.   1.
   2.   2.
   3.   3.
   4.   4.
   5.   5.
   6.   6.
   7.   7.
   8.   8.
   9.   9.
   10.   10.
C. Relative Importance of Characteristics to Topic and Audience:
   1.
   2.
   3.
   4.
   5.
   6.
   7.
   8.
   9.
   10.
D. Write a thesis statement that introduces your topic and prepares your reader for a comparison and contrast: _____
_____

Sample Data Sheet 6-2 Comparison and Contrast

A. Topic: London and Paris as a vacation spot for an American college student.
B. Characteristics of Item 1:   Characteristics: Paris
   London
   1. Language: English.   1. Language: French.
   2. Quality of food: poor to good. 2. Quality of food: good to excellent.

(Continued on following page)

Sample Data Sheet 6-2 *(Continued)*

---

    3. Quality of hotels: low-cost — clean, friendly, near transportation.

    4. Transportation: superior — subways, busses, and taxis.

    5. Museums: superior — British Museum is greatest in world; outstanding art galleries.

    6. Theaters: superior — finest theatre choice in the world for plays presented in English.

    7. Nightlife: superior — cafes, discos, gambling casinos, cinemas, night clubs, pubs, coffee and wine houses.

    8. Shopping: superior — special buys in woolens, rain wear, china, men's clothing, prints.

    9. University areas: good — Bloomsbury houses University of London, bookshops, museums, student gathering spots.

   10. City atmosphere: cosmopolitan, electric with energy.

---

    3. Quality of hotels: low-cost — often dirty, friendly to unfriendly, near transportation.

    4. Transportation: good — subways, busses, and taxis.

    5. Museums: superior — Louvre is greatest art gallery in world; many outstanding smaller museums.

    6. Theaters: superior — finest theatre choice in the world for plays presented in French.

    7. Nightlife: superior — bars, cinema, nightclubs, bistros, sidewalk cafes, coffee houses.

    8. Shopping: superior — special buys in high-price designer clothes, perfume.

    9. University areas: good — Left Bank houses Sorbonne, bookshops, museums, student gathering spots.

   10. City atmosphere: gracious, sophisticated.

C. Relative Importance of Characteristics to Topic and Audience:
    1. Museums
    2. Theaters
    3. Nightlife
    4. University areas

    Can be combined into one section entitled "Things to Do"

    5. Language
    6. City atmosphere
    7. Transportation
    8. Quality of hotels
    9. Quality of food
   10. Shopping

D. Write a thesis statement that introduces your topic and prepares your reader for a comparison and contrast: <u>London and Paris are two of the most exciting cities in the world for vacationing American college students.</u>

called for a more extensive discussion, these characteristics could each form the basis for individual paragraphs.

Third, the thesis statement in this instance does not indicate the points of comparison and contrast. The writer would introduce these points after the statement of the controlling idea. However, as a writer of a comparison and contrast paper, you always have the choice of including your points of discussion in your thesis statement or of handling their introduction separately.

Examples
1. Thesis:

   London and Paris are two of the most exciting cities in the world for vacationing American college students.

   Second Sentence:

   Both offer many activities to fill the days and nights of tourists, although a language barrier might cause problems for those people lacking a knowledge of the French language.

2. Thesis Statement:

   Although an acoustic guitar and a steel-string guitar have similar appearances, they produce different tone qualities.

The choices are yours to make. Before you write your first draft, be sure to decide which points of discussion are most important to your audience and to your purpose in writing, which points could be combined for an effective essay, and what information should be included in your thesis statement to insure reader interest and a clear introduction to your essay.

Writing the First Draft

Using your two data sheets as guides, write the first draft of your three-paragraph essay. Remember, your first paragraph serves as an introduction, while your next two paragraphs develop the two points of comparison and contrast that you have chosen. *Save your data sheets to submit with your final draft.*

Revising the Three-Paragraph Comparison and Contrast Essay

Your assignment asked you to write a three-paragraph comparison and contrast essay. Look over your two data sheets and your first draft and then analyze your work according to the adjusted basic revision questions and the special questions for this assignment.

Basic Revision Questions

1. *Is all my information accurate? Appropriate?*
   Have you bored your readers by repeating information they already know or have already considered? Have you misinformed your readers by giving them false information? Have you offered all the information needed by your readers on your points of discussion?
2. *Is this information organized so that my reader can comprehend what I have said? Could I organize my paper so that it would be more effective?*
   Does your essay have three sections: an introductory paragraph and two comparison and contrast paragraphs? Do paragraphs two and three focus on distinct points of discussion?
3. *Do I have a clear, unified focus; that is, does my essay telescope in on one major theme?*
   Do your points of comparison and contrast in paragraphs two and three relate directly to your thesis statement? In developing these paragraphs, have you accidentally added any information that does not relate to your topic?
4. *Do I offer sufficient details, examples, or explanations so that my reader gains a complete understanding of what I am discussing?*
   Are all points of discussion fully explained? Do your readers need additional clarification?

Additional Questions

1. Is my thesis statement limited, unified, precise, and clear?
2. Do paragraphs two and three have limited, unified, precise, and clear topic sentences?
3. Have I offered enough information and explanations in my introductory paragraph to develop audience interest and to prepare my reader for my comparison and contrast?
4. Are my points of comparison and contrast appropriate for my audience? Would different points of discussion be more effective or worthwhile?

EXERCISE 1

Check over your first draft. Are your thesis statement and topic sentences limited, unified, precise, and clear? Make any changes and adjustments that are necessary.

EXERCISE 2

Evaluate your essay by asking the revision questions posed in this section. If you answer either "No" or "I don't know" to any question, you probably need some revision. If you are not sure your information is accurate, check your facts in your school library. If you are not sure you have met your readers' needs, review your data sheets and your essay to see if your discussion concentrates on what your readers need to know, need to have reviewed, or need to have explained or pointed out to them. If your readers hold opinions based on misinformation or personal bias, you must check to see that you have informed them of the correct facts. If paragraphs two and three do not treat distinct points of discussion, you need to reorganize and refocus your discussions. Make all necessary adjustments to your essay.

EXERCISE 3

Put your first draft away for several days, then review your work. You should be able to evaluate your essay more effectively at this time since it is no longer fresh in your mind. Make any revisions necessary for an effective discussion.

EXERCISE 4

Write a clean draft of your revised essay in preparation for editing.

Editing

Word Choice: Transitions

Nowhere is it more necessary to make your sentences and paragraphs interact than in comparison and contrast. One chief way to achieve this interaction is through the careful choice of transitional words and phrases. Transitions, as discussed in the Reading Strategies section, are words and phrases that guide; establish order in time; or suggest contrast, likeness, and logical order. Although it is easy to forget to signal your audience when you are writing, you must always remember that your reader must be led over bridges to arrive at the destination you have chosen. The adverbs *however, therefore, for example,* and *finally* are such transitions. They point out relationships and serve as linking devices that connect the ideas in your sentences and link your paragraphs. Refer to the sentence structure chart in Unit 3 and the list of transitions in the reading lesson of this unit.

Remember that transitional words and phrases are only one linking device. There are others, such as repetition and the use of pronouns and synonyms. However, transitions serve to link sentences smoothly and effectively like careful stitches in a quilt. In comparison and contrast, these links are especially important. They help prevent confusion and the "ping pong" effect that comparison and contrast so easily leads to if one is not careful. Sometimes an entire transitional sentence is necessary. In fact, you may need to use transitional sentences to end a series, show a shift in time, or indicate a contrast.

> John struggled for years to conquer what for him was the unsolvable mystery: How to take a decent picture. In all his pictures, the horizons suggested that the world was caving in, and the lighting was

strangely dim or eerie in its high contrast. The composition invariably suggested either a pathetic lack of artistic awareness or, to be kind, an acute scarcity of imagination. At the most crucial moments he wiggled just enough to make things out of focus. This explains why no family occasions were recorded with John at the shutter.

All this failure, however, turned to success this year when he enrolled in a photography course. John's course included a series of lessons in composition, a series in lighting, and lessons in camera handling and film selection. A determined if not apt student, motivated by previous failure, John followed everything carefully and worked hard to complete every requirement successfully. *Finally* the mystery was solved.

John now knows photography is no mystery. Producing good pictures takes some effort, study, and practice.

In the above sample essay, transition words, phrases, sentences, and a whole paragraph serve as links between what John's photography was and what it is now. The following exercises are designed to help make you more conscious of the need for transitions and the links and interactions they provide.

EXERCISE 1
Go back to your reading assignment in this section and list all the transitional words and phrases you can find. Bring your list to class and compare your findings with those of others in the class.

EXERCISE 2
Examine each essay to see if there are any transition sentences or whole paragraphs of transition in any of the three essays. If so, underline them. Bring your findings to class for discussion.

EXERCISE 3
Write a transition sentence for each of the transition words from the list you made in Exercise 1.

EXERCISE 4
Using the sample paragraph on John's photography as a model, write a brief paragraph using clear transitional devices.

EXERCISE 5
Check over your three-paragraph essay. Have you built bridges for your reader? Add any necessary transitional devices that will make your discussion easier to understand and more pleasurable to read.

Sentence Structure: Review of Style

The first five units have helped you to become more aware of your need to manipulate sentences and to increase your sentence-building skills. But acquiring such improved skills constitutes only the first step towards a more effective and pleasing writing style. To be a truly effective writer, you must make conscious choices as you manipulate your sentences. In other words, as a writer, you must always try to understand the effects that addition, deletion, rearrangement, and substitution have on your reading audience. For example, as you edit your work, you should ask yourself the following questions.

1. If I join two sentences together with a coordinating conjunction, would my discussion be clearer? Better focused? More emphatic? More logical? Smoother? Would the revised sentence show the relationship of ideas more clearly?
2. If I join two sentences together by subordinating one clause to the other, would my discussion be clearer? More emphatic? Better focused? More logical? Smoother? Would the revised sentence show the relationship of ideas more clearly?
3. If I move a subordinate clause from the left side of the sentence to the right side, would the rearranged sentence be more emphatic? Clearer? More focused? Easier to read? Smoother? If I move a clause from the right side of the sentence to the left side, would the revised sentence be more emphatic? Clearer? More focused? Smoother? Easier to read?
4. If I delete unnecessary words such as "Who is," would my sentence be more direct? Easier to comprehend? More active?
5. If I reduced the repetition of nouns by creating a relative clause, would my revised sentence be clearer? More active? More emphatic? Smoother? Would the revised sentence show the relationship of ideas more clearly?
6. Would short simple sentences be more effective than a long, complex sentence? Would they be clearer? More emphatic? Easier to read and understand?
7. Have I used the passive voice when the active voice would be more exciting? Clearer? Better focused? More emphatic? Have I used the active voice when the passive voice would be more emphatic? Smoother? Clearer? Better focused?

Editing sentences, then, requires both skill and an awareness of the effects that sentence structure has on readers. Always remember that most sentences can be rewritten in many, many different ways; and that each time they are restructured, they create a different effect. For instance, notice the changes in the following sentences. Can you "feel" differences between the sentences? Can you explain what subtle differences in meaning result from each sentence manipulation?

1. The fat, sloppy boy who ate the greasy hamburger dripped onions, pickles, and relish down his chin.

2. The fat, sloppy boy ate the greasy hamburger and dripped onions, pickles, and relish down his chin.
3. The greasy hamburger, which was eaten by the fat, sloppy boy, dripped onions, pickles, and relish down his chin.
4. The fat, sloppy boy who was eating the greasy hamburger dripped onions, pickles, and relish down his chin.
5. The fat, sloppy boy eating the greasy hamburger dripped onions, pickles, and relish down his chin.
6. Eating the greasy hamburger, the fat, sloppy boy dripped onions, pickles, and relish down his chin.
7. The fat, sloppy boy ate a greasy hamburger. He dripped onions, pickles, and relish down his chin.
8. The fat, sloppy boy dripped onions, pickles, and relish down his chin while he ate a greasy hamburger.
9. The boy, fat and sloppy, dripping onions, pickles, and relish down his chin, ate a greasy hamburger.
10. The boy, fat and sloppy, dripped onions, pickles, and relish down his chin as he ate a greasy hamburger.

These are but a few of the possible arrangements of the same material; but the revisions clearly show that subtle differences in meaning, clarity, emphasis, and tone occur as sentences are restructured. Because of these subtle differences, writers must put much effort into reworking their paragraphs, adjusting their sentences for maximal effect. As you rework your own paragraphs, keep in mind the following guidelines on style.

1. The two points of a sentence that receive the most emphasis are the beginning and end. Thus, if you wish to place special focus on a word or phrase, do *not* place that word or phrase in the middle of the sentence.

    Examples
    Móther gave Dad a gíft.

    Móther gave a gift to Dád.

2. Readers can generally understand a long, complicated sentence best if few sentence structures precede the subject and verb. In other words, once readers know the who or what of a sentence and understand what action takes place, they can follow a writer's commentary with relative ease.

    Example
    ADEQUATE
    Although camera equipment, especially lens and filters, is quite expensive, often costing thousands of dollars even when purchased at a discount, more people than ever before have taken up photography as a hobby.

EASIER TO COMPREHEND
More people than ever before have taken up photography as a hobby, even though camera equipment, especially lens and filters, is quite expensive, often costing thousands of dollars even when purchased at a discount.

3. An effective way to show relationships between ideas is to combine sentences through coordination and subordination.

    Examples
    a. The magician performed all his best tricks. The audience failed to respond.

        Although the magician performed all his best tricks, the audience failed to respond.
    b. I shopped for a new school wardrobe. I didn't buy any new clothes.

        I shopped for a new school wardrobe, but I didn't buy any new clothes.

4. Deleting unnecessary words can often make a sentence more direct and emphatic.

    Example
    The dog that is nibbling on my shoe is teething.

    The dog nibbling on my shoe is teething.

EXERCISE 1

Combine the following kernel sentences to create an effective paragraph. You may add words such as conjunctions and transitionals, delete unnecessary words, substitute pronouns for nouns, and rearrange parts of sentences as you see fit.

I hate jogging.

I jog every morning at dawn.

I jog around the reservoir.

The reservoir is in Central Park.

Central Park is in New York City.

I hate jogging every morning.

It is so tedious.

Some people disagree.

For them jogging is thought conducive.

Others look at the scenery.

Scenery relieves the monotony.

The pace is wrong for me.

I cannot contemplate ideas.

I cannot contemplate vistas.

All I can think about is jogging.

I can think about nothing.

There is an advantage to jogging around a reservoir.

There is no dry shortcut home.

EXERCISE 2
Check paragraph one in the reading "Fear of Dearth" in Unit 7 and compare your version of the previous paragraph with the author's. What are the subtle differences in meaning, emphasis, and tone between the two versions? Can you suggest why and how these differences occur?

EXERCISE 3
Combine the following sentences to create an effective paragraph. You may add words such as transitionals, delete unnecessary words, substitute pronouns for nouns, and rearrange parts of the sentences as you see fit.

Captain John Smith arrived off the coast of Virginia.

His little band of colonists arrived off the coast of Virginia.

They arrived 372 years ago.

They confronted a wilderness.

The wilderness was vast.

A squirrel could travel from the Atlantic to the prairie's edge.

It would not touch the ground.

The forests were cut lavishly for three centuries.

The forests were cut wastefully for three centuries.

Americans can thank their stars.

Seventy percent of the forest still exists.

Our oil is fast dwindling.

Our trees mostly remain.

Trees are a natural resource.

The resource is of incomparable value.

EXERCISE 4
Check paragraph one in the reading "America's Green Gold" in Unit 10 and compare your version of the previous paragraph with the author's. What are

the subtle differences in meaning, emphasis, and tone between the two versions? Can you suggest why and how these differences occur?

EXERCISE 5

Check through your first draft of this unit's writing assignment. Could any sentences be adjusted by addition, deletion, rearrangements, or substitution for a better effect? If so, make these adjustments.

Punctuation: Review of Comma Usage

Review the following rules of comma usage. If you are still having difficulties with any of them, review the Punctuation sections in Units 2, 3, 4, and 5.

1. Place a comma before the conjunction in a compound sentence if the two parts of the sentence are long; if the two parts are rather short, make a conscious choice on this matter. Always consider how fast you want your reader to read and what emphasis you want placed on the second half of the sentence.
2. Use commas to separate all left-branch subordinate clauses from the midbranch.
3. Use commas to separate all long phrases on the left branch from the midbranch.
4. Use commas to separate short phrases and single words on the left branch from the midbranch if you wish to adjust your emphasis. You must make conscious choices in these cases.
5. Use commas to separate any left-branch words or phrases from the midbranch if these words or phrases might otherwise cause confusion or misreading.
6. Use commas to separate a right-branch word or phrase that describes or renames the final noun of the midbranch kernel sentence.
7. Use commas to separate right-branch subordinate clauses from the midbranch if you want to adjust emphasis. You must make conscious choices in these cases.
8. Separate all items of a series (words, phrases, clauses, or sentences) with commas.
9. Use pairs of commas to set off all midbranch words, phrases, or clauses that act as free modifiers.

EXERCISE 1

Place commas wherever needed in the following sentences.

1. Although I have never been able to learn the French language I was able to communicate in Paris through the use of a phrase book my fluttering hands and my facial expressions.

2. Early yesterday afternoon before the announcement was officially made I thought the football game would not be rescheduled.
3. Choking the man turned blue from a lack of oxygen.
4. Enrico registered for Physics 3A which was supposed to be taught by Professor Miller but when he found out that Professor Dewey was assigned to the class he transferred to Chemistry 6B.
5. No I won't help you.
6. To begin with the debate team investigated its opponent's issues before researching its own position.
7. Whenever parents say "no" to their children their children proceed to do what they want to do that is until they get caught.
8. Now she has decided to make her own clothes although she really doesn't know how to sew.
9. As soon as the United Nations was established it faced many serious problems such as vetoes war and invasions.
10. Flying over the Atlantic ocean the jet cruised at 42,000 feet not lowering its altitude until one hour out of Ireland.

EXERCISE 2

Place commas in the following paragraphs wherever you think they are needed. When you are finished, turn back to the reading in Unit 4 "Confessions of a City Woodcutter," paragraphs 28 and 29, and compare your use of commas with the author's. Be prepared to defend your system of punctuation. If you and the author have made different conscious choices, evaluate the effect these choices have on the paragraphs.

The only American houses that are built largely without the destruction of trees are concrete and stucco bungalows on desert sites mostly in Arizona and Nevada. And even with them wood scaffolding and forms for poured concrete are often used. If you live in a house you are responsible for the destruction of trees because of your need for shelter. The same applies also to those who live in apartment houses although the guilt is more removed. Aside from a few hermits who live in natural shelters such as caves all of us are responsible for the cutting of many trees.

To lessen the shock I always point out that trees and other living things cannot be preserved. Natural death overtakes them and wise use before that event is largely guiltless provided other trees or living things are allowed to replace them through natural growth or artificial generation such as forestation. Burning wood as fuel is perhaps the least harmful form of consumption since trees replace themselves very rapidly if allowed to do so. And wood fires create only the pollution that nature herself produces. The products of wood oxidation are the same as those generated by a tree that rots away unused by man. Oil coal and gas on the other hand are fossil fuels that can never be replaced and burning them produces pollution.

EXERCISE 3

Look over your writing assignment. Have you used commas correctly? Are there any sentences in which the addition or deletion of commas would make your essay more effective? Clearer? More emphatic? Make all necessary changes.

Preparing the Final Copy and Proofreading

1. Read the final copy of your essay aloud, slowly and carefully, listening for the end of every sentence in order to avoid comma splices, fused sentences, and fragments that need to be attached to main clauses.
2. Check to see that all pronouns refer back clearly and accurately to a noun immediately or closely preceding the reference.
3. Check to see if there are any vague or ambiguous sentences that need recasting.
3. Check to see that all words are spelled correctly.
5. Check to be sure your paper adheres to the rules of manuscript preparation: proper margins, double-spaced, and neatly corrected.

UNIT 7
Exposition: Cause and Effect; Effect and Cause

READING:
Exposition: Cause and Effect; Effect and Cause

Reading Strategies: Reading for Different Purposes — Reports, Articles, and Essays in Various Disciplines

One misleading idea that many students have about reading is that they should aim for the same speed no matter what they read, whether it is a newspaper, a popular magazine, a novel picked up at the supermarket, an assigned book, or a textbook. These students are self-critical when they find themselves reading their college assignments more slowly than other material and often think something is wrong. But as you may have suspected, after practicing skimming in Unit 1, close reading in Units 2 and 3, and scanning in Unit 5, your *purpose* or intention in reading helps determine your reading speed. If your intention is to relax and enjoy a magazine, a novel, or other kind of light reading, chances are you will read those materials faster than you will an assigned book or text. This difference in reading speed is also related to the difficulty of the material. Certainly you will need to spend more time on each page in your chemistry text than you would on a page in a book of short stories. The first presents concentrated information that you must comprehend; the second helps you to move forward through style and plot.

One very important thing to remember throughout your college career is that everything assigned for a class requires more than one reading in order to gain complete comprehension. In fact, some difficult material may require several readings for your complete understanding. Once you accept the fact that you will be rereading, you can feel more confident about changing your reading speed. Each of the major steps in reading — skimming, close reading, and scanning — will be done at different speeds. To review, skimming is done at a rather rapid speed so you can gain an overview, not total comprehension, of the material. In contrast, close reading slows your speed as you look for main ideas and supporting data. And scanning requires a speed somewhere between that of skimming and close reading, a speed determined by whether you are reviewing the material for an in-class discussion or studying for a test.

Reading reports, articles, or essays for various academic disciplines requires all of the skills and variations in speed discussed previously; but some very difficult materials, especially those that offer densely packed information, present additional problems. One technique that can assist you in extracting the basic concepts of an article or report involves writing brief summaries.

The Précis

The *précis* ("pray-see") is a brief summary of the essential thought of a complex piece. To get the best results from this kind of summary, carefully report the author's *thesis, main points of discussion, research methodology, major findings*, and *primary data*. Your précis should be rather short, usually under 250 words, and should never include any of your own interpretations or personal reactions. To write a précis that will help you in reviewing for exams, follow these guidelines.

1. Read carefully, using your close reading skills. Look up any words or phrases you don't understand. Find the main ideas and important supporting details and underline them. This underlined material is the basis for your précis.
2. As you write, use your own words, although you can include a few key words or phrases in quotation marks.
3. Be concise but always use complete sentences. Most passages can be reduced by two-thirds to three-fourths. Omit minor details.
4. Follow the original organization or pattern of development, maintaining the author's emphasis.
5. Include the author's name, the article title, and the sources of the article.

EXERCISE 1

Skim the essay assigned to you in this unit. Reread the essay slowly, marking the author's thesis and major points of discussion. Then write a précis of the passage, following the guidelines listed above.

Cloze Exercise: Focus on Pronouns

In the preceding units, you reviewed the functions and sentence positions of coordinators, nouns, and adjectives. Another type of word that has distinct functions in a sentence is the *pronoun*. Pronouns have four functions: they serve as substitutes for nouns, as intensifiers of nouns, as modifiers of nouns, and as interrogatives or question signals.

1. Pronouns that replace nouns belong to the following classes and serve as subjects of sentences or clauses, objects of verbs, indirect objects, and objects of prepositions.
    a. *Personal Pronouns* substitute for the names of specific persons or things: *I, we, you, he, she, it, they, me, him, her, them, us.*

Examples
He gave *it* to *me.*

John sold *it.*

   b. *Demonstrative Pronouns* substitute for the names of specific persons or things that are being pointed out: *this, that, these, those.*

Example
This became a serious problem.

   c. *Indefinite Pronouns* substitute for the names of nonspecific persons or things: *anybody, anyone, someone, somebody, everyone, everybody, each, either, neither, one, none, some, several, few, both.*

Example
Somebody answered the phone.

   d. *Reflexive Pronouns* substitute for nouns when these nouns perform action upon themselves. These pronouns appear after the verb as objects of prepositions: *myself, yourself, himself, herself, itself, themselves, ourselves.*

Examples
The man shot *himself.*

The lonely woman talked to *herself* all day long.

   e. *Relative Pronouns* substitute for nouns in forming relative clauses: *who, whom, which, what, that, whoever, whichever, whatever.*

Example
The boy *who* was waiting for his friend paced up and down the sidewalk.

2. Pronouns that intensify nouns take the same basic form as the reflexive pronoun, but *Pronoun Intensifiers* usually appear directly *after* the nouns they modify: *myself, yourself, yourselves, himself, herself, itself, ourselves, themselves.*

Example
James *himself* broke his stereo, not you.

3. Pronouns that modify nouns are called *Possessive Pronouns* since they indicate possession or ownership. They appear either before a noun or after a "to be" verb: *my, mine, our, ours, your, yours, his, hers, their, theirs.*

Examples
John sold *his* book.
This car is *mine.*

4. *Interrogative Pronouns* substitute for the names of unknown persons or things and signal that a question is being asked: *who, whom, which, what.*

Example
Who wrote this book?

Understanding these functions and positions of pronouns can help you to quickly fixate your eyes onto meaningful phrases and to anticipate what comes next in a sentence. Both skills lead towards more effective reading.

In the following Cloze exercise, four types of words have been omitted: nouns, pronouns, adjectives, and coordinators. As you work through the exercise, keep in mind the functions and possible positions of these types of words. On completion of the exercise, be prepared to justify your choice of words for each blank space.

EXERCISE 1

A great many Americans have become vegetarians. They have stopped eating _____ for a variety of _____. Some claim meat is _____, causing heart disease, high _____ pressure, diabetes, constipation, cancer, _____ obesity; some don't like _____ taste of red meat; _____ believe killing animals is _____; some belong to a _____ that proscribes eating meat. Whatever the reason for _____ meatless diets, not all _____ avoid all animal products. _____ will eat poultry, fish _____ eggs, while others will use dairy products.

Words and the Language:
The Structure of Words — Suffixes

Suffixes affect the way a word functions in a sentence. They thus contrast with roots, which establish the base meaning of words, and prefixes, which alter that meaning by extension or negation. Suffixes, generally occurring as final syllables, identify words as nouns, adjectives, verbs, or adverbs. For example, alien**ate** is a verb (many parents alienate their children), but alien**ation** is a noun

Table 7-1 Noun, Verb, Adjective, and Adverb Suffixes

Noun Suffixes	Verb Suffixes	Adjective Suffixes	Adverb Suffixes
tion, -cion, -sion	-ize	-ic	-ly
-ism	-ify	-ent	-wise
-ity, -ty	-ise	-tive	
-ness	-ate	-ly	
-ment		-ous	
-ance, -ence		-al, -ical	
-ence		-less	
-ure		-ant	
-hood		-able, -ible	
		-ful	
		-ical	
		-ive	
		-ate	

(this alienation may be temporary). Knowing the common suffixes of English can therefore increase both your reading and writing ability — as a reader you will recognize more words, and as a writer you can make more conscious choices about the most effective words for a specific situation. In other words, you can make your writing more lively and precise by knowing how to manipulate noun forms, adjective forms, and verb forms.

Examine the list of suffixes in Table 7-1 and then complete the exercises.

EXERCISE 1

Alter the following words by changing their suffixes. Use a dictionary if necessary.

1. Make the following adjectives into adverbs.

   Example
   pathetic   pathetically

   vicarious

   placid

   translucent

2. Make the following nouns into verbs.

   Example
   alienation   alienate

   human

   beauty

   nation

3. Make the following adjectives into nouns and verbs.

   Example
   meliorative   melioration   meliorate
   communal
   different

EXERCISE 2

List as many words as you can think of using four to five of the suffixes listed above.

   Example
   -ize: criticize, lionize, patronize, nationalize, mechanize

EXERCISE 3

From one of the assigned reading selections, find five words whose function will change if the suffix is changed. Now make up your own sentences, using these words with the new suffixes.

   Examples
   1. "When we were at last safely in the lane I almost *collapsed* with relief."

      I ran quickly to the safety of the *collapsible* tent.
   2. "We spent, my husband and I and the baby, a *restorative* week in paradise."

      The *restoration* of the cathedral was completed.

READINGS: SELECTION ONE

Fear of Dearth
by Carll Tucker

Ideas to Think About

1. All of us, except perhaps a few highly disciplined people, overindulge at times. Sometimes we overeat or gorge ourselves on unnutritious junk food; sometimes we avoid doing chores or homework, preferring to loll around the house watching TV or reading a detective story; sometimes we stay out late, knowing we will never be able to get up in time for school or work. The next day, however, we often feel guilty, ill, or worried. Discuss how you tend to overindulge and describe how you feel the next day.
2. Many of today's Americans are more health-conscious than people of previous generations. They diet more, exercise more, and talk on and on about physical fitness and youth. Are you one of these people? If so, describe what you do to maintain your health. If you are not one of these people, tell how you react to this national pastime.
3. In his essay, Tucker seeks to find the reasons why millions of Americans now jog. As you read, analyze all suggested reasons for this new craze and decide if they are valid.

Vocabulary

Look at each word as it is used in the article. (The number in parentheses indicates the paragraph in which it appears.) First, try to understand the meaning from the way it is used in the sentence. Second, use any clues to meaning through the structure of the word. Then, use the dictionary to clarify the meaning.

reservoir (1)	charismatic (8)
array (2)	resurgence (8)
disparate (4)	dearth (9)
predecessors (4)	penance (9)
theologians (7)	gluttony (9)

Fear of Dearth

I hate jogging. Every dawn, as I thud around New York City's Central Park reservoir, I am reminded of how much I hate it. It's so tedious. Some claim jogging is thought conducive; others insist the scenery relieves the monotony. For me the pace is wrong for contemplation of either ideas or vistas. While jogging, all I can think about is jogging — or nothing. One advantage of jogging around a reservoir° is that there's no dry shortcut home.

From the listless looks of some fellow trotters, I gather I am not alone in my unenthusiasm: Bill-paying, it seems, would be about as diverting. Nonetheless, we continue to *choose* to jog. From a practically infinite array° of opportunities, we select one that we don't enjoy and can't wait to have done with. Why?

For any trend, there are as many reasons as there are participants. This person runs to lower his blood pressure. That person runs to escape the telephone or a cranky spouse or a filthy household. Another person runs to avoid doing anything else, to dodge a decision about how to lead his life or a realization that his life is leading nowhere. Each of us has his carrot and stick. In my case, the stick is my slackening physical condition, which keeps me from beating opponents at tennis whom I overwhelmed two years ago. My carrot is to win.

Beyond these disparate° reasons, however, lies a deeper cause. It is no accident that now, in the last third of the 20th century, personal fitness and health have suddenly become a popular obsession. True, modern man likes to feel good, but that hardly distinguishes him from his predecessors.°

With zany myopia,[1] economists like to claim that the deeper cause of everything is economic. Delightfully, there seems no marketplace explanation for jogging. True, jogging is cheap, but then not jogging is cheaper. And the scant and skimpy equipment which jogging demands must make it a marketer's least favored form of recreation.

Some scout-masterish philosophers argue that the appeal of jogging and other body-maintenance programs is the discipline they afford. We live in a world in which individuals have fewer and fewer obligations. The work week has shrunk. Weekend worship is less compulsory. Technology gives us more free time. Satisfactorily filling free time requires imagination and effort. Freedom is a wide and risky river; it can drown the person who does not know how to swim across it. The more obligations one takes on, the more time one occupies, the less threat freedom poses. Jogging can become an instant obligation. For a portion of his day, the jogger is not his own man; he is obedient to a regimen he has accepted.

Theologians° may take the argument one step further. It is our modern irreligion, our lack of confidence in any hereafter, that makes us anxious to stretch our mortal stay as long as possible. We run, as the saying goes, for our lives, hounded by the suspicion that these are the only lives we are likely to enjoy.

All of these theorists seem to me more or less right. As the growth of cults and charismatic° religions and the resurgence° of enthusiasm for the military draft suggest, we do crave commitment. And who can doubt, watching so many middle-aged and older persons torturing themselves in

---

[1] Near-sightedness.

the name of fitness, that we are unreconciled to death, more so perhaps than any generation in modern memory?

But I have a hunch there's a further explanation of our obsession with exercise. I suspect that what motivates us even more than a fear of death is a fear of dearth.° Our era is the first to anticipate the eventual depletion of all natural resources. We see wilderness shrinking; rivers losing their capacity to sustain life; the air, even the stratosphere, being loaded with potentially deadly junk. We see the irreplaceable being squandered, and in the depths of our consciousness we are fearful that we are creating an uninhabitable world. We feel more or less helpless and yet, at the same time, desirous to protect what resources we can. We recycle soda bottles and restore old buildings and protect our nearest natural resource — our physical health — in the almost superstitious hope that such small gestures will help save an earth that we are blighting. Jogging becomes a sort of penance° for our sins of gluttony,° greed, and waste. Like a hairshirt or a bed of nails, the more one hates it, the more virtuous it makes one feel.

That is why *we* jog. Why *I* jog is to win at tennis.

Discussion

1. Tucker's essay follows an effect and cause format. He first describes a situation (effect) and then suggests its possible causes. Make a list of these possible causes in the order that the author discusses them. Why do you think Tucker arranges his material in this way?
2. Tucker carefully analyzes the reasons Americans jog, but then, in the last sentence, announces his own reason, one which has no similarity to the others. What is the effect of this statement on the essay? Does it change its tone? Its seriousness? Its message? How did you react to the swift reversal? Do you accept the author's pronouncement, or do you think he refuses to accept the true reason for his morning misery?
3. Which of Tucker's reasons for jogging do you believe are the most valid? Discuss why.
4. Jogging is one of today's most popular pastimes. What pastimes were very fashionable ten years ago but are now less popular? Why do you think their popularity faded? What other pastimes are now popular? Can you suggest reasons why people have become interested in them?

READINGS: SELECTION TWO
Pomp and Civil Engineering
by Samuel C. Florman

Ideas to Think About
1. Have you ever noticed "institutional advertising" — those ads that try to promote a group's reputation or a corporation's name, not sell a product? Describe one such ad and discuss its effectiveness.
2. Do you approve of doctors, lawyers, or engineers advertising their services? Why or why not? Should some professions be prohibited from advertising schedules of fees or types of services? Explain.
3. Florman begins his essay arguing against institutional advertising to promote the profession of civil engineering but then turns his emphasis towards the role of this profession. Look for this change in focus as you read through the essay. Does Florman prepare you for such a shift?

Vocabulary
Look at each word as it is used in the article. (The number in parentheses indicates the paragraph in which it appears.) First, try to understand the meaning from the way it is used in the sentence. Second, use any clues to meaning through the structure of the word. Then, use the dictionary to clarify the meaning.

erstwhile (2)	antithesis (8)
aeronautical (2)	diffidence (8)
transmuted (3)	sordid (8)
venerable (3)	lamentable (17)
array (6)	pandering (21)
anachronism (6)	transcend (21)

Pomp and Civil Engineering

Samuel C. Florman is a contributing editor of *Harper's* and the author of *The Existential Pleasures of Engineering.*

In the pages of a recent issue of *Business Week* there appeared a most peculiar advertisement. On the left-hand page was a large picture of an ambulance with lights ablaze, and above it the caption "We civil engineers believe a carload of cantaloupes shouldn't come between an ambulance and its hospital." To the right was a small picture of a civil engineer standing in front of an insignificant-looking railroad overpass. Above this picture the caption continued: "I could just imagine somebody with a coronary¹ in the ambulance that has to wait for a seventy-two car slow freight to pass . . ." and paragraphs followed elaborating the social importance of engineering. The lengthy commentary ended with "For more information about how civil engineers serve people, write to the American Society of Civil Engineers."

The advertisement's more subtle message, I suppose, is this: Civil engineers, erstwhile° heroes of a developing nation, are unhappy about having lost their appeal. No longer do they swagger through popular novels in high-laced boots, or win the pretty girl in movies about the building of the Pacific railroad. They are not to be found among the rock stars and astronauts on television talk shows, nor in *People* magazine. What little public attention is granted these days to science and technology is accorded for the most part to physicists and surgeons. And when the rare engineer does make news, he invariably represents one of the more glamorous branches of the profession: electrical, chemical, or aeronautical.° The public takes for granted its railroads, highways, bridges, tunnels, airports, aqueducts, and sewers. It is bored by dams and skyscrapers, and — as a result of environmentalism — increasingly hostile toward those who make them.

Civil engineers are understandably frustrated by this decline in status. Nonetheless, it is astonishing to see this frustration transmuted° into an advertising campaign. Professional societies send slide shows to high schools and discreet public-service announcements to local radio stations. Occasionally they lobby, and even buy space in newspapers and magazines to speak out on issues. But they don't hire advertising agencies and pay large sums to the media in an attempt to buff up their public image. Certainly not the American Society of Civil Engineers: it is venerable° (founded 1852), conservative, some would even say stuffy. When I learned that the society's board of directors had approved the campaign and announced it at this year's convention in Boston, my interest was piqued.² How had this come to pass? And what are the broader implications of this curious enterprise?

At ASCE headquarters the staff was ready with answers to my first question. The campaign had begun simply because society members *want* it. According to James Shea, who was appointed to the recently created post of director of public communications, an extensive canvass of the members in 1973 set improved public relations as a high priority. Three years later, more than 20,000 of the society's 76,000 members were surveyed, and again "gaining public recognition" was an activity most respondents thought deserved more attention. To this end, in 1977, the

---
¹ Heart attack.
² Aroused.

society's 25th year, a public-relations campaign was approved, built around the theme "Civil Engineering — A People-Serving Profession."

But public relations proved inadequate, according to Mr. Shea. "Reporters are only interested in us when the roof falls down in the Hartford Civic Center. If you want to get your message across, you have to go directly to the public, and you can only do that through advertising."

However persuasive the argument, the society's staff and officers seem nervous in anticipation of criticism. They have accumulated an array° of reports and questionnaires that support the advertising, and are prudently funding the campaign with an optional $4 contribution per member (in addition to the annual dues of $60). Partial returns indicate that at least $100,000 will be collected, and that is the amount that has been committed. Not a large sum for an advertising campaign, Mr. Shea conceded, but enough to pay for two-page spreads in Business Week, Engineering News-Record (in the interests of intramural morale), and a special executive-readership edition of Time, with some left over to pay for the society's float in the Tournament of Roses parade. (Started several years ago by the Los Angeles members, this anachronism° has become an ASCE tradition.) It is hoped that more money can be raised so that Newsweek and U.S. News & World Report can be added to the list.

I asked if the recent Supreme Court decisions about professional advertising — ruling that it may no longer be prohibited by professional societies — had anything to do with the new campaign. Mr. Shea admitted that there was some connection. "A new category of advertising is coming into being," he said, "and we hope to set the tone."

As I left ASCE headquarters, I wondered how one goes about setting the right tone for braggadocio.[3] Rationalize it as one will, to advertise is to boast — to puff: the antithesis° of the diffidence° traditional to engineering. What would the great civil engineers of the past think of this venture: John Smeaton, builder of the Eddystone lighthouse, who first assumed the title of civil engineer; John Rennie, who, after the opening of his Waterloo Bridge, said, "I had a hard business to escape knighthood"? What would be the comment of John Augustus Roebling, student of Hegel, creator of the Brooklyn Bridge? Surely these men would condemn the new campaign as a sordid° business.

Yet modesty, admirable as it may be, is not the essence of honor. In fact, to set too much store by modesty, to seek an aloof *dignity* above all, verges upon the ignoble.[4] Seen in this light, the advertising campaign is an act of courage for which the ASCE should be congratulated, having risked ridicule and charges of vanity in order to redeem the public value of a necessary discipline.

---

[3] Empty boasting.
[4] Not noble.

If professional self-acclaim is indeed to become a new category of advertising, the line between the praiseworthy and the fatuous[5] will be very thin. Thus a lot will depend on the performance of the "experts" to whom the professional societies turn for guidance.

The day after I visited ASCE headquarters, I called on the author of the campaign, Paul Lippman of Gaynor and Ducas, a small Manhattan advertising agency. He explained that the campaign is what is called in the trade "corporate advertising." Instead of trying to sell goods, its purpose is to affect the public's opinion of an institution. There is some financial motivation, to be sure, since civil engineers' salaries are to some degree related to the esteem in which civil engineering is held. But mainly the intent is to improve the image of the profession. This raises morale — a legitimate goal — and also serves to attract talented young people to the field.

"The first thing we look for," Mr. Lippman said, "is a creative rationale, a creative platform. I decided to stay away from big engineering projects. People can't relate to something like Hoover Dam. We have to be more specific and smaller in scale. So I thought we'd start with a single person, a real engineer, use his voice: "We civil engineers believe . . ." That has warmth, it's persuasive. Then I looked for a dramatic situation in which an *individual* is being helped by a civil engineer. For example, an ambulance that might be delayed by a train unless there's an overpass. Strong human interest."

Mr. Lippman admitted that he wrote the copy for the ad I saw in *Business Week,* but assured me that each of the engineers to be featured was a real person (nominated by his peers) who endorsed every word. "It could be you or your relative in that ambulance," Mr. Lippman said. "To be effective we've got to touch on the needs of individual people."

One might not care for Mr. Lippman's use of cantaloupes, but his point seems reasonable enough. Even so, there was something about the ad, and those proposed to follow, that I did not like.

I walked a few blocks from Mr. Lippman's office to Fifty-seventh Street and Madison Avenue, where excavation was proceeding for the new IBM building. Seventy feet below the surface a host of men and machines were carving an enormous hole into the rock, and I joined the people who were watching. An intricate pattern of steel and timber bracing supported the sidewalk on which we stood, suspended over the chasm. Walking along Fifty-seventh Street, past apartment houses, office buildings, stores, theatres, and art galleries, I envisioned the complex maze of pipes and cables that lay beneath the pavement. By the time I reached Carnegie Hall, its splendid tile-and-plaster ceiling suspended from 100-foot steel trusses, I knew what was wrong with the ASCE advertising campaign.

---

[5] Foolish or silly.

The essence of civil engineering lies not in what it can do for one person, but in what it does for the commonwealth. Ever since the first irrigation ditches were dug in Egypt, civil engineering has made it possible for large groups of people to live together. And ever since the building of the pyramids, civil engineering has provided the monuments and public works that inspire a sense of community.

If Mr. Lippman is right in his contention that people can no longer relate to Hoover Dam — or to Gustave Eiffel's tower, the Erie Canal, Yankee Stadium, the Golden Gate Bridge — then something lamentable° has happened to people. Not so long ago, schoolchildren studied the Seven Wonders of the Ancient World, and argued about what the seven modern wonders might be. Now it seems that no sense of wonder can be summoned at all.

An ambulance's unobstructed passage is the wrong image by which to define civil engineering. Yet it is difficult to fault the man who selected it. (Advertising, like technology, is one of those abstractions that people like to blame when the world disappoints them.) Mr. Lippman has assessed the public mood accurately: "What's in it for me?" But if civil engineers are to advertise, their proper role is to defy society's dispirited temper with symbols of civic grandeur.

If Mr. Lippman cannot find pictures of civil engineering projects to which a reader can "relate," let him start with *Twentieth Century Engineering,* the catalogue of a photography exhibit at the Museum of Modern Art in 1964. And if, after looking at the breathtaking photographs of towers, vaults, bridges, and other works, he still is at a loss for a "creative platform," perhaps he can borrow a few sentences from the catalogue's introduction by Arthur Drexler:

> Engineering is among the most rewarding of the arts not only because it produces individual masterpieces but because it is an art grounded in social responsibility. Today we lack the political and economic apparatus that would facilitate a truly responsible use of our technology. But it may be that a more skillful and humane use of engineering depends on a more knowledgeable response to its poetry.

The present rebellion against materialism and bigness, however understandable its origins, shrivels the human spirit. People begin by searching for an inner peace, and end by staring vacantly at sunsets, eating TV dinners in front of a flickering screen, and reassuring themselves that ambulances are standing by.

Civil engineering is an expression of group purpose and community pride — the counter-counterculture whose time is coming. It is sad to see the profession pandering° to the very egoism that it has a mission to transcend.°

Discussion

1. Florman claims that the present-day rebellion against materialism and bigness "shrivels the human spirit." Do you agree? Is a desire for material growth always bad? Explain.
2. Much of Florman's argument relies on information gained from interviews and on personal observations. How effective are these arguments in developing the thesis of the essay?
3. "Loaded" language (see Unit 4) is present thoughout this essay. Find two or three examples of sarcasm or emotionally charged phrases and examine the effectiveness of their use. How do they add or detract from Florman's discussion?
4. Discuss the role of civil engineering in American culture. Do you agree with Florman's view that "civil engineering is an expression of group purpose and community pride"? How would you describe the roles of the medical, legal, teaching, and accounting professions? Describe an advertising campaign you feel would be both ethical and effective for each of these professions.

274 UNIT 7 EXPOSITION: CAUSE AND EFFECT; EFFECT AND CAUSE

READINGS: SELECTION THREE

Memories of a Bilingual Education
by Richard Rodriguez

Ideas to Think About

1. Do you use the same vocabulary and level of formality whenever you speak? How does your language differ when talking to friends, parents, teachers, and members of the opposite sex?
2. How do you react when hearing people speak a foreign language on a bus, in a store, or at school? Why?
3. Rodriguez's discussion of private and public language is central to his thesis. Notice when it appears first in the essay.
4. Rodriguez makes effective use of comparison and contrast in several ways. For example, note the frequent use of sound and quotation to emphasize the contrast between private and public language.
5. A cause-and-effect pattern affects this essay in important ways. As you read, consider the major cause of the problem the author presents. What have been its effects on Rodriguez and others?

Vocabulary

Look at each word as it is used in the article. (The number in parentheses indicates the paragraph in which it appears.) First, try to understand the meaning from the way it is used in the sentence. Second, use any clues to meaning through the structure of the word. Then, use the dictionary to clarify the meaning.

preceded (1)
exotic (10)
polysyllabic (10)
incongruity (16)
inconsequential (17)
menial (27)

effusive (27)
assimilated (30)
paradoxically (31)
tenuous (31)
decadent (31)

Memories of a Bilingual Education

Richard Rodriguez is a writer living in San Francisco, California. A longer version of this essay appears as the opening chapter of his intellectual autobiography, *Hunger of Memory: The Education of Richard Rodriguez*, published in late 1981.

I remember, to start with, that day in Sacramento, in a California now nearly thirty years past, when I first entered a classroom — able to understand about fifty stray English words. The third of four children, I had been preceded° by my older brother and sister to a neighborhood Roman Catholic school. But neither of them had revealed very much about their classroom experiences. They left each morning and returned each afternoon, always together, speaking Spanish as they climbed the five steps to the porch. And their mysterious books, wrapped in brown shopping-bag paper, remained on the table next to the door, closed firmly behind them.

An accident of geography sent me to a school where all my classmates were white, and many were the children of doctors and lawyers and business executives. On that first day of school, my classmates must certainly have been uneasy to find themselves apart from their families, in the first institution of their lives. But I was astonished. I was fated to be the "problem student" in class.

The nun said, in a friendly but oddly impersonal voice: "Boys and girls, this is Richard Rodriguez." (I heard her sound it out: *Rich-heard Road-ree-guess*.) It was the first time I had heard anyone say my name in English. "Richard," the nun repeated more slowly, writing my name down in her book. Quickly I turned to see my mother's face dissolve in a watery blur behind the pebbled-glass door.

Now, many years later, I hear of something called "bilingual education" — a scheme proposed in the late 1960s by Hispanic-American social activists, later endorsed by a congressional vote. It is a program that seeks to permit non-English-speaking children (many from lower-class homes) to use their "family language" as the language of school. Such, at least, is the aim its supporters announce. I hear them and am forced to say no: It is not possible for a child, any child, ever to use his family's language in school. Not to understand this is to misunderstand the public uses of schooling and to trivialize the nature of intimate life.

Memory teaches me what I know of these matters. The boy reminds the adult. I was a bilingual child, but of a certain kind: "socially disadvantaged," the son of working-class parents, both Mexican immigrants.

In the early years of my boyhood, my parents coped very well in America. My father had steady work. My mother managed at home. They were nobody's victims. When we moved to a house many blocks from the Mexican-American section of town, they were not intimidated by those two or three neighbors who initially tried to make us unwelcome. ("Keep your brats away from my sidewalk!") But despite all they achieved, or perhaps because they had so much to achieve, they lacked any deep feeling of ease, of belonging in public. They regarded the people at work or in crowds as being very distant from us. Those were the others, *los gringos*. That term was interchangeable in their speech with another, even more telling: *los americanos*.

I grew up in a house where the only regular guests were my relations. On a certain day, enormous families of relatives would visit us, and there would be so many people that the noise and the bodies would spill out to the back yard and onto the front porch. Then for weeks no one would come. (If the doorbell rang, it was usually a salesman.) Our house stood apart — gaudy yellow in a row of white bungalows. We were the people with the noisy dog, the people who raised chickens. We were the foreigners on the block. A few neighbors would smile and wave at us. We waved back. But until I was seven years old, I did not know the name of the old couple living next door or the names of the kids living across the street.

In public, my father and mother spoke a hesitant, accented, and not always grammatical English. And then they would have to strain, their bodies tense, to catch the sense of what was rapidly said by *los gringos*. At home, they returned to Spanish. The language of their Mexican past sounded in counterpoint to the English spoken in public. The words would come quickly, with ease. Conveyed through those sounds was the pleasing, soothing, consoling reminder that one was at home.

During those years when I was first learning to speak, my mother and father addressed me only in Spanish; in Spanish I learned to reply. By contrast, English *(inglés)* was the language I came to associate with gringos, rarely heard in the house. I learned my first words of English overhearing my parents speaking to strangers. At six years of age, I knew just enough words for my mother to trust me on errands to stores one block away — but no more.

I was then a listening child, careful to hear the very different sounds of Spanish and English. Wide-eyed with hearing, I'd listen to sounds more than to words. First, there were English (gringo) sounds. So many words still were unknown to me that when the butcher or the lady at the drugstore said something, exotic° polysyllabic° sounds would bloom in the midst of their sentences. Often the speech of people in public seemed to me very loud, booming with confidence. The man behind the counter would literally ask, "What can I do for you?" But by being so firm and clear, the sound of his voice said that he was a gringo; he belonged in public society. There were also the high nasal notes of middle-class American speech — which I rarely am conscious of hearing today because I hear them so often, but could not stop hearing when I was a boy. Crowds at Safeway or at bus stops were noisy with the birdlike sounds of *los gringos*. I'd move away from them all — all the chirping chatter above me.

But then there was Spanish: *español,* the language rarely heard away from the house; *español,* the language that seemed to me, therefore, a private language, my family's language. To hear its sounds was to feel myself specially recognized as one of the family, apart from *los otros*. A simple remark, an inconsequential° comment would convey that assurance. My parents would say something to me, and I would feel embraced by the sounds of their words. Those sounds said: *I am speaking with ease in Spanish. I am addressing you in words I never use with* los gringos. *I recognize you as someone special, close, like no one outside. You belong with us. In the family. Ricardo.*

At the age of six, well past the time when most middle-class children no longer notice the difference between sounds uttered at home and words spoken in public, I had a different experience. I lived in a world compounded of sounds. I was a child longer than most. I lived in a magical world, surrounded by sounds both pleasing and fearful. I shared with my family a language enchantingly private — different from that used in the city around us.

Supporters of bilingual education imply today that students like me miss a great deal by not being taught in their family's language. What they seem not to recognize is that, as a socially disadvantaged child, I regarded Spanish as a private language. It was a ghetto language that deepened and strengthened my feeling of public separateness. What I needed to learn in school was that I had the right, and the obligation, to speak the public language. The odd truth is that my first-grade classmates could become bilingual, in the conventional sense of the word, more easily than I. Had they been taught early (as upper-middle-class children often are taught) a "second language" like Spanish or French, they could have regarded it simply as another public language. In my case, such bilingualism could not have been so quickly achieved. What I did not believe was that I could speak a single public language.

Without question, it would have pleased me to have heard my teachers address me in Spanish when I entered the classroom. I would have felt much less afraid. I would have imagined that my instructors were somehow "related" to me; I would indeed have heard their Spanish as my family's language. I would have trusted them and responded with ease. But I would have delayed — postponed for how long? — having to learn the language of public society. I would have evaded — and for how long? — learning the great lesson of school: that I had a public identity.

Fortunately, my teachers were unsentimental about their responsibility. What they understood was that I needed to speak public English. So their voices would search me out, asking me questions. Each time I heard them I'd look up in surprise to see a nun's face frowning at me. I'd mumble, not really meaning to answer. The nun would persist. "Richard, stand up. Don't look at the floor. Speak up. Speak to the entire class, not just to me!" But I couldn't believe English could be my language to use. (In part, I did not want to belive it.) I continued to mumble. I resisted the teacher's demands. (Did I somehow suspect that once I learned this public language my family life would be changed?) Silent, waiting for the bell to sound, I remained dazed, diffident, afraid.

Three months passed. Five. A half year. Unsmiling, ever watchful, my teachers noted my silence. They began to connect my behavior with the slow progress my brother and sister were making. Until, one Saturday morning, three nuns arrived at the house to talk to our parents. Stiffly they sat on the blue living-room sofa. From the doorway of another room, spying on the visitors, I noted the incongruity,° the clash of two worlds, the faces and voices of school intruding upon the familiar setting of home. I overheard one voice gently wondering, "Do your children speak only Spanish at home, Mrs. Rodriguez?" While another voice added, "That Richard especially seems so timid and shy."

That Rich-heard!

With great tact, the visitors continued, "Is it possible for you and your husband to encourage your children to practice their English when they are home?" Of course my parents complied. What would they not do for their children's well-being? And how could they question the church's authority, which those women represented? In an instant they agreed to give up the language (the sounds) that had revealed and accentuated our family's closeness. The moment the visitors left, the change was observed. "*Ahora,* speak to us only *en inglés,*" my father and mother told us.

At first, it seemed a kind of game. After dinner each night, the family gathered together to practice "our" English. It was still then *inglés,* a language foreign to us, so we felt drawn to it as strangers. Laughing, we would try to define words we could not pronounce. We played with strange English sounds, often over-anglicizing our pronunciations. And we filled the smiling gaps of our sentences with familiar Spanish sounds. But that was cheating, somebody shouted, and everyone laughed.

In school, meanwhile, like my brother and sister, I was required to attend a daily tutoring session. I needed a full year of this special work. I also needed my teachers to keep my attention from straying in class by calling out, "*Rich-heard!*" — their English voices slowly loosening the ties to my other name, with its three notes, *Ri-car-do.* Most of all, I needed to hear my mother and father speak to me in a moment of seriousness in "broken" — suddenly heartbreaking — English. This scene was inevitable. One Saturday morning I entered the kitchen where my parents were talking, but I did not realize that they were talking Spanish until, the moment they saw me, their voices changed and they began speaking English. The gringo sounds they uttered startled me. Pushed me away. In that moment of trivial misunderstanding and profound insight, I felt my throat twisted by unsounded grief. I simply turned and left the room. But I had no place to escape to where I could grieve in Spanish. My brother and sister were speaking English in another part of the house.

Again and again in the days following, as I grew increasingly angry, I was obliged to hear my mother and father encouraging me: "Speak to us *en inglés.*" Only then did I determine to learn classroom English. Thus, sometime afterward it happened: One day in school, I raised my hand to volunteer an answer to a question. I spoke out in a loud voice, and I did not think it remarkable when the entire class understood. That day I moved very far from being the disadvantaged child I had been only days earlier. Taken hold at last was the belief, the calming assurance, that I *belonged* in public.

Shortly after, I stopped hearing the high, troubling sounds of *los gringos*. A more and more confident speaker of English, I didn't listen to how strangers sounded when they talked to me. With so many English-speaking people around me, I no longer heard American accents. Conversations quickened. Listening to persons whose voices sounded eccentrically pitched, I might note their sounds for a few seconds, but then I'd concentrate on what they were saying. Now when I heard someone's tone of voice — angry or questioning or sarcastic or happy or sad — I didn't distinguish it from the words it expressed. Sound and word were thus tightly wedded. At the end of each day, I was often bemused, and always relieved, to realize how "soundless," though crowded with words, my day in public had been. An eight-year-old boy, I finally came to accept what had been technically true since my birth: I was an American citizen.

But diminished by then was the special feeling of closeness at home. Gone was the desperate, urgent, intense feeling of being at home among those with whom I felt intimate. Our family remained a loving family, but one greatly changed. We were no longer so close, no longer bound tightly together by the knowledge of our separateness from *los gringos*. Neither my older brother nor my sisters rushed home after school any more. Nor did I. When I arrived home, often there would be neighborhood kids in the house. Or the house would be empty of sounds.

Following the dramatic Americanization of their children, even my parents grew more publicly confident — especially my mother. First she learned the names of all the people on the block. Then she decided we needed to have a telephone in our house. My father, for his part, continued to use the word gringo, but it was no longer charged with bitterness or distrust. Stripped of any emotional content, the word simply became a name for those Americans not of Hispanic descent. Hearing him, sometimes, I wasn't sure if he was pronouncing the Spanish word *gringo,* or saying gringo in English.

There was a new silence at home. As we children learned more and more English, we shared fewer and fewer words with our parents. Sentences needed to be spoken slowly when one of us addressed our mother or father. Often the parent wouldn't understand. The child would need to repeat himself. Still the parent misunderstood. The young voice, frustrated, would end up saying, "Never mind" — the subject was closed. Dinners would be noisy with the clinking of knives and forks against dishes. My mother would smile softly between her remarks; my father, at the other end of the table, would chew and chew his food while he stared over the heads of his children.

My mother! My father! After English became my primary language, I no longer knew what words to use in addressing my parents. The old Spanish words (those tender accents of sound) I had earlier used — *mamá* and *papá* — I couldn't use any more. They would have been all-too-painful reminders of how much had changed in my life. On the other hand, the words I heard neighborhood kids call their parents seemed unsatisfactory. "Mother" and "father," "ma," "papa," "pa," "dad," "pop" (how I hated the all-American sound of that last word) — all these I felt were unsuitable terms of address for *my* parents. As a result, I never used them at home. Whenever I'd speak to my parents, I would try to get their attention by looking at them. In public conversations, I'd refer to them as my "parents" or my "mother" and "father."

My mother and father, for their part, responded differently as their children spoke to them less. My mother grew restless, seemed troubled and anxious at the scarceness of words exchanged in the house. She would question me about my day when I came home from school. She smiled at my small talk. She pried at the edges of my sentences to get me to say something more. ("What . . . ?") She'd join conversations she overheard, but her intrusions often stopped her children's talking. By contrast, my father seemed to grow reconciled to the new quiet. Though his English somewhat improved, he tended more and more to retire into silence. At dinner he spoke very little. One night his children and even his wife helplessly giggled at his garbled English pronunciation of the Catholic "Grace Before Meals." Thereafter he made his wife recite the prayer at the start of each meal, even on formal occasions when there were guests in the house.

Hers became the public voice of the family. On official business it was she, not my father, who would usually talk to strangers on the phone or in stores. We children grew so accustomed to his silence that years later we would routinely refer to his "shyness." (My mother often tried to explain: both of his parents died when he was eight. He was raised by an uncle who treated him as little more than a menial° servant. He was never encouraged to speak. He grew up alone — a man of few words.) But I realized my father was not shy whenever I'd watch him speaking Spanish with relatives. Using Spanish, he was quickly effusive.° Especially when talking with other men, his voice would spark, flicker, flare alive with varied sounds. In Spanish he expressed the ideas and feelings he rarely revealed when speaking English. With firm Spanish sounds he conveyed a confidence and authority that English would never allow him.

The silence at home, however, was not simply the result of fewer words passing between parents and children. More profound for me was the silence created by my inattention to sounds. At about the time I no longer bothered to listen with care to the sounds of English in public, I grew careless about listening to the sounds made by the family when they spoke. Most of the time I would hear someone speaking at home and didn't distinguish his sounds from the words people uttered in public. I didn't even pay much attention to my parents' accented and ungrammatical speech — at least not at home. Only when I was with them in public would I become alert to their accents. But even then, their sounds caused me less and less concern. For I was growing increasingly confident of my own public identity.

I would have been happier about my public success had I not recalled, sometimes, what it had been like earlier, when my family conveyed its intimacy through a set of conveniently private sounds. Sometimes in public, hearing a stranger, I'd hark back to my lost past. A Mexican farm worker approached me one day downtown. He wanted directions to some place. "*Hijito,* . . ." he said. And his voice stirred old longings. Another time I was standing beside my mother in the visiting room of a Carmelite convent, before the dense screen that rendered the nuns shadowy figures. I heard several of them speaking Spanish in their busy, singsong, overlapping voices, assuring my mother that, yes, yes, we were remembered, all our family were remembered in their prayers. Those voices echoed faraway family sounds. Another day, a dark-faced old woman touched my shoulder lightly to steady herself as she boarded a bus. She murmured something to me I couldn't quite comprehend. Her Spanish voice came near, like the face of a never-before-seen relative in the instant before I was kissed. That voice, like so many of the Spanish voices I'd heard in public, recalled the golden age of my childhood.

Bilingual educators say today that children lose a degree of "individuality" by becoming assimilated° into public society. (Bilingual schooling is a program popularized in the seventies, that decade when middle-class "ethnics" began to resist the process of assimilation — the "American melting pot.") But the bilingualists oversimplify when they scorn the value and necessity of assimilation. They do not seem to realize that a person is individualized in two ways. So they do not realize that, while one suffers a diminished sense of *private* individuality by being assimilated into public society, such assimilation makes possible the achievement of *public* individuality.

Simplistically again, the bilingualists insist that a student should be reminded of his difference from others in mass society, of his "heritage." But they equate mere separateness with individuality. The fact is that only in private — with intimates — is separateness from the crowd a prerequisite for individuality; an intimate "tells" me that I am unique, unlike all others, apart from the crowd. In public, by contrast, full individuality is achieved, paradoxically,° by those who are able to consider themselves members of the crowd. Thus it happened for me. Only when I was able to think of myself as an American, no longer an alien in gringo society, could I seek the rights and opportunities necessary for full public individuality. The social and political advantages I enjoy as a man began on the day I came to believe that my name is indeed *Rich-heard Road-ree-guess*. It is true that my public society today is often impersonal; in fact, my public society is usually mass society. But despite the anonymity of the crowd, and despite the fact that the individuality I achieve in public is often tenuous° — because it depends on my being one in a crowd — I celebrate the day I acquired my new name. Those middle-class ethnics who scorn assimilation seem to me filled with decadent° self-pity, obsessed by the burden of public life. Dangerously, they romanticize public separateness and trivialize the dilemma of those who are truly socially disadvantaged.

32   I grew up the victim of a disconcerting confusion. As I became fluent in English, I could no longer speak Spanish with confidence. I continued to understand spoken Spanish, and in high school I learned how to read and write Spanish. But for many years I could not pronounce it. A powerful guilt blocked my spoken words; an essential glue was missing whenever I would try to connect words to form sentences. I would be unable to break a barrier of sound, to speak freely. I would speak, or try to speak, Spanish, and I would manage to utter halting, hiccupping sounds that betrayed my unease. (Even today, I speak Spanish very slowly, at best.)

33   When relatives and Spanish-speaking friends of my parents came to the house, my brother and sister would usually manage to say a few words before being excused. I never managed so gracefully. Each time I'd hear myself addressed in Spanish, I couldn't respond with any success. I'd know the words I wanted to say, but everything I said seemed to me horribly anglicized. My mouth wouldn't form the sounds right. My jaw would tremble. After a phrase or two, I'd stutter, cough up a warm, silvery sound, and stop.

34   My listeners were surprised to hear me. They'd lower their heads to grasp better what I was trying to say. They would repeat their questions in gentle, affectionate voices. But then I would answer in English. No, no, they would say, we want you to speak to us in Spanish *("en español")*. But I couldn't do it. Then they would call me *Pocho*. Sometimes playfully, teasing, using the tender diminutive — *mi pochito*. Sometimes not so playfully but mockingly, *pocho*. (A Spanish dictionary defines that word as an adjective meaning "colorless" or "bland." But I heard it as a noun, naming the Mexican-American who, in becoming an American forgets his native society.) "¡Pocho!" my mother's best friend muttered, shaking her head. And my mother laughed, somewhere behind me. She said that her children didn't want to practice "our Spanish" after they started going to school. My mother's smiling voice made me suspect that the lady who

faced me was not really angry with me. But searching her face, I couldn't find the hint of a smile.

    Yet, even during those years of guilt, I was coming to grasp certain consoling truths about language and intimacy — truths that I learned gradually. Once, I remember playing with a friend in the back yard when my grandmother appeared at the window. Her face was stern with suspicion when she saw the boy (the *gringo* boy) I was with. She called out to me in Spanish, sounding the whistle of her ancient breath. My companion looked up and watched her intently as she lowered the window and moved (still visible) behind the light curtain, watching us both. He wanted to know what she had said. I started to tell him, to translate her Spanish words into English. The problem was, however, that though I knew how to translate exactly what she had told me, I realized that any translation would distort the deepest meaning of her message: it had been directed only to me. This message of intimacy could never be translated because it did not lie in the actual words she had used but passed through them. So any translation would have seemed wrong; the words would have been stripped of an essential meaning. Finally, I decided not to tell my friend anything — just that I didn't hear all she had said. 35

    This insight was unfolded in time. As I made more and more friends outside my house, I began to recognize intimate messages spoken in English in a close friend's confidential tone or secretive whisper. Even more remarkable were those instances when, apparently for no special reason, I'd become conscious of the fact that my companion was speaking *only to me*. I'd marvel then, just hearing his voice. It was a stunning event to be able to break through the barrier of public silence, to be able to hear the voice of the other, to realize that it was directed just to me. After such moments of intimacy outside the house, I began to trust what I heard intimately conveyed through my family's English. Voices at home at last punctured sad confusion. I'd hear myself addressed as an intimate — in English. Such moments were never as raucous with sounds as in past times, when we had used our "private" Spanish. (Our English-sounding house was never to be as noisy as our Spanish-sounding house had been.) Intimate moments were usually moments of soft sound. My mother would be ironing in the dining room while I did my homework nearby. She would look over at me, smile, and her voice sounded to tell me that I was her son. *Richard*. 36

    Intimacy thus continued at home; intimacy was not stilled by English. Though there were fewer occasions for it — a change in my life that I would never forget — there were also times when I sensed the deep truth about language and intimacy: *Intimacy is not created by a particular language; it is created by intimates*. Thus the great change in my life was not linguistic but social. If, after becoming a successful student, I no longer heard intimate voices as often as I had earlier, it was not because I spoke 37

English instead of Spanish. It was because I spoke a public language for most of my day. I moved easily at last, a citizen in a crowded city of words.

As a man I spend most of my day in public, in a world largely devoid of speech sounds. So I am quickly attracted by the glamorous quality of certain alien voices. I still am gripped with excitement when someone passes me on the street speaking in Spanish. I have not moved beyond the range of the nostalgic pull of those sounds. And there is something very compelling about the sounds of lower-class blacks. Of all the accented versions of English that I hear in public, I hear theirs most intently. The Japanese tourist stops me downtown to ask me a question, and I inch my way past his accent to concentrate on what he is saying. The Eastern European immigrant in the neighborhood delicatessen speaks to me, and, again, I do not pay much attention to his sounds, nor to the Texas accent of one of my neighbors or the Chicago accent of the woman who lives in the apartment below me. But when the ghetto black teenagers get on the city bus, I hear them. Their sounds in my society are the sounds of the outsider. Their voices annoy me for being so loud — so self-sufficient and unconcerned by my presence, but for the same reason they are glamorous: a romantic gesture against public acceptance. And as I listen to their shouted laughter, I realize my own quietness. I feel envious of them — envious of their brazen intimacy.

I warn myself away from such envy, however. Overhearing those teenagers, I think of the black political activists who lately have argued in favor of using black English in public schools — an argument that varies only slightly from that of foreign-language bilingualists. I have heard "radical" linguists make the point that black English is a complex and intricate version of English. And I do not doubt it. But neither do I think that black English should be a language of public instruction. What makes it inappropriate in classrooms is not something in the language itself but, rather, what lower-class speakers make of it. Just as Spanish would have been a dangerous language for me to have used at the start of my education, so black English would be a dangerous language to use in the schooling of teenagers for whom it reinforces feelings of public separateness.

This seems to me an obvious point to make, and yet it must be said. In recent years, there have been many attempts to make the language of the alien a public language. "Bilingual education, two ways to understand . . ." television and radio commercials glibly announce. Proponents of bilingual education are careful to say that above all they want every student to acquire a good education. Their argument goes something like this: Children permitted to use their family language will not be so alienated and will be better able to match the progress of English-speaking students in the crucial first months of schooling. Increasingly confident of their ability, such children will be more inclined to apply themselves to their studies in the future. But then the bilingualists also claim another very different goal. They say that children who use their family language in school will retain a sense of their ethnic heritage and their family ties. Thus the supporters of bilingual education want it both ways. They propose bilingual schooling as a way of helping students acquire the classroom skills crucial for public success. But they likewise insist that bilingual instruction will give students a sense of their identity apart from the English-speaking public.

41 Behind this scheme gleams a bright promise for the alien child: One can become a public person while still remaining a private person. Who would not want to believe such an appealing idea? Who can be surprised that the scheme has the support of so many middle-class ethnic Americans? If the barrio or ghetto child can retain his separateness even while being publicly educated, then it is almost possible to believe that no private cost need be paid for public success. This is the consolation offered by any of the number of current bilingual programs. Consider, for example, the bilingual voter's ballot. In some American cities, one can cast a ballot printed in several languages. Such a document implies that it is possible for one to exercise that most public of rights — the right to vote — while still keeping oneself apart, unassimilated in public life.

42 It is not enough to say that such schemes are foolish and certainly doomed. Middle-class supporters of public bilingualism toy with the confusion of those Americans who cannot speak standard English as well as they do. Moreover, bilingual enthusiasts sin against intimacy. A Hispanic-American tells me, "I will never give up my family language," and he clutches a group of words as though they were the source of his family ties. He credits to language what he should credit to family members. This is a convenient mistake, for as long as he holds on to certain familiar words, he can ignore how much else has actually changed in his life.

43 It has happened before. In earlier decades, persons ambitious for social mobility, and newly successful, similarly seized upon certain "family words." Workingmen attempting to gain political power, for example, took to calling one another "brother." The word as they used it, however, could never resemble the word (the sound) "brother" exchanged by two people in intimate greeting. The context of its public delivery made it at best a metaphor; with repetition it was only a vague echo of the intimate sound. Context forced the change. Context could not be overruled. Context will always protect the realm of the intimate from public misuse. Today middle-class white Americans continue to prove the importance of context as they try to ignore it. They seize upon idioms of the black ghetto, but their attempt to appropriate such expressions invariably changes the meaning. As it becomes a public expression, the ghetto idiom loses its sound, its message of public separateness and strident intimacy. With public repetition it becomes a series of words, increasingly lifeless.

• • •

44   The mystery of intimate utterance remains. The communication of intimacy passes through the word and enlivens its sound, but it cannot be held by the word. It cannot be retained or ever quoted because it is too fluid. It depends not on words but on persons.

My grandmother! She stood among my other relations mocking me when I no longer spoke Spanish. *Pocho,* she said. But then it made no difference. She'd laugh, and our relationship continued because language was never its source. She was a woman in her eighties during the first decade of my life — a mysterious woman to me, my only living grandparent, a woman of Mexico in a long black dress that reached down to her shoes. She was the one relative of mine who spoke no word of English. She had no interest in gringo society and remained completely aloof from the public. She was protected by her daughters, protected even by me when we went to Safeway together and I needed to act as her translator. An eccentric woman. Hard. Soft.

45   When my family visited my aunt's house in San Francisco, my grandmother would search for me among my many cousins. When she found me, she'd chase them away. Pinching her granddaughters, she would warn them away from me. Then she'd take me to her room, where she had prepared for my coming. There would be a chair next to the bed, a dusty jellied candy nearby, and a copy of *Life en Español* for me to examine. "There," she'd say. And I'd sit content, a boy of eight. *Pocho,* her favorite. I'd sift through the pictures of earthquake-destroyed Latin-American cities and blonde-wigged Mexican movie stars. And all the while I'd listen to my grandmother's voice. She'd pace around the room, telling me stories of her life, her past. They were stories so familiar that I couldn't remember when I'd heard them for the first time. I'd look up sometimes to listen. Other times she'd look over at me, but she never expected a response. Sometimes I'd smile or nod. (I understood exactly what she was saying.) But it never seemed to matter to her one way or the other. It was enough that I was there. The words she spoke were almost irrelevant to that fact. We were content. And the great mystery remained: intimate utterance.

46   The child reminds the adult: to seek intimate sounds is to seek the company of intimates. I do not expect to hear those sounds in public. I would dishonor those I have loved, and those I love now, to claim anything else. I would dishonor our intimacy by holding on to a particular language and calling it my family language. Intimacy cannot be trapped within words; it passes through words. It passes. Intimates leave the room. Doors close. Faces move away from the window. Time passes, and voices recede into the dark. Death finally quiets the voice. There is no way to deny it, no way to stand in the crowd claiming to utter one's family language.

The last time I saw my grandmother I was nine years old. I can tell you some of the things she said to me as I stood by her bed, but I cannot quote the message of intimacy she conveyed with her voice. She laughed, holding my hand. Her voice illumined disjointed memories as it passed them again. She remembered her husband — his green eyes, his magic name of Narcissio, his early death. She remembered the farm in Mexico, the eucalyptus trees nearby (their scent, she remembered, like incense). She remembered the family cow, the bell around its neck heard miles away. A dog. She remembered working as a seamstress, how she'd leave her daughters and son for long hours to go into Guadalajara to work. And how my mother would come running toward her in the sun — in her bright yellow dress — on her return. "MMMMAAAAMMMMMÁÁÁÁ," the old lady mimicked her daughter (my mother) to her daughter's son. She laughed. There was the snap of a cough. An aunt came into the room and told me it was time I should leave. "You can see her tomorrow," she promised. So I kissed my grandmother's cracked face. And the last thing I saw was her thin, oddly youthful thigh, as my aunt rearranged the sheet on the bed.

At the funeral parlor a few days after, I remember kneeling with my relatives during the rosary. Among their voices I traced, then lost, the sounds of individual aunts in the surge of the common prayer. And I heard at that moment what since I have heard very often — the sound the women in my family make when they are praying in sadness. When I went up to look at my grandmother, I saw her through the haze of a veil draped over the open lid of the casket. Her face looked calm — but distant and unyielding to love. It was not the face I remembered seeing most often. It was the face she made in public when the clerk at Safeway asked her some question and I would need to respond. It was her public face that the mortician had designed with his dubious art.

Discussion

1. What truths did Rodriguez learn about the relationship between language and intimacy?
2. What contrasts in sound does Rodriguez mention, and how do those descriptions of sound work to emphasize what he says about intimacy?
3. In his discussion of Black English and public instruction, Rodriguez expresses the opinion that Black English should not be a language of public instruction. What are his supports for that opinion?
4. What does Rodriguez feel are the dangers of public separateness, and what statements support this feeling?
5. What is the point of using the personal experience, his grandmother's funeral, in the conclusion? How does this fit his thesis?

WRITING:
Exposition: Cause and Effect; Effect and Cause

Writing Assignment: A Three-Paragraph Cause-and-Effect or Effect-and-Cause Essay

Another type of analysis that needs to be mastered involves seeking out the causes or effects of situations or actions. This analytical model, like the comparison and contrast model, is often used in college essay examinations and term papers and serves as an excellent approach to learning new concepts and textbook materials. For example, on your midterm examination, your history professor might ask you to evaluate the causes of the War of Roses or to discuss the possible effects of a particular Supreme Court decision on future educational policies. Or you might want to write your term paper for Sociology I on the effects of the energy crisis on the inner-city unemployment rate or on the causes of neighborhood blight in a particular section of your community. All of these assignments require you to evaluate your reading materials for cause and effect relationships and help you to develop a conceptual understanding of the situations under study. In other words, as you read and study you must always consider why a situation or action occurred and what the results were or might be.

Your writing assignment in this unit has two specific purposes: to teach you how to write a cause and effect paper; and to help you to develop an important study skill, that is, the analysis of the causes and effects of situations and actions. These two techniques are, of course, tightly interrelated, for to write a cause and effect paper requires you to evaluate and understand how things act and react upon each other. Sometimes such interactions are simple in nature and at other times quite complex. You must evaluate each situation carefully, making certain that you discover the *necessary causes* — not merely the *contributory causes* — and the *primary effects* — not merely the *secondary effects*.

Necessary causes are those that must be present for a reaction to occur; contributory causes are those that might intensify or alter the reaction. For example, if you do not study for an examination and then develop anxiety over your lack of preparation, the necessary cause of your low grade is your failure to study, not your nervous state. In this situation, your anxiety intensified the situation but did not cause it.

Primary effects result directly from a situation or action, while secondary effects are either caused by the situation or action but are of minor concern or result from the primary effect in a sort of chain reaction. For example, if a baker forgets to take bread out of an oven at a certain time, the primary effect would be burnt bread. The secondary effects might be crusted pans and loss of sales.

As you work through your assignment, keep in mind the differences between necessary and contributory causes and primary and secondary effects. To be effective, discussions should generally focus on necessary causes and primary effects, although all complementary materials can add interest. Be careful, however, that you don't mistakenly assume that first occurrences necessarily are the cause of later occurrences. Because a woman forgot to check the air pressure of her car's tires does not necessarily explain why she had a flat tire later in the day. She may have simply driven over a nail.

Assignment
Write a three-paragraph essay following one of these patterns of organization.

PATTERN 1

C (Cause) — An introductory paragraph that describes or explains a situation or action that brought about or may bring about certain effects; paragraph includes an explicit thesis statement.

E (Effect) — A discussion, explanation, or description of a primary effect.

E (Effect) — A discussion, explanation, or description of either another primary effect or a secondary effect.

PATTERN 2

E (Effect) — An introductory paragraph that describes or explains a situation or action that has occurred; paragraph includes an explicit thesis statement.

C (Cause) — A discussion, explanation, or description of a necessary cause of the action or situation.

C (Cause) — A discussion, explanation, or description of another necessary cause or a contributory cause.

Notice that Pattern 1 presents an action or a situation and then analyzes its effects; that is, the pattern controls a cause-and-effect paper. Pattern 2, in contrast, presents an action or a situation and then analyzes its causes; that is, the pattern controls an effect-and-cause paper. Each pattern has its distinct use. For example, if your reader needs to know the effects of caffeine on unborn babies or the effect of new educational policies, you would write a cause-and-effect paper. But if your reader needs to understand the cause of the Watergate scandal or the reasons for the energy crisis, you would write an effect-and-cause paper. Both papers are analytical in nature, although they focus on different aspects of situations.

Review the following sample essays before you begin your assignment. Although the patterns set up different types of analyses, they are both controlled by clear, precise, unified, and limited thesis statements. Notice, also, that the most important effect in the *C-E-E* paper and the most important cause in the *E-C-C* paper appear in the second paragraph.

As you read the sample essays, consider if they could be expanded into longer, more fully developed discussions. Sample Essay 7-1, for example, could be enlarged by the presentation of one or more effects. Perhaps a paragraph on graduates without some course work in the social sciences could be expanded to a two- or three-paragraph section through the introduction of detailed examples of educational requirements of specific schools.

SAMPLE ESSAY 7-1 CAUSE AND EFFECT

CAUSE

During the 1960s, students throughout the United States sought changes in their college curricula. Reacting to American involvement in Southeast Asia, a new emphasis on civil liberties, and increased opportunities for advanced education, students campaigned, petitioned, and even rioted for "relevant" courses and programs. Many students, especially those who faced induction into the army and possible service in Vietnam and those who were active in Civil Rights campaigns, felt universities should treat them as adults, not children, and should allow them freedom of choice in matters of required courses. Other students, especially those whose parents never had the opportunity to pursue college educations and those who majored in business and science, felt that literature, history, art, and music were irrelevant to their future careers; they sought professional training, not cultural enrichment. After much campus unrest, many colleges and universities acceded to student demands, either by reducing "general education" requirements or by increasing student course options. THESIS The effect of these curricula changes has often been the graduation of students who are trained for careers but who are not well educated.

EFFECT 1 (TOPIC SENTENCE) During the 1960s and 1970s, more students than ever before majored in the sciences, business, computer science, engineering, and psychology. At most schools, these students were no longer required to study foreign languages, literature, or the fine arts. Few were even required to take more than one course in history. The result was that students generally registered for courses in their own areas of specialization or in areas that interested them the most. Students waited in line to register for Accounting III, Advanced Organic Chemistry, and Mechanical Engineering V, but turned away from Public Speaking, Medieval History, and French. They fought over admission into American Horror Movies, Guitar I, and Assertiveness Training, but avoided the registration lines for The Art of the Italian Renaissance, Shakespearean Drama, and Baroque Music. And then they graduated with bachelor's, master's, and doctoral degrees, well-trained for professional careers but poorly trained for well-rounded lives. They could build bridges, audit accounts, or program computers, but not enjoy classical music, art, or novels. They became, in fact, proficient workers, the robots of American industry and business.

EFFECT 2 (TOPIC SENTENCE) A second effect of these academic changes in college curricula was the lowering of communication skills. Many schools no longer required first-year students to take composition courses or public speaking. Other schools either reduced required writing courses from two semesters to one or allowed students to take Writing Lyrics for Contemporary Music or Creative Writing in place of expository writing. As a result, students, lacking writing experience and ability, began to buy term papers from "scholastic papers" companies, to pay for professionally written resumés, and to fail state bar examinations at a higher rate than ever before. Eventually, this lack of communication skills started to affect the business and professional world. Engineers, unable to communicate their ideas clearly, began relying on technical writing staffs, and psychologists and business executives began to seek out ghost-writers to prepare professional papers and speeches. All in all, then, the curricula changes of the 1960s and 1970s fulfilled college students' demands for "relevancy" but robbed them of well-rounded educations and their humanistic future.

SAMPLE ESSAY 7-2 EFFECT AND CAUSE

EFFECT Each morning, as I slam my alarm clock onto the floor, a wet tongue splatters my face. If I attempt to slither under my blankets, a five-pound hunter pounces onto my stomach to claw away my protective covering. From the moment I finally get out of bed until the time I enter the kitchen, I'm stalked by this hairy nuisance, yelping at me to hurry up. And hurry is what I'm forced to do. Gulping down breakfast and leashing myself to my tormentor's collar, I begin my morning outing around the block, alternately pulled, tugged, and jerked to unexpected stops. Waiting impatiently as my leader sniffs at

THESIS a tree, I ask myself, Why, oh why, did I ever buy a dog? Why, oh, why, did I invite this bossy, domineering Yorkie to share my life?

CAUSE 1 (TOPIC SENTENCE) <u>Looking back, I think I remember feeling lonesome.</u> New to Chicago, three thousand miles from home, and beginning my first professional job after graduation from college, I felt isolated. My apartment echoed my despair, reporting only my footsteps and off-key voice. There was no one to greet me as I stepped through the door at six o'clock, no one to share my evenings except my stereo and television, and no one to talk to as I ate my microwave dinner. I guess I could have found a roommate, but I wanted, for the first time in my life, to be able to leave my socks on the couch and dirty dishes in the sink without being told to clean up my mess. I wanted my freedom, but I needed company. The only solution, or at least the only one that came to mind, was to buy a dog.

CAUSE 2 (TOPIC SENTENCE) So I visited pet shops, kennels, and city pounds in search of a special companion. <u>I wanted a dog that would not only adore me, comfort me, and amuse me, but also one that would fit into my 800-square-foot apartment, not shed on my blue suit, and not make me wheeze.</u> Lacking these qualities, sheep dogs and collies, Dobermans and boxers had to be dismissed from consideration. Then I saw Barnabas, a six-week-old Yorkshire terrier with one drooping ear. The breeder promised me this bouncing hairball would never shed, wouldn't cause allergies, and would only grow to five pounds. The perfect dog! Or so I thought! Indeed, Barney keeps his hair to himself, never overturns tables, and causes no allergic reactions; he adores me, comforts me, and amuses me, and I am lonesome no longer. I'm just a tired, dominated victim of love.

TOPICS

TUCKER
1. Write an effect-and-cause paper explaining why you enjoy or dislike a particular sport. Your audience is your classmates.
2. Write a cause-and-effect paper in which you analyze the possible effects of the depletion of one natural resource on American life. Your audience is your teacher.

FLORMAN
1. Write a cause-and-effect paper on television commercials. In this essay, be sure you focus tightly on only one type of advertisement, such as those selling beer, or one type of audience, such as children or senior citizens. Your audience is a group of college-educated adults.
2. Write an effect-and-cause paper in which you suggest possible causes for today's narcissistic society, that is, a society dominated by desires for per-

sonal fulfillment and pleasure, not community well-being. Your audience is a group of college-educated adults.

RODRIGUEZ

1. Write an effect-and-cause essay in which you suggest reasons for the demand for bilingual education in American schools. Your audience is your teacher.
2. Write a cause-and-effect paper in which you analyze the possible effects of immigration on American families, society, or individuals. Your audience is your classmates.

Brainstorming and Shaping

1. Choose your topic and audience.
2. Prepare a data sheet on your audience that is similar to Data Sheet 7-1.

Data Sheet 7-1   Audience

A. Topic: _____
B. Audience: _____
C. General Characteristics of the Audience:
   1.
   2.
   3.
   4.
   5.
   6.
   7.
   8.
   9.
   10.
D. Probable Knowledge of Reading Audience on Topic:
   1. What do my readers know about my topic? _____
   2. What do my readers need to know about my topic? _____
   3. What do my readers need to have reviewed on my topic? _____
E. Probable Opinions of Reading Audience on Topic:
   1.
   2.
   3.
   4.
   5.

As in Data Sheet 6-1, Data Sheet 7-1 has not asked you to construct a thesis statement. Before you can consider possible controlling ideas for your analytical paper, you need to investigate the possible causes or effects of the situations or actions under consideration. In addition, you must decide which causes are necessary causes or contributory causes and which effects are primary and secondary.

Remember, necessary causes are those that must be present for an action to occur; they are the primary agents of change. In contrast, contributory causes are those that intensify or alter the reaction. Primary effects are those that result directly from a situation or action, while secondary effects are those that are either caused by the situation or action but are of minor concern or those that result from the primary effect in a sort of chain reaction. To write an effective cause-and-effect or effect-and-cause paper, then, you must carefully examine two things: the audience and the cause-and-effect relationships of a situation or action.

Date Sheets 7-2 and 7-3 will assist you in recognizing the causes or effects of the situation or action under consideration for your essay. But before you begin filling out the form, be sure you spend adequate time in thinking about your topic. Check with your teacher to see if you are to expand your essay beyond three paragraphs or if you are permitted to research your topic in the school library. However, little if any research should be necessary for this assignment. Choose a topic that is familiar to you — one that you know well from personal experience or prior course work. You all have taken part in sports, watched television, and have been made aware of ecological concerns and immigration of non-English-speaking people to this country. In other words, you already know a great deal about all the suggested topics for this writing assignment. Instead of seeking out other writers' opinions, focus upon your own knowledge and experience, learning to formulate your own evaluations and opinions.

Cause and Effect

Certain aspects of the data sheets should be particularly noted. In Data Sheet 7-2, the cause is the situation or action that will bring or has brought about an effect. For example, if your topic were the energy crisis, your cause might be the high price of gasoline. Or, if your topic were alcoholism, your cause might be the lowering of the legal age for the purchase of alcoholic beverages.

Once you have limited your topic, you should then list all possible effects the situation or action could bring about or has brought about. At this point, do not worry whether these effects are primary or secondary. For example, possible effects of high gasoline prices might be the following.

1. Inflation.
2. Less driving.

Data Sheet 7-2   Cause and Effect

```
A. Topic: _____
B. Cause (present situation or action): _____
C. Possible Effects:
    1.
    2.
    3.
    4.
    5.
    6.
    7.
    8.
    9.
   10.
D. Primary Effects:
    1.
    2.
    3.
E. Secondary Effects:
    1.
    2.
    3.
F. Write a thesis statement that introduces the situation or action
   and suggests possible effects: _____
   _____
   _____
```

3. Increased use of public transportation.
4. Fewer pleasure trips in cars.
5. Business reversals for motels, hotels, and resorts.
6. Increased emphasis on fuel-economy cars.
7. More home entertainment.
8. Increased emphasis on diesel engines.
9. Increased research into gasoline substitutes.

Once you have listed all the possible effects, you must stop to evaluate the items on your list. Which are primary and which are secondary effects? Perhaps you would list the following under primary effects.

1. Inflation.
2. Increased emphasis on fuel-economy cars.
3. Increased use of public transportation.

Each person might consider different items as primary — the decision would depend on the person's background, occupation, financial status, and lifestyle. An economist, for example, might consider inflation as the primary effect, whereas a person who must drive forty miles to work every day might consider the development of fuel-economy cars as primary.

Once you have evaluated the effects, review Data Sheet 7-1. You may now need to adjust some of your decisions about your audience's needs. For example, if you know your audience is most concerned with inflation and has little interest in automobiles, you would probably want to discuss inflation in your paper. Since you will be writing only a three-paragraph paper, you need to choose the *two effects most important to your readers. Don't simply choose those effects that interest you the most.* You may, however, choose one primary effect and one secondary effect for discussion, but again be sure these are the effects that are important to the audience.

Finally, write your thesis statement, including both an introduction to the situation or action (the cause) under discussion and the possible effects. For example, a thesis statement on the high price of gasoline might read:

> The high price of gasoline, the result of the current energy crisis, has caused serious inflation and a public demand for fuel-economy cars.

Effect and Cause

In Data Sheet 7-3, your topic is the general theme of your paper, and the effect is the situation or action under consideration. If your topic were illiteracy, your effect might be sixth graders reading at the first-grade level. Or if your topic were music, your effect might be the rise of rock-and-roll in the 1950s.

Once you have chosen your general topic and specific situation or action (effect) for your writing assignment, you should list all possible causes at this time — simply list everything you can. For example, your list of possible causes of sixth graders reading at first-grade level might include the following items.

1. Poor teachers.
2. Poor books.
3. Inadequate equipment and school facilities.
4. Racism.
5. Sexism.
6. Poor health.
7. Lack of discipline.
8. Disinterested parents.
9. Parents' failure to teach self-discipline to preschoolers.
10. Lack of motivation.
11. Lack of reading readiness experience for preschoolers.

Data Sheet 7-3 Effect and Cause

A. Topic: _____
B. Effect (situation or action): _____
C. Possible Causes:
   1.
   2.
   3.
   4.
   5.
   6.
D. Necessary Causes:
   1
   2.
   3.
E. Contributory Causes:
   1.
   2.
   3.
F. Write a thesis statement that introduces the situation or action and indicates the essay will seek out possible causes. Such an indication can be made through either a brief statement of the causes or a question. _____
_____
_____

After you have completed your list of possible causes, you must stop to evaluate what you have listed. Now classify your items according to necessary causes and contributory causes. For example, do inadequate school buildings always cause poor reading skills? Are most teachers racist, sexist, or inadequate? Probably not, so you would list these under contributory causes. But lack of motivation, self-discipline, and reading readiness experience do block reading development, so they would be listed under necessary causes. Of course, two writers might disagree on which of these areas are most important, but they need only to explain their choices to their readers; they do not have to be concerned that everyone will agree with their decisions.

After you have divided your possible causes into necessary and contributory categories, you must review Data Sheet 7-1. Again, you might need to adjust your choice of causes for your paper to fit your audience's needs. For example, if your audience were the parents of three-year-olds, you would probably want to discuss parental responsibility in reading development, focusing on the need for preschool reading readiness experience at home and the need for development of self-discipline. You may, of course, choose for your essay one necessary cause and one contributory cause, but you must explain the reasons for the inclusion of contributory causes to your reader. Without such an explanation, the reader might decide you lack a good understanding of your topic.

Finally, you must write your thesis statement. You may wish to include an introduction to the causes in this statement, or you may prefer to couch your thesis in a question. For example, you might write:

> Poor reading skills among sixth graders are frequently caused by lack of self-discipline and inadequate reading readiness experiences.

Or you might ask:

> Do parents bear any responsibility for the poor reading skills of their sixth graders?

Writing the First Draft

Using your two data sheets as guides, write the first draft of your three-paragraph essay. Remember, your first paragraph introduces the situation or action under consideration, while your next two paragraphs discuss the causes or effects of this situation or action. *Save your data sheets to submit with your final draft.*

Revising the Three-Paragraph Cause-and-Effect or Effect-and-Cause Essay

Your assignment asked you to write a three-paragraph cause-and-effect or effect-and-cause paper. Look over your two data sheets and then analyze your essay according to the adjusted basic revision questions and the special questions for this assignment.

Basic Revision Questions

1. *Is all my information accurate? Appropriate?*
   Have you bored your readers by repeating information they already know? Have you misinformed your readers? Have you offered all the information needed by your readers on your points of discussion?
2. *Is this information organized so that my readers can comprehend what I have said? Could I organize my paper so that it would be more effective?*
   Does your essay have three sections: an introductory paragraph that treats the situation or action under consideration and two paragraphs that discuss the causes or effects of this situation? Do paragraphs two and three focus on distinct points of discussion?

3. *Do I have a clear, unified focus; that is, does my essay telescope in on one major theme?*
   Do your causes or effects in paragraphs two and three relate directly to your thesis statement? In developing these paragraphs, have you accidentally added any information that does not relate to your topic?
4. *Do I offer sufficient details, examples, or explanations so that my reader gains a complete understanding of what I am discussing?*
   Are all your points of discussion fully explained? Do your readers need any additional clarification?

Additional Questions

1. Is my thesis statement limited, unified, precise, and clear?
2. Do paragraphs two and three have limited, unified, precise, and clear topic sentences?
3. Have I offered enough information and explanations in my introductory paragraph to develop audience interest and to prepare my readers for my discussion on causes or effects?
4. Are my choices of causes or effects appropriate for my audience? Would different causes or effects be more effective or worthwhile?
5. Have I focused on necessary causes and primary effects? Have I explained any inclusion of contributory causes or secondary effects to my readers?

EXERCISE 1

Evaluate your essay by asking the revision questions posed in this section. If you have answered either "No" or "I don't know" to any of the questions, you probably need some revision. If you are not sure your facts are accurate, check your information in your school library, but only if your teacher permits research for this assignment. If you are not sure you have met your readers' needs, review your data sheets and your essay to see if your discussion concentrates on what your readers need to know, need to have explained, or need to have reviewed. If your readers hold opinions based on misinformation or personal bias, you must check to see that you have informed them of the correct facts. Make any revisions that seem necessary.

EXERCISE 2

Reevaluate your causes or effects. Make certain that you have correctly identified contributory causes and secondary effects. If you are not certain about your decisions, discuss your choices with friends or family. Never hesitate to discuss your ideas and evaluations with other people. Listen carefully to their comments but don't accept their suggestions or opinions without careful consideration. Remember, everyone has different backgrounds, beliefs, and lifestyles. Although your friends and family might disagree with you, you may not be wrong in your views. In fact, you both might be right, but simply have different focuses. Yet, don't hesitate to admit your error if you have reached a faulty conclusion. Listen, evaluate, and then decide if you need to adjust your views. Make any necessary corrections or adjustments to your paper.

EXERCISE 3

Put your first draft away for several days, then review your essay. You should be able to evaluate your essay more effectively at this time since it is no longer fresh in your mind. Make any revisions in organization and content that appear necessary.

EXERCISE 4

Write a clean draft of your revised essay in preparation for editing.

Editing

Word Choice: Transitions in the Longer Essay

The need to make careful transitions is especially important in writing extended discussions. You are already familiar with transitions within sentences and between sentences and realize how useful the recognition of transitions can be in your reading. These transitional devices are equally important in linking together paragraphs within essays. Like careful stitches in a quilt, transitions unite all individual parts into a finished piece with form and design. As you know, transitions guide your reader by ordering time, suggesting cause and effect or comparison and contrast, and arranging ideas in a logical order. In this way, they prevent reader confusion by unifying all points of discussion.

Examine the following excerpt. Mark all transitionals and analyze their effectiveness in unifying thought.

> From the early days of the Industrial Revolution, intellectuals of every sort predicted that the machine would make man superfluous. Right now, it would be difficult to find a social scientist who does not believe that automated machines and computers are eliminating man as a factor in the social equation.
>
> The belief that the machine turns men into robots is an a priori assumption that prevents social scientists from seeing that technology is doing precisely the opposite of what they predicted it would do. There is evidence on every hand that the human factor has never been so central as it is now in technologically advanced countries. And it is this centrality of the human factor that makes industrial societies at present so predictable.
>
> In the 19th century, which saw a Promethean effort to master and harness nature, little thought was given to the management of man. The ruling middle class could proceed on the principle that government is best when it governs least. Everyday life had a fabulous regularity. Obedience of authority was as automatic as a reflex movement. Social processes were almost as rational and predictable as the processes of nature. It was reasonable to believe in the possibility of a social science as exact as a natural science.

There was also boundless hope, a belief in automatic progress that imbued people with patience. Then came the 20th century! Have there ever been two successive centuries so different from each other as the 19th and the 20th?

— Hoffer, *"Beware the Intellectual"*

In this paragraph, pronouns, careful repetition, and transitional adverbs serve as bridges between past and present. In addition, paragraph two is a transition in itself, bridging the gap between past failure and present success.

The following exercises are designed to help make you more conscious of the need for transitions throughout your essays.

EXERCISE 1
Examine the essays in this unit to see if you can find the transitional devices each author uses. Underline them and explain how each operates to unify the discussion.

EXERCISE 2
Using the sample paragraphs on John's photography in Unit 6 as a model, write three brief paragraphs using transitions in each of them. Refer to the list of transitions if necessary. Use emphasis words, relative pronouns, pronouns, comparative adjectives, time sequence words, illustration words, comparison or contrast words, cause-and-effect relationships, words that summarize, and repetition. In short, use any of these transitions and as many as you feel are needed to guide your readers.

EXERCISE 3
Read over the draft of your writing assignment. Do all ideas flow together? Is your essay unified so that your reader can easily follow your discussion? Perhaps you should read your essay aloud, listening carefully to the discussion to judge how well ideas are interlinked. Add any transitional devices necessary.

Sentence Structure: Participles
In the last unit, you edited sentences for style by building and contracting relative clauses. Two other sentence elements used to create clarity and liveliness are the past and present participles. The present participle is formed by adding *-ing* to the verb's infinitive form (a form listed in the dictionary).

Sing/singing, jump/jumping, eat/eating, beat/beating

The past participle of regular verbs, like the past tense, adds *-d* or *-ed* to the infinitive form of the verb.

ask/asked, poke/poked, hope/hoped, jump/jumped

Irregular verbs, however, usually form their past participles by adding *-en* instead of *-ed* or by changing vowels.

be/been, sing/sung, beat/beaten, hang/hung

The present and past participles can combine with auxiliary verbs to form verb phrases *(VP)*, but they can also act as adjectives to modify nouns and pronouns.

    Adj.
1. *Turning* away, she allowed herself to cry.

    VP
2. The girl's heart *was pumping* hard.

    Adj.
3. *Speaking* loudly, he attracted too much attention.

    VP
4. His face *was twisted* with pain.

    Adj.
5. *Bitten* to the quick, his nails said something about the state of his nerves.

Because the present and past participles are formed from verbs, they give power, variety, and emphasis to sentences. In fact, much of the action and movement you communicate to your reader comes from such verbal force. But power is only one benefit of these words; economy is another. For example, you can reduce relative clauses to form adjective/noun clusters. To do so, you simply delete the relative clause, changing its verb to the participle form and placing it in front of a noun.

1. The horse *that won the race* was eligible for the Kentucky Derby.

    The *winning* horse was eligible for the Kentucky Derby.

2. The television set *that was broken* was fixed.

    The *broken* television was fixed.

3. The package *that was mailed last week* was delivered yesterday.

    The *mailed* package was delivered yesterday.

Another type of reduction of relative clauses requires the deletion of the *relative pronoun* and the conversion of the verb to a participle form. This reduction creates a *verbal phrase*, which acts as an adjective.

1. My new car, *which averages 28 miles per gallon*, saves me $5.00 a week on transportation expenses.

    Averaging 28 miles per gallon, my new car saves me $5.00 a week on transportation expenses.

2. The woman *who sells cosmetics at Macy's Department Store* refused to take my personal check.

The woman *selling cosmetics at Macy's Department Store* refused to take my personal check.

There are other advantages to verbals. Notice the change in emphasis and meaning in the following set of sentences when we create a verbal from the verb "peer."

1. James *peered* over the fence.
2. James hoped to meet his new neighbor.
3. *Peering over the fence,* James hoped to meet his new neighbor.

Sentence three combines two choppy sentences and emphasizes the action of "peering," giving the reader a feeling that James looked over the fence time and time again. In this sentence combining, the subject of the first sentence is deleted and the verb is transformed to its participle form.

A few words of caution — first, place your present participles carefully. If we had written, "He hoped to catch a glimpse of his new neighbor peering over the fence," we would have changed the meaning of the sentence entirely. Written this way, the sentence says that the neighbor is doing the peering and "he" may be trying to catch the neighbor in the act or "he" may just want to see the neighbor. Remember that every time you manipulate language, you also manipulate meaning. Remember also that verbals may stand alone or in combination with other words in verbal phrases and may even take objects. *But a verbal cannot stand alone as the predicate of your sentence.*

The star shining brightly.
The girl coming closer.

Both of these examples are sentence fragments without a verb. As long as you remember those words of caution, verbals should serve your writing needs effectively.

There are, of course, times when a good simple sentence is just what you need to communicate your ideas clearly. But the verbal is often a highly useful tool to create excitement and variety. As you combine the following sentences, decide which words and phrases you want to emphasize and whether you want to increase action. Decide where and when participle phrases would be effective. Remember that too much of anything can be as deadly as too little, so feel free to vary the sentences, but don't try to include verbals in every sentence.

> Suzy combed her hair. She put on her makeup next. She wanted to look her best. She knew it was important to look good. She was very nervous. She spilled her nail polish. She wanted her house to look its best too. The doorbell rang. It announced an important guest.

Discuss the results of your sentence combining to see if everyone in the class agrees on both the verbals chosen and the number of verbals used.

EXERCISE 1
Choose ten verbs and list their past and present participle forms.

EXERCISE 2
Create a sentence using each of the present participles on your list. Then create a sentence for each of the past participles on your list.

EXERCISE 3
Note the difference in meaning in the following.

> Leaving the room in a rage, John bumped into Mary.
>
> John bumped into Mary leaving the room in a rage.

EXERCISE 4
Write five sentences beginning with a present or past participle. Next, rewrite the same five sentences by moving your modifier. Notice what happens to the meaning of your sentences.

Punctuation: Capitalization

Capitalization gives few problems to most writers of English since set rules govern this system of punctuation. There are, however, a few instances when a writer might be confused about proper usage. To help eliminate such difficulty, you should review the following rules of capitalization very carefully.

> Rule 1: *Always capitalize the first word of every sentence.*
>
>> The dog looked like a mutated flea.
>>
>> Where did you hide the last piece of apple pie?
>>
>> Stop that!
>
> Rule 2: *Capitalize the first word of each line of poetry.*
>
>> When lilacs last in the dooryard bloomed,
>> And the great star drooped in the western sky in the night,
>> I mourned, and yet shall mourn with ever-returning spring.
>
> Rule 3: *Capitalize the pronoun "I"; capitalize the pronoun "he" when referring to the deity — He.*

After God created the heavens and the earth, He made man in His own image.

Rule 4: *Capitalize the names of holidays.*

Easter, Halloween, the Fourth of July

Rule 5: *Capitalize the names of people and the abbreviations of their names.*

John Smith, Wm. Jones, Ellen Flanagan

Rule 6: *Capitalize the titles of people if these titles precede the names. Do not capitalize these titles if they follow the names (titles of high governmental officials are capitalized at all times).*

Dr. Margaret Sanger; Senator Allan Greenbaum; Alison Richards, professor of history

Rule 7: *Capitalize the names of brands of merchandise that are copyrighted.*

Camaro, Coca-Cola, Campbell's Soups, Westinghouse

Rule 8: *Capitalize names of geographic areas, mountains, bodies of water, nations, states, counties, and cities.*

Great Britain, Suez Canal, Yorkshire, Dade County, Mississippi River, Mount Shasta, Alps, Main Street, Fifth Avenue, Atlantic Ocean, Iowa, Boise

Rule 9: *Capitalize adjectives that derive from proper nouns.*

American, Italian, New Yorker, Spanish, Michigander

Rule 10: *Capitalize nouns and adjectives related to specific religions.*

Catholicism, Islam, Baptist, Jew, Moslem, Christianity, Allah, God, the Virgin, Bible, Koran, Catholic, Jewish, Islamic, Buddhism, Lutheran

Rule 11: *Capitalize names of organizations, schools, clubs, governmental offices and agencies, and companies.*

Purdue University, the Elks Club, the Urban League, the Department of Labor, General Electric Corporation

Rule 12: *Capitalize names of wars, treaties, laws, and governmental documents.*

the Treaty of Paris, World War I, the Civil Service Act, the U.S. Constitution

Rule 13: *Capitalize titles of books, plays, magazine articles, newspapers and newspaper headlines, journals, stories, movies, records and record albums, tapes, poems, television programs and music. (Do not, however, capitalize articles, conjunctions, and prepositions unless they are the first or last words in the titles.)*

"The Johnny Carson Show," "Songs of Innocence," The *New York Times*, *Roots*, "White Christmas," *Gone with the Wind*

Rule 14: *Capitalize names of school courses.*

Chemistry 3A (but — I enjoy chemistry.)

Art 403 (but — I plan to study art.)

History 23 (but — I registered for a history course.)

Rule 15: *Capitalize North, South, East, and West only when these words refer to specific geographic areas.*

She lives in the Northwest.

Seattle is northwest of Phoenix.

Have you ever been in the South?

Turn south on the Harbor Freeway.

Rule 16: *Capitalize names of family relationships only if they are used as substitutes for people's names or as part of a name. (If the word "the" or "a" precedes the word, do not capitalize.)*

Aunt Sadie burned the chicken soup.

My aunt is a terrible cook.

I bought a gift for Mother.

I noticed a father trying to diaper his squirming son.

Rule 17: *Capitalize the words "O" and "Oh" when they are used as interjections.*

I bought a new car, but Oh, was it a lemon!

Rule 18: *Do not capitalize the names of the seasons.*

fall, autumn, winter, spring, summer

Rule 19: *Capitalize names of races; either capitalize or lowercase all colors that refer to races.*

Caucasian, Negroid, Mongoloid

Black, White, Yellow, Red, Brown *or* black, white, yellow, red, brown

Rule 20: *Capitalize all major elements in an address.*

Miss Heidi Chan
724 Michelson St.
Apartment 3A
London, SW7
Great Britain

EXERCISE 1

Correct any errors of capitalization in the following sentences.

1. I just read Steinbeck's *The Grapes Of Wrath* for my History class; the book treats the story of the migration of oklahoma farmers to california.
2. The united nations headquarters is in New York city.
3. The Los Angeles times quoted mayor Bradley on the need for Urban Renewal.
4. Although I am majoring in Chemistry at Wayne state university, I took fine arts classes such as sculpture I, drawing 3A, and piano 2.
5. During my Summer vacation, I traveled with my Father to the East and spent the fourth of July at Niagara falls.
6. I bought a new pinto from mr. Jameson, President of town motor company.
7. Uncle Toby and aunt Sadie dressed like president Lincoln and Mary Todd at our halloween party.
8. Both Christians and jews read the old testament.
9. Jerry and i joined sigma chi at the university of Michigan.
10. I spent ten hours studying for my english exam, but, oh, I hated every moment of it.

EXERCISE 2

Correct any errors of capitalization in the following paragraph.

if mr. lippman cannot find pictures of civil engineering projects to which a reader can "relate," let him start with twentieth century engineering, the catalogue of a photography exhibit at the museum of modern art in 1964. and, if, after looking at the breathtaking photographs of towers, vaults, bridges, and other works, he still is at a loss for a "creative platform," perhaps he can borrow a few sentences from the Catalogue's introduction by arthur drexler.

EXERCISE 3

Review your three-paragraph writing assignment for possible capitalization errors and comma errors. Make all necessary corrections.

Preparing the Final Copy and Proofreading

In preparing your final copy, follow the manuscript conventions listed under the section on proofreading at the end of Unit 1. Use one side of the page only. Check for correct margins and double spacing; center the title at the top of the page; indent the first sentence of each paragraph; and correct any errors neatly with correction fluid, clean erasures, or lines drawn neatly through the mistakes.

Now you are ready to proofread. Read the final copy aloud, slowly and carefully. Ask yourself the following questions.

1. Are all the words spelled correctly? Are hyphens at the ends of lines placed correctly between the syllables of divided words? If you are uncertain about either your spelling of certain words or the division of any word, check your dictionary.
2. Have you made any accidental changes in your text or omitted any words?
3. Is the punctuation correct?

UNIT 8
Exposition: Opinion

READING:
Exposition: Opinion

Reading Strategies: Reviewing for Tests

Preparing for a test is a process that begins on the first day of each new class. In fact, test preparation is a long-term procedure involving taking good lecture notes and marking textbooks properly. But once the test day approaches, perhaps two weeks ahead of time, you should begin to review and study these materials. How can you approach and conquer such a vastness of material that often seems insurmountable? First, think of your short-term preparation as one step in the process of learning. Second, organize and review your materials efficiently, just as you would organize and prepare for a mountain-climbing expedition by studying the mountain and anticipating all possible hazards. The following test review guidelines will help you to recognize, prepare for, and, in all probability, overcome many of the test-taking hazards you will encounter.

Scheduling Time

One valuable device for test preparation that students often overlook, either in their eagerness or panic, is a *time schedule*. You should plan test review time just as you schedule your regular study hours. By arranging a study schedule for specific tests, you can find sufficient time for sleeping, eating, and even recreation. Many students discover that if they allow themselves some recreational rewards, they work better once they begin to study. For these students, having a set time schedule relieves anxiety, for they know precisely the amount of time allotted for each activity. But for other students, the mere idea of a schedule often inflicts anxiety and guilt, for they worry that they will not be able to concentrate once they begin to study. You must decide for yourself whether a time schedule will work for you, but remember that the key words for any time schedule are *sensible* and *realistic*. If you do decide to try this method, don't set unrealistic goals. Even though you will be working harder than usual during times of exam review, you must try to live a normal daily life.

EXERCISE 1

When you know your exam schedule, enter it in Figure 8-1. Then write in the hours you will review for *specific* subjects. (Do not simply mark "study time.") Next allow for daily meals and some specific recreational hours.

Rereading by Scanning

When you review for an exam, you should do your rereading as *scanning*. All your close reading should have been done when topics were first introduced in lectures or textbook assignments. If your lecture notes have been properly written and your textbook accurately marked, you will have little difficulty in scanning to find main ideas and key supporting information. As you begin to scan, however, remember also to scan the chapter headings and subheadings.

Organizing the Material

Scanning your lecture notes and textbook underlining or highlighting helps you in your initial review, but this study method will not prepare you sufficiently for a test. You also need to clarify *relationships* between concepts, facts, and situations — a requirement for total comprehension of a subject. Consequently, you must *organize* your materials by condensing your notes so you can handle them easily during the final test preparation steps — anticipating test questions and recitation. In other words, these abbreviated notes will help you to see, grasp, and remember relationships and important details.

Study notes, written on 3 x 5" index cards, are useful to college students in all majors. But in addition to these cards, you may also need to prepare study sheets on standard 8½ x 11" paper. The study sheet (based on lecture notes, a course syllabus, assigned textbook, or any combination of these) can be used as a *table of contents* or *outline* of a course. The advantage of making up your own table of contents is that it gives you a clear overview from which to review, to trace a development, and to perceive and learn relationships. In other words, your own table of contents allows you to see a course as an organized whole.

EXERCISE 2

Choose one of your courses. Make up your own table of contents or outline based on the course syllabus, the lecture notes, textbook, or any combination that is appropriate and helpful.

READING: EXPOSITION: OPINION 311

Day	Time	8:00	9:00	10:00	11:00	12:00	1:00	2:00	3:00	4:00	5:00	6:00	7:00	8:00	9:00	10:00

Figure 8-1 Time schedule

Study sheets can also be used to learn *specialized vocabulary* or *terminology*. To organize vocabulary and definitions for effective study, buy either wide-margin notepaper or draw in a wide margin on the left third of a sheet of paper. List vocabulary words on the far left and the definitions to the right of the margin. Skip lines between items listed. For example, in this course you might list the terms used in this book and give their definitions, as shown below:

Syntax:	The study of sentence structure.
Diction:	Word choice.

EXERCISE 3

Make up a study sheet of specialized vocabulary and definitions.

This same wide-margin study sheet format can often be used to show historical sequence or development of ideas. In this case, dates can be listed on the left, with associated development or events given on the right. Organizing this way shows relationships through both chronology and concepts or events.

EXERCISE 4

If you have a history class or a course that deals with the chronological development of ideas or technology (even a business or engineering course might fit this category), use this study sheet format to organize for a test review.

A study sheet can show comparison and contrast or cause-and-effect relationships (similar to the data sheets in the Brainstorming sections in Units 6 and 7). Both comparison and contrast and cause-and-effect examination questions are favorites among professors for almost the same reason you might use them as organizing devices: they enable your teacher to find out how well you comprehend the course's materials. These methods are also especially helpful in gaining an understanding of difficult, complex theories or concepts.

EXERCISE 5

Write up a comparison and contrast or cause-and-effect study sheet on a situation or event studied in one of your classes.

Anticipating Test Questions

Once you have organized your materials so that you can see and understand the relationships between *major* ideas, concepts, or situations and their *supporting* ideas, evidence, or examples, you should try to anticipate which of those major ideas are likely to appear on your test. To some students, especially those who are not test-wise, anticipating test questions means "psyching out the prof," a phrase with negative connotations suggesting something not "nice," or even something unfair.

But test-wise students know that anticipating what will probably be on the test is but another logical step in the test preparation process. These students know, even if they haven't explicitly expressed this strategy to themselves, that they must consider their audience — their instructor — just as they must adjust to an audience for any other writing assignment. In other words, much of this anticipation results from an awareness of the teacher's emphasis in lectures and class discussions, not from hunches or guesses. In reviewing for tests, therefore, take each of the following steps.

1. Review all textbook assignments; review chapter headings and subheadings.
2. Look over your lecture notes to find any points repeated or written on the board.
3. Compare your notes with your textbook; material is especially important if it appears in both places.
4. Talk to your instructor. Try to find out what will be included on the test. With this approach, at best you may be able to see a sample test. And the worst that can happen to you is a negative response.

Objective Tests

Since this is a reading and writing textbook, the main focus in this unit is on writing the essay exam. However, for an objective exam, you should prepare just as you would for the essay test: by understanding the relationships between major ideas or concepts and their supports or examples. That is, if you simply memorize details or examples rather than trying to understand total relationships, a slight rewording of those examples on the test might confuse you. So even though objective tests require your recognition of one correct answer, understanding relationships will prevent your confusion during the test. In preparing for objective tests, then, be sure to review study sheets and cards in the same way you do for essay exams.

Cloze Exercise: Focus on Adverbs

In previous units, you reviewed the functions and sentence positions of nouns, pronouns, adjectives, and coordinators. Another type of word that has a distinct function in a sentence is the *adverb*. Like adjectives, adverbs are modifiers; that is, they describe, limit, or expand another word or group of words. But whereas adjectives can modify only nouns and pronouns, adverbs can modify verbs, adjectives, other adverbs, and even entire sentences.

Examples
1. An adverb modifying a verb.

    The termites *quickly* digested Fido's house.

2. An adverb modifying an adjective.

    As a result, the entire termite family grew *very* fat.

3. An adverb modifying another adverb.

    In fact, they grew *so* very fat that they could not move.

4. An adverb modifying an entire sentence.

    Consequently, the exterminators executed them on the spot.

Since adverbs modify four different types of words or groups of words, they are apt to appear almost anywhere in a sentence. Yet you can learn to anticipate their appearance in a sentence through an awareness of the specific type of modification they perform. Most adverbs provide answers to one of the following questions: *where, when, how,* or *in what manner or degree.*

Examples
1. How.

           adv.
    The gopher *daintily* ate his breakfast, my tulip bulbs.

2. When.

     adv.
    Yesterday, it entered my garden for lunch, my iris bulbs.

3. Where.

              adv.
    I guess I should plant its dinner *here*, under the shade of the elm tree.

4. In what manner or degree.

             adv.
    I certainly don't want it to be *too* hungry.

Review the above examples very carefully so you can develop an awareness of adverbial functions and can improve your ability to fixate upon meaningful phrases. Once you feel confident about the ways these words work in a sentence, complete the following exercise. In this exercise, nouns, pronouns, adjectives, conjunctions, and adverbs may have been deleted. Time yourself as you fill in the blanks; you should be able to complete the exercise within five minutes. If you take longer, you need to review the discussions preceding the Cloze exercises in Units 2, 3, 4, and 5.

EXERCISE 1

    Now, personally, I was _____ able to get my _____ flowers to blossom in _____ water. And the place _____ I made from a _____ pattern ended up costing _____ $4.65 apiece. (They were _____ excruciatingly ugly). Furthermore, when _____ am car-pooling children on _____ July day in my _____ car, my desire is _____ to lead a wholesome _____ of "Ninety-Nine Bottles of _____ on the Wall." Rather, _____ am really much more _____ to be fantasizing about an impenetrable soundproof plastic chauffeur's barrier around my seat.

    — Adapted from Goodman, *"Your Better Basic Supermother"*

Words and the Language: The Dictionary

A major guide to understanding vocabulary is the dictionary. Even if you learn how to use structural and contextual clues to identify meaning, you will sometimes need to check your inferences or reinforce your guesses with further information about a word. And sometimes you will simply have to resort to a good, up-to-date dictionary to find a word whose meaning you can't infer. Moreover, when you become familiar enough with the meaning that you are ready to use the word in speaking and writing, you may need a dictionary to check spelling, syllabication (breaking a word into its parts), pronunciation, usage, and synonyms. You may even want to know the source of a word (its *etymology*). Did it come from Old English (lord), Greek (chair), French (garage), or Latin (homicide)?

    You should carry a pocket dictionary to classes, but these paperbacks are incomplete for your general college requirements. You also need to own a standard desk dictionary. The following dictionaries are good resources both for school and professional work.

> *The American Heritage Dictionary of the English Language* (New York: The American Heritage Publishing Company; text edition, Boston: Houghton Mifflin Company).
>
> *Funk and Wagnall's Standard College Dictionary* (New York: Funk and Wagnall's; text edition, New York: Harcourt Brace Jovanovich).
>
> *The Random House Dictionary of the English Language*, College Edition (New York: Random House).
>
> *Webster's New Collegiate Dictionary* (Springfield, Mass.: G. and C. Merriam Company).
>
> *Webster's New World Dictionary of the American Language* (Cleveland: World Publishing Company).

Once you have bought your dictionary, take a few minutes to survey it. Find the introductory section that tells how to use it, for all dictionaries are not alike. Some, for example, list the most commonly used meaning first, while others list the earliest meaning first. Some put the pronunciation key at the bottom of each page, and some put it at the front or back of the book. How does your dictionary list the meanings? Where does it indicate pronunciation?

Using the Dictionary

A dictionary is a descriptive record of our language. Look at an entry from a college dictionary (Figure 8-2) to see how informative a good dictionary can be. The following list explains the various parts of the entry.

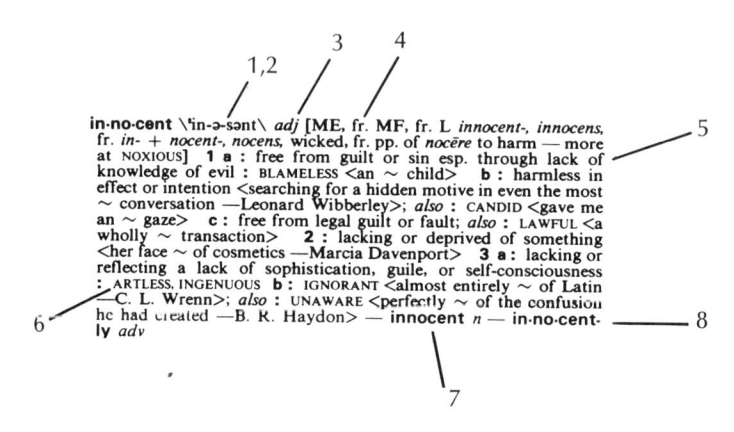

Figure 8-2   An entry from a college dictionary

1. Syllabication — the entry word is separated into syllables by dashes. When you need to hyphenate a word in your own manuscript, consult the dictionary.
2. Pronunciation — see the explanatory notes at the beginning of your dictionary to understand the markings used.
3. Part of speech for the meaning that follows, in this case an adjective.
4. Etymology — the word's history is written in brackets.
5. Definitions for word when used as an adjective.
6. Cross-reference to another word, written in capital letters, for extended meaning.
7. Form of word when used as noun.
8. Form of word when used as an adverb.

EXERCISE 1

secular   vernacular
antithesis   clandestine

Look up the above words in your dictionary. Then answer the following questions about each word.

1. How many syllables does each word have?
2. Look up the initial explanation about pronunciation in your dictionary and use that information to decipher the pronunciation markings here. How do you pronounce these words?
3. If your word is a verb, is it regular or irregular? What are its principal parts? If it is a noun, how is its plural formed? If it is an adjective, what are its inflected forms?
4. Again, referring to the notes at the beginning of your dictionary, use the etymological code to write out the abbreviations and meaning of the symbols. Has the word's meaning changed over the years, or has it remained constant? Does the etymology help you better understand the word's present meaning? If so, how?
5. How many definitions are given? Is one much more familiar than the others? Which one?
6. Are any labels used? Explain.
7. Are any synonyms or antonyms given?

EXERCISE 2

In addition to offering different presentations of abbreviations, pronunciation, foreign words, and general organization, dictionaries differ in their treatment of levels of usage. One dictionary might label a particular word "slang," while another calls the same word "informal." Following are several usage labels used in various standard desk dictionaries. Read through carefully the first few pages of explanatory notes in your dictionary to discover which of these terms it uses and what it says about each.

colloquial	formal
slang	vulgar
dialect	British
archaic	Americanism
jargon	informal

Now see if any usage labels appear in the entry for each of the following words. Write the words and the usage labels in your notebook and come to class prepared to discuss them.

cootie	kibbitz
copout	pink
copper	pine
kerosene	

EXERCISE 3

Use your dictionary to distinguish between these often confusing pairs of words.

distract, detract
elude, allude
affect, effect
disinterested, uninterested
vice, vise

allusion, illusion
elicit, illicit
eminent, imminent
respectful, respective
incredible, incredulous

EXERCISE 4

In addition to all the information contained in each entry, the dictionary also has useful supplemental material in introductions and appendices. Check the table of contents of your own dictionary for information on punctuation conventions; colleges and universities; accepted manuscript form; biographical and geographical information; tables of weights and measures; and Greek and Latin prefixes, suffixes, and roots. Many abridged dictionaries also contain informative full-page color illustrations and charts.

In your book, list three or four supplementary information sections contained in your dictionary. Under each, list two specific bits of information that you find interesting. Be prepared to discuss them in class.

READINGS: SELECTION ONE

Indian Food: A Rich Harvest
by Evan Jones

Ideas to Think About

1. Have you ever considered how your eating habits might change if certain staple foods were no longer available? What favorite meals would no longer be served if tomatoes, potatoes, corn, and chocolate were eliminated from your diet?
2. As you read through this essay, note the placement of the thesis statement and decide whether it is clearly stated. Then underline the major supports of the thesis.
3. As you read, decide which illustrations of the Indians' contribution to classic American food are most surprising.

Vocabulary

Look at each word as it is used in the article. (The number in parentheses indicates the paragraph in which it appears.) First, try to understand the meaning from the way it is used in the sentence. Second, use any clues to meaning through the structure of the word. Then, use the dictionary to clarify the meaning.

derived (2)
evolved (2)
proclivities (4)
ancestral (4)
aboriginal (5)

mentor (5)
incredible (6)
integral (6)
culinary (10)
gastronomy (12)

Indian Food: A Rich Harvest

Evan Jones, the author of *American Food: The Gastronomic Story* and *The World of Cheese*, is also an acknowledged authority on American history.

1   It is sometimes said, though probably not often enough, that no English colony in 17th-century America could have survived without the help of the Indians. Occasionally school children are told a little about Squanto, the Massachusetts native who helped the first New Englanders avert starvation by showing them how to plant corn with fish as fertilizer. But we're seldom reminded that during the first economic struggles at Jamestown some of the early Virginia settlers were sent off one year to live with nearby Indians in order to learn from experts what wild foods could be eaten.

2   Most of the classic American dishes — corn on the cob, roast turkey, candied sweet potatoes, cranberry sauce — are derived° from Indian

origins. It might have been enough had the colonists learned only how to make cornmeal bread, how to use flour made from Indian maize instead of wheat. However, early Yankees also learned that beans should be planted among the rows of corn and that they could be baked with a seasoning of maple syrup, thus establishing Boston Baked Beans as a regional specialty. New England Indians, in addition, passed on the knack of cooking shellfish by heating stones and masses of seaweed, a custom that evolved° into the shoreside ritual known today as the clambake. And in the South the natives introduced the barbecue, thereby setting an example for the thousands of contemporary backyard cooks.

3   American Indians were the first to domesticate virtually half the crops that now make up the world's total food supply. None of this food was known in Europe before 1492, and two of the crops — corn and potatoes — are now ranked with wheat and rice as the most important sources of food in the world. The American sweet potato and manioc have become close runners-up. Still, there are more than 80 other edible plants, including squashes, pumpkins, tomatoes, peppers, peanuts, a host of beans (one is the source of chocolate), as well as avocados, pineapples, and chicle for chewing gum.

4   The culinary proclivities° of the original inhabitants were almost as various. In his *Natural History of Virginia,* the colonist William Byrd described the Indians baking bread "either in Cakes before the Fire, or in Loaves on a warm Hearth, covering the Loaf first with Leaves, then with warm Ashes, and afterwards with Coals over all." The result was the bread that Southerners still call corn pone. Today in Second Mesa, Arizona, Hopi Indians, using similar methods, continue to make ancestral° corn breads, thin as paper, that have been judged "the most perfect of all known corn-foods." Other native cooks of the Southwest long ago demonstrated that dried corn, when soaked in water mixed with ashes, would swell, whiten, and take on new flavor, and the resulting hominy became a standard Indian dish throughout the country and is now served by white Americans with pride. Indeed, grits (hominy coarsely ground and boiled) is not unknown in the White House.

5   There are said to be more than 40 aboriginal° ways of using corn in cooking, from thickening soups and stews with cornmeal to making puddings by scraping and simmering fresh kernels. As famous as any corn concoction is succotash, which their Indian mentors° showed the Pilgrims how to produce by mixing corn, beans, and bear meat, and which became a traditional part of New England Thanksgiving dinners. A more surprising item of history is the fact that the original Thanksgiving didn't come to an end until after a brother of Chief Massasoit brought in a large basket spilling over with popcorn.

There is no evidence that turkey (the bird Ben Franklin wanted America to honor instead of the eagle) was served at that feast in 1621, but "Wild Turkeys of incredible° Bigness" were noted by observers of the period, and colonial wives up and down the Atlantic showed their appreciation of the Indian game bird by roasting it according to European recipes. Learning to modify the tartness of cranberries with the flavor of maple, in lieu of hard-to-get white sugar, they made cranberry sauce an integral° part of Thanksgiving. The cranberries that grew wild in the Indian country were so prized by Franklin, in fact, that they were high on the list of foods he asked his wife to send abroad when he was alone in London before the Revolutionary War.

The maple syrup that sweetened berries had been gathered by the Iroquois and other tribes for generations before the arrival of the white man. Maple sap was used in cooking as a condiment, and in the making of baked sweet breads in which ground corn was mixed with chestnuts, beans, and wild berries. It was the sweetener for a primitive corn porridge out of which New Englanders evolved the recipe for Indian Pudding, a dessert that still rates respectful attention from Yankee hostesses. And the syrup was thinned in summer with cold spring water to make a refreshing tonic, which may well have been the first soft drink available in America. Colonists who distrusted water (with considerable reason, given the lack of sanitation they had known in Europe) went a step farther than their Indian benefactors. Using their thirst to mother invention, they devised palatable brews not only from maple sugar, but from pumpkins and persimmons.

Southern Indians harvested numerous fruits, such as persimmons and peaches, and tribes throughout the continent cultivated pumpkins and squashes, introducing settlers to numerous basic cooking methods. One recipe, given a European twist or two, was simplicity itself. Describing what he called "an ancient New-England standing dish," the traveler John Josselyn reported a century before the Revolution that "the housewives manner," in following the Indian way of preparing pumpkin, "is to slice them when ripe, and cut them into dice, and so fill a pot with them of two or three gallons, and stew them upon a gentle fire a whole day, and as they sink, they fill again with fresh pompions; not putting any liquor to them, and when it is stew'd enough, it will look like bak'd apples; this they dish, putting butter to it, and a little vinegard with some spice, and ginger which makes it taste tart like an apple, and so serve it up to be eaten with fish or flesh."

Like beans, pumpkins (or pompions as some called them) were grown by Indians among their rows of corn, and so was purslane, a potherb presented to Samuel Champlain when he made one of the first landfalls on Cape Cod. There the French explorer found the natives cultivating the sunflower roots which have become known as Jerusalem artichokes. Voyagers who came after Champlain found the Chippewas eating "with fish or flesh" another equally esoteric vegetable; it was wild rice, a staple grain of the Great Lakes tribes which today is sometimes linked with caviar, lobster, Marennes oysters, and crab cakes from Chesapeake Bay.

A staple food of the South was, and still is, the sweet potato, which belongs to the morning-glory family and was most commonly baked in hot ashes by the Indians. Soon after the first white man tasted this New World vegetable, Robert Beverly of Virginia described the sweet potatoes that grew wild as "about as long as a Boy's leg, and sometimes as long and big as both the Leg and Thigh of a young Child, and very much resembling it in shape." They grew so large that in the words of an extravagant observer from the North, "You may sit on one end and roast and eat the other." They make exceedingly fine pies, of course, but it is their affinity for smoked ham that is their best claim to culinary° fame. 10

It is the white potato, however, that rules the tuber world. Its natural habitat was Latin America and it came to colonial Virginia as a luxury, imported from Bermuda for elegant dinners in plantation mansions. Even earlier, Spaniards learned about potatoes from the Indians of Peru, whose descendants still cook them in simple ways, sometimes adding sauces flavored with chili. But only after potatoes were planted in Ireland was their capacity for feeding the hungry really recognized. Now there are about 160 varieties, of which the best known may be those from Idaho. The product of high altitudes, they are considered to be the best baking potatoes anywhere (and so removed from ancient Indian culinary simplicity that chef Paul Bocuse of *nouvelle cuisine* renown has said that he never leaves America for France without taking with him one hundred pounds of Idahos). 11

It is hard to imagine what French cooking, or that of any European country, would be without potatoes, and it may be even more difficult to conceive of southern Italian fare as we know it had the Indians managed to keep tomatoes to themselves. In Aztec times red tomatoes were known in Mexico and other parts of Latin America but — in spite of the fact that Thomas Jefferson grew them at Monticello — it was not until the 19th century that recipes for cooking them began to appear generally. Today, whatever else is true, tomatoes are among the most obvious of Indian gifts to gastronomy.° 12

It is even more obvious that food is only one of many endowments to the white man. In *The Indian Heritage of America*, Alvin M. Josephy summed up the matter: "Few persons today recognize, or are appreciative of, the vast contributions made to contemporary life by American Indians." 13

Discussion

1. Jones uses comparison and contrast frequently. For example, at the end of the essay he compares the sweet potato and the white potato. Examine the comparison and contrast devices and their arrangement in those paragraphs and discuss whether or not they are effective.
2. Outline the thesis and support of Jones's essay. Discuss whether or not you feel there are any irrelevant supports. If you were editing this essay, what changes would you make in word choice or arrangement?
3. What new things did you learn about the contributions made to contemporary life by the American Indians?

324   UNIT 8   EXPOSITION: OPINION

READINGS: SELECTION TWO

from The Mysterious Rise and Decline of Monte Albán
by John E. Pfeiffer

Ideas to Think About

1. Have you ever considered the similarities between the development of a city and the growth of a human being? Both experience a birth; both grow and flourish; both decline and die. Why do you think your own hometown developed?
2. How has your hometown changed in the last few years? Has there been much new building? Have areas fallen into disrepair? Describe these changes. Explain why you think they have occurred.
3. Pfeiffer's essay is an informative article documenting the emergence of a great city. Pay attention to the organization of facts and ideas in the essay. Why do you think Pfeiffer organizes the essay as he does?

Vocabulary

Look at each word as it is used in the article. (The number in parentheses indicates the paragraph in which it appears.) First, try to understand the meaning from the way it is used in the sentence. Second, use any clues to meaning through the structure of the word. Then, use the dictionary to clarify the meaning.

imperial (2)	nomads (7)
archaeologists (4)	expediency (11)
artifacts (4)	subjugated (14)
trajectory (5)	inconspicuous (20)
emergence (6)	cumulative (20)

from The Mysterious Rise and Decline of Monte Albán

John E. Pfeiffer is the author of *The Emergence of Society* and *The Emergence of Man*. He is now writing a book on the appearance of humans on earth.

Some 2,500 years ago when Greeks were busy fighting Persians at places like Thermopylae and Marathon, Zapotec Indians across the Atlantic began building a great city, possibly the first in the New World. The job called for reshaping Monte Albán, a 1,500-foot hill overlooking the Valley of Oaxaca in Central Mexico. Cutting into the hillsides, workers constructed hundreds of terraces, stepped platforms with retaining walls designed mainly for plain and fancy residences. For the seats of the mighty,

1

the palaces and temples and major administrative centers, they leveled the entire hilltop, creating the main plaza on a 55-acre super-terrace perhaps eight times bigger than St. Peter's Square at the Vatican.

Monte Albán endured for more than a millennium.[1] It housed 20,000 to 30,000 persons at its height, and lost its position as regional capital some seven to eight centuries before the arrival of invaders from imperial° Spain. But the setting, one of the most magnificent in the ancient world, remains, together with the glamour.

I remember my first visit to the main plaza, climbing stairs to a platform where a palace had once stood and feeling as if I were on the edge of an island in the sky, among gray-black storm clouds, the valley floor far below and mountains on all sides. It was an appropriate place for people in power. Today the center is probably more bustling than it was in its prime, with a rather different cast of characters: tourists by the busload, souvenir vendors, armed soldiers on 24-hour duty to discourage looting.

The city attracts archaeologists° as well as tourists. It has been one of the world's most intensively studied sites ever since Mexican investigators spent 18 seasons digging there, starting in the early 1930's. The latest research project, launched seven years ago and still under way, is headed by 33-year-old Richard Blanton of Purdue University. He and his associates have been engaged in a kind of Operation Mountain Goat, tramping up and down the hill's steep slopes, searching for artifacts° directly underfoot and at the same time on the lookout in the middle distance for traces of ancient roadways, dams, reservoirs and especially terraces. . . .

One objective of Blanton's research is to trace the "trajectory"° of the city, to put together the equivalent of a time-lapse film of its rise and fall, and for that the terraces provide vital information. Shards, shattered bits of cooking and serving ware, are documents of a sort from which, among other things, rough dates may be read. A dish with characteristic "comb" designs scratched on the bottom is typical of what people were using between 300 and 200 B.C., while a popular item from A.D. 200 and 450 was a flared-rim bowl with snake-like carving. Populations for different periods can be estimated from the number and size of houses.

To date the investigators have identified nearly 2,100 terraces, collected about 120,000 shards and thousands of stone tools, produced 30,000 pages of maps and filled out forms specifying exactly what was found where — all of which makes up only part of the record. Monte Albán was the result of remote as well as local forces. Its unfolding story involves findings at hundreds of other sites located in continuous surveys throughout the immediate region and beyond. In some way which eludes us still, its rise was connected with the rise of other early Mesoamerican

---

[1] 1000 years.

centers, its fall with their fall, including the mysterious and relatively sudden collapse of Maya civilization. Furthermore, what we are learning from developments in the Valley of Oaxaca raises questions which apply to the emergence° of cities and states everywhere, and in our own times as well as in times past.

The Valley of Oaxaca's first migrants from a nearby valley — perhaps 50 persons — arrived some 10,000 to 15,000 years ago. They were nomads,° taking nature pretty much as they found it, living on what the good earth offered, wild plants and wild animals. When local resources became scarce, they moved to another part of the valley, rarely camping in one spot more than a month or so. This was the ancestral way of the hunter-gatherer, dating back at least two million years to the earliest members of the genus *Homo*.

Their descendants — and those of other highland people in Mesoamerica — began tinkering with nature. Instead of relying solely on what happened to be growing wild, they altered bits of the Oaxaca landscape. They proceeded to clear selected plots, plant seeds and experiment with garden produce, which merely supplemented conventional wild diets at first, and later became increasingly important. The process culminated in a heavy dependence on a variety of cultivated species including corn, beans, squash, avocados and chili peppers, and in the end of nomadic hunting-gathering as a dominant life-style. Villages appeared around 1600 B.C., settlements of one-room houses with walls of lashed-together reeds or cane plastered with clay and mud. . . .

Perched high and near the point where the three arms of the Y-shaped valley come together, Monte Albán would have made a fine fortress, but the founders built no fortifications. The site was not convenient to good farming land, raw materials or water, and hauling supplies up the hillsides meant backbreaking labor in a country where the only draft animals were human beings. "We really don't know why Monte Albán was built when it was, or why at all," Blanton explains, "but it may have been the creation of local chiefs." These leaders may deliberately have located it in an undesirable place in neutral territory — as was Brasilia on its remote Amazonian plateau or, in earlier times, Washington, D.C., in what was originally a malarial swamp area which no one wanted. It may be significant that in the beginning the center consisted of three separate districts or zones, perhaps the political bailiwicks of leaders from the valley's three arms.

Further clues to what was going on come from Monte Albán's great open terrace, the main hilltop plaza. One of its earliest buildings contained a series of figures carved in low relief on stone slabs, depicted in stylized positions with eyes closed and open mouth, and once believed to be *danzantes* or dancers engaged in some sort of ecstatic ritual. More recent studies suggest that they were dead rather than entranced — slain or sacrificed captives. We might learn more about the killing if experts learn to translate hieroglyphs[2] found at one end of the "Gallery of Danzantes," the oldest known written texts in the New World.

Monte Albán served as the base of a military league or confederation, not a tightly centralized government but a union by consent and for expediency's° sake. Populations were on the rise not just in the Valleys within a radius of 50 miles or so, where competing peoples represented a threat — and, if subjugated, a rich source of tribute in the form of cotton, tropical fruits and other valuable products.

The region suffered growing pains with the population, some 10,000 to 20,000 persons in 300 B.C., soaring to more than 40,000 by 200 B.C. Farmers under pressure to work the land more intensely, to produce more food for city folk, acquired extra hands by producing more children.

Fortification Begins to Appear

A new feature shows up in the archaeological record at Monte Albán, whose own population had tripled. You can see part of it from the top of the hill. About halfway down the west slope, just beyond a plowed field, lies a great ridge marked by a row of trees. The ridge goes on and on, an ancient semicircular defense, a double earthen wall more than a mile long, 10 to 30 feet high, and up to 60 feet thick. Furthermore, in an apparent effort to become more self-sufficient, people built behind the walls what may have been reservoirs, with a network of irrigation canals at the base of the mountain. Unguarded since its founding, Monte Albán was no longer an open city.

Its conquests are commemorated on the main plaza, in a building which, for reasons unknown, is shaped like an arrowhead and points southwest. Set into its walls are more than 40 stone slabs listing subjugated° places. A typical slab includes a "hill" sign, with a glyph above it specifying a conquered place and below it an upside-down head with closed eye, evidently a visual pun representing an overturned chief. In time this structure, known as Building J, was converted to other uses but archaeologists do not agree on its functions. It may have been an observatory.

Political patterns, reflected in living patterns, were changed in the valley's central region, the countryside immediately surrounding Monte Albán. After about 200 B.C., what had been flourishing agricultural development within a radius of ten miles of the city, collapsed. In the region as a whole many sites were abandoned as the people clustered together in the larger communities.

Danger put new life into the Oaxaca military league, starting about A.D. 200 to 300. The threat probably arose some 225 miles to the north-

---

[2] Pictorial symbols.

west on a high plain not far from the present site of Mexico City, where at about that time the supercenter of Teotihuacan was just entering its heyday period, with more than 50,000 inhabitants and dreams of conquest. It was doing business of some sort with Monte Albán, as indicated by the first traces of Teotihuacan-type pottery on the hill, and by the establishment of a Oaxaca district in Teotihuacan. Blanton speculates that "the rich Valley of Oaxaca would have been a prime target for those in Teotihuacan who were directing the expansion of their own empire."

Whatever the Teotihuacanos' intentions, the Zapotecs were never conquered. They created a state of their own with Monte Albán as capital, and a centralized government which seems to be reflected in their sculptures and relief carvings. In a study of some 200 monuments, Joyce Marcus of the University of Michigan reports a wide range of styles during the period from 200 B.C. to A.D. 200, with carvings from different valley-floor localities differing markedly from one another and from those produced by craftsmen on the hill. After that period, however, "all regional styles were abandoned . . . and those sites that continued to carve monuments did so in the Monte Albán style."

Monte Albán reached its peak around A.D. 500 to 600, when it emerged as a supercenter, an unprecedented focus of power. The entire valley of Oaxaca, some 700 square miles, contained in excess of 60,000 persons — and perhaps as many as 30,000 were living on less than three square miles of hillside. The city represented something completely new in the New World, a high-rise complex of slopes and levels, terraces above and overlooking terraces, some no larger than backyard gardens, others bigger than football fields, and all 2,100 of them occupied. . . .

At this time the city was divided into districts, as it had been a millennium ago at its founding, only now instead of three there were 14 (not counting the main plaza). Blanton discovered that all the districts were organized along similar lines, each consisting of numerous residential terraces surrounding one or two groups of mounds at least a meter high and often considerably higher, with platforms on top and facing a common patio or plaza, probably residences for the well-born and their retinues, plus an "open" mound or pair of mounds, generally with access to a major road, perhaps a civic-ceremonial area combining a ritual space with a marketplace.

It was in the main plaza, at the heart of the empire, that eventually decay set in. There was no melodramatic twilight-of-the-gods finale, no vandals breaking down the gates, no sacking. Things began coming apart in little ways. Cracks in a facade, a crumbling bit of pavement, paint peeling off an inconspicuous° temple wall — flaws like these failed to be repaired as promptly as usual and a foreman noticed and someone may have paid with his life. But in time it became clear that something more than neglect was involved as the tiny cumulative° marks of massive social change mounted too fast for maintenance crews to keep up with.

Decline started during the seventh century A.D. First walls were allowed to fall, then entire buildings. By A.D. 1000, the city's population had dropped to less than a fifth of its peak level and the great plaza was abandoned. Gradually, people moved down from the heights, most of them living on the lower slopes of the hill behind defense walls and near a major crossroads which provided easy access to the valley floor. This strategic location, together with a number of other features such as a small settlement and a public space and pyramids just outside the walls, suggests that the former imperial capital had become now more of a commercially oriented tradesmen's community than a regional capital. . . .

We know very little about why Monte Albán collapsed or why, for that matter, any other early center collapsed. (Investigators have been concerned chiefly with rising rather than falling political systems, but now, with the recent outbreak of second thoughts about man's future, more attention is being paid to decline.) Local forces were certainly at work, perhaps within the city itself. In the beginning the main plaza contained only two or three buildings and, although probably never wide open to the public, they may have been readily accessible on special occasions.

Later it became more and more secluded — staircases facing inward and stark back walls facing the rest of the city. A sign of trouble toward the end was the building of new outer defense walls and a high wall hiding an inner-sanctum zone around South Platform. Blanton describes the plaza as "a segregated closed elite-administrative place, access to which was only by way of three small and easily controlled entrances." The distance between the people and their leaders, and the possibility of restlessness that might flare up in hard times, was on the increase.

Monte Albán was not alone in decline. Its fateful century, the seventh century A.D., also saw the beginning of the end for its mammoth Valley of Mexico counterpart to the northwest. Within a century or so, Teotihuacan declined and many of its temples were burned. It dropped from a population of perhaps 150,000 persons to about a fifth of that figure, and became what one authority calls "a backwater in a highly sophisticated state whose center was elsewhere." Another backwater was in the making more than 450 miles to the east, in the tropical lowlands of Guatemala. Not long after the downfall of Teotihuacan, Tikal, one of the New World's proudest centers, also went under. The prime city of the Maya people, with its estimated 60,000 population and massive defense earthworks and white temple-pyramids rising huge and lonely out of the jungle, ended up as a ghost town, a deserted place of relics.

Centers throughout much of the southern Maya lowlands shared the fate of Tikal, in a gigantic population decline on a scale unprecedented in the annals of ancient Mesoamerican society. The cause of collapse of this early Maya civilization, which took place within two centuries or so, continues to stir up controversy among investigators. There are many theories. In fact, practically every conceivable possibility has been suggested: malnutrition and food shortages resulting from overpopulation, the spread of insect-borne diseases, warfare among lowland tribes, an uprising of commoners against the upper classes, declining soil fertility, moral decay, and so on. But the solid evidence to support these notions or any others is lacking.

One thing is certain. Decline in the Maya lowlands, as in Monte Albán itself, cannot be accounted for by local forces alone. A complex system had broken down, a network of trade and diplomatic relationships among the elites of supercenters who, on occasion at least, may have had closer ties with one another than with the people of their own states. Expanding research can be expected to help clarify the nature of changes that took place on a Mesoamerica-wide basis of social evolution on a large scale.

Discussion

1. Pfeiffer refers to Monte Albán as a "supercenter, an unprecedented focus of power." Why would such a great city arise on such a remote and undesirable hilltop?
2. Monte Albán has attracted numerous archaeologists and undergone intensive study since 1930. What is it about Monte Albán that warrants this attention? Why do archaeological sites themselves seem to hold a special fascination for both scientists and tourists alike?
3. Pfeiffer develops his points of discussion in many ways. Find examples of description, use of concrete data, and reference to other researchers. Are these passages effective? Believable? Interesting? Explain.

READINGS: SELECTION THREE
Wrong Ism
by J. B. Priestley

Ideas to Think About

1. Now that you are in college, you have probably met people from other nations, other parts of the country, and other neighborhoods. How do these people differ from your other friends? Do they use different slang? like different foods? dress differently? use different dialects? have different customs? In what ways are these people like you and your other friends?
2. How do you define and describe your nation? How do you think people from other areas of the country define and describe it? How do your views differ from those of national political leaders such as senators, congressional representatives, the president?
3. As you read through the following essay, notate where the author defines terms, classifies, uses similes, compares and contrasts, and develops cause and effect relationships. How do these techniques clarify his thesis? make his points of discussion vivid? help convince you of the validity of his views?

Vocabulary

bogus (1)
entity (4)
fervent (4)
dynamo (5)
piety (5)
imperialism (6)
paraphernalia (6)
dubious (7)
entrepreneurs (7)
impresarios (7)
sensuous (8)
ideologies (9)

Wrong Ism

John Boynton Priestley (1894–) is an English novelist, dramatist, and essayist. Among his works are *The English Novel, The Good Companion, Time and the Conways, An Inspector Calls,* and *The English*. The following excerpt is from *Essays of Five Decades*.

There are three isms that we ought to consider very carefully—regionalism, nationalism, internationalism. Of these three the one there is most fuss about, the one that starts men shouting and marching and shooting, the one that seems to have all the depth and thrust and fire, is of course nationalism. Nine people out of ten, I fancy, would say that of this trio it is the one that really counts, the big boss. Regionalism and internationalism, they would add, are comparatively small, shadowy, rather cranky. And I believe all this to be quite wrong. Like many another big boss, nationalism is largely bogus.° It is like a bunch of flowers made of plastics.

The real flowers belong to regionalism. The mass of people everywhere may never have used the term. They are probably regionalists without knowing it. Because they have been brought up in a certain part of the world, they have formed perhaps quite unconsciously a deep attachment to its landscape and speech, its traditional customs, its food and drink, its songs and jokes. (There are of course always the rebels, often intellectuals and writers, but they are not the mass of people.) They are rooted in their region. Indeed, without this attachment a man can have no roots.

So much of people's lives, from earliest childhood onwards, is deeply intertwined with the common life of the region, they cannot help feeling strongly about it. A threat to it is a knife pointing at the heart. How can life ever be the same if bullying strangers come to change everything? The form and color, the very taste and smell of dear familiar things will be different, alien, life-destroying. It would be better to die fighting. And it is precisely this, the nourishing life of the region, for which common men have so often fought and died.

This attachment to the region exists on a level far deeper than that of any political hocus-pocus. When a man says 'my country' with real feeling, he is thinking about his region, all that has made up his life, and not about that political entity,° the nation. There can be some confusion here simply because some countries are so small—and ours is one of them—and so old, again like ours, that much of what is national is also regional. Down the centuries, the nation, itself so comparatively small, has been able to attach to itself the feeling really created by the region. (Even so there is something left over, as most people in Yorkshire, or Devon, for example, would tell you.) This probably explains the fervent° patriotism developed early in small countries. The English were announcing that they were English in the Middle Ages, before nationalism had arrived elsewhere.

If we deduct from nationalism all that it has borrowed or stolen from regionalism, what remains is mostly rubbish. The nation, as distinct from the region, is largely the creation of power-men and political manipulators. Almost all nationalist movements are led by ambitious frustrated men determined to hold office. I am not blaming them. I would do the same if I were in their place and wanted power so badly. But nearly always they make use of the rich warm regional feeling, the emotional dynamo° of the movement, while being almost untouched by it themselves. This is because they are not as a rule deeply loyal to any region themselves. Ambition and a love of power can eat like acid into the tissues of regional loyalty. It is hard, if not impossible, to retain a natural piety° and yet be forever playing both ends against the middle.

Being itself a power structure, devised by men of power, the nation tends to think and act in terms of power. What would benefit the real life of the region, where men, women and children actually live, is soon sacrificed for the power and prestige of the nation. (And the personal vanity of presidents and ministers themselves, which historians too often disregard.) Among the new nations of our time innumerable peasants and laborers must have found themselves being cut down from five square meals a week to three in order to provide unnecessary airlines, military forces that can only be used against them and nobody else, great conference halls and official yachts and the rest. The last traces of imperialism° and colonialism may have to be removed from Asia and Africa, where men can no longer endure being condemned to a permanent inferiority by the color of their skins; but even so the modern world, the real world of our time, does not want and would be far better without more and more nations, busy creating for themselves the very paraphernalia° that western Europe is now trying to abolish. You are compelled to answer more questions when trying to spend half a day in Cambodia than you are now travelling from the Hook of Holland to Syracuse.

This brings me to internationalism. I dislike this term, which I used only to complete the isms. It suggests financiers and dubious° promoters living nowhere but in luxury hotels; a shallow world of entrepreneurs° and impresarios.° (Was it Sacha Guitry who said that impresarios were men who spoke many languages but all with a foreign accent?) The internationalism I have in mind here is best described as world civilization. It is life considered on a global scale. Most of our communications and transport already exist on this high wide level. So do many other things from medicine to meteorology. Our astronomers and physicists (except where they have allowed themselves to be hush-hushed) work here. The UN special agencies, about which we hear far too little, have contributed more and more to this world civilization. All the arts, when they are arts and not chunks of nationalist propaganda, naturally take their place in it. And it grows, widens, deepens, in spite of the fact that for every dollar, ruble, pound or franc spent in explaining and praising it, a thousand are spent by the nations explaining and praising themselves.

This world civilization and regionalism can get along together, especially if we keep ourselves sharply aware of their quite different but equally important values and rewards. A man can make his contribution to world civilization and yet remain strongly regional in feeling: I know several men of this sort. There is of course the danger—it is with us now —of the global style flattening out the regional, taking local form, color, flavor, away for ever, disinheriting future generations, threatening them with sensuous° poverty and a huge boredom. But to understand and appreciate regionalism is to be on guard against this danger. And we must therefore make a clear distinction between regionalism and nationalism.

It is nationalism that tries to check the growth of world civilization. And nationalism, when taken on a global scale, is more aggressive and demanding now than it has ever been before. This in the giant powers is largely disguised by the endless fuss in public about rival ideologies,° now a largely unreal quarrel. What is intensely real is the glaring nationalism. Even the desire to police the world is nationalistic in origin. (Only the world can police the world.) Moreover, the nation-states of today are for the most part far narrower in their outlook, far more inclined to allow prejudice against the foreigner to impoverish their own style of living, than the old imperial states were. It should be part of world civilization that men with particular skills, perhaps the product of the very regionalism they are rebelling against, should be able to move easily from country to country, to exercise those skills, in anything from teaching the violin to running a new type of factory to managing an old hotel. But nationalism, especially of the newer sort, would rather see everything done badly than allow a few non-nationals to get to work. And people face a barrage of passports, visas, immigration controls, labor permits; and in this respect are worse off than they were in 1900. But even so, in spite of all that nationalism can do—so long as it keeps its nuclear bombs to itself—the internationalism I have in mind slowly creating a world civilization, cannot be checked.

Nevertheless, we are still backing the wrong ism. Almost all our money goes on the middle one, nationalism, the rotten meat between the two healthy slices of bread. We need regionalism to give us roots and that very depth of feeling which nationalism unjustly and greedily claims for itself. We need internationalism to save the world and to broaden and heighten our civilization. While regional man enriches the lives that international man is already working to keep secure and healthy, national man, drunk with power, demands our loyalty, money and applause, and poisons the very air with his dangerous nonsense.

Discussion

1. What is Priestley's thesis and where is it stated? What are his major supports of this thesis?
2. Priestley claims that, because England is a very small nation, the regionalism and nationalism of its people are quite similar. The United States, however, is a large nation. Is there much difference between the regionalistic and nationalistic attitudes of its people? Do the attitudes of the people differ from those of their national political leaders? Cite examples of such differences. Why do you think these differences occur?
3. How does Priestley define nationalism, regionalism, and internationalism? Do you accept these definitions as valid? Why?
4. The author avoids offering concrete examples and facts to substantiate his

thesis; instead, he relies on emotionally charged language and general references to incidents and situations. How does this technique affect the reader? What is his specific purpose in writing this essay? Locate examples of emotionally charged language and discuss the effect on the reader.
5. What dangers does the author see in nationalism? in internationalism?
6. Where does the author employ comparison/contrast? Why?
7. What does Priestley see as the cause of nationalism?

WRITING:
Exposition: Opinion

The Three-Paragraph Essay Exam

Have you ever wondered how you were able to make such a good grade on a particular test? That is, even though you had studied hard and prepared well, you were surprised at your own performance. Maybe you thought, "Boy, was I lucky!" On the other hand, have you ever left a test situation wondering what happened to you? Maybe you were just as well prepared as you had been for the "lucky" examination, but this time when you began to write, you rambled, babbling in bits and pieces about the material you thought you had known so well. And then a poor grade confirmed your fears. If you prepare equally well for every test and then find luck playing a major role in your actual test performance, you need some specific test-taking skills that you can rely on.

An important test-taking skill is understanding the most widely used types of examination questions, those requiring you to respond with thesis and support or comparison and contrast essays. Such test formats appear often in all college courses because they measure students' comprehension of assigned material. Questions that require these kinds of essay responses test understanding of *relationships*, the key to *analysis* (breaking things down to their component parts) and *synthesis* (bringing things together into a whole). Furthermore, these types of answers reveal students' ability to express their understanding of relationships.

Thesis and Support

A basic three-paragraph thesis and support essay exam uses essentially the same *T-R-I* pattern of organization you followed for the one-paragraph essay in Unit 3. Here, however, you will find variations on that pattern, some of which allow you to make choices based on the test question. The three-paragraph examination essay is organized according to the following pattern.

Paragraph 1
T — Thesis statement.

R — Restriction to three major supports (optional).

S — Support 1.

Paragraph 2
S — Support 2.

Paragraph 3
S — Support 3.

C — Conclusion.

The *thesis statement* should be an explicit and *immediate* response to the test question. Because you will be writing under the pressure of time, the most effective way to begin your answer is simply to turn the test question around and make it your thesis. Do not waste time providing background information or restating your thesis.

In formulating your thesis statement, you have two choices open to you.

Choice 1 — You can use the exact wording of the question for your thesis. A distinct advantage to this method is that it helps you set up an accurate focus for your discussion, in a sense *forcing* you to follow through on the question as it is asked of you. The only disadvantage is that your professor may become bored, since many other students will use the same opening sentence.

Choice 2 — You can rephrase the question in your own words. The advantage to this method is that it indicates your understanding of the question and your ability to express yourself as an individual. But the danger is that you may misinterpret the question, a situation that can lead you into an incorrect or unfocused answer.

Example

In his book *Wealth and Poverty* George Gilder claims that "women prefer to avoid full commitment to the work force." Do you agree or disagree with this statement? Explain.

THESIS

I disagree with George Gilder's view that women prefer to avoid full commitment to the work force.

THESIS

Although some women may lack a total commitment to their jobs, more and more women now seek to develop fulfilling careers.

EXERCISE 1

Look at the following forty-five-minute sample essay question. Using the choices shown in the preceding list, formulate an appropriate brief thesis to prepare for a logical discussion of the topic.

According to some critics of the state college system, general education courses should be abolished. Do you agree or disagree? Why or why not?

Before discussing your answer, let's examine the process that leads to an effective thesis. In trying to set up your thesis statement, you may have found that you had to deal with more than one simple question, a common problem in essay questions. First of all you must respond to an introductory statement, then take a stand by stating an opinion, and finally discuss the reasons for your views.

Whenever you are asked to agree or disagree, you are expected to take a stand and state your position in the thesis statement. But when you are given a brief passage to respond to, as in Exercise 1, your options are more complicated. Remember, responding to the introductory statement in a test question is not the same thing as providing your own introduction or supplementary background. As mentioned earlier, you do not need to do so. However, when an introductory comment is part of the test question, you can't ignore it. You must assume it is important in some way and then make a decision about how much of it to include in your thesis or whether to include it at all. For example, in composing the thesis for Exercise 1 following the format of Choice 1, you probably included the entire introductory statement along with your answer to the question.

> According to some critics of the state college system, general education courses should be abolished. I disagree with these critics.

If, on the other hand, you used Choice 2, perhaps your thesis looked something like this:

> I disagree with the idea that general education courses should be abolished.

or:

> I disagree with critics of the college system who want to abolish general education courses.

Whichever way you phrased your thesis, you undoubtedly were aware that at least part of the introductory statement was vital to an effective response. But a thesis statement is only a beginning, the first part of the first paragraph of an exam answer. In other words, a good first paragraph is like a good road map that tells you where you are going and how to get there.

Some of you may have learned to outline first before starting an essay — this method is fine if you are comfortable using it — but a sound thesis statement (T) with a *restriction to three major supports* (R) can serve the same purpose and also save you time under test pressure. Why three? Three is a generally accepted number of supports needed to validate or prove a thesis. One or two supports are usually not enough proof, although sometimes, depending on the subject matter and question, more than three are needed, each in a fully developed paragraph.

The test question determines the type of support needed.

details	classifications
causes	trends
effects	theories
characteristics	examples
explanations	

EXERCISE 2
To the preceding list, add some other possibilities for major types of supports. Think about some of the subjects you are studying this semester. What types of materials might you use in your final exam?

    A glance at your thesis statement for Exercise 1 will show that you have included a response to the first part of the question. But now you must confront the second part — why you agree or disagree with the given statement. The logical response to *why?* is *because,* so the major supports to the question would be explanations. The method for incorporating these explanations into your opening paragraph involves the following two steps.

1. First make an explicit statement indicating that your opinion is based on three reasons.
2. Then briefly summarize these reasons, using transition words to separate and emphasize them. (This step is always optional, depending on the wording of the test question. But if you can include a brief summary, you will have a well-drawn road map to rely on.)

EXERCISE 3
Go back to the thesis statement you composed in Exercise 1. Add a *restriction* (R) to your thesis, using the two-step method. This restriction is your brief summary of the three major supports you will use in the essay to prove why you agree or disagree.

    Example
    (T) I disagree with the critics of the state college system who want to abolish general education courses. (R) My first reason for objecting to this idea is that. . . . Another reason I disagree is that. . . . Finally, I object because. . . .

Paragraph One: Support 1

Once you have set up a thesis statement and restriction to three major supports, you are ready to complete the first paragraph. Remember you must be careful to organize your essay according to the order you have set up in your restriction; this means that your first paragraph, according to the pattern on page 336, will include the following items.

1. A thesis statement.
2. A restriction to three major supports.
3. A discussion of the *first* major support (evaluation) listed in the restriction, using specific details or examples to develop this major support. Do not

assume that your reader will know what you are trying to say; begin with an explicit restatement of your first support, e.g., "I object to this idea because. . . ."

Paragraph Two: Support 2
The second paragraph of a test essay focuses on the second major support stated in your restriction. Because of time pressure, the most effective method to make your point clear is to begin with a *topic sentence referring explicitly* to the second major support, e.g., "The second (or next) reason I disagree is that. . . ." Develop the paragraph with specific examples and concrete details.

Paragraph Three: Support 3 and Conclusion
The third paragraph of a test essay consists of a discussion of the third major support stated in the restriction. Because of time pressure, the most effective method to make your point clear is to begin with a *topic sentence referring explicitly to the final support* and to include the specific examples and concrete details necessary to develop fully that final point. In addition, this third paragraph could include a brief sentence to *summarize* or *round off* the essay, such as, "For all these reasons, I believe that general education courses are a necessary part of college learning." In this last section, be careful not to introduce a whole new topic; keep the focus on what you have already discussed.

EXERCISE 4
Write a forty-five-minute three-paragraph essay in response to the following question.

> In some European universities, students begin to concentrate on their major field of interest as soon as they enter college. Some American students feel that they too would like to avoid the general education courses required in most U.S. colleges. Other students approve of the general education requirements. Do you agree or disagree that general education courses are necessary?

> GUIDELINES
> 1. Do not generalize; be specific.
> 2. Support all major assertions, using any methods of paragraph development that seem relevant to your discussion. You might wish to use some of the following formats.
>   a. Concrete details, specific examples, or illustrations.
>   b. Cause-and-effect relationships.
>   c. Definition of terms.
>   d. Comparison and contrast relationships.

Comparison and Contrast Essay

As stated earlier, comparison and contrast is another type of essay test question used extensively to determine how well students understand relationships. As you know, the word *contrast* means to show the differences between things, while *compare* usually means to show similarities. But whenever you are asked to *compare, make a comparative study,* or *write a comparative analysis,* you are usually expected to show *both* the similarities and differences. Once you master the organizing patterns of comparison-contrast, you can use the same methods of organization for either a short paragraph answer or a longer essay, but you should always organize your material both *logically* and *fairly*. *Logically* means that in comparing or contrasting two general subjects you must treat the same specific points for both and discuss these points *in the same order* for both subjects. *Fairly* means that you try to present an equally full discussion for both subjects.

Example
Look at the following paragraph from a Unit 6 reading selection.

> There are factors involved in railroad engineering which can be found in other areas of the mechanical arts, factors so obvious that they tend to be overlooked in most histories of inventions. In art or science, invention can be done for its own sake. The individual's urge to create and explore is satisfied. The end can be an original theory, an imaginative formula, or simply a beautiful object. But in engineering, invention must have a practical end. It must not only work satisfactorily, it must work within a given cost range and yield a predictable profit.
>
> — White, *"Rails: From Old World to New"*

1. In the first sentence *(T)* and second sentence *(R)*, what are the main idea and restriction?

   The main idea is that certain factors about invention in railroad engineering (and "other areas of the mechanical arts") are often overlooked. The restriction sets up the contrast between engineering and "art or science."

2. What is the main point of contrast between engineering and art or science? List the details or examples that support the main point of contrast.

   Art or science   *Engineering*
   The end (of invention) can be . . . But the end must be . . .
   a.   a.
   b.   b.
   c.   c.

3. Now determine how logically and fairly the author has developed his paragraph.

As stated earlier in this section, you should organize your material both logically and fairly, even under the stress of a test. But suppose you were given a comparison-contrast question that also required you to state which of two things is the more successful, more valuable, or more effective? Or which of the two things is worse? Keeping in mind that you must choose one thing over the other, can you foresee that being fair could become a problem? Can you foresee that making such a choice might influence you to discuss the subject of your choice a little more fully than the other one? This kind of reaction to a comparison-contrast question involving choice is to be expected and is acceptable as long as you don't totally overlook the main points of comparison between the two subjects.

Organization: Paragraph One

Even if the test essay is a comparison-contrast, you must always begin with a thesis statement that responds immediately and directly to the question asked. And if possible, you should also add the restriction, stating the points you will be comparing or contrasting; that is, if there are a *limited* number of points (three or four) to be covered, you can state them. But if you must cover many points, you can omit the restriction.

EXERCISE 5

Set up a thesis (*T*) and restriction (*R*) for the following test question after you have read the guidelines.

> Which had a worse effect on America, the Korean or Vietnam War? Consider our military preparedness, public attitudes, and the physical impact on our armed forces.

GUIDELINES

1. Some key words for this question are "worse," "Korean," and "Vietnam War." *Worse* means you must make a choice; *Korean* and *Vietnam* are your choices. And since two military actions are mentioned, you cannot simply choose one and then ignore the other; that is, the question implies comparison and contrast, even if those words are not used explicitly.
2. Check to see what other key words in the question indicate the main points you must compare and contrast.

Organization: The Divided or Separated Pattern

Once you have set up your thesis in response to the question and have either added a restriction or made an outline list on another paper to remind yourself of the points to discuss, you have two choices available for your pattern of organization. One is the divided pattern; the other is the point-by-point pattern. You will see that making a choice between the two patterns depends on matters such as the question, the subject matter, and the length of time you have been allotted for this question. The important thing is to master both patterns so that during the test you can make a quick decision as to which pattern would be most effective. Briefly, in the *divided* pattern, you discuss fully all the points about one subject and then go on to the second subject, discussing all the same points in the same order. Although the purest form of this pattern is found mainly in a test essay, you may also find it in passages of other types of essays. For example, look at the following paragraphs.

> The Valley of Oaxaca's first migrants from a nearby valley — perhaps 50 persons — arrived some 10,000 to 15,000 years ago. They were nomads, taking nature pretty much as they found it, living on what the good earth offered, wild plants and wild animals. When local resources became scarce, they moved to another part of the valley, rarely camping in one spot more than a month or so. This was the ancestral way of the hunter-gatherer, dating back at least two million years to the earliest members of the genus *Homo*.
>
> Their descendants — and those of other highland people in Mesoamerica — began tinkering with nature. Instead of relying solely on what happened to be growing wild, they altered bits of the Oaxaca landscape. They proceeded to clear selected plots, plant seeds and experiment with garden produce, which merely supplemented conventional wild diets at first, and later became increasingly important. The process culminated in a heavy dependence on a variety of cultivated species including corn, beans, squash, avocados and chili peppers, and in the end of nomadic hunting-gathering as a dominant life-style. Villages appeared around 1600 B.C., settlements of one-room houses with walls of lashed-together reeds or cane plastered with clay and mud.
> — Pfeiffer, *"The Rise and Decline of Monte Albán"*

The main idea of this two-paragraph passage is a contrast between the earliest and later inhabitants of Oaxaca.

Earliest migrants	*Later descendants*
1. Nomads took nature as they found it.	1. People tinkered with nature.
2. Food included "wild plants and wild animals."	2. Bits of the Oaxaca landscape were altered.
3. Typical hunter-gatherers moved to another area when local resources became scarce.	3. Dependence on cultivated species marked end of nomadic hunting-gathering and beginning of villages.

A test question on this passage might be: How did the descendants of the original inhabitants of Oaxaca differ from their ancestors? A good answer could be set up in the following way.

1. You would write a thesis statement with a *modified* restriction, such as, "The descendants of the original Oaxacan inhabitants differed from them in three ways." The restriction here indicates that three major points will

be discussed, but it does not summarize those points of contrast because the points are based on chronological development and cannot be easily reduced to specific categories.
2. You would organize the essay answer, like the original paragraph, according to the divided pattern, first discussing all three major points about the earliest Oaxacan settlers and then discussing the same points in the same order about the descendants.

You will notice that in the above sample passage from "The Rise and Fall of Monte Albán," the author shows only differences (contrasts) between the two topics. In other situations, however, only the similarities (comparisons) or both similarities *and* differences between two things might be discussed. In either case, you use the basic pattern shown previously, discussing the same parallel points in the same order for both subjects. However, you may have to make some minor adjustments in your thesis statement, stating explicitly that your two subjects are either similar in certain ways or both similar and different in certain ways. In addition, if there are many points to be covered, you may want to group together first all the similarities and then all the differences.

Organization Choice 2: The Point-by-Point Pattern

After you have set up your (T) and (R) for a point-by-point pattern, you discuss the first point about the first topic and then the same point about the second. Then, in a like manner, you discuss the second point about both topics and continue in the same way until every point has been covered. Remember always to begin with the first topic and then to proceed to the second. For example, look at the following paragraphs.

> Reforestation by scattering seedlings from helicopters rather than relying on the wind, or planting seedlings that have been grown in nurseries to a size where their chance of survival is greater, also speeds up the tree-growing process. A Douglas fir seedling, raised in a greenhouse in its own individual plastic tube, reaches plantable size (6 to 8 inches) in five to seven months. A natural seed may take several years to reach the same size — if it survives at all.
> One forested acre, left to nature, would grow a stand of mature trees in 250 years. That same acre, properly managed, could grow a stand ready for cutting every 50 years — thus providing five harvests instead of one in the same time span, with six times the volume of wood of the unmanaged forest.
> —Wigner, *"America's Green Gold"*

The main idea of this two-paragraph passage is that controlled reforesting, as opposed to natural reforesting, "speeds up the tree-growing process." And since the author begins first with a reference to controlled reforesting ("scattering seedlings from a helicopter"), it should be considered as the first topic and natural reforesting as the second topic. Arranged graphically, the passage looks like this.

Controlled
1. Faster tree-growing process (more effective).
2. Use of helicopters to scatter.
3. Increased survival with nursery-grown seedlings.

Example
Greenhouse-grown seedlings plantable in five to seven months.

Natural
1. Slower process (less effective).
2. Reliance on wind to scatter.
3. Decreased survival chances implied with natural growth.

Example
Equal natural seed growth rate after several years.

EXERCISE 6
Using the point-by-point pattern, answer the following question: Why is controlled reforesting more effective than nature's reforesting?

Choosing the Right Pattern

Now that you are familiar with both the divided and point-by-point organizational patterns, you may wonder which one is more effective in a test situation. The choice, as mentioned earlier, is often determined by the complexity of the subject matter or by the time allotted for the answer — is it to be one paragraph or a longer essay? You can prepare yourself for a decision before being faced with an actual choice; consider the following advantages and disadvantages of each pattern under certain circumstances.

1. If the subject matter is complicated, requiring an extended discussion of each point in order to show important relationships between two (or more) topics.

   Divided pattern
   Gives the effect of two separate discussions, causing loss of emphasis about important relationships.

   Point-by-point pattern
   Stresses important relationships by dealing fully, one point at a time, with both topics.

2. If subject matter is uncomplicated, requiring only brief details of comparison or contrast, perhaps for a one-paragraph answer.

   Divided pattern
   Allows for quick, clear build-up of pertinent facts.

   Point-by-point pattern
   Creates an annoying ping-pong effect, back and forth between briefly stated items.

3. If a forty-five-to fifty-minute answer is required.

Divided pattern
Causes time management problems, e.g., if four key points of comparison and contrast are needed, you can very easily spend too much time on the four points of one topic and run out of time to complete the four points about the other topic, resulting in an unbalanced essay.

Point-by-point pattern
Allows better time control over each key point, e.g., if you cover only three out of four points for both topics, they are at least balanced and fully developed in relationship to each other.

Brainstorming and Shaping

Brainstorming here takes the form of a review of test preparation covered in this unit. To get ready for examinations, follow these procedures.

1. Set up a time management schedule using the plan recommended in the Reading Strategies section of this unit under the topic "Scheduling Time."
2. Anticipate the questions you may be asked on your exams; check your texts for main ideas and review lecture notes for topics stressed by the instructor. Then prepare data sheets listing main points and supporting examples and details for both the thesis and support essay and the comparison and contrast essay. Review the methods shown in these sections of this unit.
    a. The Reading Strategies section under the topic "Organizing the Material."
    b. The Writing Assignment section under the topic "The Three-Paragraph Essay Test" or "Comparison and Contrast Essay Test."

Writing the Essay Exam

Your instructor will give you an essay exam based on the assigned reading in this unit.

Revising the Three-Paragraph Essay Exam

Even though examinations are written under the stress of time, you should always allot yourself at least a few minutes to check your essays and make necessary changes and corrections. As part of your test preparation, keep the following review questions in mind to use when checking your answers before handing in your paper.

Basic Revision Questions

1. *Have I answered the exact question asked of me?*
    Many students fail their exams simply because they do not pay enough attention to or misunderstand the question asked. Read the question care-

fully and ask your teacher for a clarification if you do not understand what is expected of you.

2. *Does my main thesis respond quickly to the question and focus clearly on what I want to say?*
Once you determine that you have understood the question, you must check to see that the thesis is clearly written, not vague or ambiguous. Get to the point immediately and stay with it.

3. *Do I have a clearly stated topic sentence for each of my paragraphs?*
Be sure you offer sufficient supports for your thesis and express them through a limited, precise topic sentence.

4. *Do I have enough accurate examples and details to back up or develop my main supports?*
Make certain that all items in each paragraph contribute to a full, logical, intelligent discussion.

Editing

Word Choice: Tone

The word *tone* has special applications in art, music, and literature; in all three of these areas, tone is associated with the word *quality* — quality of sound, pitch, color, shade, words, phrases, or sentences. In expository writing, the word choices that express your attitude toward your content and reader help create tone, establishing the general effect, atmosphere, and quality of what you say. In fact, tone is as vital to the overall effect of what you write as it is to the overall effect of any music or artwork.

But in writing, your purpose and reading audience suggest all your choices, including the tone you want and the word choices necessary to create it. For example, when writing a term paper, you want a professional tone; for a letter to your best friend, you would prefer a friendly tone (unless you are angry with this friend). In your letter, you would use many adjectives, probably expressed in colloquial language, that would reflect your feelings. You might even use slang or occasional sentence fragments for effect. However, in a term paper, you would not use contractions or colloquialisms, and your vocabulary would probably include longer words and more impersonal, denotative words that might tend to be abstract. Your personal attitude would be more muted. You might evaluate a work in your term paper for an art class by saying, "The work is a fine graphic illustration." In a letter to a friend you might say, "What a great poster!"

Words chosen to create a desired tone reflect the writer's attitude. For instance, a writer who chooses colloquialisms, slang, contractions, and popular diction in an angry letter of complaint would be at a disadvantage, for such word choices lessen the writer's credibility. Note the following examples. Which one would be taken more seriously by the reader? Which one would be considered no more than a crank letter?

Examples

This product is garbage. In fact, it's a rotten, lousy piece of junk, and the idiot who made it should be canned or shot. I want my money back!

This merchandise, purchased at your Westland branch store on Monday, August 12, 1981, is defective. Since it does not perform according to the claims made in your advertisement, I would appreciate an immediate refund.

All of us have had enough experience with defective products to sympathize with the writer of the first statement. However, consider the audience in each case. The first claim is made with such hostile and insulting words that its chances of being regarded seriously are slim. In fact, it is a kind of shouting match that might make the reader want to return the insults or even break into laughter. In contrast, the tone of the second letter is as firm and as uncomplimentary as the first, but it is more credible and would alienate the reader less. In all probability, this more business-like tone would be more apt to convince the reader to grant the desired refund. Yet, a semiformal tone need not and should not be stiff and pompous like a legal contract; instead, it should be temperate and rather objective. As such, it is usually the most effective choice for writing college papers, business letters, and persuasive essays of all kinds.

Levels of formality are only one concern. When creating tone, consistency is another. Whatever tone you select should be maintained carefully throughout your essay, with word choices staying at the same level of formality. For example, when writing an essay on excessive television viewing as a cause of children's reading problems, you should use the words *children* or *youngsters* and not switch to *brats, little monsters,* or *kids;* these inappropriate slang terms would jar your audience and diminish your credibility as an authority. Remember, choose words that best suit your purpose for writing, remain consistent, and, unless you want to incite a riot, be careful not to alienate your audience with inappropriate language choices.

EXERCISE 1

Examine the first paragraph of each of the essays in this unit. List the specific word choices that create the tone of each paragraph. Which seems most formal? Which is least formal? Why?

EXERCISE 2

Write the opening paragraph of a letter in which you complain about the faulty wiring in your new car. The local service man has refused to repair it without charge. Address your letter to the national sales manager requesting that the manufacturer honor its warranty.

EXERCISE 3

Now write a similar paragraph of complaint, but this time address it to Ralph Nader or your best friend. How might the word choices you make affect the tone of the letter? Should the tone be the same as that in your first letter? Why or why not?

Sentence Structure: Noun Choices — Contracting and Expanding through Noun Clauses and Verbals

In the previous units, you explored some ways of contracting and expanding modifiers, those parts of sentences functioning as adverbs and adjectives. In this unit, you will explore substitutions for the noun parts of the sentence. As you know, modifiers expand or limit nouns and verbs, the core or kernel of each sentence.

```
                           CORE
      The  /\  company  /\  manufactures  /\  boxes  /\.
         Slot A        Slot B            Slot C    Slot D
```

POSSIBLE MODIFIERS

Slot A

   small

   local

   famous

Slot B

   which is owned by a local family

   that is most successful

   that hired the new computer technician

Slot C

   delicate

   shipping

   colored

   jewelry

Slot D

   covered with red leather

   of heavy cardboard

Just as the modifiers in this sentence can be one adjective (small, colored) or many words in an adjective clause or phrase (that is most successful, covered with red leather), so nouns and verbs can be either single words or whole clauses or phrases. Thus another of your many stylistic choices in writing is to expand and contract sentences through use of noun clauses and verbal phrases.

A noun clause, another way of indicating relationships between ideas, is a dependent clause that functions as a noun within a larger sentence. The clause contains a subject and a verb and is ordinarily signaled by words such as *that, what, whatever, whoever, why,* and *how.*

1. The mayor hoped *that the local company would manufacutre velvet boxes.* (works as a direct object)
2. He didn't know *that the company was bankrupt.* (works as a direct object)
3. *That the company treasurer stole funds* was obvious to the bank. (works as a subject)
4. The treasurer took *whatever he could get.* (works as a direct object)

EXERCISE 1

Add words in the following sentences to complete the noun clauses. Note the kinds of words in italics that introduce the clauses.

Example

Whoever wrote that letter to the editor was well informed about the housing project.

1. Mr. Tiffany wants *whatever* _____.
2. *Whoever* _____ received a D in the class.
3. The workman rejected *what* _____.
4. The senator suggested *that* _____.
5. The book revealed *that* _____.
6. The secretary asked *why* _____.
7. The mechanic told us *how* _____.
8. *What* _____ puzzled the attorney.
9. The parents gave their children *whatever* _____.
10. The General recommended *that* _____.

In some of these sentences, you may have added a verbal phrase instead of a clause. Sentence 7, for example, could easily by completed with a clause: The mechanic told us *how he had repaired the carburetor* — or with a verbal phrase: The mechanic told us *how to start the car properly.* The clause can be identified because it contains a subject and verb and, without the introductory word, can stand alone as an independent sentence. That is not true of the verbal. Here you have a verb that functions as a noun or modifier in the sentence.

You have already been introduced to one kind of verbal, the participle, which functions as a modifier. In this unit, you meet two other kinds of verbals — the *infinitive* and the *gerund*. The gerund looks just like a present participle, that is, it is a verb with *-ing* as a suffix, but it *functions* as a noun. The infinitive is a verb preceded by "to" and, though it can function as a modifier, it is most useful for you now to consider its *noun function*.

Like the participle, the gerund and the infinitive are powerful writing tools. They not only can be used as nouns, but they also retain many verb functions. For example, they can have objects, subjects, and modifiers, so they often take on aspects of an independent sentence within another sentence. By means of a gerund, part of the sentence:

Professor Renton wrote a biology textbook.

can become the object of the preposition "after":

Professor Renton became famous *after writing a biology textbook.*

the subject of the following sentence:

Writing a textbook enabled Professor Renton to supplement his income.

or the direct object of the following sentence:

Professor Renton knew *writing a biology textbook would be difficult.*

Likewise, by converting the verb "wrote" to its infinitive form, part of the original sentence can become the subject or object of a new sentence:

To write a biology textbook meant that Professor Renton had to give up his vacation.

Professor Renton decided *to write a biology textbook.*

EXERCISE 2

Make the following italicized verbs into gerunds by adding *-ing* after them, and into infinitives by adding "to" in front of them. Then rewrite the sentences using the new verbal phrases.

Example
Mother Teresa *loves* all people.

    loving all people (gerund phrase)

    to love all people (infinitive phrase)

Loving all people makes Mother Teresa strong.

Mother Teresa wants *to love all people.*

1. Mother Teresa *spreads* peace.
2. Mother Teresa *cares* for the poorest of people.
3. She *founded* her own order in Calcutta, India.
4. She *runs* a leprosy center in India.

5. Paramedics *staff* the leprosy center.
6. She *teaches* job skills such as weaving and spinning.
7. She *encourages* usefulness to fellow men and women.
8. Her school *teaches* literacy.
9. In 1939 she *moved* to Calcutta, the British capital of India.
10. In 1948 she *left* the convent for the slums.

A word of caution. English tends to be a noun-heavy language. Sentences can easily accumulate too many nouns and noun-heavy modifiers such as prepositional phrases. You will often find such heavy writing in textbooks, and you will likely find it slow, boring, and difficult to comprehend. Noun clauses, especially if they occur at the beginning of sentences, may have this effect. In contrast, verbals tend to make writing more fluid and clear. Your ear should be able to tell when these structures are effective in individual sentences and paragraphs. Do they sound good? Are the ideas clear?

EXERCISE 3

Read over one of your past writing assignments to see if you can effectively (1) contract two sentences into one by making one into a noun clause or verbal, or (2) expand a sentence by adding a noun clause or verbal. Read these editing efforts aloud to make sure they enhance the focus of each paragraph.

Punctuation: Apostrophes and Quotation Marks

Two punctuation marks that can cause difficulty for a writer are the apostrophe and quotation marks. To prevent any confusion about their use, study the following rules very carefully.

APOSTROPHES

Apostrophes have three primary roles: to indicate missing letters, to indicate possession, and to form certain plurals.

Rule 1   *Use apostrophes in verbal contractions to indicate missing letters.*

do not — don't
I had — I'd
cannot — can't
he will — he'll
would not — wouldn't
is not — isn't

Rule 2   *Use apostrophes to show possession.*
If you have difficulty deciding whether or not to indicate possession, rewrite your sentence using an "of" phrase. For example, *the boy's*

book can be rephrased *the book of the boy; my mother's home* can be rewritten *the home of my mother;* and *her brothers' room* can be rewritten *the room of her brothers.*

a. *Form the possessive of singular nouns by adding apostrophes and the letter "s" — 's.*

>   John's coat
>   Chicago's downtown
>   the cat's claws

b. *Form the possessive of plural nouns that do not end in "s" by adding apostrophes and the letter "s" — 's.*

>   children's
>   women's
>   mice's

c. *Form the possessive of plural nouns ending in "s" by adding apostrophes.*

>   my two brothers' room
>   the horses' stable
>   the boys' school

d. *Do not add apostrophes to the following pronouns:* mine, yours, your, my, his, hers, their, theirs. *These words are already possessive.*

Rule 3 *Form the plural of letters, numbers, symbols, and words being discussed by adding apostrophes and the letter "s" — 's.*

>   F's — He received F's in all his classes.
>   1980's — The government hopes for economic improvements in the 1980's.
>   but's, if's — Don't give me any more of your if's and but's.
>   4's — The dress buyer at Macy's Department Store ordered too many size 4's.

QUOTATION MARKS

Quotation marks are used in the following ways: to enclose dialogue or the exact words of a speaker; to enclose quotations; to indicate copyrighted titles; and to set off words or phrases.

Rule 1 *Use quotation marks to enclose dialogue or the exact words of a speaker.*

My boyfriend told me, "I can't afford to pay for prom tickets."

"Please," she said, "I need you. I can't face the future alone."

   a. *Do not use quotation marks to enclose indirect quotations.* An indirect quotation does not use the exact words of a speaker; it is a paraphrase of the conversation.

My brother told me that he didn't want to go with him.

My teacher told us not to do the exercises on page 3.

Rule 2   *Use quotation marks to enclose quotations.*

In his article on advertisements promoting civil engineering, Samuel C. Florman stated: "The present rebellion against materialism and bigness, however understandable its origins, shrivels the human spirit."

   a. *If a quotation appears within material you are about to quote, use single quotation marks for the interior quotation.*

"In the pages of a recent issue of *Business Week* there appeared a most peculiar advertisement. On the left-hand page was a large picture of an ambulance with lights ablaze, and above it the caption 'We civil engineers believe a carload of cantaloupes shouldn't come between an ambulance and its hospital.' "

Rule 3   *Use quotation marks to indicate copyrighted titles of material contained within books or magazines, of acts and scenes of plays or television programs, and of newspaper headlines.*

"Yankees Lose the Pennant" — headline

"Pomp and Civil Engineering" — an article in this book

"Another Murder" — the second act of a television play

Rule 4   *Use quotation marks to set off words and phrases.*

   a. *To set off words under discussion.*

He defined the word "pomposity" in reference to people who use only many-syllable words.

According to the *OED*, "artificial" has changed meaning since the Renaissance.

   b. *To set off words for emphasis.* (Be cautious when using quotation marks in this way; emphasis can also be achieved through careful word choice and sentence structure.)

How can you call such poor economic conditions "a slow-down"?

My husband gave me a "can-opener" for my birthday!

Rule 5 *Do not use quotation marks for slang terms. If you are embarrassed to use such words, avoid them. If you believe a slang expression is a good choice, simply use it without quotation marks.*

The kids in my class resented the new attendance rules.

Her behavior turned me off.

Rule 6 *Place commas and periods within quotation marks; place colons and semicolons outside of quotation marks.*

When I think of Martin Luther King, I think of his statement, "I have a dream."

President Kennedy said, "Ask what you can do for your country"; I did, but I didn't like the answer.

EXERCISE 1

Correct any errors of apostrophe and quotation mark usage in the following sentences.

1. My history textbook has a chapter entitled After the Civil War.
2. Mary said that "she couldn't afford to buy a new car."
3. Although my doctor wasn't available last night, I could get medical attention at the hospitals' emergency room.
4. My teacher said, "Either hand in your late assignment's or be prepared for Fs on them."
5. The Milwaukee Journals banner headline said Earthquakes Rock Turkey.
6. Do you know the meaning of plagiarism?
7. The "guys" at work think I'll get the promotion.
8. My political science textbook states: "President Truman had a sign on his desk which said "The Buck Stops Here."
9. The advertisement in the magazine claimed that "childrens' rooms often harbor germs."
10. Josh sold me his book's on stamp collecting because they're too elementary for him.

EXERCISE 2

Write complete sentences that use the following words as possessives.

Example
England   England's flag is red, white, and blue.

1. countries
2. men

356   UNIT 8   EXPOSITION: OPINION

3. Mr. Chan
4. sheep
5. New Jersey
6. essays
7. babies
8. newspapers
9. Louise
10. mothers

EXERCISE 3

Make verbal contractions out of the following.

1. is not
2. cannot
3. he would
4. I will
5. they are
6. are not
7. have not
8. she would
9. it is
10. you are

EXERCISE 4

Review your sample essay exam for possible errors with periods, semicolons, commas, apostrophes, and quotation marks. Make any necessary corrections.

Preparing the Final Copy and Proofreading

Proofreading your test essay, like revising it, will be done under psychological stress and time pressure. In a test situation you can only expect to find the most glaring errors, those that will make the worst impression on your reader (your teacher). The following questions will help you anticipate the kinds of errors to seek out as you proofread.

1. Are there enough appropriate transition words or phrases to clarify the flow of the discussion? Have you shown clearly where you shift from comparing to contrasting? Where you give examples? Where you move on to a new point? Where you add a point? Review "Word Choice: Transitions" in Unit 6 in the Editing section.

2. Is the spelling as accurate as possible?
3. Are any reference pronouns vague or ambiguous, causing sentence meanings to be unclear? Reference pronouns should refer clearly to the noun or pronoun immediately preceding them. Avoid vague "this" or "that," referring to a whole phrase or clause. Are the sentences correctly punctuated?
4. Are any apostrophes (for possession) omitted? Read aloud to detect comma splices or fragments.
5. Are there any subject/verb agreement errors?
6. Are there any awkward tense shifts that might confuse or annoy your reader?

UNIT 9
Exposition: Analysis and Evaluation

READING:
Exposition: Analysis and Evaluation

Reading Strategies: Analysis and Evaluation

One of the biggest academic challenges you face in college is the reading assignment that seems so complicated and difficult to understand that your first impulse is to say, "I *hate* this!" If you take the next big step and admit you probably hate the assignment because you don't understand it, you have made a positive move in the learning process, because the next logical step toward learning is to ask, "What should I look for to make all this clear to me?" The answer to that question is, "Ask questions." When you read to analyze or separate material into its component parts, you ask questions of it to gain insights into both content and form. The questions are divided into four categories, some of which will overlap in certain readings. Not every category or question, however, may be relevant for every reading assignment.

Speaker/Writer

What is the tone or attitude of the writer toward the subject matter? (See Unit 8, Word Choice.) Toward the audience? Does the writer's attitude change? If so, where? Why?

Write down adjectives to describe tone or attitude, such as *formal, informal, calm, angry, playful, emotional, reasonable, gentle, ironic, sincere, arrogant.* In other words, describe the general qualities of the "voice" speaking.

EXERCISE 1

In the essay assigned for this unit, underline key words or phrases that reveal the speaker's tone; look for connotative language. Then evaluate the author's tone. How effective is it? How well does it contribute to the communication of ideas here?

Audience/Reader
1. Who makes up the author's "intended audience"? *Intended audience* suggests that the essay may not have been originally intended for "us," a college audience. For example, articles in medical journals are not usually intended for the general public, and an eighteenth-century essay was not intended for a twentieth-century college audience.
2. How does the intended audience influence the tone, language level, and use of connotative language? If the intended audience is not clear, try examining the word choices for tone and levels of formality to find an implied audience. How does the language usage *reveal* the kind of audience the author is trying to reach?
3. Is the writer trying to change the audience's beliefs or make it take some kind of action? If so, the writing is persuasive. Determine the belief or action (see Appendix A).
4. Is the writer relating a sequence of events? If so, the essay is narrative.
5. Is the writer describing one or more things? If so, the writing is descriptive.
6. Is the author defining or giving information to the audience? If so, the writing is explanatory or informative.

Note: Essays (and, of course, books) may be combinations of persuasion, narration, description, and/or explanation.

EXERCISE 1

In the essay assigned for this unit, apply the above audience criteria. Decide whether the essay includes narration, description, explanation, or persuasion. If it includes persuasion, what beliefs does the author want changed or what action taken? Then *evaluate* the importance of the audience for this essay (see Appendix A).

1. Decide why you think the author has either judged the audience well or else has made some faulty assumptions. That is, does the author offend the audience? How? Does he or she choose appropriate or inappropriate language? How can you tell?
2. Determine the value of your audience analysis; what did it reveal about communication?

Argument/Discussion
1. What is the author's purpose in writing the essay or book? The purpose may be implied rather than stated openly.

This question refers to the author's thesis statement; it is extremely important to find the main idea. Look for it near the beginning of the essay, perhaps after an introduction, or look at the ending. Check the title for a clue.

EXERCISE 1

In the essay assigned for this unit, underline the thesis statement or write in your own words a one-sentence summary of the thesis.

2. What are the main assertions used to support or develop the thesis?

The main assertions, but not all of them (the next question will clarify this point) will be found in the topic sentences or controlling ideas of certain paragraphs.

3. How are the main assertions supported?

This question refers to either of the following aspects of the selection.

THE TYPE OF EVIDENCE USED
1. Documented facts or figures from an outside source.
2. Opinions of authorities on a subject.
3. Historical events or evidence.
4. Examples or illustrations.
5. Details.
6. Analogy (comparing two unlike things to prove a point or to clarify a complicated topic).

THE KIND OF PARAGRAPH PATTERN USED
1. Narration.
2. Description.
3. Comparison and contrast.
4. Definition.
5. Cause and effect.
6. Explanation.
7. Question and answer.
8. Problem and solution.
9. Persuasion.
10. Analysis.

Don't be dismayed to find that categories overlap. Establishing categories is the simplest way to clarify the analysis, but the method is not meant to be rigid.

EXERCISE 2

In the essay assigned for this unit, underline all the main assertions, then choose three of them and determine how they are supported.

4. Is the argument an appeal to reason or emotion or to both? If both, is there a pattern such as a rise and fall to the emotional appeal? (See Appendix A.)

Look closely for connotative language revealing emotional undertones. Although this is an analytical question, it leads to an evaluation of whether the author uses appropriate appeals and whether the subject matter and audience consideration calls for a basically reasoned approach, an emotional approach, or a combination of the two. How effective is the author's approach?

5. What is the basic premise of the essay, the underlying foundation on which the argument is built? Is it stated explicitly, or is it an implicit assumption? Is there more than one premise?

Finding the answer to this question is important because it ties things together and leads directly to an overall evaluation of the essay and to a perception of relationships among the premises, thesis, and main assertions. Are the assertions arranged in a progression? Are any assertions unnecessary or unrelated to the premises or thesis?

Style and Language

1. How much connotative language is used? Evaluate how connotative language contributes to the emotional appeal. Decide whether a close examination of connotative language reveals the author's attitudes in a way not readily apparent when skimming.
2. What kinds of images, similes and metaphors are used? How extensively are they used? Evaluate the effect of this usage.
3. What sentence patterns or structures are characteristic of this author? Look for use of verbals, coordination, subordination, and modification patterns. Is there a great deal of variety?
4. Where does the writer vary sentence length? Evaluate whether this variation is for emphasis or emotional impact.
5. What references, allusions, and repetitions are used? Evaluate whether they add to or detract from the overall effect of the writing.

EXERCISE 1

In the essay assigned for this unit, locate, with the help of your teacher, any historical references or any allusions to famous literature. Evaluate how much they add to the writing; would the essay have been as effective without them?

Cloze Exercise: Focus on Prepositional Phrases

Another type of word that has a distinct function in a sentence is the *preposition*. Prepositions combine with nouns, pronouns, or groups of words to form *prepositional phrases*, groups of words that act as adjectival or adverbial modifiers in sentences. Become familiar with the prepositions in Table 9-1 and then review the manner in which these prepositions combine with other words to form phrases. Once you can identify prepositional phrases quickly, you will be better able to anticipate meaning from context and to fixate your eyes on large units of meaning — the prepositional phrases and the words they modify.

Table 9-1 Prepositions

about	besides	on
above	between	onto
across	beyond	out
after	by	outside
against	despite	over
along	down	since
among	during	through
around	except	throughout
as	for	to
at	from	toward, towards
atop	in	underneath
because of	inside	until
before	into	up
behind	like	upon
below	near	with
beneath	of	within
beside	off	without

Examples

PREPOSITIONAL PHRASES

off the boat, without food, during the examination, towards him, like a clown

Notice how prepositional phrases serve as modifiers in the following sentences.

1. The cowboy *on the black-and-white pinto* won first prize.

(Here the prepositional phrase acts as an adjective modifying *cowboy*, a noun.)

2. The car crashed *into the fence.*

(Here the prepositional phrase serves as an adverb modifying *crashed*, a verb.)

3. Arriving *after dinner,* I missed a gourmet feast.

(Here the prepositional phrase acts as an adverb modifying *arriving*, an adjective.)

4. Ice cream *without hot fudge* is *like Thanksgiving without turkey.*

(Here all three prepositional phrases act as adjectives; *without hot fudge* and *like Thanksgiving* modify *ice cream*, a noun; and *without turkey* modifies *Thanksgiving*, a noun.)

Notice also that these prepositional phrases generally stand next to the words they modify and enable you to fixate on large units of meaning.

The car / crashed into the fence.

The cowboy on the black-and-white pinto / won first prize.

In the following Cloze exercise, nouns, pronouns, adjectives, adverbs, conjunctions, and prepositions may have been deleted. Fill in the spaces with appropriate words, trying to anticipate words from context and to fixate on large units of meaning. Time yourself. If you need more than ten minutes to complete this exercise, you should review the discussions preceding the Cloze exercises in Units 1 through 6.

EXERCISE 1

This view of prizes as a reflection of hardihood and a reward for risk stems straight from the 19th century; the rodeo, for all its new trappings, has remained unchanged in attitude, essence, and, largely, in procedure since it took shape at Pecos, Prescott and Miles City. But its time-honoured _____ and a good deal _____ its individualism face alteration _____ a syndicate or entrepreneurs _____ have borrowed concepts from _____ stratified professional sports like _____ and baseball. In 1978 _____ launched "major league" rodeo _____ six teams (of 15 _____ and 3 women), a _____ draft, a league commissioner, _____ the prospect of future _____ in cities from coast _____ coast. The first six _____ were organized into an _____ Conference (Denver, Los Angeles, _____ Salt Lake City). The _____, from April 15 to September 15, _____ in a World Championship _____ which the Denver Stars defeated the Tulsa Twisters.

— Adapted from O'Neil, *"Modernized Ritual of Rodeo"*

Words and the Language: Technical Words

As we noted briefly in the Words and the Language section in Unit 8, specialized dictionaries may be needed for technical words not found in ordinary desk dictionaries. Because these technical words express theories, laws, concepts, and terms of particular subject fields such as chemistry, physics, biology, literature, history, and social sciences, they are often not included in standard dictionaries.

As a college student, you must familiarize yourself with the technical vocabulary used in your textbooks and by your professors. In some courses, most of the ideas expressed require a working knowledge of words used only in that particular field. So to be successful in these classes, you must develop some method of listing and studying these words in order to master them. One method is simply to underline your textbooks and define words in the margins; another method is to keep a separate vocabulary section in your notebooks; and a third method is to make study sheets or note cards. Whichever method used, you need to compile a fairly complete list to consult for periodic study and examination review.

What are some approaches to finding technical word definitions? The following guidelines can help you organize your search.

1. Read your textbooks carefully to see whether the authors have defined technical words when they first introduce them.
2. Sometimes textbook writers assume you already know certain terms and therefore do not define them. If you have a more elementary textbook on the subject, check that book's index for word locations and definitions within the text.
3. Check the back of your textbooks; you will often find a *glossary*, a brief dictionary of key terms used in the book.
4. If you cannot find the specialized meaning of a word in a standard desk dictionary, consult an unabridged dictionary in the library.
5. In none of the above approaches provides sufficient information, consult a specialized dictionary. You can find this kind of dictionary listed in the library card catalogue under the subject, for example, geology, psychology, economics, or chemistry. Scan the cards for "Dictionary." Or you can reverse the process, looking under "Dictionary" for the subject. You can also ask the reference librarian to direct you to the appropriate section in the reference room.
6. For studying science, memorize some commonly used Latin and Greek prefixes, suffixes, and roots to give you clues to meanings of words otherwise hard to understand or remember. Such a list appears in Appendix D.

As we pointed out in Unit 8 in the Reading Strategies section, study sheets and cards are especially helpful when reviewing for exams. But to be even more efficient in your study habits, prepare your vocabulary study aids ahead of time, before you confront new terminology. The following exercises suggest specific ways to organize specialized vocabulary.

EXERCISE 1

Make a specialized vocabulary sheet for each course that uses technical terms or specialized words.

1. Write each word or term in a phrase or sentence so that you will remember the appropriate context.
2. For each word or term, include a memory device — a related foreign or English word, an example, or a diagram.

Set up your vocabulary sheet as shown in Figure 9-1.

EXERCISE 2

As an alternative to study sheets, make study cards for each course using specialized vocabulary, as shown in Figure 9-2.

Figure 9-1 Vocabulary sheet for specialized words

Word/Term	Phrase/Sentence	Meaning	Memory Device
omnivore	Omnivores eat everything.	eats both meat and vegetable food	Omnivores are both carnivores and herbivores. God is omnipotent, all-powerful.

Figure 9-2 Study cards using specialized vocabulary

Side 1

Loss Leader

Marketing 101

Side 2

A retail product advertised and sold at a low price, so that customers come into a store and buy other products as well as the loss leader.

Example: A food market advertises coffee at a low price. Customers come in for the coffee but also buy other products sold at regular prices.

1. On one side of a 3 x 5" card, write the term or phrase and the course title.
2. On the other side of the card, write the definition and either an example, a sentence using the word/phrase, or a diagram.

EXERCISE 3

Use the list of Latin and Greek prefixes, suffixes, and roots in Appendix D to answer the following questions.

1. Would an *intramural* game be played between opposing schools or between opposing teams within the same school?
2. How old is an *octogenarian?*
3. Does *homeopathy* or *allopathy* recommend that the disease be treated with the same medicine that in large doses might cause it?
4. Would *hypobole* or *hyperbole* mean exaggeration?
5. If a high school places its students in classes *heterogeneously* rather than *homogeneously*, does it set up classes with students of similar abilities?
6. *Lithography* is a printing term. Can you guess what it means?
7. What does a *hydropathist* do?

READINGS: SELECTION ONE
Why Man Explores   (2)
by Norman Cousins

Ideas to Think About
1. Have you ever been so curious about something that you went out to investigate it? Perhaps you drove around an unfamiliar neighborhood, or hiked through a new area. Why did you take time for these activities?
2. In the introductory paragraph, Cousins poses the question, "Why explore?" He then tells us what first must be explored before answering this question: the nature of the human mind. Notice his response to his question in each paragraph.
3. Paragraph 5 relates a personal experience. Consider how it fits the discussion of the nature of the human mind and reasons we explore.

Vocabulary

Look at each word as it is used in the article. (The number in parentheses indicates the paragraph in which it appears.) First, try to understand the meaning from the way it is used in the sentence. Second, use any clues to meaning through the structure of the word. Then, use the dictionary to clarify the meaning.

phenomenon (1)
conceive/inconceivable (1)
comprehend/incomprehensible (1)
emancipate (2)
prospect (2)

accumulation (3)
infinity (5)
unencumbered (6)
proximity (6)
incontestable (6)

Why Man Explores   (2)

Former editor of *Saturday Review* magazine, Norman Cousins is currently Senior Lecturer in the Medical Humanities at the University of California's School of Medicine, in Los Angeles. In this essay, Cousins suggests that by extending the frontiers of space, man discovers his own human potential.

The question "Why explore?" pertains to the nature of the human mind. The phenomenon° of a journey to the planets is the phenomenon of intelligence. The fact that we can conceive° of the inconceivable° and comprehend° the incomprehensible° is perhaps the highest exercise of the human brain, symbolized so dramatically by the exploration of space.

Our question, therefore, involves not just science but philosophy. The answer has to come out of our view of life, out of our concept of history, out of our understanding of human progress, and mostly out of instinctive awareness that we can always do better than we are doing if we emancipate° ourselves from our fears in order to search the horizon for new prospects.° So, naturally, we look to our traditions and our philosophy as we expand the human presence in the universe.

Some historians see history as an accumulation° of error. But history is also the story of the defiance of the unknown and of what happens when man tries to extend his reach. Not all problems are old problems; therefore, new approaches and new truths have to be discovered. In order to answer the question "Why explore?," it becomes necessary to refer to the phenomenon of human progress. I have a theory that progress is what is left over after one meets an impossible problem.

The reason it is safer to travel in a Boeing 747 than to sit in your bathtub is that adequate thought has been given to all the things that can go wrong when you are in a 747, but not enough thought to what can go wrong in a bathtub. What I am trying to suggest is that the more difficult and complex the undertaking, the more likely it is that knowledge will be gained that can be applied more fruitfully far beyond the undertaking itself.

Several years ago I was in war-torn Biafra with some other people. We were in a jeep. A plane loomed behind us out of the sun and dived down on the jeep in a strafing run. We plunged into a ditch, face down in the mud. I could contemplate that even as we were pressing our faces into the muddy earth in safety from our brothers, men found it possible to walk erect on the moon. That evening the war suddenly came to a halt, at least for a few hours. The word had spread through Biafra that human beings were setting foot on the moon for the first time. Suddenly everyone had a new perspective. It didn't last long enough to cause the war to end altogether, but for a few moments at least we could contemplate the possibilities of human grandeur and meditate on our station in infinity.° In that sense the most significant achievement of that first lunar voyage was not that man set foot on the moon but that he set his eye on the earth. He was able for the first time to develop a true perspective of that beautiful, wet, blue ball, as Archibald MacLeish has described it, which possessed the millions of conditions that existed in the precise and exquisite combination to make life possible.

The effect is philosophical. To be able to rise from the earth; to be able, from a station in outer space, to see the relationship of the planet Earth to other planets; to be able to contemplate the gift of life unencumbered° by proximity,° to be able to meditate on journeying through an infinity of galaxies; to be able to dwell on the encounter of the human brain and spirit with the universe — all this enlarges the human horizon. It also offers incontestable° proof that technology is subordinate to human imagination. We are going into space not because of our technology but because our imagination requires it.

So long as human beings do not persuade themselves that they are creatures of failure, so long as they have a vision of life as it ought to be, so long as they can comprehend the full meaning and power of the unfettered mind, so long as they can do all these things, they can look at the world and, beyond that, the universe with the sense that they can be unafraid of their fellows and can face choices not with dread but with great expectations.

Discussion

1. What in your own experience would make you agree that technology is subordinate to human imagination? What, if anything, in your experience would make you disagree?
2. What does Cousins mean when he says, " . . . progress is what is left over after one meets an impossible problem"? How does this definition fit his theory that we are going into space because our imagination requires it?
3. What is the thesis of the essay? How effective are Cousins's supports?
4. How does the brief narrative about Cousins's experience in Biafra serve his thesis?
5. Notice the repetition of "so long" as in paragraph 7, a one-sentence paragraph. Decide if you like its effect as a conclusion and whether or not you think it necessary to the thesis of the essay.

READINGS: SELECTION TWO
Beware the Intellectual
by Eric Hoffer

Ideas to Think About
1. What is an intellectual? Have you ever met one? Do you consider yourself an intellectual?
2. Would you prefer living in the nineteenth or the twentieth century? How are these centuries similar? How are they different?
3. Note the many uses of definition in this essay. Look for the definition of words like "intellectual" and "compassion" — words we use all the time but have difficulty defining precisely.

Vocabulary
Look at each word as it is used in the article. (The number in parentheses indicates the paragraph in which it appears.) First, try to understand the meaning from the way it is used in the sentence. Second, use any clues to meaning through the structure of the word. Then, use the dictionary to clarify the meaning.

a priori (2)
certitudes (6)
absurdities (7)
apocalyptic (10)
irrationality (10)
hordes (11)

clamor (12)
propensities (13)
protagonists (14)
perpetrated (15)
deviation (19)

Beware the Intellectual

A self-educated author of numerous books on social philosophy, Eric Hoffer is a former migratory worker, gold miner, and longshoreman.

From the early days of the Industrial Revolution, intellectuals of every sort predicted that the machine would make man superfluous.[1] Right now, it would be difficult to find a social scientist who does not believe that automated machines and computers are eliminating man as a factor in the social equation.

The belief that the machine turns men into robots is an a priori° assumption that prevents social scientists from seeing that technology is doing precisely the opposite of what they predicted it would do. There is evidence on every hand that the human factor has never been so central

---
[1] More than sufficient, excessive.

as it is now in technologically advanced countries. And it is the centrality of the human factor that makes industrial societies at present so unpredictable.

In the 19th century, which saw a Promethean[2] effort to master and harness nature, little thought was given to the management of man. The ruling middle class could proceed on the principle that government is best when it governs least. Everyday life had a fabulous regularity. Obedience of authority was as automatic as a reflex movement. Social processes were almost as rational and predictable as the processes of nature. It was reasonable to believe in the possibility of a social science as exact as a natural science.

There was also boundless hope, a belief in automatic progress that imbued people with patience.

Then came the 20th century! Have there ever been two successive centuries so different from each other as the 19th and the 20th?

The 19th century was stable, predictable, rational, hopeful, free, fairly peaceful and lumpy with certitudes.°

The 20th century has been hectic, soaked with the blood of innocents, fearful of the future, stripped of certitudes, unpredictable and absurd. The history of the 20th century is a succession of disastrous absurdities°: the First World War, the Russian Revolution, the Versailles Peace Treaty, Prohibition, the wild '20's, the Great Depression, the Roosevelt Administration, the Hitler Revolution, the Second World War, the Holocaust, the absurd 1960's and now the Carter Presidency.

What was it that made the 20th century so different from the 19th? The First World War was the sharp dividing line between the two centuries. But it was not the First World War itself, but its aftermath, that shaped our century. Without the breakdown of Czarist Russia and the humiliation of Germany by the Versailles Treaty, there would have been neither a Lenin nor a Hitler Revolution.

We have the testimony of highly reliable observers on the fabulous stability and hopefulness of the pre-war decade. To Alfred North Whitehead, who was immersed in the new physics, "the period 1880 to 1914 was one of the happiest times in the history of mankind."

It is impressive how logic and hope kept 19th century thinkers from contemplating an unpleasant, let alone apocalyptic,° denouement as the fulfillment of the Industrial Revolution. Few in the 19th century were aware of the explosive irrationality° of the human condition. No one suspected that once nature had been mastered, industrial societies would enter a psychological age in which man would become a threat to mankind's survival.

No one foresaw the disintegration of values and the weakening of

---

[2] Superhuman.

social discipline caused by the elimination of scarcity. A logician like Marx could not foresee the downfall of capitalism by ever-increasing efficiency rather than by ever-increasing misery. Hardly anyone in the 19th century foresaw the chronic unemployment and the loss of a sense of usefulness caused by increased ambition. No one feared that drastic change would upset traditions, customs and other arrangements that make life predictable. Finally, no one foresaw that the education explosion made possible by advanced technology would swamp societies with hordes° of educated nobodies who want to be somebodies and end up being mischief-making busybodies.

Strangely, those whom thinkers of the 19th century viewed with alarm were the masses. Some thought that the masses loathed continuity and that their clamor° for change would topple all that was noble and precious. Others believed that, once the masses were given political power, only education and prosperity could preserve social stability. How naive to believe in a stabilizing power of prosperity and education after we have seen what affluence and education have done!

To Freud it seemed that individuals composing the masses support one another in giving free reign to their indiscipline. No one had an inkling that anarchy, when it came, would originate not in the masses but in violent minorities, including the minority of the educated. Everything that was said about the anarchic³ propensities° of the masses fits perfectly with the behavior of students, professors, writers, artists and the hangers-on during the righteous '60's.

The masses are the protagonists° of stability, continuity and law and order. It is curious that Disraeli — remarkable man — should have had a truer world view of the nature of the masses than his liberal contemporaries. He sensed the conservatism and patriotism of common people. Could it be that, as a genuine conservative, Disraeli was more attuned to the eternal verities of man's existence? Considering also how timely and relevant were Disraeli's ideas about what makes nations strong and great, it is legitimate to wonder whether you have to be a conservative if you want to be up to date.

The 20th century saw not only the fulfillment of the Industrial Revolution but also the fulfillment of wars planted in the preceding century. There is hardly an atrocity perpetrated° in the 20th century that had not been advocated by some intellectual in the 19th.

The 19th century was dominated by men of action; the intellectuals just talked. And no one expected savage words to have consequence. The intellectuals entered the 19th century convinced that it was going to be their century. Had they not made the French Revolution? They saw them-

---

³ Without government or law.

selves as the coming ruling class. But the Industrial Revolution gave power to the middle class, and the intellectuals were left out in the cold.

It is the predicament of the middle class that, although it excels in mastering things, it is awkward and almost helpless when it comes to managing men. Thus, when the human factor became more and more central, the middle class, drained of confidence by the First World War and a great Depression, found itself in deep trouble.

The stage was set for the entrance of the intellectuals. To an intellectual, power means power over man. He cannot conceive of power moving mountains and telling rivers where to flow. He is in his element commanding, brainwashing and in general making people love what they hate. He glories in the role of medicine man and charismatic leader. And feels godlike when he makes words become flesh. Thus, he has made the 20th century a century of words par excellence. In no other century have words become so dangerous. A failure to recognize this fact can have disastrous consequences.

Now, viewed from any vantage point, the 19th century was a sharp historical deviation.° About 150 years ago, the Occident was catapulted into a trajectory away from the ancient highway of history. We can now see that the trajectory is the loop that turns upon itself and is curving back to where it started. We can see all around us the lineaments of a pre-industrial pattern emerging in post-industrial society. We are not plunging ahead into the future, but falling back into the past. The explosion of the young, the dominance of the intellectuals, the savagery of our cities, the revulsion from work are all characteristics of the decades that preceded the Industrial Revolution. We are returning to the rocky highway of history and are rejoining the ancient caravans.

The significant point is that the people who are rejoining the ancient caravan are not what they were in pre-industrial days. They are more dangerous. The unspeakable atrocities of the 20th century have demonstrated that man is the originator of a great evil that threatens the survival of mankind. The central problem of the post-industrial age is how to cope with this human evil.

It is conceivable that if the exhaustion of raw materials and sources of energy make it imperative for a society to tap the creative energies of its people, it may in doing so also tap a new source of social discipline, for the creative individual, no matter how highly educated, must be hardworking and disciplined if he's to accomplish much.

There is no invention that will take the hard work out of creating. Moreover, since the creative flow is never abundant, the greatest society is likely to be disciplined by a new chronic scarcity. The trouble is that the coming of the creative society will be slow and faltering, and we must find other defenses against evil.

What I'm going to advocate may seem far-fetched. But in this case, all suggestions are legitimate. As things are now, it may well be that the survival of the species will depend upon the capacity to foster a boundless capacity for compassion. In the alchemy of man's soul, almost all noble attributes — courage, love, hope, faith, beauty, loyalty — can be transmuted into ruthlessness. Compassion alone stands apart from the continuous traffic between good and evil proceeding within us. Compassion is the antitoxin of the soul. Where there is compassion, even the poisonous impulses remain relatively harmless. 23

Compassion seems to have its roots in the family. It is conceivable that the present weakening of the family may allow compassion to leak out into wider circles. So, too, the cultivation of esprit de corps, which is the creation of family ties between strangers, may spread compassion. 24

The question is: can we make people compassionate by education? It is natural to assume that the well-educated are more humane and compassionate than the uneducated. But, believe it or not, the reverse seems to be true. When Gandhi was asked what it was that worried him most, he replied, "The hardness of heart of the educated." 25

We have seen the highly educated German nation give its allegiance to the most murderously vengeful government in history. The bloody-minded professors in the Kremlin, as Churchill called them, liquidated 60 million Russian men, women and children. We have also seen a band of graduates of the Sorbonne, no less, slaughter and starve millions of innocents in Cambodia and Vietnam. The murder weapons that may destroy our society are being forged in the work factories of our foremost universities. In many countries, universities have become the chief recruiting ground of mindless terrorists. 26

I've never been a teacher or a parent, and my heart is savage by nature and therefore unfit to tell people how to implant compassion. We feel close to each other when we see our planet as a tiny island of life in an immensity of nothingness. We also draw together when we become aware that night must close in on all living things, that we are condemned to death at birth and that life is a bus ride to the place of execution. All of our struggling and vying is about seats in the bus, and the ride is over before we know it. 27

Discussion

1. Hoffer's essay offers a series of definitions. It explores such notions as "the masses," "power," "intellectuals," and "compassion." Explain Hoffer's definition of any one of these concepts. Do you agree with his definition? Is it indicative of the world you live in? Write your own definition of the word you have chosen.
2. Hoffer defines power as "making people love what they hate." Explain his

definition. Have you ever tried to make someone love something you knew they hated? Did you succeed? Is it possible to succeed? Explain.
3. Notice the choice of words throughout the essay. Does the essay seem formal or informal? Was this article written for "the masses"? For whom was it written?
4. Hoffer contends that compassion is the only antidote for the spread of evil in the world. How can compassion counteract evil? Are you a compassionate person? How do you know when you are being compassionate?

378   UNIT 9   EXPOSITION: ANALYSIS AND EVALUATION

READINGS: SELECTION THREE

The Fallacy of the Energy-Civilization Equation
by George Basalla

Ideas to Think About

1. Do you believe that our twentieth-century technological use of energy has made us more "civilized"? What does the word "civilized" mean to you?
2. What energy-using conveniences would you be willing to give up? That is, would you go without such things as air conditioning, heating, electric can openers, a toaster, lights, TV, or gasoline?
3. Notice how much of Basalla's essay is devoted to defining and explaining "the existence of an energy-civilization equation" as an ideological concept. Where in the essay does Basalla begin to trace the history of this equation? Where does he change to another kind of discussion?

Vocabulary

Look at each word as it is used in the article. (The number in parentheses indicates the paragraph in which it appears.) First, try to understand the meaning from the way it is used in the sentence. Second, use any clues to meaning through the structure of the word. Then, use the dictionary to clarify the meaning.

apocalyptic (2)
ideological (4)
aesthetic (9)
assimilates (16)
imperative (19)
veneration (20)

mystique (23)
manifestations (25)
precariously (27)
integrity (30)
disparate (30)
correlation (34)

The Fallacy of the Energy-Civilization Equation

George Basalla is associate professor in the history of science and technology at the University of Delaware.

Among the critics of energy conservation are those who claim that as we use less energy we will become less civilized. They believe that the retreat from high energy consumption will lead mankind directly back to the caves that provided his first shelter. The immediate response to this warning is that the first substantial use of petroleum dates not to the Stone Age but to the period of the Civil War. And furthermore, that even a fifty percent reduction in our total consumption of energy would not transport us back to Paleolithic times,[1] nor even to the Dark Ages, but to the 1950's.

Nevertheless, apocalyptic° visions of an American society forced to reduce its energy consumption continue to haunt us. We foresee a doomed civilization, with tractors paralyzed in the fields, abandoned automobiles rusting on weed-choked freeways, factories as quiet as tombs and our haggard descendants facing a life of everlasting drudgery. These are strange visions for a nation that uses a 5,000-pound automobile to drive a mile in order to buy a half-dozen cans of beer that will be drunk in an overcooled room and the empties thrown on the trash heap instead of being delivered to an aluminum recycling center.

How did it come about that a people who use and waste vast amounts of energy believe that the alternative to high energy consumption is the primitive life endured by early man? And, even if the choice is not between the Stone Age and life in the twentieth century, what is the relationship between energy use and level of civilization?

The current approach to the energy problem ignores the fact that for almost two centuries energy consumption in the West has had an ideological° component. High energy consumption has not only been associated with physical comfort, economic well-being and military strength, it has also been identified with the idea of civilization itself.

The tendency of the Western nations to equate energy use with level of civilization was accurately and satirically described by British author Aldous Huxley. Said Huxley, because we use a hundred and ten times as much coal as our ancestors, we naively think that we are a hundred and ten times better intellectually, morally and spiritually.

When energy consumption thus serves as a measure of the height of civilization reached by a nation, then changes in energy use will have wide implications. As less energy is available per capita, the nation is thought to lose its standing among the world's civilizations.

Those countries with high rates of energy consumption are ideologically committed to maintaining them, and those with lower rates are motivated to copy their energy-hungry, civilized superiors. This ideological commitment helps to explain why so many of the less industrialized nations felt it necessary to have their own nuclear reactors. It was not necessity that drove them to acquire them but the feeling that they might be left behind in this latest event in the energy-civilization race.

To simplify consideration of these matters, I will assume the existence of an energy-civilization equation. Although no one has ever formally written out such an equation, it has pervaded western thought for the past two centuries. It can be found in the physical, life and social sciences, and in technology, philosophy and popular culture.

---

[1] Stone Age.

9   The left side of that equation contains energy, a well-defined physical concept. On the opposite side appears civilization, which is a subjective evaluation of the intellectual, moral and aesthetic° accomplishments of a society. The two sides of the equation are directly related, so that high energy consumption results in high civilization and low energy consumption in a low level of civilization.

10   The energy-civilization equation originated in the early nineteenth century. Prior to that time, the introduction of new energy sources was not linked to the advancement of culture. Take the example of the Middle Ages, which witnessed a great power revolution. Although the waterwheel, windmill and effective harnesses for draft animals transformed social and economic life, no medieval thinker was ever moved to claim that they were the ultimate sources of the cultural and spiritual achievements of the time.

11   The rose window of Chartres, the philosophy of St. Thomas Aquinas, or any other of the accomplishments of the age were never related to the energy that had recently been put to new and practical uses. And conversely, medieval man never feared that dry streams, windless days and bad harnesses would mark the end of civilization. Yet, by the 1800's, the energy-civilization equation found easy acceptance, and claims and warnings of this sort were gaining in popularity.

12   The formulation of the energy-civilization equation was made possible by the Scientific Revolution of the seventeenth century. The emergence of modern science and the subsequent identification of scientific and technical advancement with human progress provided the kind of intellectual environment in which a newly introduced power source would be dealt with differently than it had been in the Middle Ages. The Scientific Revolution created a world view in which energy and civilization could be directly related.

13   In the 17th century, Sir Francis Bacon listed the great inventions that had changed the course of civilization; they were the compass, gunpowder and the printing press. With the rapid growth of science and technology, it was an easy matter to extend Bacon's original list by adding new inventions. By the late 18th century, an obvious addition to that list was the steam engine, which produced large amounts of power and had noticeable social and economic effects. It quickly became the symbol of industrialization and the social, economic and cultural changes that accompanied it.

14   The steam engine appeared to offer strong evidence that energy could be converted into civilization. However, neither the steam engine nor any other mechanical device could provide a proper theoretical basis for the energy-civilization equation. Only the sciences could supply such a foundation, and they did so during the 19th century. First physics and chemistry and then the biological, social and behavioral sciences were called upon to offer theoretical justification for linking energy with civilization.

Among the great successes of nineteenth-century physics were the discovery of the laws of conservation of energy and the establishment of a science of thermodynamics. Early in the century scientists had their first glimpse into the possibility of energy conversion. At that time they were interested in the conversion of heat to light, light to chemical action, chemical action to motion, motion to electricity, electricity to magnetism and so forth.

Some men of science were not satisfied to confine the conversion series to the boundaries of the physics and chemistry laboratory. Is it not possible, they argued, to convert physical forces or energies into biological ones? After all, it occurs naturally every time an animal assimilates° its food. And cannot the series be extended from the biological to the nervous forces that energize the nervous system? And why stop here? Can we not take the next step, the one that connects nervous forces to the mind and to the study of moral and intellectual energy?

If one answered "yes" to these questions, then there existed no theoretical barrier between the physical concept of energy and the moral and intellectual progress that characterized civilization. It was in this way that the energy-civilization equation finally found an apparently respectable place for itself among the sciences.

Once the path had been opened between physical energy and culture, it was possible to imagine energy conversion sequences that began in the firebox of a steam engine, or in the windings of an electric dynamo, and ended in the world of morality, social and intellectual concern and artistic creation. Most scientists preferred to work on the first few links of the sequence, links that were clearly empirical. On the other hand, there were those who saw no problem in speaking of vital mental and social energies and in determining their relationship to the energy of the physical sciences. Some cases in point:

- Wilhelm Ostwald, German chemist, 1919 Nobel prizewinner and creator of Ostwald's energetic imperative°: Do not waste energy! He attempted to develop an energetic basis for all the sciences.
- Henry Adams, American historian and author of the famous essay, "The Virgin and the Dynamo," which evaluated the effects of the two great and different energies upon the course of Western civilization, concluding that the force of electricity was every bit as mysterious and powerful as the religious force produced by medieval Catholicism's veneration° of the Virgin Mary.
- Frederick A. Soddy, British scientist, 1921 Nobel prizewinner and a pioneer in the study of the atom. Soddy believed atomic energy would lift civilization to heights undreamed of, if atomic warfare could be averted and a new economic system established for a more equitable distribution of goods and services.
- Henry Ford and Thomas A. Edison, who followed Soddy's lead in

dealing with energy and economics. Ford proposed using an abandoned Muscle Shoals, Alabama, hydroelectric plant to produce enough cheap power to supply a city 75 miles long and 15 miles wide. Edison proposed financing the scheme through Energy Dollars, imprinted with a depiction of the hydroelectric plant because energy was the true basis of money. Politics intervened to kill the grandiose scheme.

23 And the energeticists marched on. The dream of hydroelectric plants and a new society persisted to the time of Franklin Delano Roosevelt's administration, when they became part of the Tennessee Valley Authority program. The TVA mystique° was to reappear in such unlikely and remote areas of the world as Aswan, Egypt, and the Mekong River delta in Vietnam.

24 It would be foolish to argue that hydroelectrical establishments have no influence on their social and intellectual milieu.[2] However, it is also true that they have not created the revolutionary changes promised by their promoters. We have yet to create a new civilization merely because we harnessed the power of some wild river. There remains a considerable gap between the Utopian societies projected and the economic and ecological liabilities of power dam construction.

25 I have touched upon but a few of the many manifestations° of the energy-civilization formulation. Sigmund Freud linked sexual energy, and its sublimation, to civilization. Some current anthropological and sociological thought links energy and cultural achievements. There is astronomical speculation that ranks the civilizations of yet to be discovered extra-terrestrial beings according to their supposed access to different amounts of energy. The disclosure of new energy sources — coal, petroleum, the atom, the sun — is accompanied by highly exaggerated claims that they would be the basis for a new society and a higher civilization. Finally, a National Science Foundation course describes energy as follows: "Energy is the source and control of all things, all values and all the actions of human beings and nature." That is the sort of description that at one time would have sufficed to define God!

26 Having resolved the historical question of the origins and diffusion of the energy-civilization equation, we are still left wondering about its ultimate validity.

27 In this equation, slight increases or decreases in energy use cause large fluctuations in the level of civilization. If man uses less coal or electricity, then he is surely doomed to wear animal furs, gnaw on bones and pass his time shaping stone tools. On the other hand, if he only adopts solar, fusion or some other new energy source, then the gates of the Garden of Eden will be opened to him. We should be suspicious of a

---

[2] Environment.

formulation that places mankind so precariously° between apocalypse and utopia. And we should be cautious in accepting an equation that does not reflect the fact that the vast increases in energy consumption over the past few decades have not necessarily enhanced our chances of reaching a new stage in civilization.

Perhaps one reason why our rapidly increasing energy consumption has not placed us upon a new plateau of civilization is the way in which we choose to use that excess energy. The crude formula linking civilization with energy has no place for questions of choice. It deals with energy expended per capita and does not ask if the energy was squandered on trivialities, wasted in destructive wars, or utilized to advance the social, moral and cultural accomplishments we identify with civilization.

Another weakness of the equation grows out of the vague way energy is defined within its context. There is no quarrel when the term is limited to the physical domain. But what are we to make of the analogical[3] reasoning that led to the writing of serious essays on moral energy, sexual energy or religious energy?

If the energy-civilization formulation encouraged the loose definition of energy, what did it do for the definition of civilization? Immediately we are faced with an entirely different situation. Energy has its roots in the physical sciences, so that no matter how it is misapplied the original concept maintains its integrity.° Civilization, on the contrary, never has had the kind of precise determination we associate with an accepted scientific concept. Civilization has always been a value-laden word that has changed over time and has been redefined again and again in order to meet current political, social or cultural needs or desires. It is an ill-fated formula that would attempt to link closely two such disparate° entities as energy and civilization.

Yet, even if we attempt to make the equation workable by focusing upon one nation at a given time and assuming that its people will agree on what is meant by civilization, we find grave difficulties. When the English economist and philosopher Stanley Jevons was predicting the imminent[4] decline of British civilization in the 1860's he supposed that coal, iron and railroads had raised England to the pinnacle of culture. Not so, responded the contemporary literary critic Matthew Arnold. Let us suppose, said Arnold, that two hundred years from now England was to be swallowed up by the sea. Then when the rest of the world recalled England's greatness, they would undoubtedly remember the Age of Shakespeare as her golden hour and not the time of Alfred, Lord Tennyson and Queen Victoria. The Elizabethans managed quite well without the steam engine to produce a culture that is admired throughout the world.

Should a twentieth-century opponent choose to enter into the debate

---
[3] Dealing with partial comparisons.
[4] Close at hand.

with Matthew Arnold over this matter, he would probably draw upon statistics proving modern superiority in life expectancy, literacy, nutrition, public hygiene, speed of transportation, equality of opportunity and so on. In short, he would shift the argument to the arenas of quality of life and economic growth. Matthew Arnold would reply to his modern critic as he did to Jevons, by defining national greatness as that quality that excites love, interest and admiration for a nation and its deeds. And Arnold would be correct in doing so, because throughout its history the energy-civilization equation has stressed the highest cultural achievements of man, and not the more mundane[5] aspects of his life. After all, the steam engine was praised not merely because it could pump drinking water to city dwellers but because it was a dispenser of culture.

33   A persistent critic would then respond that there just might be a connection between the availability of potable water and the creation of high culture. Must not the artist and scientist be fed, clothed and sheltered before he can address himself to artistic and scientific affairs? There is no simple reply to this question. However, I believe it calls for something far more profound[6] than the energy-civilization equation, which has often been put forth as the definitive answer.

34   There is a great danger in assuming that cultural attainments must wait upon the fulfillment of creature comforts, that man could not study the stars, think about gods or ornament a piece of pottery until he had a full stomach, a roof over his head and a wall around his city. The more historians and anthropologists learn about the early history of mankind, the more they are convinced that science, religion, and art were always part of his existence, and not refinements he cultivated after reaching a certain stage of economic stability. Neither historical nor anthropological research supports the popular view that economic necessity is prior to, and prepares the way for, the moral, intellectual and aesthetic life of man. Therefore I, for one, would reject the simple correlation° of energy consumption, economic growth and civilization.

35   In the final analysis, it is not crucial that all of my criticisms of the energy-civilization equation be accepted. It is much more important that the equation is recognized as a pervasive,[7] if often implicit,[8] element in both popular and sophisticated approaches to energy and society. If the equation is as worthless and potentially dangerous as I think it is, then it should be exposed and discarded, because it supplies a supposedly scientific argument against our efforts to adopt a style of living based upon lower levels of energy consumption. If it is a generalization of great truth,

---

[5] Commonplace.
[6] Deep.
[7] Spread out.
[8] Suggested, not stated.

then it deserves a more refined handling than it has received from its supporters to date.

Discussion

The following questions are specifically based on the analysis and evaluation questions listed in the Reading Strategies section of this unit. Even though some questions overlap the categories, this overlap helps you to see important relationships that link speaker, audience, argument, and language to the essay as a total unit.

SPEAKER/WRITER

1. What is Basalla's attitude toward his subject matter? Describe the general qualities of the "voice" speaking.
2. How objective is he? How and where does he reveal his bias?
3. What does knowing his profession add to your acceptance of him as an authority? Does he seem to be a "good man speaking well"?

AUDIENCE/READER

1. What assumptions does Basalla seem to make about his audience; that is, does he intend his essay for the general reading public, the scientifically based reader, or both? Try to see if his assumptions about probable audience help to explain his language level and tone toward the reader. If he had simplified the language, what would he have gained or lost?
2. Basalla tries to inform his readers as well as persuade them. Find the section that informs or explains and summarize it. Then determine where he persuades the reader to change certain beliefs. Does he also try to make his audience take action? Explain.

ARGUMENT/DISCUSSION

1. Basalla previews his thesis in the title. Then he devotes almost two-thirds of the essay to explaining that the concept of increased energy usage has been linked historically to the advancement of civilization. Why do you think he withholds his explicit thesis statement until the last third of the essay? What is his thesis and where is it stated?
2. Why is it important to understand the historical background of the energy-civilization equation? What are the main assertions in the explanatory section? What methods does he use to support them? Look for documented facts and figures from outside sources, opinions of authorities, historical evidence, details, examples, and analogy and mark them for discussion.
3. What are the main assertions or reasons Basalla uses to develop his thesis? What methods does he use to support these assertions? Does he define his terms? Find examples of definition. Look for the use of comparison and contrast in his argument.
4. Is this essay an appeal to reason or emotion? Find examples in the text

to support your answer. Consider the subject matter. How effective is Basalla's choice of appeal?
5. If we accept the first, explanatory, part of the essay as Basalla's premise for his thesis, how effective is the overall argument? Are the assertions arranged in a clear, logical progression? Are any assertions irrelevant? Does he overgeneralize anywhere? Oversimplify? Does he consider possible refutations to his argument? Where? Are there any false analogies? Are the cause-and-effect relationships valid?

STYLE/LANGUAGE

1. Locate any connotative language and decide if it adds to or detracts from the overall effect.
2. Find and evaluate significant references, allusions, and repetitions. What do they add to the style?
3. Look for characteristic sentence patterns; decide whether variety and length make the essay lively or emphatic.

WRITING:
Exposition: Analysis and Evaluation

Writing Assignment:
A Five-Paragraph Analytical Essay

Throughout this semester, you have practiced writing different types of short essays. These writing assignments have helped you not only to organize your thoughts and to become familiar with different rhetorical patterns, but also to develop methods of analysis. Now that you have developed analytical tools for reading and writing and have trained yourself to make conscious choices as you write, you are ready to attempt a longer essay. Most college assignments require a fuller discussion than can be presented in three paragraphs, so, as you tackle more complex problems and investigate more serious issues, you will need to expand your essays. For example, your sociology professor might assign an analysis of the effects of poverty on teenagers in a large city, or your history teacher might request an explanation for Hannibal's defeat in the Alps. Neither of these assignments could be fulfilled in two pages.

The first step in developing longer discussions is to learn to generate a five-paragraph essay. Although this type of essay cannot handle the in-depth discussions mentioned in the last paragraph, its structure is easily adaptable to an assignment of any length. As a five-paragraph essay has a distinct introduction and a distinct conclusion, it establishes a pattern that can be expanded to a five-, ten-, or even twenty-page paper. All the writer must do is to mentally substitute the word "section" for the word "paragraph," that is, to view an informative essay as having five or more sections: an introduction, a conclusion, and three or more discussion sections. Each of these sections can vary in length from one paragraph to two or three pages or more.

You should have little difficulty in making the transition from a three- to five-paragraph essay because you will need to learn only one new technique, the writing of a conclusion. Since you are already familiar with the *T-R-I-I-I* pattern*, you have only to add one more point of discussion and a conclusion to this pattern to form a *T-R-I-I-I-C* essay. Perhaps at this point, you should review the writing assignment in Unit 3, paying particular attention to instructions on writing the introduction and on developing points of discussion. When you are certain that you have control of the *T-R-I-I-I* essay, study the following assignment.

Assignment

Write a five-paragraph essay following the *T-R-I-I-I-C* pattern of organization.

---

* Adapted from theories outlined in Richard E. Young, Alton L. Becker, and Kenneth L. Pike, *Rhetoric: Discovery and Change* (New York: Harcourt, Brace, and World, 1970).

Paragraph 1: Introduction.
Paragraph 2: First point of discussion.
Paragraph 3: Second point of discussion.
Paragraph 4: Third point of discussion.
Paragraph 5: Conclusion.

Paragraph 1, the introduction, opens the discussion and includes the following.

1. A thesis statement and a restriction or restatement.
2. An introduction to the points of discussion.
3. Complementary materials to develop reader interest and to explain the topic under discussion.

Paragraphs 2, 3, and 4 develop the points of discussion. Each paragraph is, in fact, a *T-R-I-I-I* paragraph that includes a topic sentence, a restriction or restatement, and three illustrations.

Paragraph 5 serves as a conclusion, a discussion that rounds out the essay. This discussion could be any one of the following.

1. A summary of major points.
2. An evaluation of materials discussed.
3. A solution to a problem discussed in the essay.
4. A recommendation of an action.
5. A projection into the future.
6. An answer to a question posed in the thesis statement.
7. A conclusion drawn from the ideas and information presented.

There is no way to develop this section; the writer must *choose* an effective way to draw the discussion to a satisfactory close. The following guidelines and examples, however, can help you to compose this part of your essay.

1. Include a topic sentence in the conclusion.
2. Never introduce a new topic in the conclusion. Instead, expand only on the information you have already presented.
3. Avoid beginning your conclusion with "in conclusion" or "in summary." These phrases contain no information, are overused, and tend to bore your reader.
4. Never simply repeat or simply rephrase your introduction. A conclusion should round out, not merely repeat, your thesis.

Examples: Concluding Paragraphs

The Los Angeles Dodgers thus failed to win the Western Division of the National League in 1980 for three reasons. Injuries, especially to Reggie Smith, Davey Lopes, Dusty Baker, and Ron Cey, not only frequently left the batting line-up without four of the team's power hitters, but also seriously weakened its defensive ability. Injuries and sore arms among the pitching staff reduced the effectiveness of both starters and reliefers. And outstanding play by the Houston Astros in the final month of the season left the Dodgers with no room for error, an impossible situation for a crippled ball club. Yet the team fought with determination, pride, and spirit, and as Vince Scully, the team's announcer, said, "See you next spring."

Much new information on earthquakes has been acquired within the past ten years. Most geologists now agree that the plate tectonics theory explains the causes for earth tremors and that, as a result of ongoing research, they will soon be able to make accurate predictions of the time and place of an impending episode. But can such knowledge help prevent disaster? At times, yes. If a quake were predicted for a sparsely populated area, an evacuation of residents and even farm animals could probably be accomplished quickly enough to prevent deaths and injuries. But could Tokyo, Teheran, San Francisco, or Rome be evacuated within a day or two? Would an attempt at evacuation cause panic, traffic accidents, and looting? Would more deaths and injuries occur as a result of an attempted evacuation than from an earthquake itself? No one knows the answers to these questions, but someday soon, someone — a governor, mayor, scientist, or army officer — will be forced to decide on an appropriate action. And in that person's hands will rest the lives of millions.

In view of the poor hotel accommodations, mediocre food, and jam-packed days of sightseeing set up by government agencies, prospective travelers to the People's Republic of China should carefully evaluate their health, endurance, and flexibility before committing themselves to such a trip. Senior citizens, those with physical handicaps, and those who insist on American-style accommodations, should perhaps visit Japan, Hong Kong, or Singapore rather than China. Or, if these people genuinely wish to visit China, they should consider a cruise ship that stops at several Chinese ports throughout the trip. Until China can upgrade its restaurants and hotels and can handle larger crowds without putting their visiting guests through daily marathon races, only healthy, experienced travelers, especially those more interested in archaeology, anthropology, history, and art than in feasts and comforts, should plan a tour of China within the next five years.

TOPICS
COUSINS
1. Analyze the psychological characteristics needed by future settlers in space. Your intended audience is NASA.
2. Discuss possible new frontiers available on earth for a person with a pi-

oneering spirit. This frontier may be a physical place or an intellectual aspiration. Your intended audience is your classmates.
3. Discuss one field of exploration of the sixties and seventies that has come to an end or is about to be completed. Your intended audience is a convention of history teachers.

HOFFER
1. Discuss the purposes of a college education. Your intended audience is your parents.
2. Choose one human characteristic and discuss how it affects society. Your intended audience is your teacher.
3. Define the role of the intellectual in society. Your intended audience is Eric Hoffer.

BASALLA
1. Evaluate the effectiveness of your city's public transportation system. Your intended audience is a city official.
2. Discuss the effect of increased energy costs on your life. Your intended audience is your parents.
3. Forecast the effect that total depletion of all oil supplies would have on your life. Your intended audience is your classmates.

Brainstorming and Shaping

EXERCISE 1
1. Choose a topic from the preceding suggestions.
2. Review the sample data sheets.
3. Fill in Data Sheet 9-1. Note that you are to choose a very general topic at this time. You cannot limit your topic before you become aware of your readers' needs.
4. Now fill in your Data Sheet 9-2. At this point you must narrow your topic, limiting it to one that can be handled in five paragraphs. For example, in five paragraphs you could analyze one character in a novel but not the entire book, or you could summarize the major features of a particular car but not describe all its parts. Your narrowed topic should derive primarily from information listed in items 6 and 7 of your Data Sheet 9-1, but you might also want to consider information listed in item 8. Carefully adjust your final narrowed topic to avoid angering or insulting your reader.
5. Choose three points of discussion for your paper. These points will usually be found listed in item 4 of your Data Sheet 9-2, but you might wish to include one point from item 5.

Data Sheet 9-1 Audience

A. General Topic: _____
B. Audience: _____
C. What Does My Audience Probably Know About My Topic?
   1.
   2.
   3.
   4.
   5.
   6.
D. What Does My Audience Probably Need to Have Reviewed?
   1.
   2.
   3.
   4.
E. What Does My Audience Probably Need to Know About My Topic?
   1.
   2.
   3.
   4.
   5.
F. What Are My Audience's Possible Biases or Attitudes on My Topic?
   1.
   2.
   3.

Sample Data Sheet 9-1 Audience

A. General Topic: The retail shoe business.
B. Audience: College students majoring in business.
C. What Does My Audience Probably Know About My Topic?
   1. The recent rise in the prices for shoes.
   2. Busiest days of the week — Friday and Saturday.
   3. Occurrence of yearly fads in shoe styles.
   4. Many new shoe stores in new shopping malls and centers.
   5. Special sales periods — after Christmas and Easter; summer.
   6. Many part-time shoe clerks.

(Continued on following page)

Sample Data Sheet 9-1 *(Continued)*

D. What Does My Audience Probably Need to Have Reviewed?
   1. The number of sizes available.
   2. The variety of shoe styles available.
   3. The hours of business for shoe stores.
   4. Difficulty in getting proper fit.
E. What Does My Audience Probably Need to Know About My Topic?
   1. Overhead costs of shoe stores.
   2. Markup and markdown procedures.
   3. Cost to set up shoe store.
   4. Anticipated margin of profits.
   5. Problems of buying merchandise.
F. What Are My Audience's Possible Biases or Attitudes on My Topic?
   1. Some find retail business exciting.
   2. Some find retail business dull, too much work, unglamorous.
   3. Some believe huge profits available.

Data Sheet 9-2   Content

A. Specific Topic: _____
B. Purpose: _____
C. Audience: _____
D. Possible Major Points of Discussion:
   1.
   2.
   3.
   4.
   5.
   6.
   7.
   8.
   9.
   10.
   11.
   12.
   13.
E. Possible Minor Points of Discussion:
   1.
   2.
   3.
   4.

Sample Data Sheet 9-2   Content

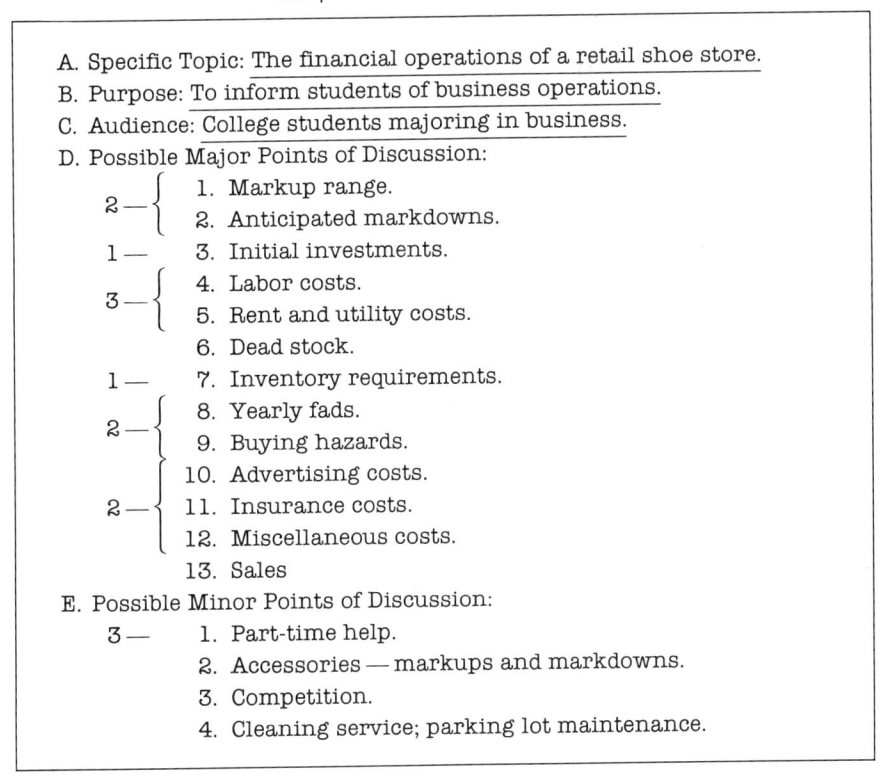

A. Specific Topic: <u>The financial operations of a retail shoe store.</u>
B. Purpose: <u>To inform students of business operations.</u>
C. Audience: <u>College students majoring in business.</u>
D. Possible Major Points of Discussion:
    2 — { 1. Markup range.
            2. Anticipated markdowns.
    1 — 3. Initial investments.
    3 — { 4. Labor costs.
            5. Rent and utility costs.
            6. Dead stock.
    1 — 7. Inventory requirements.
    2 — { 8. Yearly fads.
            9. Buying hazards.
           10. Advertising costs.
    2 — { 11. Insurance costs.
           12. Miscellaneous costs.
           13. Sales
E. Possible Minor Points of Discussion:
    3 — 1. Part-time help.
          2. Accessories — markups and markdowns.
          3. Competition.
          4. Cleaning service; parking lot maintenance.

6. Decide on the order of your points of discussion. In general, the most important point should be the first discussed, while the least important point should be second. This arrangement allows you to start and end your discussion strongly. However, there is no set rule for arranging your ideas. Make a conscious choice based upon your data and your audience's needs.
7. Fill out Data Sheet 9-3. You should write out your thesis statement, topic sentences, restrictions, and restatements in full sentences. All other entries may be notated by single words or phrases.
8. Review Data Sheet 9-3, checking to see if all information in each paragraph relates to its topic sentence. Check to make certain that all topic sentences relate to your thesis statement. Consider whether your points of discussion are arranged in an effective way.

Data Sheet 9-3 Outline — *T-R-I-I-I-C*

Introduction: Materials to be included (you need not adhere to the following order):
  A. Thesis Statement: _____
  B. Restriction or Restatement: _____
  C. Introduction of Points of Discussion:
    1.
    2.
    3.
  D. Complementary Materials (you might want to include some of the material listed in item 5 of Data Sheet 9-1:_____
  _____
  _____

Paragraph 2: First Point of Discussion:
  A. Topic Sentence: _____
  B. Restriction or Restatement: _____
  C. First Illustration: _____
  D. Second Illustration: _____
  E. Third Illustration: _____
Paragraph 3: Second Point of Discussion:
  A. Topic Sentence: _____
  B. Restriction or Restatement: _____
  C. First Illustration: _____
  D. Second Illustration: _____
  E. Third Illustration: _____
Paragraph 4: Third Point of Discussion:
  A. Topic Sentence: _____
  B. Restriction or Restatement: _____
  C. First Illustration: _____
  D. Second Illustration: _____
  E. Third Illustration: _____
Paragraph 5: Conclusion:
  A. Topic Sentence: _____
  B. Discussion: _____

WRITING: EXPOSITION: ANALYSIS AND EVALUATION 395

Sample Data Sheet 9-3   Outline — *T-R-I-I-I-C*

Introduction: Materials to be included (you need not adhere to the following order):
  A. Thesis Statement: Shoe stores require one of the highest investments of all retail operations.
  B. Restriction or Restatement: No other retail shop requires such a large capital outlay or operates on such a narrow net profit margin.
  C. Introduction of Points of Discussion:
    1. Initial investment.
    2. Gross profits.
    3. Net profits.
  D. Complementary Materials (you might want to include some of the material listed in item D of Data Sheet 9-1): Definitions; brief reference to business conditions.
Paragraph 2: First Point of Discussion:
  A. Topic Sentence: A capital outlay of $75,000–$100,000 is required today to open a moderate-sized store.
  B. Restriction or Restatement: Of this money, at least $30,000–$50,000 is needed for the physical set-up of the shop.
  C. First Illustration: Lease and licenses.
  D. Second Illustration: Fixtures, windows, and stockroom.
  E. Third Illustration: Initial inventory.
Paragraph 3: Second Point of Discussion:
  A. Topic Sentence: Anticipated gross profits on sales should range between 20 and 40 percent.
  B. Restatement or Restriction: This figure depends on an effective and efficient buying policy.
  C. First Illustration: Buying.
  D. Second Illustration: Markup range.
  E. Third Illustration: Markdown range.
Paragraph 4: Third Point of Discussion:
  A. Topic Sentence: Net profits on sales should range between 10 and 25 percent.
  B. Restriction or Restatement: This figure fluctuates with economic conditions.
  C. First Illustration: Operation costs.
  D. Second Illustration: Labor costs.
  E. Third Illustration: Stock depreciation.
Paragraph 5: Conclusion:
  A. Topic Sentence: The retail shoe business thus requires a large capital outlay and offers a low profit margin.
  B. Discussion: Evaluation of possible profits.

Writing the First Draft

Write the first draft of your *T-R-I-I-C* paper following your completed outline in Data Sheet 9-3. *Do not discard your data sheets as they must be submitted with the final draft of your essay.*

Sample First Draft

Shoe stores require one of the highest financial investments of all retail operations. No other retail store involved in personal furnishings requires such a large capital outlay or operates on such a narrow net profit margin. This profit margin, a figure derived from subtracting overhead costs from gross profit, is generally quite small and can fluctuate widely. Inflation can cause buyer resistance, operating expenses can increase unexpectedly, and increased competition can decrease customer draw. As a result, the retail shoe business is not stable.

A capital outlay of $75,000-$100,000 is required today to open a moderately-sized shoe store. Of this money, at least $30,000-$50,000 is needed for the physical set-up of the shop. A merchant usually deposits two months rent in addition to the first months rent when leasing a store, must pay for licenses and make deposits with local business agencies and utility companies. This can run up to $5,000--$15,000. Fixtures, carpeting, windows and window displays, and shelving also are expensive. They can run between $20-$60,000. This money must be spent before one shoe is sold. A minimum opening inventory generally costs $40,000-$80,000, but not all needs cash payment.

Anticipated gross profits on shoes should range between 20-40%. This figure depends on the merchant's effective and efficient buying policy. He needs to offer his customers the types and colors they want. He needs to order the correct range of sizes. He needs to have the current fads in stock. He normally marks staples only 35-45% but will mark-up stylish shoes at least 50-65%, sometimes more. He also must anticipate mark-downs for sales. Mark-downs usually range from 20% of retail price to a give-away price of one dollar.

The net profits on sales should range between 10-25%. This figure fluctuates with economic conditions. One item of overhead involves rent, utilities, equipment, theft, and advertisements. Another is labor. Shoe clerks, mostly men, are higher paid than other retail clerks and get between $12,000 and $25,000 a year. Part-time help costs at least $4.00 and hour. Then there is the problen of stock depreciation. Unsold shoes at the end of a season have less value than when first bought. This must also be deducted.

The retail shoe business thus requires a large capital outlay and offers a low profit margin. A normal shoe store costs at least $75,000 to set up and net profits on sales can average around 10-25%. Thus if a merchant takes in $225,000 in shoes sold and makes a 15% net profit, he has only $33,750. Considering he has worked in his store and his labor is worth $25,000, his net profit on his inventory would be only $8,750 or 11½%. Considering the risks involved, this business may not be enticing to prospective merchants.

Revising the Five-Paragraph Analysis Essay

Your assignment asked you to write a five-paragraph *T-R-I-I-I-C* essay, similar to the sample first draft just preceding. Study the revised sample essay, noting the changes made in content and organization. Then look over your own first draft, analyzing it according to the following revision questions.

Basic Revision Questions

1. Is all my information accurate? Appropriate?
2. Is this information organized so that my reader can comprehend what I have said? Could I reorganize my paper so it would be more effective?
3. Do I have a clear, unified focus; that is, does my essay telescope in on one major theme?
4. Is my thesis statement limited, unified, precise, and clear?
5. Do my informative paragraphs and my conclusion have limited, unified, precise, and clear topic sentences?
6. Do I offer sufficient details, examples, or explanations so that my reader gains a complete understanding of what I am discussing?

Sample Revised Draft

(See the end of the Editing Section for the final draft.)

> Neighborhood family shoe stores require greater financial investments than most other small retail businesses. No other retail stores involved in personal furnishings require such a large capital outlay or operate on such a narrow net profit margin. This profit margin, a figure derived from subtracting overhead costs from gross profit, is generally quite small, seldom in fact more than 25%, and can fluctuate widely. Inflation can cause buyer resistance, operating expenses can increase unexpectedly, and increased competition can decrease customer draw. As a result, each year many shoe merchants are confronted by severe financial problems, often even bankruptcy.
>
> A capital outlay of $75,000-$150,000 is normally required today to open an average sized neighborhood family shoe shop, one specializing in medium priced shoes. Of this money, at least $30,000 to $50,000 is needed for the physical set-up of the store. A merchant

must generally pay his landlord a two months' rent deposit plus the first month's rent upon leasing a store, must pay for licenses, and make deposits with local governmental agencies and utility companies. These initial expenditures can run close to $5,000 to $15,000. Fixtures, carpeting, electrical signs, windows and window displays, and shelving are also very expensive. They can run between $20,000 and $60,000, depending on the store layout and original condition upon leasing and upon interior design. This money must be spent before one shoe is sold. A minimum inventory generally costs $40,000-$80,000, but not all needs cash payment since credit is usually extended to merchants with past retail business experience and good financial records.

Anticipated gross profits on sales should range between 20% and 40%. This figure depends on the individual merchant's effective and efficient buying policies. He needs to offer his customers the types and colors of shoes that they want. For example, in working class areas, a merchant might need to stock work boots while in a white-collar area he might need to stock golf shoes and high-styled women's pumps. He needs to order the correct range of sizes, perhaps concentrating on the mid ranges (6-9, narrow and medium for women, 8-11, B's and D's for men, and 3 infants to 4 youths in B's and D's for children) and carry only a few styles in extra narrows and wides. He needs to have current fads, such as this year's fast seller Cherokee, in stock. He normally marks up staple shoes, such as nurses' oxfords and work boots, only 35% to 40% but will mark up stylistic shoes, such as ladies' pumps and men's cowboy boots, at least 50% to 65%, sometimes even more. He also must anticipate mark-downs for sales. Mark-downs could range from 20% of retail price to a give-away price of one dollar.

The net profit on sales should range between 10% and 25%. This figure fluctuates with economic conditions. For example, if there is a business slow-down in the country, sales will decline and more merchandise will have to be marked down. Some basic items of overhead include rent, utilities, advertising, insurance, equipment replacement and repair, and theft. But a major cost for all shoe stores is salaries. Shoe clerks, mostly men, are higher paid than most other retail clerks and get a base salary between $12,000 and $25,000 a year. If the sales clerk receives commission on total sales, the base salary is naturally lower. Part-time help, that is, extra clerks working on Fridays and Saturdays, earn between $4.00 and $6.00 an hour, again depending on a store's commission policy. Then there is the problem of stock depreciation. Unsold shoes at the end of a season have less value than when first purchased. For example, if a merchant has to carry over white dress shoes from August to the following June, he has a dead investment, money tied up in merchandise that bears no profit. For inventory purposes, he must mark down the value of these shoes and inventory them at the depreciated rate.

The retail shoe business thus requires a large capital outlay but offers a low profit margin. An average neighborhood family shoe store costs at least $75,000 to set up and shows a net profit on sales of approximately 15-20%. Thus if a merchant takes in $225,000 a year, a very good sales figure for this size store, and makes a 15% net profit, he has only made $33,750. Considering he has worked in his store and his labor is worth $25,000 (the minimum salary as a buyer/manager at a major department store), his net profit on his investment would be only $8,750 or 11.5%. Considering the risks involved, this is a rather low economic gain in today's financial world.

Editing

Word Choice: Point of View and Voice

The term "point of view" refers to the position from which observations are made by the writer. Point of view is also the focal point, place, or idea from which the discussion proceeds. In expository writing you have three possible "voices" to express point of view.

1. First person — *I, me, we, us.*
2. Second person — *you.*
3. Third person — *he, him, she, her, they, them, it.*

The first person can be used effectively when you want to present yourself openly and honestly as a limited authority, one who uses personal opinion and experiences to develop and support a thesis. For example, if your topic is "the purpose of a college education," your audience is made up of parents, and you have chosen your experience and opinions and the experience and opinions of friends to support your thesis, first person — *I* or *we* — is the voice to use to present your point of view.

The second person, *you,* is sometimes forbidden by instructors who feel it establishes too informal a tone for expository writing. Other instructors allow *you* in a limited way for specific purposes. As "you" can see, second person was the chosen voice throughout this book for the specific purpose of giving directions in a deliberately informal way. In your own writing, if you had to write about how to make or do something, a process analysis, *you* might be the chosen voice. The *you* may be explicitly stated or understood.

> After you dig a hole for the seeds, drop them in, cover them carefully, and water lightly.

The imperative mood with an exclamation point is another limited way to use *you.* Use this approach to grab your reader's attention. However, use it only rarely. The exclamation point is to be avoided most of the time.

> Some people think that students simply accept their college education without questioning its purpose. Don't believe it!

The third person is the voice most widely accepted and frequently used for expository writing: *he, him, she, her, they, them,* and *it.* The subject/noun (singular or plural) being discussed — students, plants, advertising, energy costs, characteristics, new frontiers — is the focal point, place, or idea from which the discussion proceeds. The appropriate personal or indefinite pronoun — *she, her, it, he, him, they, everyone, all, each, some* — is the reference that clusters around the focal subject.

> This city's public transportation system is outmoded. It consists mainly of ancient, gas-guzzling buses that pour noxious, stifling fumes into our already smog-laden atmosphere.

Keep in mind that the generic pronoun *he,* traditionally used in referring to both male and female, has become objectionable to many people on sexist grounds. You can avoid this kind of reference by changing the subject and reference pronoun to the plural.

Traditional:
After only two semesters, a student will often begin to question his own purposes.

Contemporary:
After only two semesters, student*s* often begin to question *their* own purposes.

Traditional:
An intellectual owes his allegiance to something more than just his mind.

Contemporary:
Intellectual*s* owe *their* allegiance to something more than just *their* minds.

Another important thing to avoid when you use this point of view is the pompous-sounding *one.* Unfortunately, many students have been taught to use this word in the mistaken notion that it expresses objectivity or authority. But anyone who has read a paper filled with *one* hopes . . . *one* is impressed . . . *one* finds that . . . finds *oneself* bored silly. This deadening construction gives only the illusion, not the reality, of authority or objectivity.

However, no matter which voice you choose, be sure to be consistent throughout your essay.

EXERCISE 1

To discover the flexibility of your written voice, experiment in your first draft by altering the point of view until you gain the most appropriate means of expressing your observations for your intended audience. Analyze and briefly evaluate on a separate sheet of paper why this point of view is the most effective choice.

EXERCISE 2
Why are the following student observations examples of inconsistent points of view?

1. As I stood there hypnotized, staring down from the edge of the diving board, I could see my girlfriend's face beaming in anticipation. A lone arrogant bird flew silently overhead, mocking my fear.

(If the writer is "hypnotized, staring down," he can't also have the point of view of seeing a bird flying silently overhead.)

2. Basalla uses the example of the Middle Ages to support his assertion that the "energy-civilization equation" evolved later in man's history. No one in the Middle Ages ever related medieval cultural accomplishments to any recently discovered practical uses of energy.

(Although the first sentence is attributed to Basalla's point of view, the next sentence is presented from the student writer's point of view.)

Once you have examined your paper for consistency in point of view, you should look for misleading or confusing shifts that make your writing difficult to follow. So edit carefully shifts in tense, person or number, and voice.

SHIFTS IN TENSE

Because a verb carries a sense of time as well as meaning, the writer who carelessly shifts tenses either *within* a sentence (intrasentence) or *between* sentences (intersentence), confuses the reader's sense of time.

Intrasentence Inconsistency:
Yesterday while I *waited* forty-five minutes for a local bus scheduled to arrive within ten minutes, I *see* two classmates drive happily past me.

Revision:
Yesterday while I *waited* forty-five minutes for a local bus scheduled to arrive within ten minutes, I *saw* two classmates drive happily past me.

Intersentence Inconsistency:
George Basalla *says* that Western nations have tended to associate the advancement of civilization with increased energy usage. He *felt* that equation was a false assumption.

Revision:
George Basalla *says* that Western nations have tended to associate the advancement of civilization with increased energy usage. He *feels* that equation was a false assumption.

SHIFTS IN PERSON OR NUMBER

Shifts in person or number often occur when the student writer has no particular focus in mind — *anybody/everybody* — or wants to state some general idea applicable to all. One common shift is from the third person (*he, she, it, one, they*) to second person (*you* — stated explicitly or implied); another is from singular (*he, she, it, a person, an individual*) to plural (*they*).

Intrasentence Person Inconsistency:
Gasoline is an important commodity for *me* because *you* need it in order to maintain *your* way of life.
(Vague *you*, implying anybody.)

Revision:
Gasoline is an important commodity for *me* because *I* need it in order to maintain *my* way of life.

Intersentence Person Inconsistency:
One purpose of a college education is to offer specialized training to *those* who want it. *You* need that training to prepare *you* for a career.

Revision:
One purpose of a college education is to offer specialized training to *those* who want it. *Some* students need that training to prepare *them* for a career.

Intrasentence Number Inconsistency:
(singular)   (plural)
Every student thinks *they* are overly pressured.

Revision:
(plural)   (plural)
All students think *they* are overly pressured.

SHIFTS IN VOICE

Since the shift from active to passive voice almost always involves a change in subject, a shift in voice may make a sentence awkward or unclear to the reader. In the *active* voice, the subject performs the action (Tom threw the ball); in the *passive*, the subject receives the action (The ball was thrown by Tom).

Intrasentence Voice/Subject Inconsistency:
After *I had researched* my material, the writing of the paper *was begun*.

Revision:
After *I had researched* my material, *I began* writing the paper.

Intrasentence Voice Inconsistency:
He submitted his final copy after his paper *had been proofread.* (Proofread by whom? Meaning is unclear.)

Revision:
He submitted his final copy after *he had proofread* his paper.

Intersentence Voice/Subject Inconsistency:
First *I use* some brainstorming techniques. *I make* a data sheet of details. Then the general organization *is structured.* Now *I am ready* to write my rough draft.

Revision:
First *I use* some brainstorming techniques and then *make* a data sheet of details. Next, *I structure* the organization. Now *I am ready* to write my rough draft.

EXERCISE 3

Test yourself on correcting unnecessary shifts in the following sentences. Change the word order if necessary. Some sentences are correct; next to these, write a C.

1. According to Asimov, our planet is full. He believes there are no more frontiers on Earth.
2. Every talk show host seems to have their own unique personality and interview technique.
3. As soon as we reached the beach, the picnic was ready to be eaten.
4. Each student finds a solution for themselves.
5. Wherever it was found, greed is one human characteristic that affects society.
6. He waited a long time for the bus to come, feels frustrated, and then leaves in a rage.
7. Anybody who was concerned can give their opinion to the committee.
8. I stood at the edge of the diving board and looked nervously down at the water far below. I realized I am terrified to make my first dive.
9. Fifty years ago this was an open field; today it is a maze of condominiums and gaudy motels.
10. One student told the committee he hates the general education requirements. He wanted some changes to be made by them.

EXERCISE 4

Examine your own five-paragraph essay for any awkward, confusing, or unnecessary shifts in tense, person, number, or active/passive voice.

Sentence Structure: Parallel Structure for Style and Coherence

In Unit 2, you learned to coordinate words and sentences by means of a coordinator such as *and* or *but*. Now is the time to look at coordination in a more sophisticated way, as a stylistic device used consciously to shape your reader's response. Such a conscious, stylistic use of coordination is called *parallelism*. In mathematics we talk about parallel lines; in writing we talk about parallel grammatical structures — words, phrases, clauses, and sentences. Parallelism calls attention to particular ideas, achieves variety or complexity in sentence structures, and helps the reader follow your pattern of thought within a long paragraph or essay.

To create parallelism, you arrange equally important ideas into a series of identical grammatical structures. Notice, for example, the different uses of parallel structures in the following excerpts from reading selections.

> Under the pressure of the fullness, the wilderness *is disappearing;* competing plants and animals *are dying* out; the weather *is changing* and the soil *is failing.*
>
> — Asimov, *Our Destiny in Space*

Asimov uses a parallel noun and the *be* + *-ing* form of a verb four times. These parallel patterns combine to give force to what he says. Try reading the sentence aloud so that you can hear the rhythm that parallel structure gives to his sentence.

> We foresee a doom*ed* civilization with tractors paralyz*ed* in the fields, abandon*ed* automobiles rusting on weed-chok*ed* freeways, factories as quiet as tombs and our haggard descendants facing a life of everlasting drudgery.
>
> — Basalla, *"The Fallacy of the Energy-Civilization Equation"*

Basalla uses parallel adjectives in a series to create a tone that reinforces his thesis. For example, if you read his sentence aloud, you will hear how the repeated *-ed* sound of the participles adds to the serious message of the sentence.

Both examples use parallel patterns you can easily incorporate into your own writing.

EXERCISE 1

Create three sentences similar in structure to Asimov's sentence. Now do the same for the sentence from Basalla.

> *Example*
> With the heat of the day, the clean air is dissipating; headaches and bad tempers are taking over; the temperature is rising and the city is choking.

Now look at the following segment of a sentence by Asimov: ". . . one might pick up as much of one's belongings as one could carry and travel to the other side of the hill,

where	conditions	might be better
where	a new life	might be built
and where	a new chance	might be taken."

And in the sentence below he notes in parallel structure specific examples of people seeking "the other side of the hill."

The Greeks and Phoenicians	colonized	the shores of the Mediterranean
The Russians	pushed	into the Ukraine and Siberia
The Bantus		into Eastern and Southern Africa
The Polynesians		from island to island

Asimov left out the verb after the Bantus and Polynesians, because he knew that he had already established the parallel pattern in his readers' minds; they would know that "pushed" is meant. Read these two examples of parallel structure aloud to listen to their rhythmic beat. Can you hear how Asimov uses parallelism to control readers' responses?

EXERCISE 2

Find at least four other examples of parallelism in the Asimov article. (Examples occur, for instance, in all but one of the last eight paragraphs.) Write them down. Then create your own parallelism by imitating Asimov's structures but substituting your own ideas.

Example
"Space settlements must be designed from scratch, with a particular purpose, a particular ecological balance, a particular way of life."

Similar Parallel Structure:
Our family started on vacation last summer with a particular itinerary,
   a particular set of friends to visit, and a particular kind of experience in mind for each week.

A word of caution. If you set up two or more elements within a sentence in such a way that your reader expects them to be parallel, be sure you follow through. Sometimes writers start with one kind of structure and then shift unexpectedly to another, often after an *and*. Such lack of parallelism sidetracks your reader. You should watch for this error when you revise your drafts.

EXERCISE 3

All of the following sentences contain elements that should be parallel. Rewrite the sentences, putting them into correct parallel structures.

Example
The people left the auditorium quietly and with quickness.

Revised
The people left the auditorium quietly and quickly.

Example
She potted the plant, watered it, and she set it in the window.

Revised
She potted the plant, watered it, and set it in the window.

1. Mr. Jones wore a brown suit and his shoes were black.
2. Mr. Casey likes to eat at a restaurant better than eating at home.
3. William Schilling fixes cars, is a repairman of household appliances, and is skillful with carpentry.
4. The long-distance run will leave Sam weary, with sore muscles, and his feet ached.
5. With very strong opinions and because he was talkative, the committee chairman dominated the meeting.
6. Mr. James had the choice of buying a new car or to rent a used one.
7. This story shows the animalness and the passion that prevailed in war and how they changed.
8. The child was unfriendly, cross, and he was difficult to care for.
9. He joined the army because he was patriotic and because of not being able to get a job.
10. The old man lived on money from Social Security, from his insurance and his daughter.

EXERCISE 4

Now go back to the essay you have written for this unit. Edit it for faulty parallelism. More important, see if there are places where you can add parallelism to add style to your writing and to help your reader follow your argument. After you have finished editing your paper, read it aloud so your ear can tell you if your style is effective.

Punctuation: Parentheses, Dashes, and Colons

Three other punctuation marks — *parentheses,* the *dash,* and the *colon* — need to be reviewed, for they not only help clarify writers' discussions, but also adjust emphasis within sentences. Although these three punctuation marks are employed less often than commas, semicolons, and apostrophes, they serve as useful tools for writers as they manipulate their materials to communicate ideas to their readers.

PARENTHESES ( )
1. Parentheses are most often employed to enclose complementary material that the writer does not want to emphasize. In other words, a writer might want to offer extra information, explanations, or instructions to the reader but doesn't want much attention to be placed on them. Notice that in the following examples, the materials within the parentheses could very well be eliminated without loss of meaning or could simply be placed in a footnote at the bottom of the page.

   Examples
   1. Having invited twenty-four relatives for Thanksgiving dinner, I had to bake three pies (pumpkin, pecan, and apple), roast two turkeys, and bake a peck of potatoes.
   2. The City Council approved three new bus routes (see Appendix B for route maps) that are to begin on November 1, 1983.
   3. My sister (the one who lives in Boise) called last night to wish me a happy birthday.
   4. When developing pictures, be sure to keep your tongs separate so your chemicals won't be contaminated. (You can use your hands instead of tongs, but these chemicals often irritate skin.)

   Notice that the first letter within the parentheses is not capitalized unless an entire sentence is enclosed and is not attached to another sentence. Notice also that placing materials within parentheses slows down reading speed. For this reason, you should avoid overusing them.
2. Parentheses can be used to enclose letters and numerals when presenting a series of items.

   Example
   This year, as usual, I received an assortment of gifts destined to be sold at my next garage sale: (1) a footrest upholstered in lavender stripes; (2) a gilded music box that plays "The Blue Danube"; and (3) a ceramic vase embossed with pink and blue daisies.

DASHES —
Like parentheses, dashes are generally used to add information to a sentence. But unlike parentheses, dashes bring emphasis to the interjected materials. For this reason, they should be used with caution. Too many dashes can make your writing hiccup across a page, forcing your reader to stop and start again and breaking up your stylistic flow of words.

1. Dashes are employed to set off items of a series (see the first sentence of this section on punctuation).

    Example
    Needing a new car, I visited three automobile agencies — Ford, Buick, and Oldsmobile — but didn't see anything I wanted to buy.

2. Dashes can be used to indicate a change in tone of voice or change in thought.

    Example
    Looking over my monthly bills, I realized that I charged over three hundred dollars at the local department stores — I think I'll burn all my credit cards.

3. Dashes are used to force emphasis on words, phrases, or clauses. Note that in the following examples, the dashes act like arrows pointing to the material that follows.

    Examples
    Just as I was about to step off the curb, something swished in front of me — a black cat.

    After buckling my seat belt, I gripped the arm rests with all my strength — this was my first airplane flight — and counted to ten before I screamed.

    Remember: Dashes force a great deal of emphasis onto the words that follow them so don't use them as substitutes for commas and parentheses. In addition, remember that a dash is twice as long as a hyphen, so if you type your school assignments, use a double hyphen to indicate a dash - -.

COLONS :

Colons, perhaps the least employed punctuation mark, have many different uses that must be understood by all serious writers. As you study the following ways this punctuation mark is used, notice that its primary role is that of a connector.

1. A colon is used after a salutation in a business or formal letter (a comma is used in an informal letter).

    Examples
    Dear Sir:

    Dear Dad,

2. A colon is used to connect a long or formal quotation to a sentence.

    Example
    In his inaugural address, John F. Kennedy attempted to reawaken the patriotism of the American people by suggesting they look to the prob-

lems of the nation rather than to their own needs: "Ask not what your country can do for you; ask what you can do for your country."

3. A colon is used to introduce a list that relates to the ideas discussed in the sentence.

   Examples
   The little boy, afraid that his teacher would send a note home to his parents, gave three reasons why his homework wasn't done: his baby sister tore up his arithmetic problems; his dog hid his geography book; and his grandfather wanted to play checkers.

   I did not win the dance contest for the following reasons: clumsiness, lack of talent, and unfair competition.

   Notice that when the items of the series are quite long, as in the first example, they are separated by semicolons. Also note that colons are not used after words such as *are* and *such as*. When these types of words are used, no punctuation mark is needed.

   Example
   I have many outstanding characteristics such as beauty, brilliance, and humility.

4. Colons may be used to connect clauses of a compound sentence when the second clause serves as an explanation of the first.

   Example
   Beverly Sills is the most successful opera singer of the century: she has sung at La Scala, the Metropolitan Opera House, and the New York Opera House and is now managing artistic director of the New York City Opera Company.

5. Colons are used to notate hours and minutes, volume number and page numbers, and Biblical chapter and verse numbers.

   Examples
   The time is 12:30. (hour and minutes)

   The source of the information is *The New Republic* 32: 45–50. (volume number and page numbers)

   The story of creation is found in *Genesis* 1:1–10. (Biblical chapter number and verses)

6. Colons are used to connect subtitles to the information that is to follow.

EXERCISE 1

Supply the appropriate parentheses, dashes, and colons in the following sentences. Be prepared to justify the choices you make.

1. My typewriter needs a great deal of maintenance a new ribbon, greasing, and several new keys, but I don't have the money to pay for this work.
2. Walking into my bathroom, I skidded across a wet floor the pipes were leaking again.
3. Reading the Book of Job 42 107, I realized the need to accept the omnipotence and omniscience of God.
4. Beginning the new semester, I had to purchase three new books a chemistry lab book, a chemistry textbook, and a sociology textbook I did not need any new materials for math or physics.
5. Of all the famous speeches in American history, perhaps the most famous sentence is the opening line to Lincoln's Gettysburg Address "Four score and seven years ago, our fathers brought forth on this continent a new nation, conceived in liberty and dedicated to the proposition that all men are created equal."
6. Many of the changes in American education have come about as the result of Title VIII see Appendix B.
7. Preparing to leave for Europe on a month's vacation, I packed the following items 1 three pairs of jeans and three shirts 2 two changes of underwear and three pair of socks 3 a poncho 4 an extra pair of shoes 5 two sweaters 6 three books 7 my toilet articles.
8. I recently purchased a new stereo I don't really know why since my old one was quite good and now I have almost no money to spend on Christmas presents.
9. I refused to vote for either candidate for mayor this year one was incompetent and one was too radical.
10. I arrived at the party at 7 45 and left at 8 30 it was a dull, dull gathering of dull, dull people.

EXERCISE 2

Review your first draft, checking all punctuation marks for possible errors. Remember, you have choices to make in many instances, so always consider the effects your choices make on your essay.

Final Draft of Sample Essay

Neighborhood family shoe stores generally require greater financial investments than most other small retail businesses. In fact, no other retail stores involved in personal furnishings necessitate as much capital outlay or operate on such narrow net profit margins. This profit margin, derived by subtracting overhead costs from gross profits, is generally quite small, seldom more than 25 percent, and can fluctuate as business conditions change. For example, inflation can cause prices to escalate, bringing about buyer resistance; operating expenses can increase unexpectedly; and competition, especially from new shopping malls, can decrease customer draw. As a result, each year many shoe merchants are confronted by severe financial problems, often even bankruptcy.

In today's economic market, a capital outlay of $75,000 to $150,000 is usually required to open an average-size neighborhood family shoe store, one specializing in medium-priced merchandise. Of this money, at least $30,000 to $50,000 is needed for the physical set-up of the shop. First, a merchant must give his landlord two months' rent deposit on signing the store lease, pay the first month's rent, buy business licenses, and make cash deposits with local governmental agencies and utility companies. These initial expenditures can run from $5,000 to $15,000. Second, the merchant must build store windows and shelving; have carpeting laid; purchase chairs, fitting stools, display counters, fixtures, signs, and fitting devices; and have proper lighting installed. These items can cost between $20,000 and $60,000, depending on the store's size, layout, and condition upon leasing. Third, a minimum inventory generally costs $40,000 to $80,000. However, cash payment is normally required for only one-half of the inventory, since credit is generally extended to merchants with past retail business experience and good financial records. With two to three stock turnovers anticipated during a fiscal year, total yearly inventory for sale would range between $80,000 and $240,000.

Gross profits on the sale of this merchandise should run between 20 and 40 percent, depending on the merchant's buying and pricing policies. Effective buying would include stocking the store with the styles and colors in demand by neighborhood customers, an adequate range of sizes, and a selection of current fast-sellers — the shoe fads that seem to change every year. For example, in a working-class area, a merchant would need to stock different types of work boots, while in a white-collar area, he or she would need to carry golf shoes and high-styled women's dress shoes. With a $40,000 stock, the merchant would need to concentrate on mid-range sizes (6–9, narrow and medium for women; 8–11, B's and D's for men; and 3 infant size to 4 youth in B's and D's for children), while with an $80,000 stock the merchant could carry longer size ranges and some extra-narrow and extra-wide shoes in limited styles; and during each season, he or she would need to carry a good selection of the current "hot" shoe such as this year's best-seller, the "Cherokee." The merchant normally would mark up staple shoes, such as nurses' oxfords and work boots, only 35 to 40 percent but would mark up stylish shoes, such as high-heel pumps and cowboy boots, at least 50 to 65 percent, and sometimes even more. Markdowns could range from 20 percent of retail to a giveaway price of one dollar.

The net profit on sales should range between 10 and 25 percent depending on business fluctuations and overhead costs. For example, if there is a business slowdown in the store's shopping area, sales would decline and more merchandise would have to be marked down. But under normal conditions, the costs of doing business have an effect on profits equal to effective buying. In other words, each month a merchant must pay out money for rent, utilities, advertising, insurance, equipment, repair of damaged shoes, and labor. Of these items, the most expensive is the wages of the shoe clerks, who earn base salaries between $12,000 and $25,000 a year, depending on the store's commission policy. In addition, a supplementary staff of part-time salespeople generally work on Fridays and Saturdays, earning between $4.00 and $6.00 an hour, again depending on the store's commission policy. Finally, stock depreciation also affects net profits. Shoes left unsold by the end of a season have less value to the merchant than when first purchased. If, for example, a merchant has to carry over white dress shoes from August to the following June, he has a dead investment, money tied up in stock that bears no profit. For inventory purposes, he must mark down the value of these shoes and inventory them at a depreciated rate.

The retail shoe business, especially neighborhood family stores, thus requires a large capital outlay but offers a low profit margin. An average family shoe store costs at least $75,000 to set up and shows a net profit on sales of approximately 15 to 20 percent. Therefore, if a merchant grosses $225,000 a year, a very good sales figure for this size shop, and makes a 15 percent net profit, he has made only $33,750. Considering he has worked in his store and his labor is worth at least $25,000 (the minimum salary as a buyer/manager at a major department store), his net profit on his investment would be only $8,750 or 11.5 percent. With the risks involved in this type of business, this is a rather low economic gain in today's financial world.

Preparing the Final Copy and Proofreading

1. Read the final copy aloud, slowly and carefully, listening for the end of every sentence in order to avoid (a) comma splices, (b) run-on or fused sentences, or (c) fragments that should be attached to a main clause.
2. Make certain that all the reference pronouns refer clearly and accurately back to the noun or pronoun *immediately preceding* the reference.
3. Check to see if there are any vague or ambiguous uses of *this* or *that* referring to a whole clause or phrase. If so, add a noun to clarify the

reference, e.g., *this situation, this statement, that person, that idea, this feeling,* etc.
4. Check to see that all words are spelled correctly. Is the hyphenation at the ends of lines divided correctly according to your college dictionary?
5. Check to see that the punctuation is accurate, indicating the meaning you intend.
    a. Are apostrophes for possession in their proper place?
    b. If quotation marks were used, do they enclose *both* the beginning and end of the quotation? Are all periods and commas inside the quotation marks? Are other punctuation marks placed according to their usage in the quotation?

UNIT 10
Review

READING:
Review

The reading selections in this unit have no vocabulary lists for study or questions to guide your analysis. Now that you have improved your reading and analytical skills, you should be capable of working through your assignment without our assistance. Remember, however, to skim through your assignment before you start to study it slowly and make certain you understand all words used by the author. When you have completed your reading, ask yourself questions about the essay in preparation for class discussion.

READINGS: SELECTION ONE

The Prodigal Son
Luke, XV: 11–32, New Testament

And he said, A certain man had two sons: and the younger of them said to his father, Father give me the portion of thy substance that falleth to me. And he divided unto them his living. And not many days after the younger son gathered all together, and took his journey into a far country; and there he wasted his substance with riotous living. And when he had spent all, there arose a mighty famine in that country; and he began to be in want. And he went and joined himself to one of the citizens of that country; and he sent him into his fields to feed swine. And he would fain have been filled with the husks that the swine did eat: and no man gave unto him. But when he came to himself he said, How many hired servants of my father's have bread enough and to spare, and I perish here with hunger! I will arise and go to my father, and will say unto him, Father, I have sinned against heaven, and in thy sight: I am no more worthy to be called thy son: make me as one of thy hired servants. And he arose, and came to his father. But while he was yet afar off, his father saw him, and was moved with compassion, and ran, and fell on his neck, and kissed him. And the son said unto him, Father, I have sinned against heaven, and in thy sight: I am no more worthy to be called thy son. But the father said to his servants, Bring forth quickly the best robe, and put it on him; and put a ring on his hand, and shoes on his feet: and bring the fatted calf, and kill it, and let us eat, and make merry: for this my son was dead, and is alive again; he was lost, and is found. And they began to be merry. Now his elder son was in the field: and as he came and drew nigh to the house, he heard music and dancing. And he called to him one of the servants, and inquired what these things might be. And he said unto him, Thy brother is come; and thy father hath killed the fatted calf, because he hath received him safe and sound. But he was angry, and would not go in: and his father came out, and entreated him. But he answered and said to his father, Lo, these many years do I serve thee, and I never transgressed a commandment of thine: and yet thou never gavest me a kid, that I might make merry with my friends: but when this thy son came, which hath devoured thy living with harlots, thou killedst for him the fatted calf. And he said unto him, Son, thou art ever with me, and all that is mine is thine. But it was meet to make merry and be glad: for this thy brother was dead, and is alive again; and was lost, and is found.

READINGS: SELECTION TWO

from America's Green Gold
by Kathleen K. Wigner

Kathleen K. Wigner lives in Los Angeles, California, and is an associate editor of *Forbes*. Articles that she has written for *Forbes* have been reprinted in the *Eastern Review* and several conservation trade magazines. She is the author of three books of poetry, *Encounters, Country Western Breakdown,* and *Three Way Driving.*

1   When Captain John Smith and his little band of colonists arrived off the coast of Virginia 327 years ago, they confronted a wilderness so vast that it was said a squirrel could travel from the Atlantic to the prairie's edge without ever once touching ground. For nearly three centuries after that, the forests were cut lavishly and wastefully; yet Americans can thank their stars that a full 70% of that forest land still exists. Our oil is fast dwindling, but our trees mostly remain, a natural resource of incomparable value.

2   From these forests may come — not *the* answer — but one major answer to the nation's energy woes. And we're not just talking about woodburning stoves. Already ethanol made from wood is being mixed with gasoline in California to power cars. Scientists at the University of California's Lawrence Berkeley Laboratory hope to design a full-size demonstration plant by 1981 that could refine tons of wood chips into fuel oil. Wood by-products are already being used to make many chemicals, such as plastics and synthetic fibers, now made from oil. Georgia-Pacific sells wood ash to Vermont farmers as a substitute for chemical-based fertilizer.

3   Alone, wood cannot free the U.S. from its economic dependency on a handful of shaky Middle Eastern nations. It can help, however, and help importantly. It is estimated that before the year 2000 Americans could be getting 10% of their energy from wood. That's no small amount. To the extent that wood-based energy replaced oil, it could reduce the U.S.' energy import bill by at least $10 billion a year at 1979 prices.

4   The abundance and availability of this renewable resource has contributed importantly toward making the U.S. the best-housed nation in the world — by far. Foreigners visiting this country for the first time are amazed to see how lavishly Americans use wood for housing; for them it is a scarce material. And, although some people may deplore the fact, wood — provided at reasonable cost — has helped bring about today's information explosion.

5   U.S. forests today cover 740 million acres — an area greater in size than the entire U.S. east of the Mississippi. Giant redwood and Douglas fir, plus lesser giants like Sitka spruce and Western red cedar, run in a green belt down the mountainous slopes of the West Coast from Alaska to California, a display of conifers (cone-bearing trees also known as soft-

woods, though the lumber they yield may be very hard) unequaled in the world. Another belt, 800 miles to the east, covers the Rocky Mountains from Canada to Mexico with more conifers — Ponderosa pine, Englemann spruce, white fir and larch. Hardwoods (whose seeds are covered rather than bare like softwoods') such as maple, elm, oak and birch blanket the eastern U.S. On the flat, sandy regions of the South flourish straight, fast-growing pines such as loblolly, longleaf and slash pine.

Some 488 million acres of America's forests are classified as "commercial," meaning they grow enough trees per acre to be usable for commercial purposes. Although the U.S. ranks behind the Soviet Union and Canada in its abundance of softwoods, the principal source of lumber and paper, the U.S. is well ahead of its chief rivals in its ability to utilize high-quality softwoods. They grow faster in the U.S. because of the milder climate, and can be brought to market faster over a far better transportation network. Best of all, U.S. forest technology leads the world and has enabled the American industry to get far more out of each forest acre than any of its rivals.

At a time when the very fate of the Free World hangs on the continuing availability of energy and raw materials, it is a dismaying sight to see self-righteous environmentalists trying to prevent the nation from utilizing this great resource. They forget that while we have been using our forests more extensively, we have also learned how to rebuild them better and faster. Since 1952, the first year records were kept, the annual net growth of wood has risen 56%. This means that while we are using more and more forest products, wood growth has exceeded harvest, leading to an increase in standing timber. This is the precise opposite of the situation in oil. The nation is harvesting no more trees today than it harvested in 1900, even though we are consuming eight times as much paper and 70% more lumber.

Nor has the U.S. reached a limit on its potential to grow more wood on the existing land base. At present, without management, we are only growing trees at an estimated 61% of our productive capacity. With proper management, the U.S. could double, perhaps triple, the productivity of its forests within fifty years.

While the future for wood seems secure, the short-term prospects for America's forest products companies are less glowing. Persistent interference and mismanagement by the federal government continues to shackle the companies that buy timber from federal lands. Moreover, wood and paper are cyclical businesses, and next year the swing is likely to be down. The squeeze on mortgage money has already hit residential construction. As a result, lumber and plywood prices are tumbling. Paper, whose use is closely tied to gross national product, will also be hurt by the expected recession.

But it is important to remember that growing trees is a long-term business, and for those companies that have taken the lead in growing the forests of the future, that future is bright indeed. Beyond lumber and paper lies a world of uses for wood which look more and more likely as the price of oil soars toward $50 a barrel.

Remember this: The world is consuming not only oil but all the major natural resources at a frightening rate. There is a real question as to whether there are enough resources around to maintain living standards in the West and Japan and at the same time to improve standards even modestly in the poorer nations of the world. But trees, unlike oil or copper or iron ore, are renewable. Moreover, we are constantly finding new ways to use trees more effectively. Thus we use more wood products without cutting additional trees. Technology shows us how. As recently as 1950, for example, only 21% of a typical tree went into the end products; the rest was wasted, either burned in dirty, smoky wigwam burners or left to rot in the forests. Today, companies can use around 60% of a tree. As new technologies are developed to turn more wood scraps into marketable products, that percentage will grow.

Improved tree-use begins in the forests themselves. Paul Bunyan–like machines now can pull trees right out of the ground — roots and all — thus harvesting at least 20% more wood weight per acre than could older harvesting methods. This year Georgia-Pacific unveiled a prototype of what it calls a biomass harvesting machine (nicknamed "Jaws 3" by its operators) whose circular blades cut an eight-foot swath of weeds and brush. Like Sherman marching through Georgia, the G-P-designed-and-manufactured machine sweeps up the forest underbrush in flat southern pine country — thereby preparing the land for planting more productive trees — and chops it into wood chips for boiler fuel for several Arkansas mills. In one hour it scrapes up wood chips equal to as much as 1,000 gallons of fuel oil.

Sawdust and shavings from sawmills and plywood mills can go into products like particleboard or waferboard or be burned as fuel. Just burning the trash left on the forest floor, a study by Louisiana-Pacific found, would save the U.S. one month's worth of imported oil every year, reducing our annual oil import bill by more than $4 billion.

Growing trees as crops is another way U.S. companies are boosting forest yields. "Until recently," says Jack Wolff, vice-president for land and timber at Weyerhaeuser Co., "the U.S. has been living off a wild, naturally created forest resource, just as agriculture stabilized food supply, so too foresters have become tree farmers, managing the forests from planting to harvest."

Many of the techniques to help trees grow to cutting size faster are not spectacular — thinning young stands to give remaining trees more growing room, removing tall trees to let in more sunlight, controlling disease and insects and fertilizing selectively. But the results of using these techniques assiduously can be spectacular. Crown Zellerbach found that merely thinning a test plot of hemlock caused the remaining trees to gain more than two feet a year in height, while an unthinned plot lost 78% of its trees to natural causes.

Reforesting by scattering seedlings from helicopters rather than relying on the wind, or planting seedlings that have been grown in nurseries to a size where their chance of survival is greater, also speeds up the tree-growing process. A Douglas fir seedling, raised in a greenhouse in its own individual plastic tube, reaches plantable size (6 to 8 inches) in five to seven months. A natural seed may take several years to reach the same size — if it survives at all.

One forested acre, left to nature, would grow a stand of mature trees in 250 years. That same acre, properly managed, could grow a stand ready for cutting every 50 years — thus providing five harvests instead of one in the same time span, with six times the volume of wood of the unmanaged forest.

Forest geneticists object to words like "supertrees" or "clones," but that's exactly what they are developing in their laboratories to improve tomorrow's trees. A number of forest products companies, like Weyerhaeuser, Georgia-Pacific and Union Camp, have invested considerable time and millions of dollars to grow the forests of the future. Using only the seeds from superior trees or grafting, geneticists hope to pass along valuable genetic traits such as faster growth or better resistance to insects and disease. While the full harvest of this work may take as long as 50 years or more, success in the laboratories would allow companies to cut their old-growth trees faster than they could if they had to rely on a natural growth process. The Forest Service has estimated that in the first generation alone genetics could add up to 15% more wood to a Douglas fir, and gains of 10% to 20% have already been made in the first generation of genetically improved Southern pine.

For two years Simpson Timber Co. of Arcata, Calif. has been growing test-tube redwoods. Using a process called tissue culture, scientists take a tiny portion of a redwood tree, put it in a test tube with different chemicals — and there it grows, needles, roots and all. The plantlet (so-called to distinguish it from a seedling) is then transferred to a nursery when it has grown to a viable size.

Getting more redwood per acre is particularly important because redwoods are now in short supply, because much of the land they are able to grow on has been taken by the federal government to create Redwood National Park. Simpson estimates that by using genetically superior planting stock, which will represent the best traits of only around 200 superior trees, it can increase timber growth at least 50% per acre.

Weyerhaeuser, the nation's third-largest forest products company, is clearly betting its future on research and development. Weyerhaeuser is particularly rich in trees, but many are old trees. In order to cut those trees that are no longer growing and replace them with faster-growing timber of equal volume, the company last year opened a lavish $40 million technology center near its Tacoma, Washington headquarters, with approximately 100 laboratories that will accommodate up to 800 employees. At it and eight smaller research laboratories across the country and in Indonesia, Weyerhaeuser is furthering what it calls the "high-yield forest." At the technology center, in a basement laboratory environmentally controlled for temperature and humidity, a Weyerhaeuser tissue specialist works with other geneticists to produce trees of identical quality. Elsewhere, in seedling nurseries, young trees grow from seeds that come from seed orchards designed to produce fast-growing new forests.

"We are involved in a high-cost project in which you don't see the benefits until you cut the tree," says Rex B. McCullough, a geneticist involved in Weyerhaeuser's tree improvement program. Weyerhaeuser is now spending about $140 million a year on reforestation and forest management. Since 1966 it has planted 1.2 billion seedlings, says C. W. Bingham, a company senior vice president. "In addition, we have rehabilitated 251,000 acres which had been covered with low-value species, and have fertilized a total of 1.4 million acres."

What happens in the laboratories and in the forests is of more than academic interest. At present the U.S. gets 2% of its energy from wood. The ability to increase that level — and to meet future demand for existing and new wood products — depends on getting higher yields from the forests.

Woodburning stoves? They are pleasant and even useful on a limited scale, but using all the forest for kindling wood is not the answer to the energy shortage. There are better uses for trees. Turned into lumber, they save energy because of their insulating qualities, which are superior to those of aluminum, brick, stone or concrete. As a building material, lumber requires a far smaller expenditure of energy to make than any of these alternatives. In a few areas of the country, however, especially in communities close to forests, trees *can* provide fuel. In Vermont, for example, wood chips sell for just $14 a ton. A ton of wood chips has the energy content of a barrel of oil. With fuel oil currently costing nearly $36 a barrel in Vermont, it clearly pays to burn wood chips.

The biggest users of wood for energy today are, naturally, the forest products companies themselves. By using solid wastes or pulping wastes, they have been able to generate 45% of their power needs. Louisiana-Pacific's Samoa, Calif. wood products plant, for example, generated enough power last year from wood wastes to run its large complex, provide power for the 100 homes nearby and sell the leftover power to Pacific Gas and Electric. Indeed, L-P estimates that if the costs of purchased energy had risen an additional 20% in 1978, its earnings would have dropped only 5%.

But what about wood as fuel for other industries without easy access?

The potential for fast-growing trees to be used exclusively for fuel is one idea being explored. Such "biomass plantations" were used extensively in Europe and in the eastern U.S. during the 19th century to produce firewood from hardwood harvested on a short growing cycle and quickly regenerated by sprouting new trees from the cut stumps. In Woodland, Me. Georgia-Pacific has established an experimental plantation of crossbred poplar seedlings to find out how quickly they will reach usable size. G-P hopes it will get a 20-to-30-foot tree in seven years or less. These trees could then be used for both pulp wood and fuel. Other fast-growing hardwood species such as cottonwood, sycamore, red alder and aspen are also promising, provided they do as well in the wilds as they have done in the laboratories. And there is considerable energy potential in new-grown hardwoods, the most desirable fuel wood, 55% of which go unharvested.

Recent studies for the U.S. Energy Research and Development Administration point to the future economic feasibility of changing the physical nature of wood on a large scale. For example, getting oil from wood chips is in the research stages in Albany, Ore. at a plant funded by the Department of Energy. Scientists there claim they can produce a barrel of industrial-grade oil for about $26. There is a possibility for producing natural gas, too. If wood is burned in an inadequate supply of oxygen, it is converted into methane, hydrogen, and other gases. "Wood gasification is cheaper than coal gasification and not all that complicated," enthuses Dr. C. Edward Taylor, corporate manager of environmental controls for Louisiana-Pacific, which is planning to use wood gas in two of its gas-fired kilns. "And there is no sulfur to clean up afterwards."

To overcome bulk and transportation problems, a company in Brownsville, Ore. is reducing the wood's moisture, pulverizing it and then compressing it into pellets the size of dog kibble. The company claims the pellets can then be shipped and burned like coal at competitive prices.

Hard on the heels of last spring's lines at the filling station, gas-thirsty Californians began receiving their first shipments of "gasohol" made from gasoline and the alcohol produced from wood sugars at Georgia-Pacific's Bellingham, Wash. pulp mill. The beauty of alcohol made from wood — as opposed to corn, for example — is that it comes from pulping process by-products. Delivered to California, G-P's alcohol costs around $1.50 a gallon. People in the New York area are already paying as much as $1.14 a gallon for gasoline. With the next turn of the OPEC screw and with U.S. decontrol imminent, $1.50-a-gallon gasoline is clearly in the offing.

Wood has considerable promise as a feedstock for the chemical industry, which now depends heavily on oil. Wood chemicals themselves are not particularly new. Turpentine, for example, was an important industry in southern forests for centuries. Tall oil (from the Swedish *tallolja*, meaning pine oil) is still an important ingredient in adhesives, printing inks and detergents and accounts for about $250 million in wood chemicals sales a year. Union Camp Corp. turns mill wastes worth a few cents a pound into flavors and fragrances worth more than $1 a pound. Some of Champion International's by-products go into soil conditioners. ITT Rayonier's pulp mill in Hoquiam, Wash. produces a popular synthetic vanilla, called vanillin. Pulping by-products even go into L-Dopa, the drug used to treat Parkinson's disease.

Wood can also be used to produce such basic chemicals as phenols, acetones, benzenes, ammonias and formaldehydes. Until recently, however, wood chemicals haven't been competitive with most oil-and-coal-based products but some forest products executives, such as G-P's Chairman Robert Flowerree, believe that escalating costs of fossil fuels could soon create a demand for these wood chemicals.

So, what are we waiting for? Why isn't the U.S. charging ahead with programs to use its forests more extensively? The answer is almost embarrassingly predictable: We are being stalled by that strong alliance between a meddling, cumbersome bureaucracy and single-issue, self-appointed guardians of the environment. The large forest companies that have been pioneering much of the research and development together own only 14% of America's commercial forest land. By far the biggest chunk, half the trees usable for lumber or paper, is owned by the federal government through its National Forest System. Here politics and single-minded environmentalists have been creating chaos over the past decade. As *Forbes* has previously written (Oct. 15, 1977), an estimated 6 billion board feet of timber in the national forests is wasted every year simply because mature trees are left to rot and die. That's more than *half* of the 11 billion board feet the service will sell this year.

Even this deadwood would be usable if sold as salvage, but salvage sales are minimal because the Forest Service claims Congress does not appropriate enough money to get the job done. Forest fires, like the ones that raged through Idaho this year, threatening lives and leaving behind thousands of charred acres, are the price paid for this neglect.

In addition, some 62 million roadless acres, about one-third of national forest acreage, have been locked away since 1970 while the Forest Service studied them as possible additions to the 16-million-acre National Wilderness Preservation System, where tree cutting is not allowed — which means, in effect, that the timber will be left to insects, decay, windstorms and forest fires.

The Forest Service is also hampered by a management policy almost as awkward as its name — "nondeclining even flow." Don't be intimidated by the scientific sound of the term. All it means is that you can't cut any more national forest trees than you grow in a given year. This policy makes absolutely no sense. More or fewer trees may have reached their maximum potential and be ready for cutting. No matter, "nondeclining even flow" it must be. The result is that in the national forests, mature, fully grown trees may stand for years, even decades, depriving newer trees of a chance for life and depriving the nation of potential energy and materials.

Then there is the issue of clear-cutting. Some environmentalists object to it because cutting an entire section of a forest, rather than a tree here and a tree there, leaves unsightly bald spots on lush green hillsides. The loggers won the right to clear-cut, but the size of those cuts was reduced drastically, adding to the cost of tree harvesting.

Such government shortsightedness has had the effect of creating an artificial timber shortage, especially in the West, where many companies depend on Forest Service sales for their mills. From 1976 to 1978, the wholesale price index for softwood lumber rose by almost 55%, reflecting the higher prices paid for scarce Forest Service timber. Is this inflation? Or bureaucratic rigidity?

There have recently been a few signs of progress. In April of this year, President Carter recommended opening up 36 million wilderness acres to timber cutting. In June he tried to halt lumber's inflationary spiral by asking the Forest Service to raise the allowable cut by as much as 3 billion board feet a year. But environmentalists, who seem to care little about inflation or the price of housing, cried that the 15 million additional acres the Carter Administration recommended for wilderness were insufficient. So the battle continues to rage in the courts and in Congress. Says a frustrated Richard Madden, chief executive of Potlatch: "It takes 25 to 70 years to grow a tree, so we need some stability in government policy. What we're doing now has to have some relationship to what we're doing in 30 years."

While it is largely government mismanagement that is responsible for many of the problems in the Pacific Northwest, it is the absence of a comprehensive government policy that is hobbling development in the eastern half of the U.S. where much of the commercial forest land is in the hands of several million small private owners.

Here the problems are different, especially in the South. Take a look at Alabama, where individuals own about 16 million acres, or 75% of that state's commercial forests. About 300,000 acres are harvested in Alabama every year, but less than 1 acre in 12 is being replanted or reseeded by man. As a result the land is growing wood at only half its potential. The same holds true throughout much of the South. Because pine is a fast-growing tree, pine growth still continues to exceed loss. But the U.S. Forest Service estimates that 1 million acres of valuable pine forests are lost each year because independent landowners didn't regenerate cutover lands.

What happens in the South matters. Today the South produces a third of the nation's softwood plywood, 60% of its pulpwood and 56% of its newsprint. One study predicts that by the year 2000 the South will provide the majority of the nation's wood supply, producing twice as much as the region does today.

There are some incentives for the small southern tree farmer. In some states such as North Carolina, Virginia and Mississippi, forest products companies pay a special tax which, along with matching state funds, is used to finance reforestation. Big forest companies also provide management assistance to small owners in exchange for an option to buy their trees at competitive prices. Industry- and state-operated nurseries provide top-quality pine seedlings to improve reforestation. Lobbying is going on in Washington to let a small timber owner postpone taxation on any portion of his harvest reinvested in a new crop of trees.

In New England, the one bright spot is Maine, where the pulp and paper industry got its start well over 100 years ago. Although Maine has been logged over as many as five times in U.S. history, it still ranks as the nation's most heavily forested state. Big companies like International Paper, Great Northern Nekoosa and Diamond International own about 50% of Maine's forests, giving them a unique degree of control over supply. As a result, many papermakers are expanding into lumber, using only leftovers for pulp.

In the rest of New England, trees provide scenery and firewood, but a study by the Yale School of Forestry and Environmental Science recently concluded that unless these forests are better managed, New England could lose the very mixture of forest, farm and village that makes it so attractive. Today many of the trees are stunted and twisted as they compete for growing space. But with the proper management, New England's abundant hardwoods could provide an area highly dependent on imported oil with fuel to see it through the cold winters.

Finally, a more rational wood and forest policy could do a lot to improve the U.S.' balance of payments. The U.S. is still a net *importer* of wood products — in fact, the largest one in the world. This year two-thirds of U.S. newsprint and one-third of its softwood lumber will be imported from Canada, which accounts for 70% of total U.S. wood imports overall. Last year our trade deficit in forest products was a record $2.9 billion. There are compelling economic reasons for our imports from Canada — lack of newsprint capacity for one. But Canada is a special case. We could substantially reduce our trade deficit in forest products simply by lifting the prohibition against exporting logs from U.S. national forests.

The U.S. is and will remain a voracious consumer of forest products. But with our climate, land mass and technology we should be able to produce enough for our present needs with plenty to spare. That "spare" could be a big help in the energy shortage, but, unfortunately, the bureaucracy and the ideologues are fiddling while the Middle East burns.

READINGS: SELECTION THREE

Our Destiny in Space
by Isaac Asimov

American author, educator, and professor of biochemistry at Boston University School of Medicine, Isaac Asimov is the author of 143 books, a noted contributor to science fiction, and a thoughtful commentator on the consequences of technology.

1 The Earth is full! Four billion people have crammed into every desirable and fruitful area and have spilled over into all the barren and inhospitable areas. Under the pressure of the fullness, the wilderness is disappearing; competing plants and animals are dying out; the weather is changing and the soil is failing. And yet there is perhaps an even more fundamental danger to humanity in the Earth's fullness than is represented by any sort of physical deterioration. Humanity began as a thin cluster of primitive hominids in East Africa about four million years ago. About two million years ago, the first hominids appeared who were sufficiently close in structure to the human being to be placed into genus *Homo.* It was not until 150,000 years ago that the hominid brain developed to a size sufficient to produce the first organisms we can classify as *Homo sapiens,* and it was only 50,000 years ago that "modern man," *Homo sapiens,* made his appearance on the Earth.

2 His increase in range was slow indeed. It was not till 30,000 years ago that human beings began to enter Australia and the American continents, and even as late as 300 years ago, those continents were but thinly occupied.

3 Then came the Industrial Revolution and the Earth filled with what was, on the evolutionary scale, an explosion. In a couple of centuries, the world population quintupled from 0.8 billion to 4.2 billion, and now Earth bears all the human load it can manage and, in many places, somewhat more than it can manage.

4 Consider, then, that we and our hominid ancestors evolved on an essentially empty Earth. There was always the possibility, during times of stress, that one might pick up as much of one's belongings as one could carry and travel to the other side of the hill, where conditions might be better, where a new life might be built and where a new chance might be taken.

5 This was true even after civilization appeared, very late in human history. The Greeks and Phoenicians colonized the shores of the Mediterranean; the Russians pushed into the Ukraine and Siberia; the Bantus into eastern and southern Africa; the Polynesians from island to island across the Pacific. In modern times, Europeans flooded into the Americas and

Australia. In every case, a thin wave of early migrants was replaced by a much denser wave of later ones.

By the 1920's, however, the freedom to migrate vanished. No nation, no region, any longer welcomed newcomers; all nations, all regions, had the power to exclude. Even when migration did take place with permission, migrants had to fit into the full society, too massive to change for them. There was no chance of building a new society.

The frontiers, open for millions of years, closed in decades, and there is no longer the other side of the hill. People cannot even make room for themselves by the desperate method of war; war has become too dangerous for that.

So even if we solved all the problems that now afflict humanity, we would still be living in a full world without the psychological stimulant of a frontier.

Yet, there *is* still a frontier, still another side of the hill. It just happens to be someplace other than on Earth itself.

Up there is the moon, to begin with, and all the space between the moon and Earth. That, too, is a frontier. That, too, represents new space for humanity — better space in some ways than anything we have yet seen, for it is empty, so that we can design it from scratch. We have already penetrated the new frontier. Human beings have lived in it for as much as six months at a stretch. Human beings have reached the moon itself on six different occasions and have returned safely.

Two nations have led the way into space. These are precisely the new nations that have in recent history filled a frontier. The American West and the Russian East offered each country examples of the exhilaration of expanding into empty spaces.

In the old days, moving to a new region might mean hardship, suffering, even death. One went with a backpack or a handcart or a wagon train or a horse or in a ship. The new frontier is, on the other hand, a full rocket-ship away. To move to the other side of the hill beyond the atmosphere means high technology and an enormous expense.

Whereas migration could once be indulged in after no more than inner communion or an impulse, it now involves the support of those who might not intend to migrate, and who must be convinced of the value of the adventure.

The nations of the Earth now spend a total of $400 billion *each year* on their competing military machines, whose only possible use is to kill people and destroy civilization. To spend 10 percent of that on the new frontier would seem unthinkable — unless it could be justified.

And of course it can be, to those with a certain vision.

It may well be that the most efficient scheme that will be developed to provide a basic energy source that will last for billions of years will be to collect solar energy in power stations orbiting the Earth and to beam that energy down to Earth's surface by microwaves.

There will be other ways of obtaining energy on the Earth's surface (nuclear fusion, for one), but this "orbital energy" will be the only kind we have ever obtained that will not be tied down by global geography.

Orbital energy need not be associated directly with any region on Earth and could rightly be taken to be a planetary resource. The expense and difficulty of building the numerous space stations required to supply the Earth with enough energy would make it natural to have it a global project. The necessity of maintaining the stations after they were set up would be a matter of global interest.

In this way, the building, maintenance and utilization of orbital energy would be a natural way of pushing the nations into globalism through that strongest of all motivations — self-interest.

The building of such space stations would be much more practical if mining operations were initiated on the moon. That would make available metals, glass, concrete, soil, even oxygen, for space construction and space life. Only carbon, hydrogen and nitrogen, of the vital elements, are lacking on the moon and would have to be supplied by Earth.

If lunar materials are available, many structures on the moon and in space can be built along with the solar power stations. There can be observatories designed to study the Universe from outside the atmosphere. There would be laboratories designed to perform experiments seen as too dangerous for Earth, or experiments difficult to perform under surface-Earth conditions. Nuclear fission and nuclear fusion stations in space might avoid undesirable radiation risks or other unpleasant side effects and could serve as a backup for orbital solar energy.

Whole sections of industry (thoroughly computerized and automated) could be shifted into space for a great variety of useful reasons:

1. Conditions in space — vacuum, zero gravity, hard radiation, high and low temperatures — are ideal for some industrial operations difficult or impossible to carry through on Earth's surface. These would include making electronic equipment requiring high vacuum; fashioning special alloys that can be mixed under gravity-free conditions; even manufacturing ball bearings more perfectly in the absence of gravity. And any operation that offers danger is safer in space than on Earth's surface.

2. Pollution would no longer be a problem since space offers millions of times the diluting factor that Earth's surface does and has no ecological balance of its own to be disturbed in the process. Nor will the pollution remain in Earth's vicinity, for the solar wind will constantly sweep it away into the vastness of the outer solar system and beyond.

3. Earth's surface, liberated of much of its industry, can revert to a desirable percentage of parkland and wilderness.

In order to build and maintain all these structures, it would be most economical to house engineers, construction workers, administration personnel and all their families in space. We will have to have fully equipped space settlements.

It is these space settlements that are more important than all else combined. Whatever material benefits space might bring to Earth, none can, in the long run, be greater than the psychological benefits of offering a new frontier, a place where people can go to start a new life if they wish to.

Space settlements must be designed from scratch, with a particular purpose, a particular ecological balance, a particular way of life. It would be tempting to design them as American middle-class suburbs, but some could be built with a strongly Marxist life-style or an Amish one or an Islamic one or as anything a group of settlers could agree on.

Not all the designs might prove viable over the long run, but how else are we to find out but by trying? However they start out, they may develop into a space-oriented society, unlike anything we have on Earth.

The details, in fact, don't matter. What does count is that those settlements will be *there* and that they can be a goal for the restless on Earth. Only a few of them may leave the Earth, perhaps even only a few of the discontented, but the mere opportunity to escape will be a tremendous psychological lifesaver.

In 1845, when the United States was driving for the possession of the Oregon Territory and tension with Mexico was rising, John Louis O'Sullivan wrote in the *United States Magazine and Democratic Review:* "Our manifest destiny is to overspread the continent allotted by Providence for the free development of our yearly multiplying millions."

"Manifest destiny" drove four generations of Americans through growth and expansion and freewheeling optimism until the Great Depression sobered us.

But there is now a new manifest destiny for us if we have the courage to grasp it. It is not reserved for Americans only but is a challenge for all humanity. It will be to our credit if we lead the way, but if we do not, some other nation surely will. It is an enterprise that would be shorn of discreditable aspects, since we will not have to spread outward at the expense of American Indians and Mexicans.

And once the first step is taken and we are out in the space of the Earth-moon system, no further step will require as great a hurdle, no later hill to be crossed will be as steep.

Manifest destiny will continue to exist, but the leaders will no longer be Americans or citizens of any earthly nation. The leaders will be the space settlers themselves.

The space settlers will be used to space travel; they will live with it every day. Exports and imports will, for them, mean space travel; construction and maintenance of the various structures in space will, for them, mean space travel; tourism will mean space travel.

They will be used to living in small, enclosed worlds with a carefully balanced and closely cycled ecology, with a limited population and with variable gravitational forces.

They will be able to build better and larger spaceships than we can since they won't have to fight an intense gravitational field, and they will be able to live in those spaceships for longer periods than we would, for obvious psychological reasons. A large spaceship would be very much like a home-world to them.

The space settlers would therefore be the cutting edge of future humanity, the explorers, the pioneers. It will be they who will carry humanity outward to the asteroid belt, where thousands of small worlds could be mined and converted into new homes. It will be they who will colonize the solar system generally.

There may well come a time when the space settlers will wish to be entirely free. Making use of advanced propulsion mechanisms and of nonsolar energy, they may decide to break loose, turn their settlements into independent worlds and wander off into interstellar space.

The solar system will then have "gone to seed" as an indefinite number of world-ships drift outward in every direction, their citizens learning to be at home in distant space, learning to use what dark bodies may exist there as material-replacement and energy sources. Eventually, they may reach other stars and find other intelligences and join them in a great brotherhood of all creatures capable of penetrating space.

There is the manifest destiny of humanity. We have been in the womb of Earth for millions of years and lived out the childhood of our species. It is time we moved out into near space and entered the adolescence of our development, so that someday we might move into far space and attain full adulthood.

That is, if we have the courage to follow that destiny, if we have no failure of nerve, if we do not fall back to a few more decades of quarreling with one another over the dying body of an Earth we are destroying and complete the process by destroying ourselves.

WRITING: Review

Writing Assignment: An Extended Essay

The *T-R-I-I-I-C* pattern discussed in Unit 9 can serve as a guideline for most of your college writing assignments. You could, of course, add as many *I*'s as necessary, increasing the scope of a paper to four to ten or more points of discussion. The more points of discussion, however, the more detailed your introduction should be. In other words, a twenty-page paper would generally have a one- or two-page introductory section. But no matter how long your paper might be, always try to incorporate the following characteristics of an effective paper.

1. The paper is adjusted to the needs of the reader.
2. The paper is clearly organized so that the reader can follow the discussion with ease.
3. All information included in the paper is correct, for any problems of accuracy might break the reader's trust in the writer.
4. The paper is unified, with all points of discussion relating directly to the thesis statement.
5. Each paragraph is unified, with all points of discussion relating directly to its topic sentence.
6. All points of discussion are fully developed.
7. Concrete descriptions and specific examples supplement discussion to assist reader comprehension.
8. The paper is carefully revised, edited, and proofread to create an effective, interesting communication.

Assignment

Write an essay using an extension of the *T-R-I-I-I-C* pattern. Check with your instructor for the approximate length.

TOPICS

1. Analyze your relationship with a brother or sister. Your reading audience: your parents.
2. Analyze your views on forgiveness of a person who has violated your trust. Your audience is your religious leader or a person over forty.

WIGNER

1. Analyze a source of energy other than wood that "self-righteous environmentalists" have overlooked or neglected. Intended audience: the Sierra Club.
2. Analyze the world in which you would live if this nation's forests were depleted. Intended audience: your classmates.
3. Discuss the possible effects on human life if the world's present sources of energy are depleted. Intended audience: the United Nations' General Assembly.

ASIMOV

1. Analyze the probable effects on human life if your city were without electricity for one month. Intended audience: local citizens.
2. Discuss the possible effects on human life if the world's population continues to increase. Intended audience: the United Nations' General Assembly.
3. Compare and contrast life in our modern society with life in a space colony. Intended audience: your classmates.

Brainstorming and Shaping

Complete the following data sheets. You may add as many points of discussion as you feel necessary to develop your thesis completely.

Data Sheet 10-1 Audience

A. General Topic: _____
B. Audience: _____
C. What Does My Audience Probably Know About My Topic?
   1.
   2.
   3.
   4.
   5.
   6.
   7.
D. What Does My Audience Probably Need to Have Reviewed?
   1.
   2.
   3.
   4.

(Continued on following page)

Data Sheet 10-1 *(Continued)*

E. What Does My Audience Probably Need to Know About My Topic?
   1.
   2.
   3.
   4.
   5.
   6.
   7.
F. What Are My Audience's Possible Biases or Attitudes on My Topic?
   1.
   2.
   3.
   4.

Data Sheet 10-2   Content

A. Specific Topic: _____
B. Purpose: _____
C. Audience:
D. Possible Major Points of Discussion:
   1.
   2.
   3.
   4.
   5.
   6.
   7.
   8.
   9.
   10.
   11.
   12.
E. Possible Minor Points of Discussion:
   1.
   2.
   3.
   4.

Data Sheet 10-3   Outline

Introduction: Materials to be included (you need not adhere to the following order):
  A. Thesis Statement: _____
  B. Restriction or Restatement: _____
  C. Introduction of Points of Discussion: _____
    1.
    2.
    3.
  D. Complementary Materials (you might want to include some of the material listed in item 5 of Data Sheet 10-1:
Section 2: First Point of Discussion:
  A. Topic Sentence: _____
  B. Restriction or Restatement: _____
  C. First Illustration: _____
  D. Second Illustration: _____
  E. Third Illustration: _____
Section 3: Second Point of Discussion:
  A. Topic Sentence: _____
  B. Restriction or Restatement: _____
  C. First Illustration: _____
  D. Second Illustration: _____
  E. Third Illustration: _____
Section 4: Third Point of Discussion:
  A. Topic Sentence: _____
  B. Restriction or Restatement: _____
  C. First Illustration: _____
  D. Second Illustration: _____
  E. Third Illustration: _____
Section 5: Conclusion:
  A. Topic Sentence: _____
  B. Discussion: _____

Revising the Essay

Always remember that writers and readers have precarious relationships: writers promise to inform, persuade, or entertain, to communicate clearly, and to treat their readers with respect; readers promise to be attentive and to evaluate the writers' evidence fairly. But if writers fail to honor their commitments by offering misinformation, by confusing readers through errors of grammar, spelling, or punctuation; by presenting awkward sentences; by failing to organize ideas in a way that readers can comprehend easily; or by insulting or boring readers; then readers may put aside the communication, dispute the evidence, or deny the writers' conclusions. In other words, once writers lose control of their material, they no longer are puppeteers; their readers take control.

Revision, then, involves content and its organization, two of the most important "strings" in the writer's performance. To insure that these two aspects of your essays are effective, that is, they work to fulfill your purpose in writing and to strengthen your relationship with your reader, you should ask yourself the following questions as you review your first drafts.

Basic Revision Questions
1. Is all my information accurate? Appropriate?
2. Is this information organized so that my reader can comprehend what I have said? Could I organize my paper so it would be more effective?
3. Do I have a clear, unified focus; that is, does my essay telescope in on one major theme?
4. Is my thesis statement limited, unified, precise, and clear?
5. Do my informative paragraphs and my conclusion have limited, unified, precise, and clear topic sentences?
6. Do I offer sufficient details, examples, or explanations so that my reader gains a complete understanding of what I am discussing?
7. Have I offered enough information and explanations in my introduction to develop audience interest and to prepare my reader for my discussion?
8. Does my conclusion round out my discussion effectively? Have I accidentally added new and distracting materials?

APPENDIX A
Supplementary Writing Lesson

Writing: Persuasion

Throughout this text, the writer/audience relationship has been emphasized, for if you wish to create effective communication, you must not only supply readers with information, but also adjust your discussion on the basis of their knowledge, opinions, and biases. In other words, you must manipulate content, organization, and style whenever you set out to inform or entertain. But when you hope to persuade your readers to act or not to act in a given situation, to accept your personal viewpoint on a particular issue, or even to buy a product, you may need to make many more adjustments in the presentation of materials. In fact, neglecting to control all aspects of a persuasive paper generally leads to failure. Your goal in persuasion, then, is to convince readers either to agree with your point of view or at least to consider your argument valid (supported by reliable evidence), even if they prefer not to act or believe as you hope they will.

The Writer's Authority

To be effective, all writers must control their materials, prove their authority on the topic under consideration, and adjust to their readers' emotional makeup. Although there has been little previous discussion on either of these last two aspects of writing, you have been taught to base your content on your audience's needs. In doing so you have, in fact, been proving your authority and adapting your discussion to the psychological characteristics of your audience. Yet, since the primary goal in each writing assignment has been to inform, most of your attention in the Brainstorming and Shaping sections has been focused on content. Now, however, as you approach the art of persuasion, you will probably have to make some changes in your approach.

In order to persuade effectively, you must first make certain that your readers see you as worthy of respect; that is, they must believe you are knowledgeable and ethical. If they doubt that you really know your materials well, they are apt to dismiss your entire argument; and if they feel you are offering them only information that proves your point and have eliminated contradictory materials, they will refuse to respond in a positive way. For example, do you usually place much trust in television commercials, a form of persuasion? Do you react to all political speeches in a similar way? Consider why you respond positively to some speeches, advertisements, or persuasive essays and letters, but negatively to others. These negative responses often derive from the lopsided arguments presented to you or from your distrust of the speaker or writer.

When writing persuasive essays and letters, then, you must first show your readers that you are trustworthy. Their good faith in you can be established in the following ways.

1. *By proving you are knowledgeable on your subject.*
   If you have a reputation as an authority on a subject, your name might be the only proof you need. For example, if you are a champion skier and are trying to persuade friends to buy a particular type of ski equipment, they will tend to accept your expertise without added comment. But if your readers do not know of your background, you will have to inform them of your experience and competition record or prove through your discussion that you know much about the sport.
2. *By proving you have researched your topic thoroughly.*
   Offering a bibliography and footnote citations shows readers that you have not only checked your information carefully, but also incorporated the information of experts into your discussion. Such citations are usually necessary in highly technical discussions.
3. *By proving you have played fair.*
   Intelligent readers expect you to consider all aspects of a topic. If you fail to discuss material that might weaken your argument, they will deny you their trust. Therefore, always bring up all aspects of a topic and then try to show whether or not they are pertinent to your view. For example, if you want to persuade readers to allow the construction of a nuclear reactor near your community, you must not neglect discussing reactor safety. Perhaps you might persuade readers that there are ample back-up systems to prevent radioactive leakage or that some safety must be sacrificed temporarily if this country hopes to lower its dependence on foreign oil.
4. *By proving you are not interested solely in personal gain.*
   Never allow readers to feel you will benefit more from your proposal than they will. For example, if you promote a certain candidate for mayor, don't let the readers think you will be rewarded for your efforts with an administrative position at city hall. Or if you are trying to sell a product, assure readers that the product is fairly priced, well made, and worth purchasing.

5. *By proving you respect the readers.*
   Don't threaten or belittle your readers. Don't, for example, tell them that this country will fall into a depression if they block the construction of nuclear reactors; suggest, rather, that this country would have a better chance at economic recovery if such reactors were built. Don't suggest they would be foolish to miss the opportunity to buy some merchandise on sale; suggest, instead, that summer is a good time to shop for ski equipment.

The Readers' Emotions

Another technique to consider when writing persuasions involves an appeal to emotions. Whereas writers of informative essays usually attempt to be very objective in their presentation of facts and ideas and avoid evoking the audience's sympathy, compassion, and biases, writers of persuasion often attempt to elicit emotional responses.

If, for example, you are seeking donations from a group of business people for a home for abused children, you might describe in great detail the bruises, broken bones, and scars of a battered three-year-old girl in order to bring out the group's compassion. Or if you hope to win support for your candidate for the Senate, you might talk about her home life, children, marriage, and charity work. These aspects of the woman's life have no direct bearing on her ability to be a good legislator, but they might reinforce the readers' belief in the American family and bring about kind feelings for the candidate.

Modifying Your Purpose in Writing

Before beginning to write a persuasive essay or letter, then, you must carefully evaluate your specific purpose, the characteristics of the reading audience, and all available information on your topic, seeking the best approach to draw out the desired reader reaction. Indeed, at times you may need to moderate your original purpose for writing, seeking a limited positive response rather than chancing a negative one.

For example, if you originally hoped to convince your political science teacher to raise your grade on a term paper but found out from his former students that he never changes grades, you might try to convince him to allow you to write another paper for extra credit. Or if you originally hoped to convince members of a local chapter of the Chamber of Commerce to sponsor a Christmas pageant at a neighborhood park but learned that this group's bylaws prohibit funding of religious events, you might try instead to encourage the donation at the pageant of gifts that would be distributed to needy children.

Organization and Tone

In planning your paper, you will also need to decide on an appropriate organization and tone so as to achieve the best possible results. You might wish, for example, to persuade fellow university students holding views similar to yours to act on a particular issue rather than to simply agree in relative silence. Both of you might resent a raise in tuition, but they merely gripe to each other about the administration's plans while you want them to sign petitions, attend a rally, or appear at a meeting of the school's Board of Regents. Your open letter to the student body to appear in the school newspaper could be very straightforward, stating your opinion strongly and encouraging classmates to act.

But if you were to write letters to persuade eighteen-year-old men who are fervently against this nation's military build-up to register for the draft, you would probably need to approach your topic indirectly. Announcing your purpose at the beginning of the letter might anger them, and then the letters might end up in the trash basket, unread. If, however, you slowly lead up to your thesis, appealing to their patriotism, informing them of imminent dangers to the nation's safety, and then discussing the failure of the army to attract sufficient enlistments, you might convince them of the validity of your views. They might still refuse to register for the draft, but you will have given them some positive ideas to consider; that is, you have put a wedge into their convictions that could possibly bring about future changes in their attitudes.

Reading: Persuasion

With some understanding of the art of persuasion, you should now take time to examine the persuasive works of other writers. Evaluate some advertisements in magazines, read several editorials in your school and local newspapers, and review the following essays in this text that contain some elements of persuasion.

"Mankind's Better Moments," Barbara Tuchman (Unit 3)
"Reflections on My Brother's Murder," David Finn (Unit 5)
"Memories of a Bilingual Education," Richard Rodriguez (Unit 7)
"Pomp and Civil Engineering," Samuel C. Florman (Unit 7)
"Beware the Intellectual," Eric Hoffer (Unit 9)
"Why Man Explores #2," Norman Cousins (Unit 9)

As you read, examine first the theses and points of view expressed in the editorials or essays and then evaluate the ways the authors established their authority and appealed to your emotions. Does understanding the techniques used in the essays alter your reactions? Consider the possible reasons for your positive or negative responses.

Assignment

There are three options in this writing assignment: a persuasive letter to your local newspaper in response to a recent editorial; a persuasive essay directed at an audience that is in general agreement with your point of view; and a persuasive essay directed at an audience that is in general *dis*agreement with your point of view. Your teacher will assign the specific format and essay length for you to follow, but you should study all three presentations for use in other situations.

Option 1:
A Persuasive Letter to the Editors of a Newspaper

Since your reading audience, the readers of a newspaper, includes people of different educational, financial, and ethnic backgrounds, you will need to take a middle stance, that is, one that is neither too straightforward nor too indirect. For your ideas to be evaluated fairly, you will need to argue politely and offer concrete information. Because of space restrictions in most newspapers, you should keep your letter to less than 500 words, and shorter if possible. This brevity forces you to state your thesis immediately and then either to back up your points with concrete information or to refute (argue against) the newspaper's thesis by the presentation of materials that contradict it. You must, in either case, establish your authority on the topic and may arouse the emotions of both the editors and other readers of the paper.

Example: Option 1
Dear Editor:
Your recent editorial backing the imposition of parking fees at the county zoo has prompted me to reply. To impose such charges will limit attendance at the zoo and block access to the city's poor. Certainly there must be other available ways to raise funds for the construction of new zoo exhibits and the acquisition of new animal species. — THESIS

    The county zoo has been one of the last free educational and recreational facilities within the area. Entrance fees are now required at our art and natural science museums, public tennis courts, and botanical gardens. Parking fees are paid at county beaches, the local observatory, and the county fairgrounds. To now impose parking fees of two dollars per car at the zoo not only will limit the number of times the average young family can afford to come, but also will probably keep out all our underprivileged children, those who desperately need an opportunity to have an outing away from the ghettoes and to learn about the animals of the world. It appears that the local government counts dollars, not young lives. — AUTHORITY (SHOWS KNOWLEDGE OF SUBJECT) / APPEAL TO EMOTIONS

    Yet if the county needs added resources to support our expanding zoo, why doesn't it impose an excise tax on the sale of liquor, wine, and beer? Why doesn't it mount a campaign for donations for new buildings or ask citizens to

AUTHORITY (SHOWS WRITER HAS NOTHING PERSONAL TO GAIN AND IS RESPONSIVE TO OTHERS)

APPEAL TO EMOTIONS

"adopt" an animal by funding its purchase or upkeep? Perhaps charging a fee for parking takes less effort, but our children are relying on us. To help our children, then, I hereby pledge to donate a dime to the zoo for every alcoholic drink I take and have already mailed the zoo twenty-five dollars to cover last year's glasses of wine. I challenge my fellow citizens to follow suit. Let's give the zoo back to all our children!

Option 2: A Persuasive Essay Directed at an Audience in General Agreement with Your Views

In this type of persuasive essay, you would state your thesis and offer some general background information on the issue to be discussed in the first paragraph. In the following sections of the essay, you would explain the situation thoroughly and then make an emotional appeal to your readers, urging them to action.

Section 1: Thesis statement and background information.
Section 2: Discussion of the situation.
Section 3: A call to action.

Example: Option 2

BACKGROUND INFORMATION

THESIS

AUTHORITY (A FELLOW STUDENT)

BACKGROUND

The university's administration announced last week that it is considering raising our tuition from $100 per unit to $150 per unit. According to Chancellor Adams, this increase has become necessary because of the effects of inflation on the university's operating budget. The cost of maintaining buildings, labs, and campus lawns and gardens has doubled since 1975, faculty salaries must be raised to keep them on par with the rising cost of living, and student facilities such as counseling and health-care offices must be emphasized. While acknowledging that the university faces difficult fiscal problems, I insist that tuition cannot be increased.

We students, as well as the university, are confronted by economic problems. Our dorm fees have gone up from $2,500 a year to $3,000 a year; books and supplies have increased 10 percent in cost since 1979; supplementary health-care fees have been charged for the first time in the school's history; and lab fees in the art and science departments have more than doubled since 1979. Those of us who live off campus must also pay escalated prices for gasoline and car expenses and $75 a year for on-campus parking, a rise of $25 over last year. And finally, all of us need clothes and shoes, the prices of which have increased dramatically within the past few years. To add another $25 per unit for tuition would mean an extra $1,500 per year for those of us who carry the standard fifteen units per semester.

If the university or government were to increase the number of available scholarships, make more on-campus jobs available, or provide increased loans, perhaps most of us could sustain a tuition hike. But fewer scholarships have been available this year than last, and university budget cuts have reduced the number of available work-study jobs. Even the state and federal governments have turned away from our needs by cutting the size and number of loan guarantees. The question then arises: where can we get the extra $1,500 a year? Our parents? Not really. Most of them are also suffering economic hardships during the current inflationary period. No, increased tuition means the end of education for many of us.

DISCUSSION OF SITUATION

But we need not sit back and simply wait for the administration to deny us our future. We must fight and protest and stand up to those who try to balance the budget by stamping out a portion of the student body. Write letters of protest to the Chancellor, the alumni associations, and members of the Board of Regents! Sign our protest petitions that are to be sent to the administration's finance committee! And come — all of you — to the scheduled Board of Regents meeting, Tuesday, December 12, at 7:00 p.m. in Bishop Hall. Let us be united and fight! Let us insist on our right to an education!

CALL TO ACTION

Option 3:
A Persuasive Essay Directed at an Audience in General Disagreement with Your Views

The most difficult type of persuasive writing involves trying to convince people who disagree with you to accept at least some of your views. Assuming readers have sound reasons to support their own position, you must somehow create an atmosphere that will enable them to evaluate your comments fairly. If, however, they feel at all threatened by your presentation or think you are not playing entirely fair with them, that is, that you are manipulating information to your own advantage, they will either debate your points of discussion or dismiss your argument entirely.* If, for example, you bluntly tell readers who favor freedom of abortion that to abort a fetus is to murder it, they will find

---

* Adapted from theories outlined in Richard E. Young, Alton L. Becker, and Kenneth L. Pike, *Rhetoric: Discovery and Change* (New York: Harcourt, Brace, and World, 1970).

your essay offensive and stop reading. Or if you propose an increase in sales taxes to finance better public transportation but fail to mention that bond issues will also be needed, they might deny your authority and refuse to consider your views with open minds.

Persuading this type of reader thus requires you to show evidence of your knowledge and good faith. Often, in fact, you will need to propose a compromise acceptable to both of you. To reach such a compromise, you must first acknowledge the strengths of the reader's position as well as the validity of your own views and then go on to suggest ways the two can work together. This compromise, rather than a call to action, closes out your discussion.

Section 1: Thesis statement treating the general topic of discussion and background information on the situation.
Section 2: A review of the readers' views on the situation and an acknowledgment of their strong points.
Section 3: A review of your views with an emphasis on your strongest points.
Section 4: Proposal of a compromise.

Example: Option 3

THESIS

Chancellor Adams announced this week that the university is considering a raise in tuition from $100 per unit to $150 per unit, to become effective at the beginning of the fall term. The student body's first reaction was, of course, fear and anger, but, now that it has had time to evaluate the issue fairly, it has asked me, as senior class president, to present its views to the Board of Regents.

BACKGROUND AND
SHOW OF GOOD
FAITH AND AUTHORITY

READERS' VIEWS

All of us — students, faculty, and administrators — have been confronted by economic hardships brought about by the current inflationary period. We students can thus appreciate the budgetary problems facing the university. To continue in existence, the school must keep buildings, classrooms, labs, and campus areas in good repair and so must meet the escalating costs of materials, equipment, and salaries of the maintenance departments. To maintain the school's high academic standards and its reputation for excellence, it not only must increase faculty salaries according to the cost-of-living index, but also match faculty salaries at other universities in order to recruit promising young professors. And finally, the university needs to improve counseling and on-campus health facilities with monies allocated three years ago; these funds, however, no longer are sufficient to meet construction costs. In reviewing the school's operating expenses, student body officers have found little room for budget cuts and have indeed become aware of what increases are necessary.

But students also have faced increased financial burdens within the past few years. Our dorm fees have risen 20 percent, our books and school supplies have gone up 10 percent, and we have had to pay new fees for on-campus health services, something we never have had to do in previous years. Additionally, we have had to meet rising transportation costs for both our personal cars and public busses. Finally, the cost of clothing, food, insurance, and recreation has jumped far faster than have our salaries from our part-time jobs. Now, with a possible $50-a-unit increase in tuition, many of us will have to transfer to less expensive schools or to quit college entirely. WRITER'S VIEW

Although our two situations may seem incompatible, we should be able to reach some type of compromise. Most students polled feel that they could probably afford a modest increase in tuition, perhaps $10 per unit. Other monies needed by the university could be raised through a joint effort of the student body and the administration. For example, special solicitations of our neighborhood businesses, alumni societies, and local philanthropists should bring in some additional revenues. Furthermore, the student council has offered to sponsor a movie preview to fund the needed expansion of counseling and health facilities. Finally, student body officers have offered to meet with Board members to seek new sources of income. If we work together, with mutual respect and mutual understanding, we should be able to survive the current financial crisis in an equitable way. Our education and our university are too important to both of us to allow our differences to block communication. COMPROMISE

TOPICS

OPTION 1
Write a letter arguing against a view expressed in a recent editorial in your city's newspaper. Audience: readers of "Letters to the Editor."

OPTION 2
Write a persuasive essay to urge your readers to act on a certain situation. Possible topics include a reduction in classes being offered, a fund-raising affair, and a campaign for office. Audience: classmates at your school.

OPTION 3
Write a persuasive essay concerning a local, state, or national situation and present a compromise between your views and the views of your reader. Pos-

sible topics include tax increases; reduced funding for education, health, or recreation; or proposed legislation. Audience: a group with views very different from yours.

Brainstorming and Shaping

Fill out the following data sheets that have been constructed to assist you in setting up a persuasive argument. After they are completed, review the materials on each sheet before you decide upon the most effective approach to take for your given audience. Remember, if your audience has beliefs similar to yours, you can adopt a straightforward approach to your topic and lead up to an appeal to action. If, however, your audience disagrees with your basic point of view, you should plan out an appropriate compromise that has a good chance of being accepted.

Date Sheet A-1   Audience

A. Topic: _____
B. Audience: _____
C. What are my readers' probable opinions (intellectual responses) on the issue under discussion?
   1.
   2.
   3.
   4.
   5.
D. What are my readers' biases (emotional responses) about the issue?
   1.
   2.
   3.
E. What are the general characteristics of my readers?
   1.
   2.
   3.
   4.

Data Sheet A-2   Writer

A. What are my opinions about the situation under discussion?
   1.
   2.
   3.
   4.
   5.
B. What are my biases about the issue?
   1.
   2.
   3.
C. What could I hope to persuade my audience to do or believe? _____

D. If necessary, what compromise would I accept? _____

E. The specific purpose of my persuasive paper based upon my evaluation of the audience's characteristics, biases, and opinions. _____

After you have completed the data sheets, outline your paper and write a first draft.

Revising and Editing

When you have completed the first draft of your persuasive paper, check it over to see if you have followed the assigned format, adjusted your persuasion to your audience's needs and personality, and proven your authority on the issue at hand. Then proceed to revise and edit the paper according to the principles discussed in Units 1–10.

APPENDIX B
Additional Cloze Exercises

With a knowledge of the distinct functions of each part of speech, you should be better able to anticipate words and meaning as you read. You should also be able to fixate your eyes on large sections of sentences since you now understand the possible positions within a sentence of some of these types of words. Now you must read, read, and read again, because the more you read, the more effective your skill will become. You should also occasionally review this book's reading selection discussions to reinforce your language awareness. In addition, you should review the discussions on sentence structure and word choice in the Editing section of each unit. Remember that an understanding of the structure of the English language; an ability to anticipate the meaning of new words through context; and a knowledge of roots, prefixes, and suffixes will help you to read faster and to comprehend the reading material more fully.

In the following Cloze exercises, any of the seven parts of speech in the English language may have been deleted. Fill in the spaces with appropriate words. Try to anticipate words from context and to fixate your eyes on units of meaning. Time yourself. If you take more than ten minutes for each exercise, you need to review the preceding units. Be prepared to defend your word choices during class discussions on these exercises.

EXERCISE 1

One misleading idea that _____ students have is that _____ should aim for the _____ reading speed no matter _____ they read, whether it _____ a newspaper, a popular _____, a novel picked up _____ the market, an assigned _____ for reading outside class, _____ a textbook. These students _____ self-critical when they _____ themselves reading their college _____ more slowly than when _____ for recreation. They think _____ is wrong. But as

449

_____ have learned in this _____, your purpose or intention _____ reading determines your reading _____. If your intention is _____ relax and enjoy yourself _____ a magazine or a _____, you will probably read _____ than you will read _____ class-assigned book or _____. And this difference in _____ speed is not only _____, but also is proper. _____ remember that your reading _____ will depend on your _____ in reading and in _____ difficulty of the reading material.

EXERCISE 2

In this troubled world of ours, pessimism seems to have won the day. But we would do _____ to recall some of _____ positive and even admirable _____ of the human race. _____ hear very little of _____ lately. Ours is not _____ time of self-esteem or _____ as was, for instance, _____ 19th century, whose self-esteem _____ be seen oozing from _____ portraits. Victorians, especially the _____, pictured themselves as erect, _____, and splendidly handsome. Our _____ looks more like Woody _____ or a character from _____ play. Amid a mass _____, we see our species — _____ cause — as functioning very badly, _____ blunders when not knaves, _____ violent, ignoble, corrupt, inept, _____ of mastering the forces _____ threaten us, weakly subject _____ our worst instincts; in _____ decadent.

— Adapted from Tuchman, *"Mankind's Better Moments"*

EXERCISE 3

I'm sandwiched in silence. My father _____ not a talker and _____ is my son. Talking _____ to be going out _____ style and this worries _____, because I'm used to _____. My generation talked all _____ time. We thought we _____ change the entire world _____ talk. Talking shaped our _____, marked them around the _____ and mouth, sharpened, mobilized, _____ grooved them. We licked _____ lips with speech. You _____ parse our faces. We _____ simple, declarative, compound-sentence _____. Talk was our life _____.

— Adapted from Broyard, *"The Silent Generation: An Essay"*

EXERCISE 4

When Captain John Smith _____ his little band of _____ arrived off the coast _____ Virginia 372 years ago, _____ confronted a wilderness so _____ that it was said _____ squirrel could travel from _____ Atlantic to the prairie's _____ without ever once touching _____. For nearly three centuries _____ that, the forests were _____ lavishly and wastefully; _____ Americans can thank their _____ that a full 70 percent _____ that forest land still _____. Our oil is fast _____, but our trees mostly _____, a natural resource of _____ value.

— Adapted from Wigner, *"America's Green Gold"*

EXERCISE 5

The first paragraph of _____ essay should act as _____ introduction to your essay's _____. Your thesis statement can _____ at any point in _____ paragraph, but it must _____ limited, clear, precise, and _____ in the same way _____ your topic sentences are _____. Here, however, the extent _____ your topic will be _____ as you will have _____ paragraphs to develop your _____ of discussion. Yet the _____ paragraph must include more _____ a thesis statement. It _____ include any material necessary _____ set up your discussion _____ to develop reader interest. _____ ways to develop the paragraph _____ offering a discussion of _____ historical background to your _____, offering a discussion of _____ contemporary interest in your _____, and introducing your points _____ discussion.

APPENDIX C
Taking Lecture Notes

Why Take Notes?

The ability to take good notes is an invaluable study skill since so many college courses involve lectures. Some professors lecture on materials not readily found in textbooks; other professors use their lectures to supplement the assigned textbooks with important additional information. You should thus think of your lecture notes as another type of "textbook," an accurately handwritten record of the teacher's ideas. Later you will study this record in order to recapture and understand the ideas. Students who think they can simply listen without taking notes will find, if they are like most people, that within twenty-four hours they have forgotten half of what they "learned."

Setting Up the Notebook

1. *Prepare a separate notebook* or section for each course. Always use a standard-size notebook with 8½ x 11" pages. This size allows plenty of room so that your writing will be easy to read. Although many students prefer to use spiral notebooks, they should consider using a large loose-leaf notebook because of the following advantages.
    a. It enables you to insert any supplementary handouts corresponding with the lecture.
    b. It enables you to spread out the pages to organize the material in significant ways when you begin studying for tests.
    c. It allows you to add your own study sheets in topical or chronological order when you review.
2. *Prepare the pages* according to the system developed at the Cornell University Study Center. Draw a vertical line 2½ inches from the left edge of each sheet. This margin will become the *recall* column for key words and phrases

when you review. Take notes to the right of the line. This format has become so widely accepted that many college bookstores now stock three-ring paper with this type of margin.
3. *Label* each day's set of notes. At the top of the first page, write the date and topic. On each subsequent page, mark the date and page number. This method prevents loss or mix-up of notes.
4. *Write in ink* on one side of the page only. Not only will the notes be longer-lasting and more legible, but you will have the reverse side to add your notes — for example, supplementary details from textbooks or outlines and study guides.

Listening

Effective listening, like effective studying, is an active not a passive process. You must deliberately *intend* to listen and remain alert. The following suggestions can help you activate the listening process.

1. *Prepare* to listen well.
    a. If the lecture supplements or correlates with the textbook, be sure to read the assignment before going to class; even if you don't completely understand the assignment, you will be more alert and will pick up the items with which you are already somewhat familiar.
    b. Before going to class, review the notes from the preceding lecture so that you'll have some sense of continuity. Also, speculate on some points that may be covered in the new lecture.
2. Consciously assume a physical position of *alertness* — if you slump physically you will probably slump mentally. Some students find that they pay closer attention if they sit near the lecturer. For one thing, they are not so easily distracted by noticing a classmate's new hairdo or by trying to overhear a whispered conversation in front of them. For another, they are too embarrassed to "drift" if they are sitting close to the teacher!
3. *Do not be distracted* by the lecturer's method of delivery, accent, or mannerisms. Concentrate on what is said, not on how it is said.
4. If and when it is appropriate to do so, *ask a question*. Although some lecturers follow a time schedule that doesn't allow for questions, others encourage them. One way to formulate useful questions is to note unclear points as you read the assignment. Then if a point is not clarified in the lecture, you can ask about it. Don't feel embarrassed to ask; probably if you don't understand, others don't either.

Taking Notes in Class

1. Discipline yourself to take *legible* notes; do not plan to rewrite them. Although some students feel more secure if they recopy or type their notes,

this process is often only mechanical and wastes time. Legible writing requires allowing enough space between letters. Printing or even a combination of script and printing, can also be helpful.
2. Don't try to take notes in *precise outline form,* using Roman numerals, capital letters, Arabic numerals, and small letters. In fact, just trying to remember which capital letter or Roman numeral comes next can slow down your notetaking.
   a. Record your notes in simple paragraph form if that method is appropriate for a rather rambling lecture style.
   b. Use an informal outline form if the lecture is reasonably well organized.

   Main points begin at the margin.
      Secondary points or supporting materials are indented.
         Additional subordinate material or examples are indented further.

   c. Leave a line or two when the lecturer moves from one concept, idea, or topic to another. Even if you have been taught *waste not, want not,* notetaking is *not* the place to skimp on using paper! In fact, under pressure it is not always possible to tell the difference between a main point and a secondary point; when in doubt, skip lines. You can always link the material later.
3. Devise your own set of *abbreviations* to give you extra time to listen and to write. But do *not* use so many abbreviations that you won't be able to decipher your notes weeks later.
   a. One basic rule is to abbreviate a special term that will be repeated throughout a lecture. For example, if the word *government* will probably recur, write *govt.* — *government* at the top of the page of first use and use the abbreviation thereafter.
   b. Another rule is to include some commonly used abbreviations.

& — and	cont. — continued
w/ — with	mo. — month, monthly
co. — company	∴ — therefore
etc. — and so forth	intro. — introduction
e.g. — for example	yr. — year
i.e. — that is	wk. — week

4. Use *symbols* to mark important points to remember later, such as an asterisk★, arrow, underline, double or triple underline, square box, brackets, circled question mark. Also, write down the teacher's example and mark it *Ex.* Examples are important because they often clarify abstract ideas. And if a student contributes an example, include it and mark it *St. Ex.,* because often the simplicity of a student's example clarifies a point even more than the teacher's example does. Also, if a discussion takes place, record it

briefly, marked *Disc.*, since it may later help you to recall the flow and development of the lecture.
5. Listen and watch for important *signals* that indicate emphasis. These types of clues not only mean that something should be included in your notes, but also that it might be on the test. Be aware of the following techniques used by lecturers.
   a. They write on the board. Whenever the teacher writes something on the board, write it down and mark it *B* so that when you review for the test, you'll remember that it was emphasized.
   b. They use repetition. Whenever the teacher repeats a statement, record and underline it or mark it with a special symbol such as *R*.
   c. They use voice signals. Whenever the teacher's voice slows down or becomes louder, write down the exact words. The pause is another important form of emphasis and one that is sometimes used together with repetition. The speaker may pause both before and after making a statement and then repeat the statement.
   d. They use key words and introductory phrases. The lecturer may use numbers with *nouns*, such as, "There are three main *characteristics* . . ." or "There are four *steps* in this process. . . ." or "Two important *causes* were. . . ." Be sure to write down the statements that follow these emphasis words. The following list includes some of the signal words to listen for and mark for special attention when you review for tests (refer to the Reading Strategies section in Unit 6 for other important signal words).

advantages of/in	categories of
benefits of/in	characteristics of
criticism of	description of
disadvantages of/in	kinds of
causes (of)	parts of/in
effects of	types of
results	history of
comparison(s) between	function(s) of
similarities between	methods of
contrast(s) between	parts of/in
difference(s) between	purposes of/in
	steps in
	uses of/for

Listen also for phrases such as

The basic idea here is . . .

Pay special attention to . . .

Don't overlook . . .

Consider that . . .

Don't forget that . . .

The main point to remember . . .

6. Leave *blank spaces* for words, phrases, or statements you miss. Right after the lecture ask the instructor or a classmate to help you fill in whatever you have missed.
7. *Mark off any assignments* that are given within the lecture. The symbol used should be outstanding so that you don't miss it later. Also, note and mark any books or other references mentioned; these can be valuable guides to further reading.
8. Pay as *close attention* at the end of a lecture as at the beginning. Of course, you should arrive on time; the teacher may open the lecture by announcing a quiz or postponing an assignment. And continue taking notes until the lecture ends; sometimes the teacher summarizes the topic or gives a helpful overview that ties loose ends together.

After the Lecture

To avoid forgetting the material recorded during the lecture, you should read through your notes as soon as possible after class. Underline or box in the main ideas. Then use the left margin *recall* column to jot down key words or phrases related to the ideas on the right. Next, to implant the lecture firmly in your mind, *recite* aloud, using the recall column as a guide. Using this process makes you an active rather than passive student; it also gives you a head start on your exam study!

APPENDIX D

Latin and Greek Prefixes, Suffixes, and Roots Commonly Used in Technical Vocabulary

Table D-1 Latin Prefixes and Suffixes

Latin Element	Meaning	Scientific Word
aqua-, aqui-	water	aquiculture
bi-	two	bipodal
centrum-	center	centrifugal
epi-	upon	epidermis
homo- (contrast with Greek *homo* below)	human	*Homo sapiens*
inter-	between	intermolecular
intra-	among	intramolecular
-ped, -pod	foot	quadruped
per-	through	permeable
peri-	around	peristalsis
semi-	half	semiotic
spir-	breathe	spiracle
sub-	under	subglacial
super-	above, in addition	superfetation
trans-	across, through	transhumance

Table D-2 Greek Prefixes and Suffixes

Greek Element	Meaning	Scientific Word
anthropo-	human	anthropogenic
astro-	star	astrophere
auto-	self	autosome
bio-	life	bionomics
centro-	center	centromere
chromo-	color	chromosomes
cosmo-	world, universe	cosmogeny
cyto-	cell	cytogenetics
eu-	well, true	euglena
gen-	origin, people	genetics
hetero-	other, difference	heterosis
homo-, hom-	same	homomorphic
hydro-	water	hydrostatic
hyper-	too many	hyperostasis
iso-	same	isometry
lith-	stone, rock	lithophyte
-logy	study	geology
lumin-	light	luminance
micro-	very small	microcyte
neura-	nerve, nervous system	neuraxon
-onomy	science	taxonomy
pathos-	suffering	pathogenic
pneumo-	lung, respiratory organ	pneumonic
-philous	having affinity for	acidophilous
photo-	light	photosynthesis
-phyll, -phy	leaf	chlorophyll
-plasia, -plasy	development, formation	homoplasy
-plasm	formative material	protoplasm
proteo-	protein	proteolysis
pseudo-	false	pseudomorph
-stasis	slowing; stable	homeostasis
thermo-	heat	thermotaxis

APPENDIX D LATIN AND GREEK PREFIXES, SUFFIXES, AND ROOTS

Table D-3 Greek Number Elements

Greek Number Elements	Meaning	Scientific Term
centi	hundred	centimeter
di, bi	two	dicotyledon, biceps
dica, deci	ten	dicarboxylic, decimeter
hemi	half	hemisphere
hept	seven	heptahedron
hex	six	hexachloride
kilo, milli	thousand	kilometer, millimeter
mono, uni	one	monad, unicellular
multi	many	multicellular
nona	nine	nonagon
oct, octa, octo	eight	octamerous
omni	all	omnivore
pent	five	pentamerous
poly	many, excessive	polyzoic
tertr, quadr	four	tetrad, quadrant
tri	three	trisulfide

Table D-4 Greek and Latin Roots

Root	Meaning	Example	Definition
aer	air	aerospace	pertaining to science of flight
agrari, agri	land	agriculture	science, art, business of farming
ann	year	annual	yearly
aqua	water	aquatic	having to do with water
arche	main, beginning	architect	planner, deviser
belli	war	bellicose	warlike
cent	hundred	century	one hundred years
chronos	time	chronological	referring to events in order of time
cor, cordis	heart	cordial	hearty, warm, sincere
cratos	rule, strength	democratic	pertaining to rule by the people
demos	people	democracy	rule of people
deus	god	deicide	killing of a god
ego	I	egotism	large sense of self-importance
gen(er)	born	gender	classification of sex
geo	earth	geography	study of the earth
homo	like	homogeneous	like, similar
hydro	water	hydraulics	science of behavior of fluids
ignis	fire	ignite	to set fire to
junctum	join	junction	point of joining
micro	small	microscopic	extremely small
mor, mort	to die	mortuary	place for preparing dead bodies
multus	much, many	multiple	very many
octo	eight	octagon	eight-sided figure
pan	every, all	pantheon	all the gods of a people
pater	father	paternal	fatherly
pathy	feeling	pathetic	causing or arousing pity
philos	lover, friend	philanthropic	having love for mankind, generous
primus	first	prime	of the first importance
pseudos	false	pseudonym	false name
psyche	mind, soul	psychology	study of the mind's workings
pugno	fight	pugnacity	state of liking to fight
sophos	wise	philosophy	love of wisdom
totus	entire	total	all, add, sum
verto	to turn	divert	to turn away
via	by way of	viaduct	arches used to carry a road

CREDITS *(Continued from page iv)*

Gwendolyn Brooks, "Helen" from "Maud Martha" in *The World of Gwendolyn Brooks*. Copyright 1951 by The Curtis Publishing Company. Copyright 1953 by Gwendolyn Brooks Blakely. Reprinted by permission of Harper & Row, Publishers, Inc.

Anatole Broyard, "The Silent Generation: An Essay," *The New York Times*. © 1980 by The New York Times Company. Reprinted by permission.

Laurence Cherry, excerpted from "The Magic of Memory" by permission of the author. This material originally appeared in *Science Digest*, Special Edition (Summer 1980).

Agatha Christie, reprinted by permission of Dodd, Mead & Company, Inc. and Hughes Massie Limited from *An Autobiography* by Agatha Christie. Copyright © 1977 by Agatha Christie Limited.

Consumer Reports, "Vegetarianism." Copyright 1980 by Consumers Union of United States, Inc., Mount Vernon, NY 10550. Adapted by permission from *Consumer Reports*, June 1980.

Norman Cousins, "Man Explores." From Omni (November 1981). Adapted from *Why Man Explores*, published by the U.S. Government Printing Office, Washington, D.C.

Joan Didion, "In the Islands" from *The White Album* by Joan Didion. Copyright © 1979 by Joan Didion. Reprinted by permission of Simon & Schuster, a Division of Gulf & Western Corporation.

David Fenn, "Reflections on My Brother's Murder," *Saturday Review* (May 1980). Copyright © 1980 by *Saturday Review*. All rights reserved. Reprinted by permission.

Samuel C. Florman, "Pomp and Civil Engineering." Copyright © 1979 by Harper's Magazine. All rights reserved. Reprinted from the November 1979 issue by special permission.

Ellen Goodman, "Your Better Supermother" from *Close to Home* by Ellen Goodman. Copyright © 1979 by The Washington Post Company. Reprinted by permission of Simon & Schuster, a Division of Gulf & Western Corporation.

George H. Haas, excerpted by permission of the author from "Confessions of a City Woodcutter," *Quest/79* (October 1979).

John Heminway, from "The Other Side of Bull Mountain," *Quest/80* (April 1980). Reprinted by permission of the Author and his Agents, Raines & Raines. Copyright © 1980 by John Heminway.

Eric Hoffer, "Beware the Intellectuals," *Saturday Review* (24 November 1979). Copyright © 1979 by *Saturday Review*. All rights reserved. Reprinted by permission.

Evan Jones, "Indian Food: A Rich Harvest," *Saturday Review* (25 November 1978). Copyright © 1978 by *Saturday Review*. All rights reserved. Reprinted by permission.

John Leo, excerpt from "Memory: The Unreliable Witness." Copyright 1980 Time Inc. Reprinted by permission from *Time* (5 January 1981).

Philip Morrison, "Man Explores." From *Omni* (November 1981). Adapted from *Why Man Explores*, published by the U.S. Government Printing Office, Washington, D.C.

Paul O'Neil, excerpted from "The Modernized Ritual of Rodeo," *Smithsonian* Magazine (1979) by permission of the author.

John E. Pfeiffer, excerpted from "The Mysterious Rise and Decline of Monte Albon," *Smithsonian* Magazine (February 1980) by permission of the author.

J. B. Priestley, "Wrong 'Ism" from *The Moment and Other Pieces* (London: Heinemann, 1966). © J. B. Priestley 1966. Reprinted by permission.

Richard Rodriguez, "Memories of a Bilingual Education," which appeared in *American Educator/American Teacher*, a publication of the American Federation of Teachers, and in slightly altered form in *Hunger of Memory* by Richard Rodriguez. Copyright © 1981 by Richard Rodriguez. Reprinted by permission of David R. Godine, Publisher.

Robert P. Solomon, "We Better Not Make Book on U.S. Literacy." First appeared in

The Los Angeles Times (4 August 1980). Reprinted by permission of the author.

Barbara Tuchman, "Mankind's Better Moments," *American Scholar* (Autumn 1980). Reprinted by permission of Russell & Volkening as agents for the author. Copyright © 1980 by Barbara Tuchman.

Carll Tucker, "Fear of Dearth," *Saturday Review* (27 October 1979). Copyright © 1979 by *Saturday Review*. All rights reserved. Reprinted by permission.

Frank Waters, "Rain Song" from *The Book of the Hopi* by Frank Waters. Copyright © 1963 by Frank Waters. Reprinted by permission of Viking Penguin Inc.

Webster's New Collegiate Dictionary, definition of *innocent*. By permission. © 1974 by G. & C. Merriam Co., Publishers of the Merriam-Webster Dictionaries.

John H. White, Jr., from "Rails: From Old World to New" by John H. White, Jr. from *The Smithsonian Book of Invention*, © 1978 Smithsonian Institution. Reprinted by permission.

Kathleen K. Wigner, "America's Green Gold," *Forbes* (24 December 1979). Reprinted by permission.

Index

Abbreviations, 455
Abstract words, 64–68
Active voice, 151–153, 402–403
Adjectives
  adjective clause, 202–207
  function, 65–67, 218–219
  participles, 301–304
  placement, 157–158, 218–219
  relative, 66–67
Adverbs, 72–73, 202–205, 250–251, 313–315
Affixes. *See also* Roots
  prefixes, 219–221, 459–461
  suffixes, 262–264, 459–461
"America's Green Gold," 417–425
Analogy, 148
Analysis (writing), 240–248, 288–300, 387–395
Anticipation (reading), 128–129
Apostrophes, 352–353
Argument/discussion (reading), 360–361
Asimov, Isaac (essay), 426–430
Audience, 22–24, 58–59, 102–105, 145–146, 185–191, 240–243, 289–290, 360, 431, 437–446. *See also* Preface, Brainstorming, Revision, and Data sheets
Autobiography (Christie), 8–10
Auxiliary verbs, 24–26, 302

Basalla, George (essay), 378–386
"Beware the Intellectual," 372–377
Bound modifiers, 208–210
Brainstorming, 21–22, 60–62, 109, 149–150, 194–196, 244–248, 293–298, 346, 390–395, 432–434, 446–447
Brandt, Anthony (essay), 96–101
Brooks, Gwendolyn (excerpt), 11–14
Broyard, Anatole (essay), 222–225

Capitalization, 304–307
Cause/effect
  reading selections
    Florman, 268–273; Rodriquez, 274–287, Tucker, 265–267
  reading, 79
  transitional signals, 216
  writing, 147, 288–300
Character (reading), 7
Cherry, Laurence (essay), 83–87
Christie, Agatha (excerpt), 8–10
Clarity, 103–105, 252–254
Clauses
  adjective clause, 202–207
  adverbial clause, 204
  bound/restrictive, 208–210
  dependent, 155–159, 202–207
  free/nonrestrictive, 208–210
  independent, 26–30, 155–159

465

Clauses (*cont.*)
    noun clauses, 349–352
    relative, 202–207
    subordinate, 155–159, 202–207
Cloze exercises, 128–129, 164–166, 218–219, 260–262, 313–315, 362–364, 449–451
Cohesion, 404–405. *See also* Transitionals
Colloquial language, 198–199
Colon, 408–409
Comma, 71–75, 117–123, 159–161, 207–210, 256–258
Comma splice, 117–119
Comparisons
    comparison words, 215–216
    contrast words, 216
    simile, 67–68
    metaphor, 67–68
Comparison/contrast essay
    reading selections
        Broyard, 222–225; O'Neil, 232–239; White, 226–231
    reading, 78
    signal words, 215–216
    writing, 147, 240–248
Complex sentence. *See* Subordination *and* Relative clauses
Compound sentences. *see* Coordination
Conclusions, 388–389.
Concrete diction, 64–68
"Confessions of a City Woodcutter," 137–144
Conjunctions, 71, 116–118, 120, 128–129, 165–166
Connotation, 113–116
Context clues (vocabulary), 1–6, 80–82
Contractions, 352–353
Controlling ideas (reading), 33–39
Coordination, 68–75, 254
Coordinators, 71, 116–118, 120, 128–129, 165–166
Cousins, Norman (essay), 369–371

Dangling modifiers. *See* Adjectives *and* Adverbs
Dash, 407–408

Data sheets
    audience, 110–111, 194, 244–245, 293, 391–392, 432–433, 440
    content, 245–247, 295–298, 392–393, 433–434, 447
Definition
    reading selections
        Goodman, 131–133; Haas, 136–144; Morrison, 134–135
    reading, 4–6, 80
    writing, 145–150
Demonstrative pronouns. *See* Pronouns
Denotation, 113–116
Dependent clauses. *See* Clauses
Description
    essay, 58–60
    reading selections
        Heminway, 50–57; Thoreau, 43–44; Waters, 45–49
    reading, 41–42, 79
Details, 147
Diction. *See* Words
Dictionary, 315–318
Didion, Joan (essay), 15–18
Direct object. *See* Nouns *and* Pronouns
Direct question, 187–188
Division by parts, 148

Editing. *See* Words, Sentences, Punctuation
Emphasis, 157–159, 252–254, 302–303
Essay examinations, 336–347
Essays (writing)
    cause/effect, 288–300
    comparison/contrast, 240–248
    conclusions, 388–389
    definition, 145–150
    descriptive, 58–60
    informative, 102–108, 387–395, 431–435
    introductions, 102–108, 185–196, 240–248, 288–300, 388–389
    narrative, 19–31
    persuasive. *See* Appendix A, 437–446
    problem/solution, 185–196
    question/answer, 185–196
Etymology. *See* Roots

Examinations. *See* Study skills *and* Test taking
Examples, 78
Exclamation mark, 30–31, 399–400
Exposition
  reading, analysis and evaluating, 359, 387–395
  writing. *See* essays
Extended examples, 78

"Fallacy of the Energy-Civilization Equation," 378–386
"Fear of Dearth," 265–267
Figures of speech, similes and metaphors, 67–68
Finn, David (essay), 170–173
Florman, Samuel (essay), 268–273
Formal diction. *See* Words
Fragments, 118–121, 209, 303
Fused sentence, 117–120

Generalizations versus specificity, 33–35
Gerunds, 349–352
Goodman, Ellen (essay), 131–133
Grammar, 164–165. *See also* Sentences
Greek roots. *See* Roots

Haas, George H. (essay), 137–144
Heminway, John (essay), 50–57
Hyphen. *See* Dash, Dictionary
Hoffer, Eric (essay), 372–377

Implied meaning, 129–130
"In the Islands," 15–18
Indefinite pronouns. *See* Pronouns
Indentation. *See* Manuscript format
Index, use of. *See* Study skills
"Indian Food: A Rich Harvest," 319–323
Indirect objects. *See* Nouns *and* Pronouns
Indirect questions, 187–188
Inferences, 129–130
Infinitive, 349–352
Inflections. *See* Affixes
Intended audience. *See* Audience
Intensive pronouns. *See* Pronouns
Interrogative pronoun. *See* Pronouns

Intonation, 26–31
Introductory paragraphs. *See* Paragraph

Jargon, 199
Jones, Evan (essay), 319–323

Kernel sentences (main sentences), 26–31, 125

Latin roots. *See* Roots
Lecture notes, 453–457
Levels of generality (reading), 77–80
Luke (parable), 416

"Magic of Memory," 83–87
"Mankind's Better Moments," 88–95
Manuscript format, 31–32
Maud Martha (excerpt), 11–14
"Memories of a Bilingual Education," 274–287
Metaphor, 67–68
"Modernized Ritual of Rodeo," 232–239
Modification
  adjectives, 66–67, 151–158, 202–207, 218–219, 301–304
  adverbs, 250–251, 301
  clauses, 26–30, 155–159, 202–207, 208–210
  phrases, 301–304, 362–364
Morrison, Philip (essay), 134–136
My Journal (Thoreau), 37, 43–44
"Mysterious Rise and Decline of Monte Albán," 324–330

Narrative
  reading selections
    Brooks, 11–14; Christie, 8–16; Didion, 15–18
  reading, 6–7
  writing, 19–31
Negation (definition). *See* Definition
Note-taking. *See* Study skills
Nouns
  abstracts, 64–68
  concrete, 64–66
  function, 166, 349–352
Numbers, plural. *See* Apostrophes

Old English roots. *See* Roots
O'Neil, Paul (essay), 232–239
Opening paragraph. *See* Paragraphs
Opinion, 79
"Other Side of Bull Mountain," 50–57
"Our Destiny in Space," 426–430

Parable, 416
Paragraphs
  concluding, 388–389
  controlling idea (reading), 33–39
  introductory, 387–388
  organization. *See* Patterns
  supporting material, 78–80
  topic sentence, writing, 103–105, 185–186
  transitions, 72–73, 214–218, 250–251, 300–301
Parallelism, 404–406
Parenthesis, 406–407
Participles
  past, 301–304
  present, 301–304
Parts of speech
  adjectives, 65–66, 157–158, 202–207, 218–219, 301–304
  adverbs, 72–73, 202–205, 250–251, 301, 313–315
  conjunctions, 71, 116–118, 120, 128–129, 165–166
  nouns, 64–66, 166, 349–352
  prepositions, 362–364
  pronouns, 202–207, 260–262, 302–303
  verbs, 24–26, 151–154, 204–206, 302, 401–402
Passive voice, 152–153, 402–403
Patterns, writing
  C/C, 240–248
  C/E, E/C, 288–300
  DEE, 145–150
  ECC, 240–248
  FD, 58–60
  P/S, Q/A, 185–196
  SNE, 19–31
  TRIII, 102–108
  TRIIIC, 387–395, 431–434
  See also Persuasion

Period, 30–31
Person, 399–400
Personal pronouns. *See* Pronouns
Persuasion, 437–446
Pfeiffer, John E. (essay), 324–330
Phrase reading, 125–127
Phrases
  gerund, 349–352
  infinitives, 349–352
  participle, 301–304
  prepositional, 362–364
  verb, 24–26, 301–304
Pitch, 27
Plot, 6
Point of view, 399–400
"Pomp and Civil Engineering," 268–273
Precis, 260
Predicate. *See* Verbs
Prefixes, 219–221, 459–461
Prepositional phrases, 362–364
Prepositions, 362–364
Priestley, John Boynton (excerpt), 331–335
Problem/solution essay, 185–196
"Prodigal Son," 416
Pronouns
  demonstrative, 261
  function, 260–262
  indefinite, 261, 400
  intensifiers, 261–262
  interrogatory, 262
  personal, 261, 399
  possessive, 262
  reflexive, 261
  relative, 202–207, 261, 302–303
  shift-in-person, 402
Proofreading, 30–31, 76, 124, 161, 210–211, 258, 308, 356–357, 412–413
Proper nouns. *See* Nouns
Punctuation
  apostrophe, 352–353
  capitalization, 304–307
  colon, 408–409
  comma, 71–75, 117–123, 159–161, 207–210, 256–258
  comma splice, 117–119
  dash, 407–408

exclamation point, 30–31
parenthesis, 407
period, 30–31
question mark, 30–31
quotation marks, 353–355
semicolon, 71–75, 117–118

Question
  direct, 187–188
  indirect, 187–188
  punctuation, 30–31
Question/answer essays, 185–196
Question mark, 30–31
Quotation marks, 353–356
Quotations, in reading, 79

"Rails: From Old World to New," 226–231
"Rain Song," 45–49
Reading for different purposes, 259–260
Reading strategies
  anticipation, 1–4
  Cloze exercise, 128–129
  controlling idea, 33–39
  exposition, 82
  kinds of reading
    description, 6–7
    exposition, 82
    narrative, 41–42
  levels of generality, 77–80
  phrase reading, 125–127, 128–129
  reading for different purposes, 259–260
  reading persuasion, 440–441
  recognizing transitions, 213–218
  reviewing for tests, 309–313
"Reflections of My Brother's Murder," 170–173
Relative clauses, 201–207, 302–303
Relative pronouns. *See* Pronouns
Restrictive clause, 208–210
Revision, 22–24, 63–64, 112, 150–151, 196–198, 248–250, 298–300, 346, 397–399, 434–435, 447
Rhythm. *See* Parallelism
Rodriguez, Richard (essay), 274–287
Roots (word derivation), 167–169, 462
Run-on sentences, 404–406

Scanning, 163–164, 310
Semicolons, 71–75, 117–118
Sentence combining, 158–159, 205–206, 254–255, 303–304
Sentences
  comma splice, 117–119
  complex, 155–159, 201–207, 302–303
  compound, 68–75, 155–159
  definition of, 26–27
  fragments, 29–30, 118–121
  fused, 117–121
  kernels, 26–30
  parallelism, 404–406
  run-on, 404–406
  simple, 155–159, 303
  style, 252–255
  variety, 156–159, 302–304
Setting, 7
"Silent Generation: An Essay," 222–225
Simile, 67–68
Skimming, 1–4
Slang, 198–199
Solomon, Robert C. (essay), 174–177
Speaker-writer (reading), 359
Specificity, 33–35
Spoken voice, 26–27
Steps in a process (reading), 79
Strong verbs, 24–26, 151–154
Study skills, 299–313, 336–346, 453–457
Style
  reading language, 352
  review (writing), 252–255
Subjects. *See* Nouns *and* Pronouns
Subject/verb agreement, 69
Subordination, 155–159, 202–207
Subordinators, 116–124
Suffixes, 262–264, 459–461
Supporting ideas
  analogy, 148
  cause/effect, 79
  comparison/contrast, 78
  definitions, 80
  description, 79
  example, 78
  extended examples, 78
  graphic aids, 78–79

Supporting ideas (*cont.*)
  opinion, 79–80
  quotations, 79
  parts of the whole, 79, 339–340
  process, 79
Surveying, 1–2
Syllabification. *See* Dictionary
"Symbol of Success: The Real Horatio Alger," 96–101
Synonyms, 5

Technical words. *See* Words
Tenses. *See* Verbs
Test taking, 309–313, 336–346
Thesis statement, 36–39
  reading, 360–361, 388
  writing, 185–186, 248, 337–338
Thoreau, Henry David, *Journal*, 37, 43–44
"To be" verbs, 24–25
Tone, 252–254, 347–349, 359 (reading)
Topic sentence, 103–105, 185–186, 388
Transitionals
  adverbs, 72–73, 119–120, 301
  recognizing (reading), 213–218
  words, 72–73, 214–218, 250–251, 300–301
Tuchman, Barbara W. (essay), 88–95
Tucker, Carll (essay), 265–267

Underlining. *See* Reading strategies

"Vegetarianism," 178–184
Verbals
  gerund, 349–352
  infinitive, 349–352
  participles, 301–304
Verbs
  function, 24–25
  passive, 152–153
  phrases, 204–206, 302
  shifts in tense, 401–402
  strong and weak, 24–26, 151–154
  to be, 25

Vocabulary
  lists, 8, 11, 15, 43, 45, 50, 83, 88, 96, 131, 134, 137, 170, 174, 178, 222, 226, 232, 265, 268, 274, 319, 324, 331, 369, 372, 378
  specialized vocabulary, 312
  strategies for learning
    affixes, 219–221, 262–264, 459–461
    context, 1–6, 39–40, 80–82
    dictionary, 315–318
    roots, 167–169
  types, 4–5
Voice, 399–400
  shifts in, 402–403

Waters, Frank (essay), 45–49
"We'd Better Not Make Book on U.S. Literacy," 174–177
White, John H., Jr. (essay), 226–231
"Why Man Explores," 134–135
Wigner, Kathleen K. (essay), 417–425
Words (writing)
  appropriate usage, 198–202
  cliché, 199–202
  colloquial usage, 198–199
  definitions, 146
  denotation/connotation, 113–116
  formal usage, 199–202
  jargon, 199
  pompous diction, 199
  slang, 198–199
  stock terms, 198–200
  technical, 364–368
Words in context (reading)
  affixes, 167–169
  contrast and negation, 80–82
  definition, 4–6
  inference, 129–130
  restatement and example, 39–40
"Wrong Ism," 331–335

"Your Better Supermother," 131–133

Common Problems in Usage

accept/except   **Accept** is a verb meaning *to receive willingly:*

> The actor **accepted** the Oscar for his role in the motion picture *Reds*.

Except, when used as a verb, means *to exclude:*

> The discussion on tax reforms was **excepted** from the agenda.

a lot of (NOT *alot* or *lots*)   **A lot of** is a colloquial term used to mean *a great deal of* or *many:*

> He has **a lot of** money.

Alot and *lots* are unacceptable forms of this phrase.

already/all ready   **Already** is an adverb meaning *previously* or *prior to a given time:*

> They have **already** announced the news.

All ready means *prepared:*

> Are you **all ready** for your vacation?

because (NOT *on account of*)   *On account of* is a nonstandard phrase; **because** should be used in its place:

> She bought a new car because her old car was no longer dependable.
> (DO NOT USE: She bought a new car *on account of* her old car was no longer dependable.)

as/like   **As** is a conjunction used to introduce clauses:

> We talked about old times **as** we had always done.

Like is a preposition that introduces phrases:

> Although we had just met, we talked **like** old friends.

could have (NOT *could of*)   *Could of* is not an acceptable phrase. The correct form of this phrase is **could have:**

> He **could have** been elected president if he had used more television advertisements.

The same guideline applies to *would of* and *should of*, two unacceptable phrases which should be replaced by **would have** and **should have,** respectively.

effect/affect   **Effect** is usually used as a noun meaning *something that results from an action:*

> Airborne sulphur from midwestern factories has lasting bad **effects** on New England forests.

Affect is a verb meaning *to produce a reaction:*

> Acid rain **affects** the ability of trees to absorb ground water.

etc. (NOT *and etc.*)   **Etc.** is an abbreviation of the Latin phrase *et cetera*, meaning *and others*. *And etc.* is redundant since it means *and and others.*

fewer/less   **Fewer** pertains to countable quantities:

> There are **fewer** desks in this room today than there were yesterday.